DATE DUE		NOV 04
AUG 1 2 '05		
GAYLORD		PRINTED IN U.S.A.

Table of Contents

ASTRO BOY®

6

by
Osamu Tezuka

translation
Frederik L. Schodt

lettering and retouch
Digital Chameleon

Dark Horse Comics®

publisher
MIKE RICHARDSON

editor
CHRIS WARNER

consulting editor
TOREN SMITH for STUDIO PROTEUS

collection designers
DAVID NESTELLE and LANI SCHREIBSTEIN

English-language version produced by **DARK HORSE COMICS** and **STUDIO PROTEUS**

ASTRO BOY® VOLUME 6

The artwork of this volume has been produced as a mirror-image of the original Japanese edition to conform to English-language standards.

Published by
Dark Horse Comics, Inc.
10956 SE Main Street
Milwaukie, OR 97222

www.darkhorse.com

To find a comics shop in your area, call the Comic Shop Locator Service toll-free at 1-888-266-4226.

First edition: August 2002
ISBN: 1-56971-681-1

10 9 8 7 6 5 4 3 2 1
Printed in Canada

A NOTE TO READERS

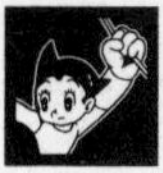

Many non-Japanese, including people from Africa and Southeast Asia, appear in Osamu Tezuka's works. Sometimes these people are depicted very differently from the way they actually are today, in a manner that exaggerates a time long past or shows them to be from extremely undeveloped lands. Some feel that such images contribute to racial discrimination, especially against people of African descent. This was never Osamu Tezuka's intent, but we believe that as long as there are people who feel insulted or demeaned by these depictions, we must not ignore their feelings.

We are against discrimination, in all its forms, and intend to continue to work for its elimination. Nonetheless, we do not believe it would be proper to revise these works. Tezuka is no longer with us, and we cannot erase what he has done, and to alter his work would only violate his rights as a creator. More importantly, stopping publication or changing the content of his work would do little to solve the problems of discrimination that exist in the world.

We are presenting Osamu Tezuka's work as it was originally created, without changes. We do this because we believe it is also important to promote the underlying themes in his work, such as love for mankind and the sanctity of life. We hope that when you, the reader, encounter this work, you will keep in mind the differences in attitudes, then and now, toward discrimination, and that this will contribute to an even greater awareness of such problems.

— Tezuka Productions and Dark Horse Comics

"ONCE UPON A TIME" ASTRO BOY TALES, PART 1

First serialized from January 24th to December 23, 1967 in the *Sankei* newspaper.

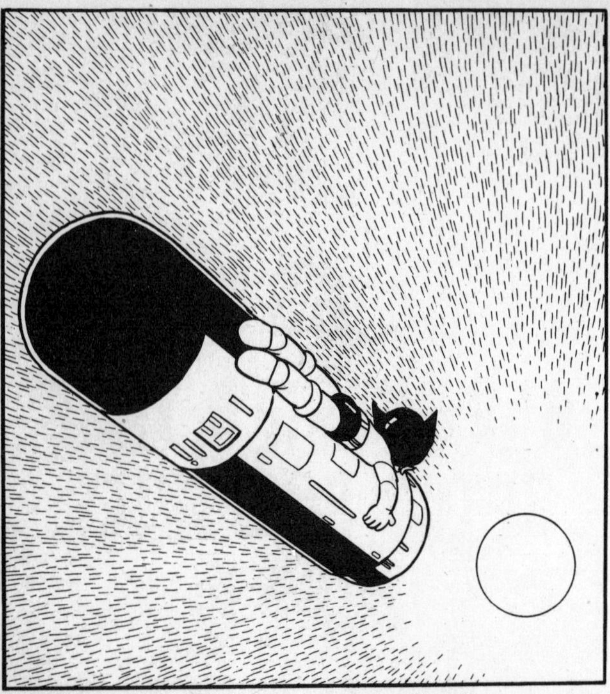

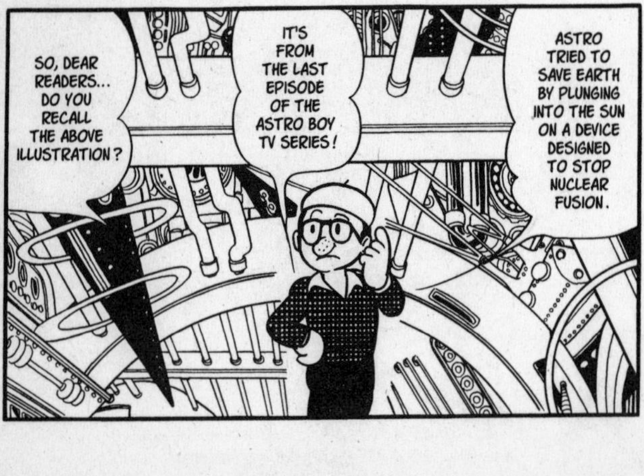
SO, DEAR READERS... DO YOU RECALL THE ABOVE ILLUSTRATION?
IT'S FROM THE LAST EPISODE OF THE ASTRO BOY TV SERIES!
ASTRO TRIED TO SAVE EARTH BY PLUNGING INTO THE SUN ON A DEVICE DESIGNED TO STOP NUCLEAR FUSION.

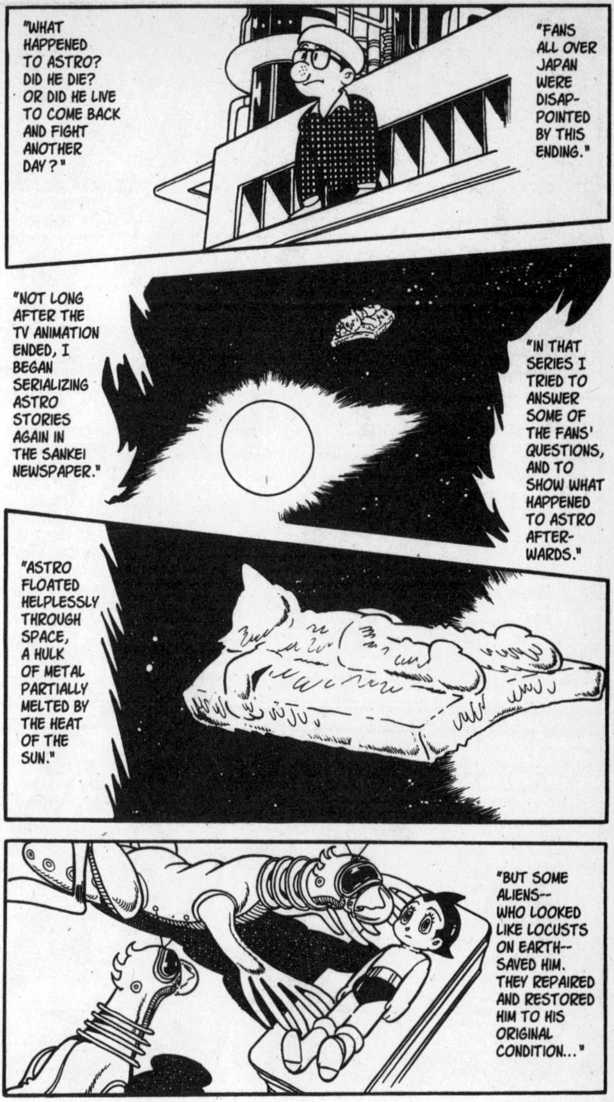
"WHAT HAPPENED TO ASTRO? DID HE DIE? OR DID HE LIVE TO COME BACK AND FIGHT ANOTHER DAY?"
"FANS ALL OVER JAPAN WERE DISAP-POINTED BY THIS ENDING."
"NOT LONG AFTER THE TV ANIMATION ENDED, I BEGAN SERIALIZING ASTRO STORIES AGAIN IN THE SANKEI NEWSPAPER."
"IN THAT SERIES I TRIED TO ANSWER SOME OF THE FANS' QUESTIONS, AND TO SHOW WHAT HAPPENED TO ASTRO AFTER-WARDS."
"ASTRO FLOATED HELPLESSLY THROUGH SPACE, A HULK OF METAL PARTIALLY MELTED BY THE HEAT OF THE SUN."
"BUT SOME ALIENS-- WHO LOOKED LIKE LOCUSTS ON EARTH-- SAVED HIM. THEY REPAIRED AND RESTORED HIM TO HIS ORIGINAL CONDITION..."

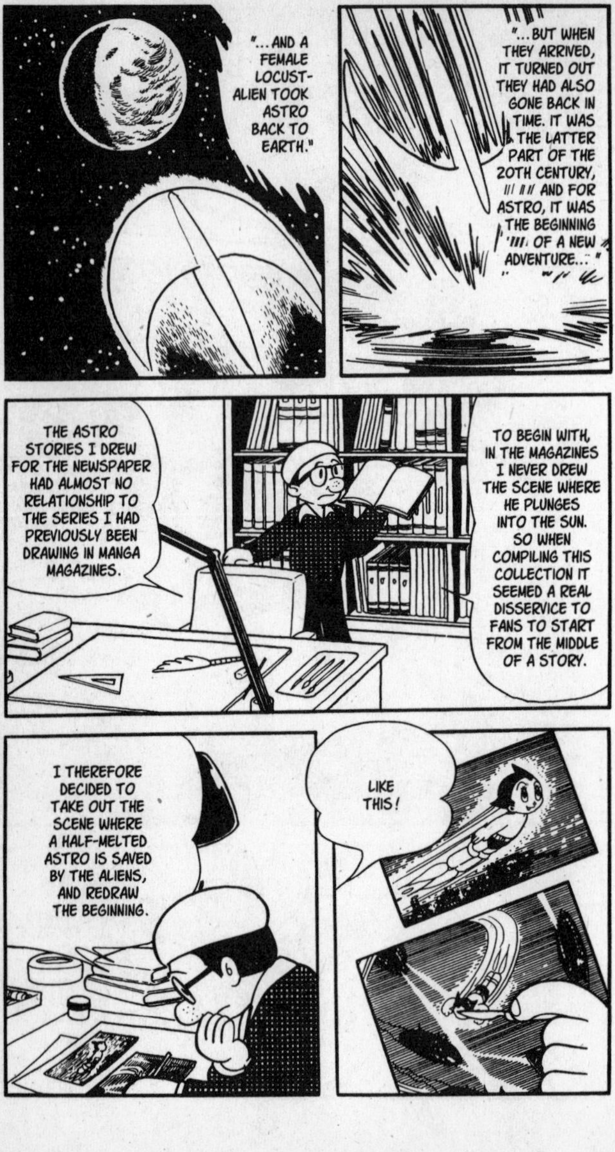
"...AND A FEMALE LOCUST-ALIEN TOOK ASTRO BACK TO EARTH."
"...BUT WHEN THEY ARRIVED, IT TURNED OUT THEY HAD ALSO GONE BACK IN TIME. IT WAS THE LATTER PART OF THE 20TH CENTURY, AND FOR ASTRO, IT WAS THE BEGINNING OF A NEW ADVENTURE..."
THE ASTRO STORIES I DREW FOR THE NEWSPAPER HAD ALMOST NO RELATIONSHIP TO THE SERIES I HAD PREVIOUSLY BEEN DRAWING IN MANGA MAGAZINES.
TO BEGIN WITH, IN THE MAGAZINES I NEVER DREW THE SCENE WHERE HE PLUNGES INTO THE SUN. SO WHEN COMPILING THIS COLLECTION IT SEEMED A REAL DISSERVICE TO FANS TO START FROM THE MIDDLE OF A STORY.
I THEREFORE DECIDED TO TAKE OUT THE SCENE WHERE A HALF-MELTED ASTRO IS SAVED BY THE ALIENS, AND REDRAW THE BEGINNING.
LIKE THIS!

BEGINNING OF THE CONTRADICTION

IT WAS A WARM SPRING EVENING. ROBOTS OFTEN HAVE THEIR ELECTRO-BRAINS PROGRAMMED TO FEEL PLEASURE WHEN IT'S GOOD WEATHER, SO ON THE SPUR OF THE MOMENT ASTRO DECIDED TO TAKE A JAUNT OUT BY THE HARBOR.

AS HE SURVEYED THE HARBOR HE THOUGHT, "HMM , THAT'S ODD..." THERE WERE AT LEAST TEN SHIPS-- PATROL BOATS AND MINESWEEPERS-- ALL GATHERING, LOOKING FOR SOMETHING, THE BEAMS FROM THEIR SEARCHLIGHTS CRISS-CROSSING THE SURFACE OF THE WATER.

"THERE MUST BE SOMETHING IN THE SEA!" HE THOUGHT, IN A SURGE OF EXCITEMENT. PLUNGING INTO THE WATER, HE ENCOUNTERED A HUGE SWIRL OF BUBBLES, AND FELT A SURGE OF RADIATION. SOMETHING VERY STRANGE WAS GOING ON.

I WONDER WHAT COULD HAVE HAPPENED!?

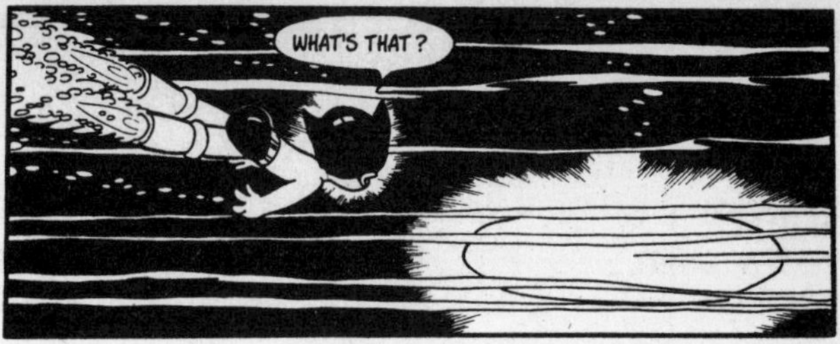
WHAT'S THAT ?
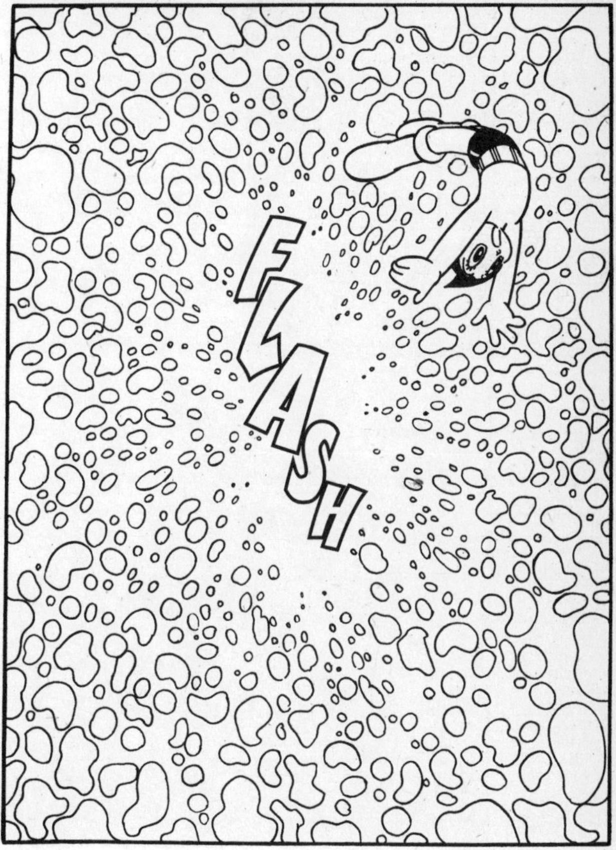
FLASH

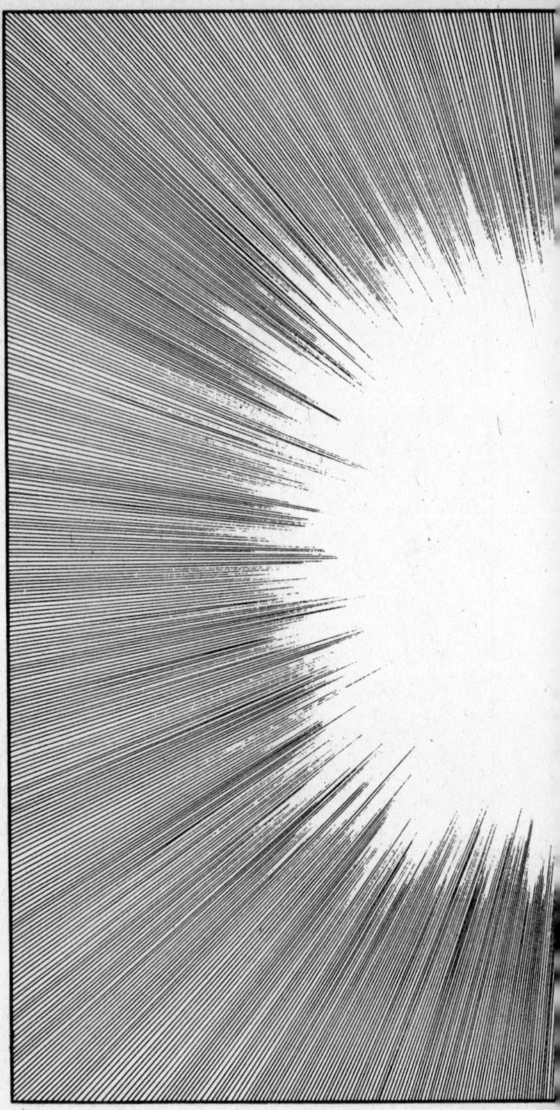

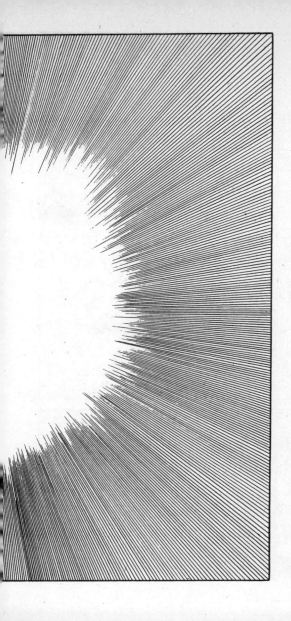

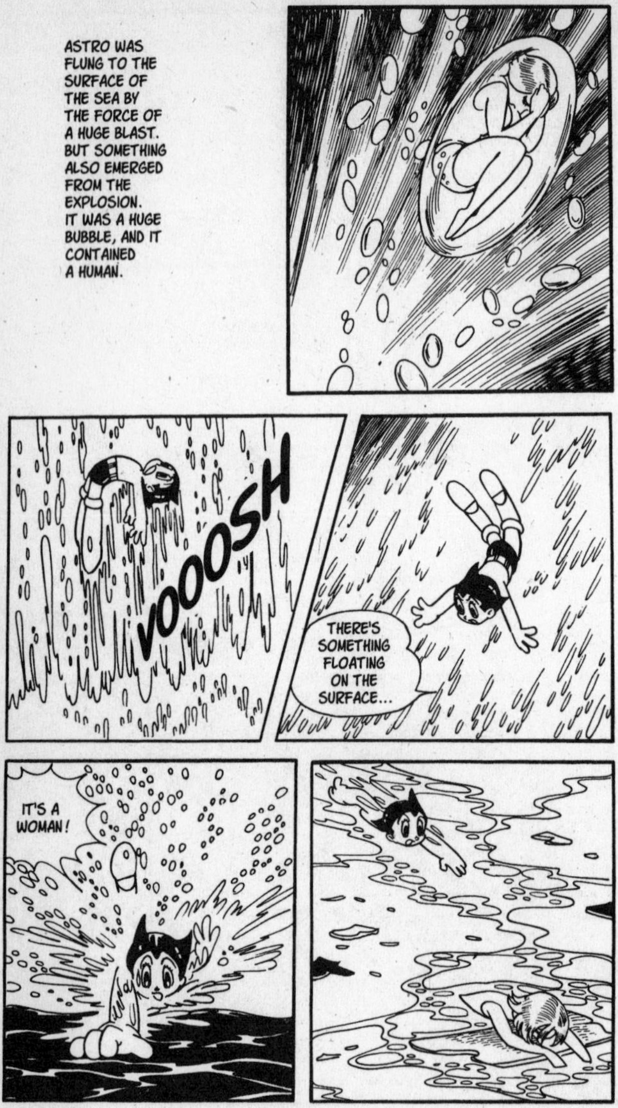
ASTRO WAS FLUNG TO THE SURFACE OF THE SEA BY THE FORCE OF A HUGE BLAST. BUT SOMETHING ALSO EMERGED FROM THE EXPLOSION. IT WAS A HUGE BUBBLE, AND IT CONTAINED A HUMAN.
VOOOSH
THERE'S SOMETHING FLOATING ON THE SURFACE...
IT'S A WOMAN!

THE WOMAN WAS UNCONSCIOUS AND NOT MOVING, AND ASTRO KNEW HE HAD TO HELP HER, BUT HIS ELECTRO-BRAIN ALSO TOLD HIM SHE WAS NOT HUMAN.

HE DECIDED TO TAKE HER TO LAND, TO A DESERTED PIER NEARBY. THERE, HE TRIED TO RESUSCITATE HER UNCONSCIOUS FORM BY GENTLY SHAKING HER. AND THEN HE NOTICED SOMETHING STRANGE.

HER HEART WAS STILL BEATING, BUT SHE WAS NOT BREATHING. NO AIR WAS GOING IN AND OUT OF HER NOSTRILS AT ALL-- WHILE SHE HAD A NOSE, IT DEFINITELY WAS NOT FUNCTIONING AS ONE.

WOW. THIS LADY'S GOT HOLES IN HER *SIDES*, AND I CAN HEAR AIR GOING IN AND OUT OF THEM...

HUMANS DON'T BREATHE THROUGH THEIR SIDES...

THAT'S WHAT *INSECTS* DO!

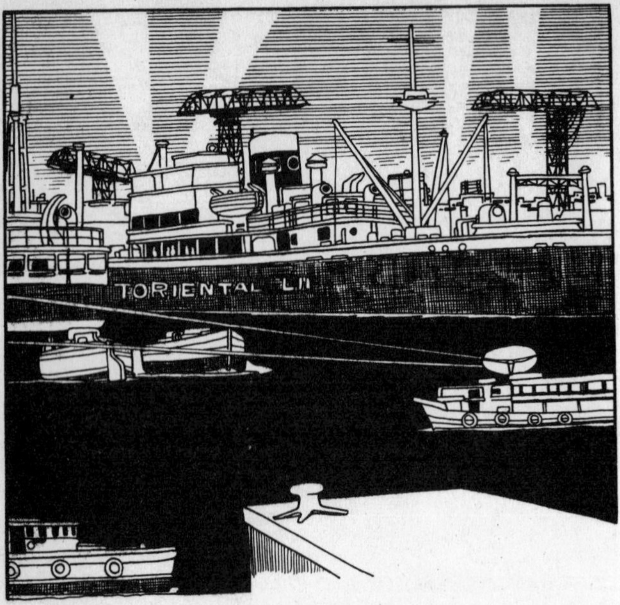
ORIENTAL LI

THE WOMAN OPENED HER EYES, AND STARED AT ASTRO.

"WHAT HAPPENED, LADY? IF YOU CAN TALK, SAY SOMETHING TO ME," HE BEGGED.

"I CAN TALK," SHE REPLIED. "YOU'RE A ROBOT, AREN'T YOU...?"

"OF COURSE I AM, BUT HOW'D YOU KNOW?"

THE WOMAN DIDN'T ANSWER DIRECTLY, AND MERELY SAID, "IF YOU'RE A ROBOT, YOU'LL KEEP WHAT I TELL YOU A SECRET, RIGHT?"

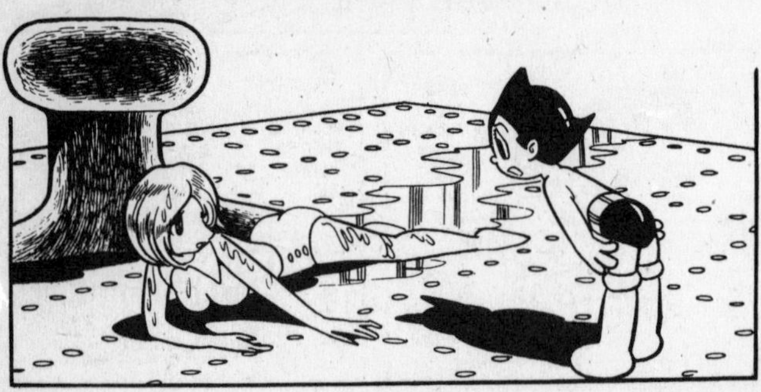

YOU SEE...

...I CAME FROM A FARAWAY PLANET.

WOW? REALLY?

I LOOK LIKE I'M FROM EARTH NOW, BUT I'M REALLY NOT...

THE INSECT-WOMAN'S PLANET HAD A VERY ADVANCED CIVILIZATION. THE PEOPLE IN THE CAPITAL LOOKED JUST LIKE LOCUSTS, BUT THEY WORE BEAUTIFUL CLOTHES AS THEY BUSILY HOPPED ABOUT. WITH THEIR POWERFUL HIND LEGS, THEY COULD TRAVEL OVER 50 YARDS IN ONE LEAP.

ONE THING ODD ABOUT THEM, THOUGH, WAS THAT THEY HAD FACES EXACTLY LIKE THOSE OF HUMANS. THEY HAD HAIR ON THEIR HEADS, EYEBROWS, AND THE MALES HAD BEARDS, TOO. FROM THE PERSPECTIVE OF HUMANS THEY LOOKED SHOCKING, EVEN HILARIOUS. BUT THE LOCUST-PEOPLE CONSIDERED THEMSELVES PERFECTLY NORMAL.

19

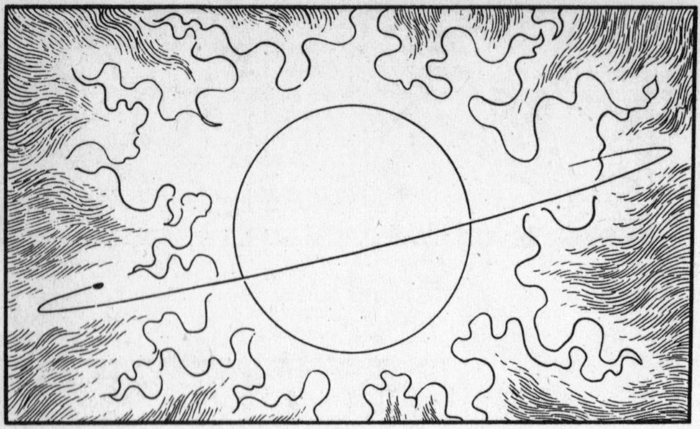

MR. AND MRS. OHARA WERE A NEWLY MARRIED COUPLE.
FOR THEIR HONEYMOON, THEY TOOK OFF ON A SPACE ROCKET, VISITING A VARIETY OF PLANETS. BUT THE MAN--OR THE MALE LOCUST--WAS EMPLOYED AS A SCIENTIST, AND IT WAS TIME FOR HIM TO RETURN.

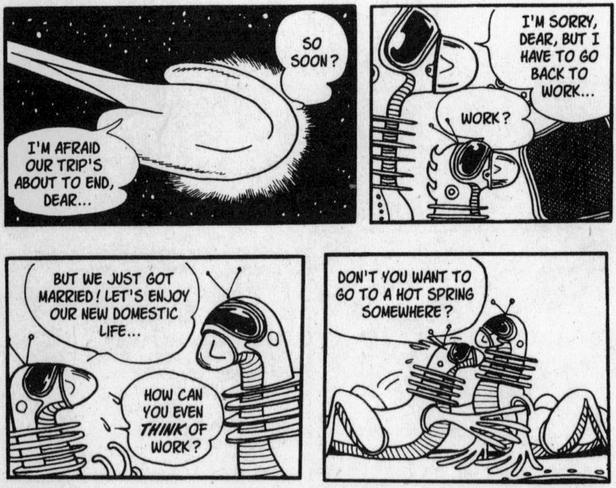
SO SOON?
I'M AFRAID OUR TRIP'S ABOUT TO END, DEAR...
I'M SORRY, DEAR, BUT I HAVE TO GO BACK TO WORK...
WORK?
BUT WE JUST GOT MARRIED! LET'S ENJOY OUR NEW DOMESTIC LIFE...
HOW CAN YOU EVEN *THINK* OF WORK?
DON'T YOU WANT TO GO TO A HOT SPRING SOMEWHERE?

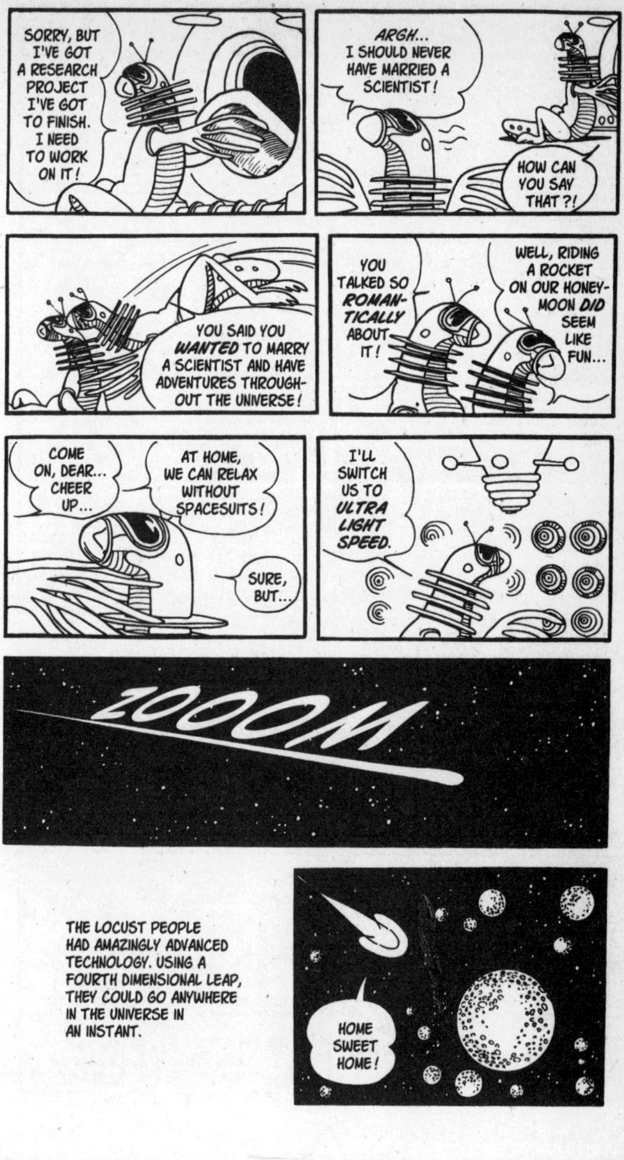
SORRY, BUT I'VE GOT A RESEARCH PROJECT I'VE GOT TO FINISH. I NEED TO WORK ON IT!
ARGH... I SHOULD NEVER HAVE MARRIED A SCIENTIST!
HOW CAN YOU SAY THAT?!
YOU SAID YOU WANTED TO MARRY A SCIENTIST AND HAVE ADVENTURES THROUGHOUT THE UNIVERSE!
YOU TALKED SO ROMANTICALLY ABOUT IT!
WELL, RIDING A ROCKET ON OUR HONEYMOON DID SEEM LIKE FUN...
COME ON, DEAR... CHEER UP...
AT HOME, WE CAN RELAX WITHOUT SPACESUITS!
SURE, BUT...
I'LL SWITCH US TO ULTRA LIGHT SPEED.
ZOOOM
THE LOCUST PEOPLE HAD AMAZINGLY ADVANCED TECHNOLOGY. USING A FOURTH DIMENSIONAL LEAP, THEY COULD GO ANYWHERE IN THE UNIVERSE IN AN INSTANT.
HOME SWEET HOME!

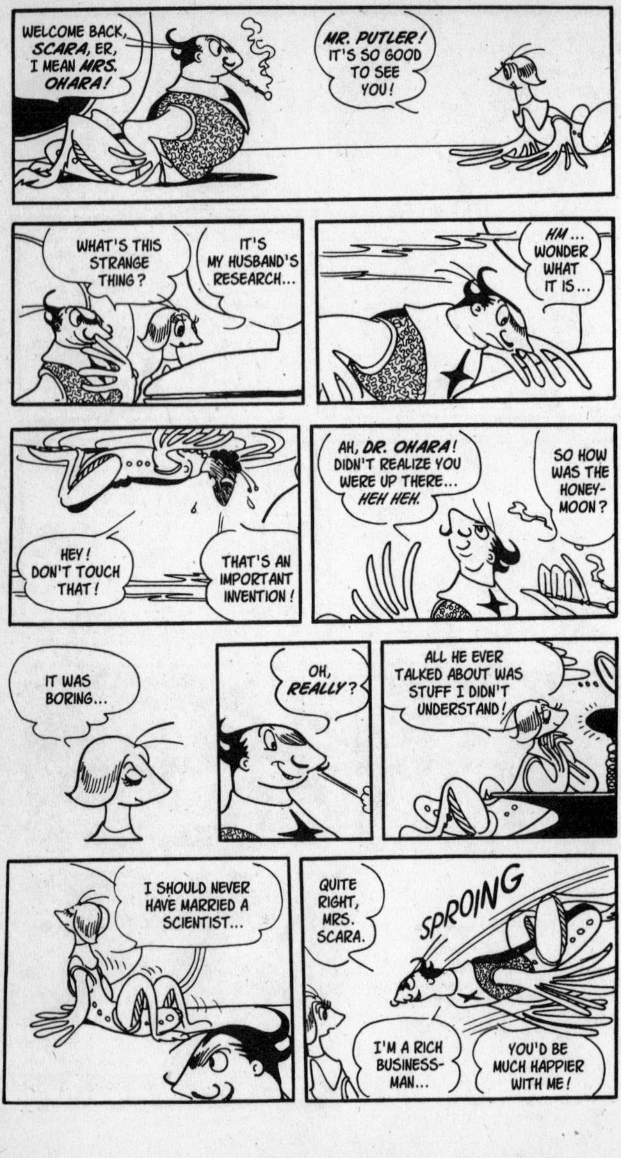
WELCOME BACK, SCARA, ER, I MEAN MRS. OHARA!
MR. PUTLER! IT'S SO GOOD TO SEE YOU!
WHAT'S THIS STRANGE THING?
IT'S MY HUSBAND'S RESEARCH...
HM... WONDER WHAT IT IS...
HEY! DON'T TOUCH THAT!
THAT'S AN IMPORTANT INVENTION!
AH, DR. OHARA! DIDN'T REALIZE YOU WERE UP THERE... HEH HEH.
SO HOW WAS THE HONEY-MOON?
IT WAS BORING...
OH, REALLY?
ALL HE EVER TALKED ABOUT WAS STUFF I DIDN'T UNDERSTAND!
I SHOULD NEVER HAVE MARRIED A SCIENTIST...
QUITE RIGHT, MRS. SCARA.
SPROING
I'M A RICH BUSINESS-MAN...
YOU'D BE MUCH HAPPIER WITH ME!

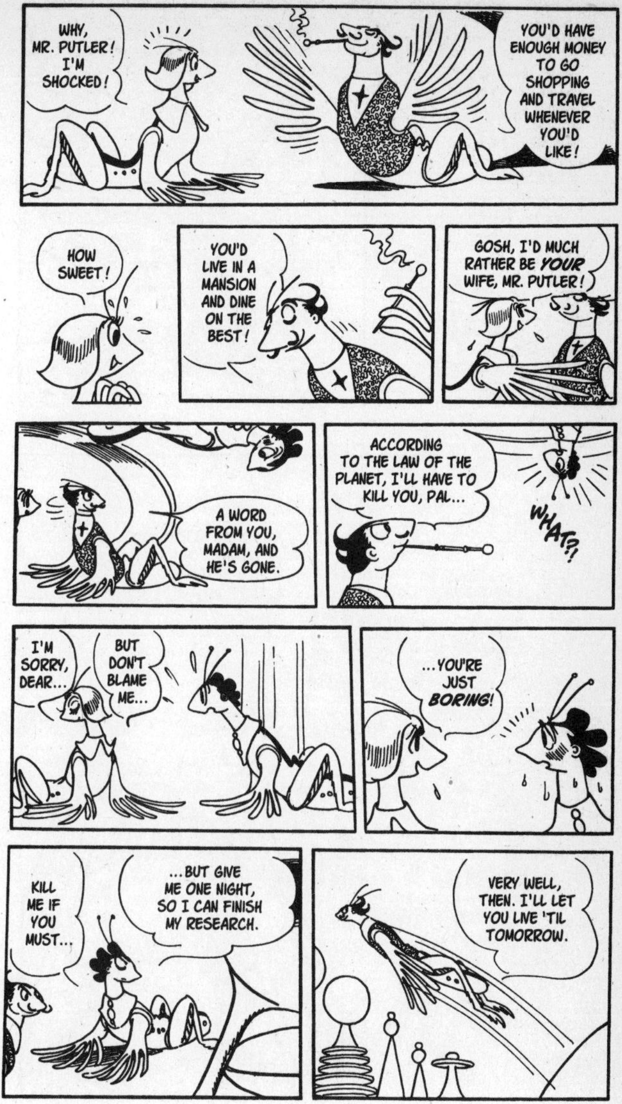
WHY, MR. PUTLER! I'M SHOCKED!
YOU'D HAVE ENOUGH MONEY TO GO SHOPPING AND TRAVEL WHENEVER YOU'D LIKE!
HOW SWEET!
YOU'D LIVE IN A MANSION AND DINE ON THE BEST!
GOSH, I'D MUCH RATHER BE *YOUR* WIFE, MR. PUTLER!
A WORD FROM YOU, MADAM, AND HE'S GONE.
ACCORDING TO THE LAW OF THE PLANET, I'LL HAVE TO KILL YOU, PAL...
WHAT?!
I'M SORRY, DEAR...
BUT DON'T BLAME ME...
...YOU'RE JUST *BORING*!
KILL ME IF YOU MUST...
...BUT GIVE ME ONE NIGHT, SO I CAN FINISH MY RESEARCH.
VERY WELL, THEN. I'LL LET YOU LIVE 'TIL TOMORROW.

THE RITUAL WAS WELL
ESTABLISHED ON THE
PLANET. WHY, YOU ASK?
WELL, ITS PEOPLE HAD
EVOLVED FROM INSECTS,
AND AS SOME READERS
MAY KNOW, TWO MALE
GRASSHOPPERS AND
KATYDIDS WILL BATTLE
TO THE DEATH OVER A
FEMALE. IN OTHER WORDS,
IN ORDER TO BE WITH
THE FEMALE, ONE OF
THE MALES MUST DIE.
AND SO IT WAS ON THIS
PLANET. THERE WAS
NOTHING THE POOR
SCIENTIST COULD DO
ABOUT IT WHEN THE
BUSINESSMAN TRIED
TO TAKE HIS WIFE...

WHEN HE PLEADED,
"WON'T YOU CHANGE
YOUR MIND, DEAR?"
HIS WIFE MERELY REPLIED,
"NO, I DON'T WANT TO."

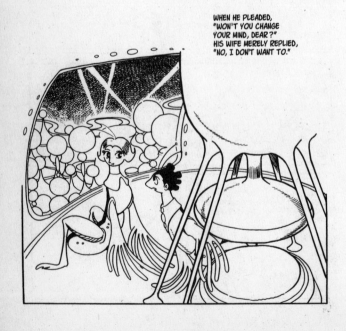

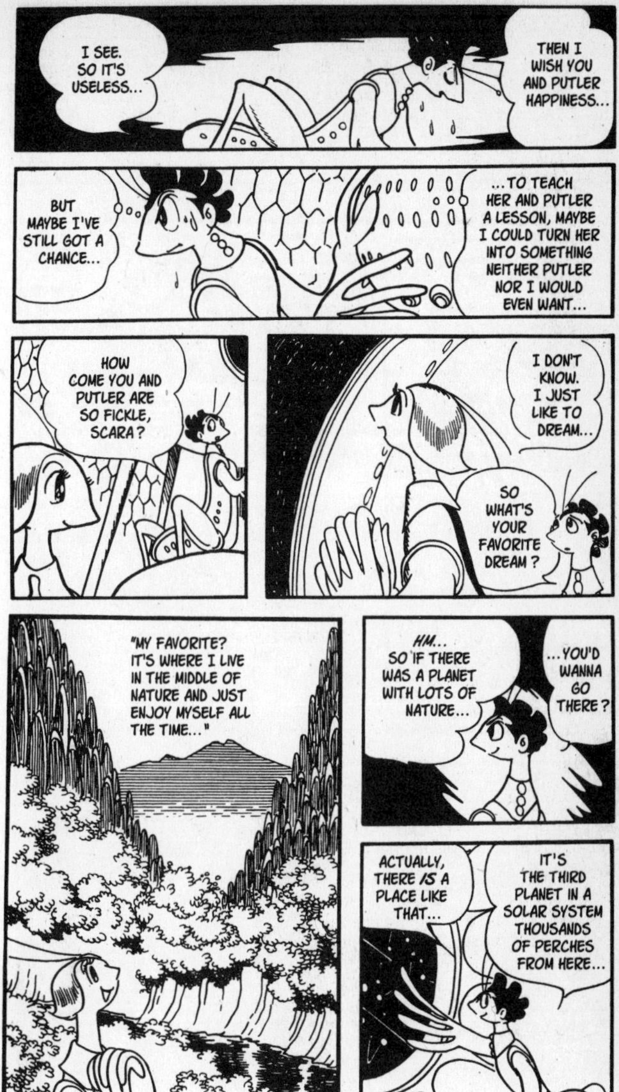
I SEE. SO IT'S USELESS...
THEN I WISH YOU AND PUTLER HAPPINESS...
BUT MAYBE I'VE STILL GOT A CHANCE...
...TO TEACH HER AND PUTLER A LESSON, MAYBE I COULD TURN HER INTO SOMETHING NEITHER PUTLER NOR I WOULD EVEN WANT...
HOW COME YOU AND PUTLER ARE SO FICKLE, SCARA?
I DON'T KNOW. I JUST LIKE TO DREAM...
SO WHAT'S YOUR FAVORITE DREAM?
"MY FAVORITE? IT'S WHERE I LIVE IN THE MIDDLE OF NATURE AND JUST ENJOY MYSELF ALL THE TIME..."
HM... SO IF THERE WAS A PLANET WITH LOTS OF NATURE...
...YOU'D WANNA GO THERE?
ACTUALLY, THERE IS A PLACE LIKE THAT...
IT'S THE THIRD PLANET IN A SOLAR SYSTEM THOUSANDS OF PERCHES FROM HERE...

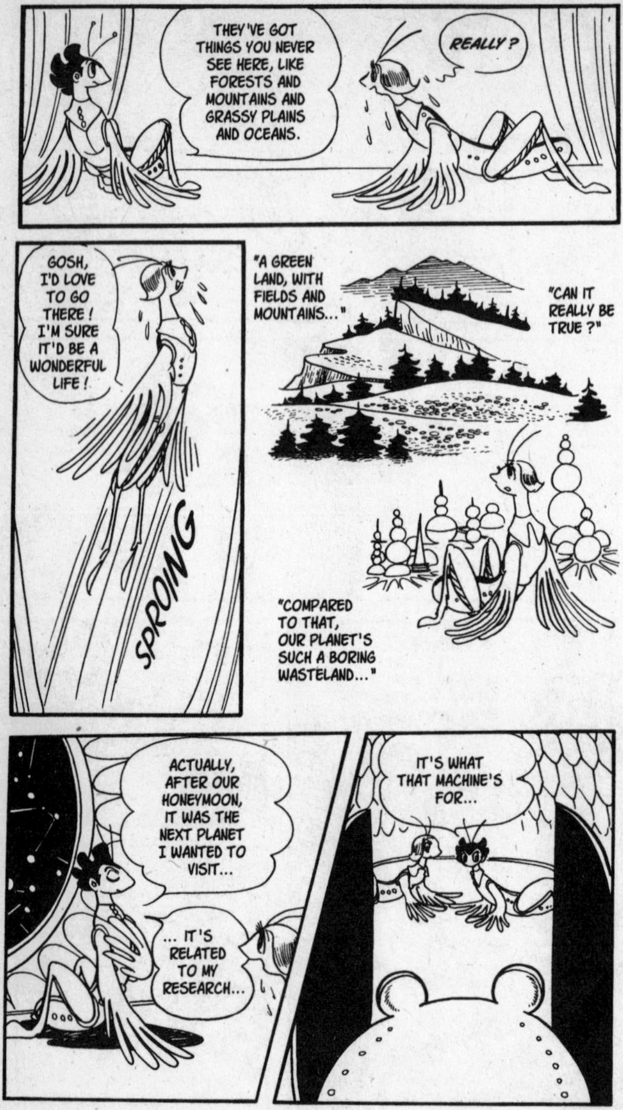
THEY'VE GOT THINGS YOU NEVER SEE HERE, LIKE FORESTS AND MOUNTAINS AND GRASSY PLAINS AND OCEANS.
REALLY?
GOSH, I'D LOVE TO GO THERE! I'M SURE IT'D BE A WONDERFUL LIFE!
SPROING
"A GREEN LAND, WITH FIELDS AND MOUNTAINS..."
"CAN IT REALLY BE TRUE?"
"COMPARED TO THAT, OUR PLANET'S SUCH A BORING WASTELAND..."
ACTUALLY, AFTER OUR HONEYMOON, IT WAS THE NEXT PLANET I WANTED TO VISIT...
... IT'S RELATED TO MY RESEARCH...
IT'S WHAT THAT MACHINE'S FOR...

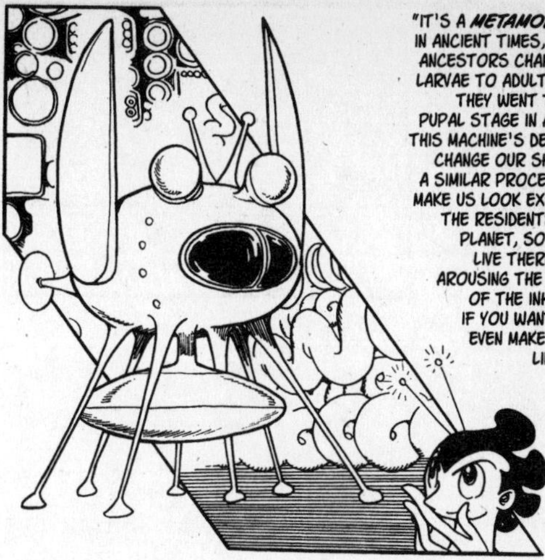

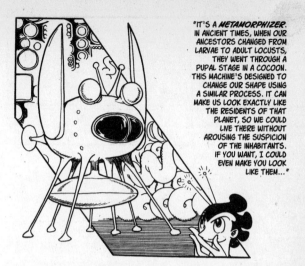

"IT'S A ***METAMORPHIZER***. IN ANCIENT TIMES, WHEN OUR ANCESTORS CHANGED FROM LARVAE TO ADULT LOCUSTS, THEY WENT THROUGH A PUPAL STAGE IN A COCOON. THIS MACHINE'S DESIGNED TO CHANGE OUR SHAPE USING A SIMILAR PROCESS. IT CAN MAKE US LOOK EXACTLY LIKE THE RESIDENTS OF THAT PLANET, SO WE COULD LIVE THERE WITHOUT AROUSING THE SUSPICION OF THE INHABITANTS. IF YOU WANT, I COULD EVEN MAKE YOU LOOK LIKE THEM..."

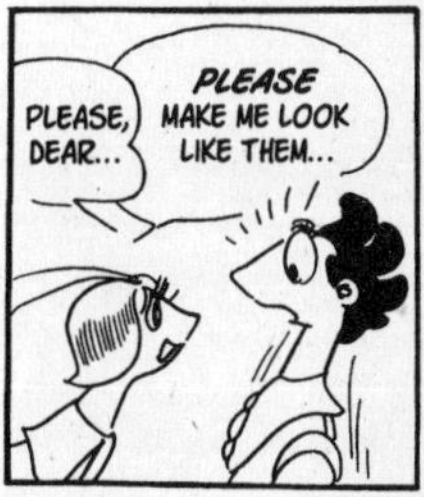
PLEASE, DEAR...
PLEASE MAKE ME LOOK LIKE THEM...

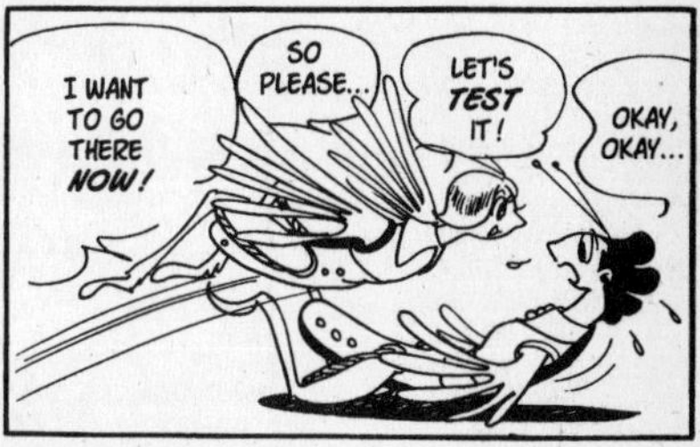
I WANT TO GO THERE NOW!
SO PLEASE...
LET'S TEST IT!
OKAY, OKAY...

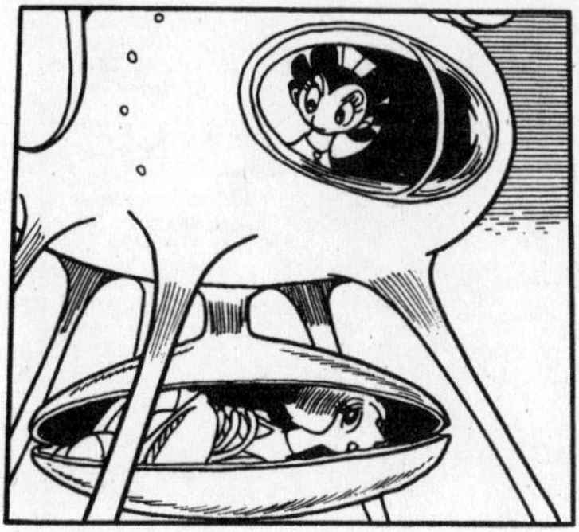

"YOU SURE ARE IN A HURRY, SCARA... BUT IF YOU INSIST... GET IN THE CASE UNDER THE MACHINE. I'LL BE IN THE UPPER PART, SETTING THINGS UP SO WE CAN CHANGE YOUR SHAPE. BUT YOU'LL HAVE TO STAY STILL FOR AT LEAST AN HOUR, OR YOU MIGHT TURN INTO SOMETHING REALLY WEIRD..."

THE METAMORPHIZER MADE A SOUND LIKE BEATING INSECT WINGS, AND THEN, WITH A HISS, EMITTED STEAM...

"IN AN HOUR YOU'LL BE TRANSFORMED INTO A NEW PERSON," THE SCIENTIST SAID...

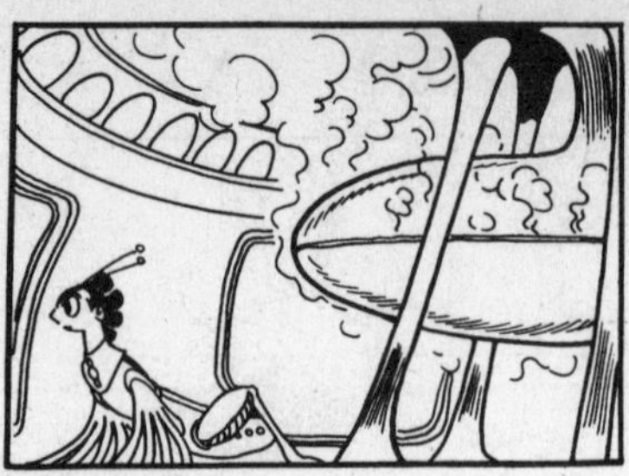

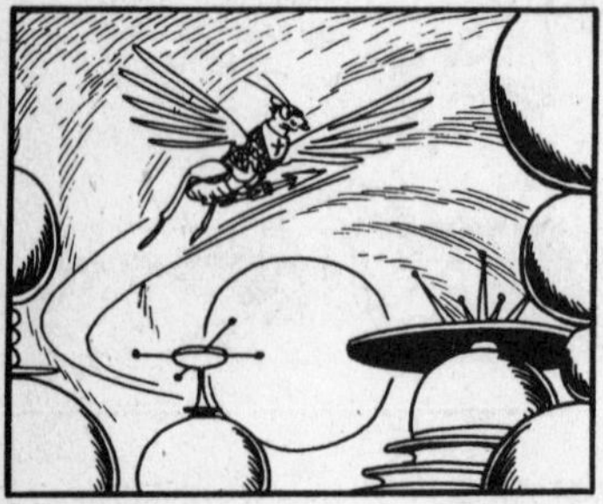

BUT THEN HE ALSO REALIZED THAT A NEW DAY WAS DAWNING, AND THAT PUTLER WOULD BE COMING TO KILL HIM. HE GLANCED OUT THE WINDOW AND SIGHED.

OUTSIDE IN THE EARLY MORNING SKY, HE COULD SEE A SHAPE SPRINGING TOWARD HIM.

"PUTLER'S FINALLY HERE...," HE THOUGHT, NOTING THE BIG WEAPON HE HAD BROUGHT WITH HIM.

"AS PROMISED, I'VE COME FOR YOU, DR. OHARA, JUST LIKE I SAID I WOULD," PUTLER ANNOUNCED.

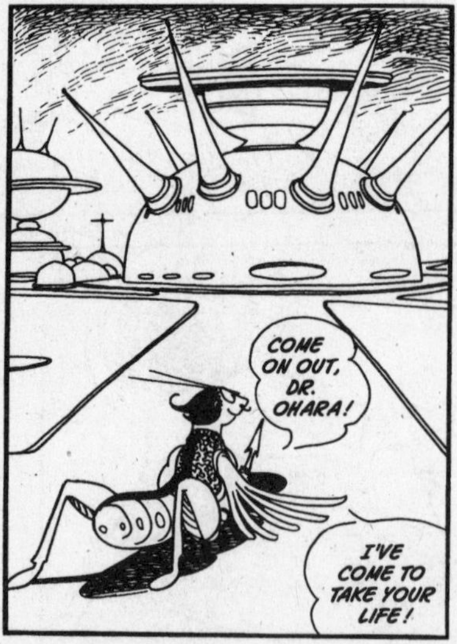
COME ON OUT, DR. OHARA!
I'VE COME TO TAKE YOUR LIFE!

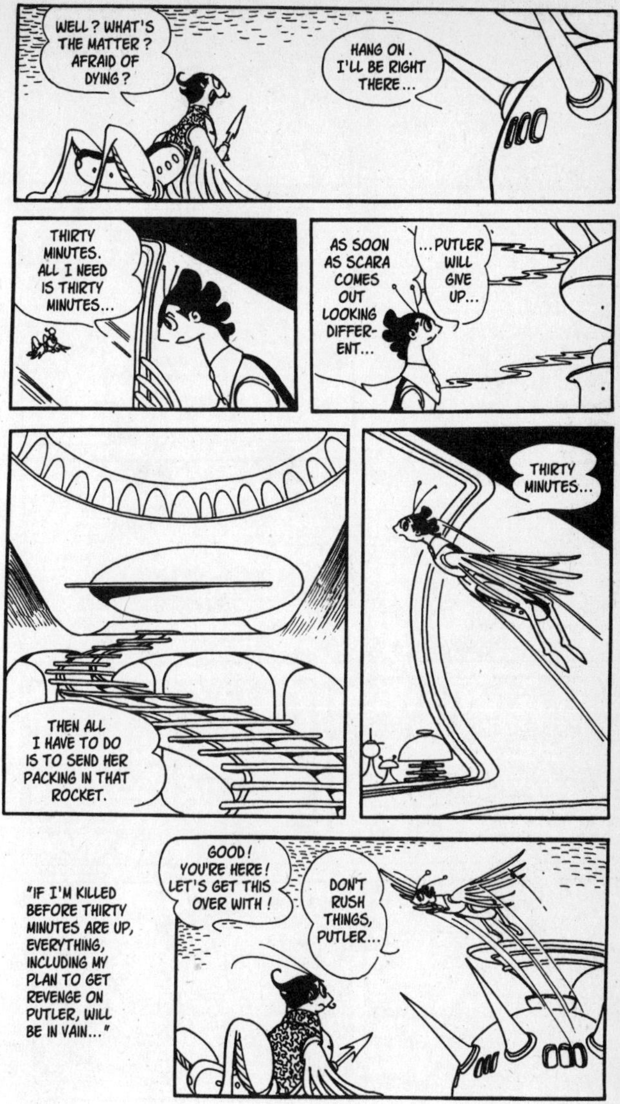
WELL? WHAT'S THE MATTER? AFRAID OF DYING?
HANG ON. I'LL BE RIGHT THERE...
THIRTY MINUTES. ALL I NEED IS THIRTY MINUTES...
AS SOON AS SCARA COMES OUT LOOKING DIFFER-ENT...
...PUTLER WILL GIVE UP...
THEN ALL I HAVE TO DO IS TO SEND HER PACKING IN THAT ROCKET.
THIRTY MINUTES...
"IF I'M KILLED BEFORE THIRTY MINUTES ARE UP, EVERYTHING, INCLUDING MY PLAN TO GET REVENGE ON PUTLER, WILL BE IN VAIN..."
GOOD! YOU'RE HERE! LET'S GET THIS OVER WITH!
DON'T RUSH THINGS, PUTLER...

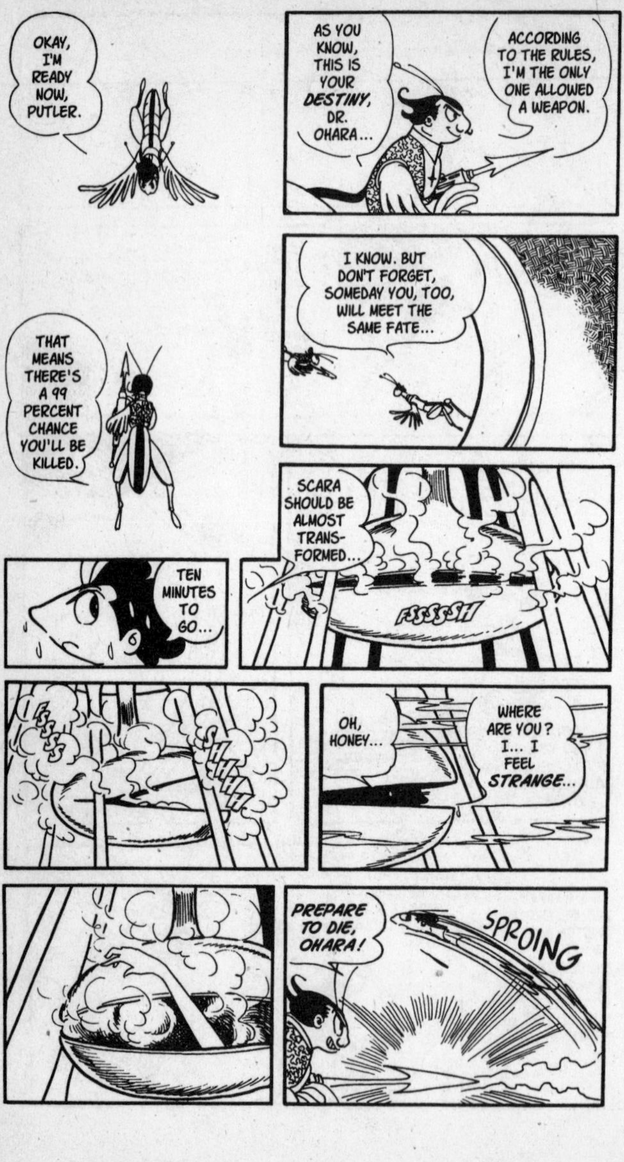
OKAY, I'M READY NOW, PUTLER.
AS YOU KNOW, THIS IS YOUR *DESTINY*, DR. OHARA...
ACCORDING TO THE RULES, I'M THE ONLY ONE ALLOWED A WEAPON.
I KNOW. BUT DON'T FORGET, SOMEDAY YOU, TOO, WILL MEET THE SAME FATE...
THAT MEANS THERE'S A 99 PERCENT CHANCE YOU'LL BE KILLED.
TEN MINUTES TO GO...
SCARA SHOULD BE ALMOST TRANS-FORMED...
FSSSSH
FSSSS
OH, HONEY...
WHERE ARE YOU? I... I FEEL *STRANGE*...
PREPARE TO DIE, OHARA!
SPROING

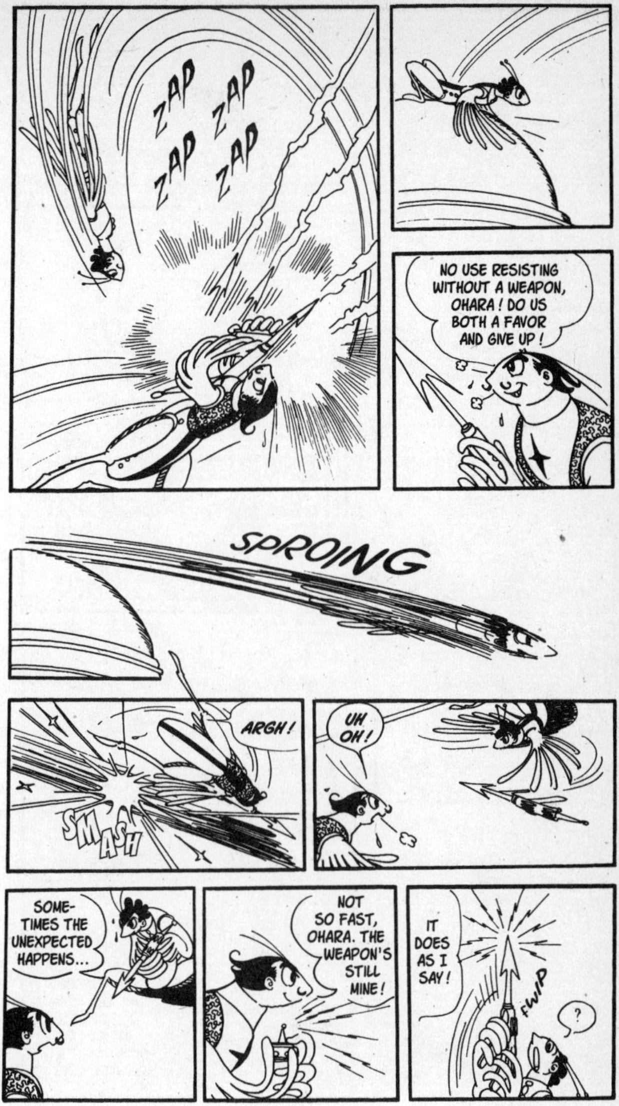
ZAP ZAP ZAP ZAP
NO USE RESISTING WITHOUT A WEAPON, OHARA! DO US BOTH A FAVOR AND GIVE UP!
SPROING
ARGH!
SMASH
UH OH!
SOME-TIMES THE UNEXPECTED HAPPENS...
NOT SO FAST, OHARA. THE WEAPON'S STILL MINE!
IT DOES AS I SAY!
FWIP
?

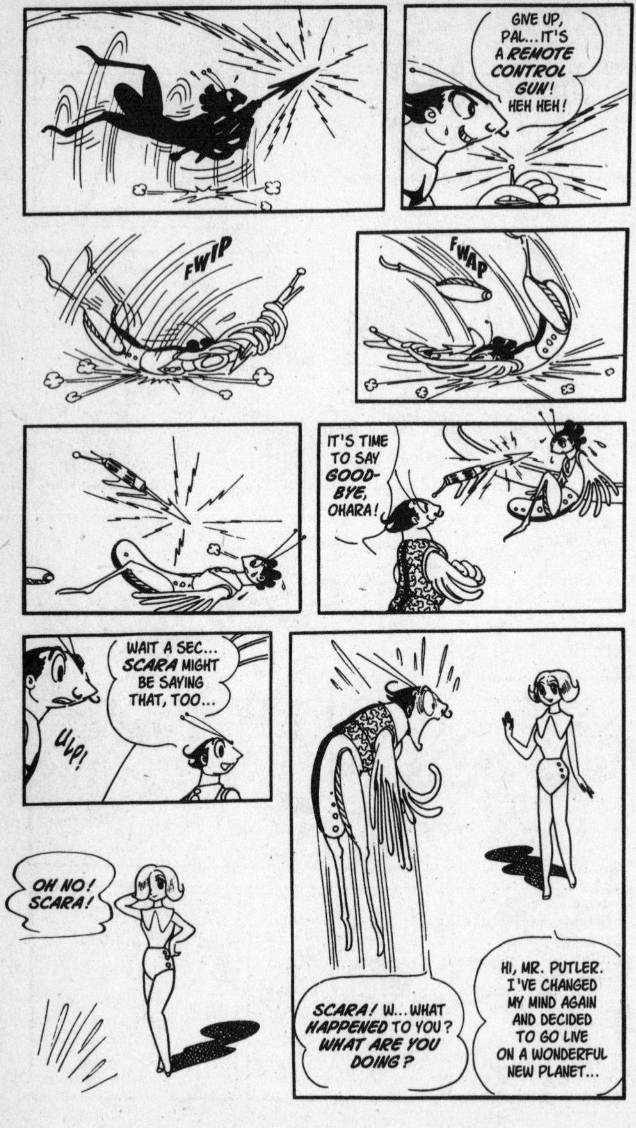
GIVE UP, PAL... IT'S A REMOTE CONTROL GUN! HEH HEH!
FWIP
FWAP
IT'S TIME TO SAY GOOD-BYE, OHARA!
WAIT A SEC... SCARA MIGHT BE SAYING THAT, TOO...
ULP!
SCARA! W... WHAT HAPPENED TO YOU? WHAT ARE YOU DOING?
HI, MR. PUTLER. I'VE CHANGED MY MIND AGAIN AND DECIDED TO GO LIVE ON A WONDERFUL NEW PLANET...
OH NO! SCARA!

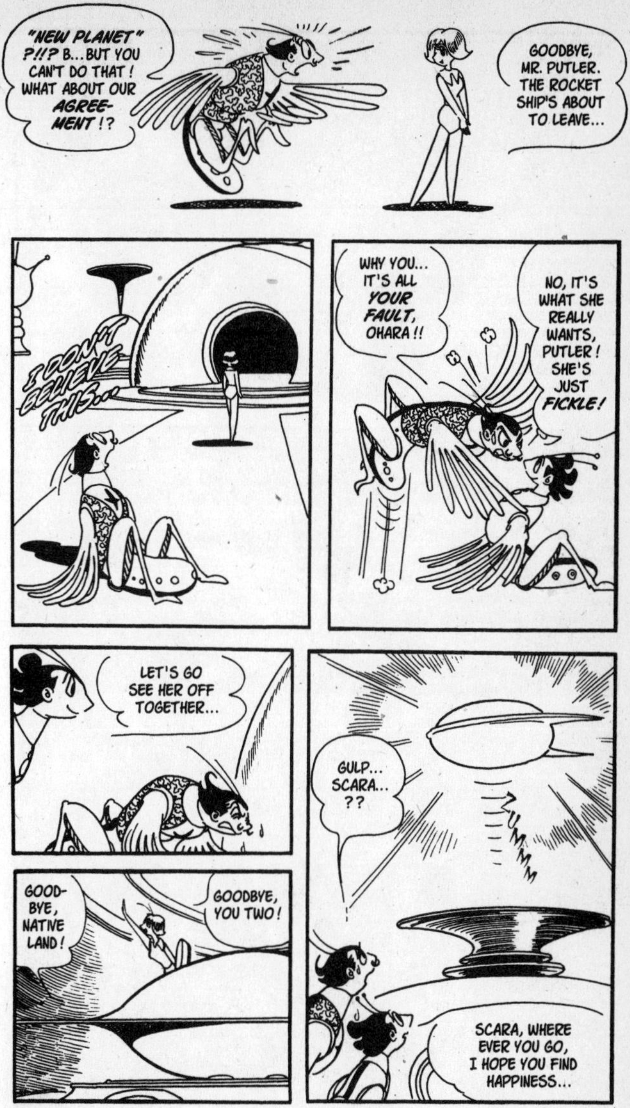
"NEW PLANET" ?!!? B...BUT YOU CAN'T DO THAT! WHAT ABOUT OUR AGREE-MENT!?
GOODBYE, MR. PUTLER. THE ROCKET SHIP'S ABOUT TO LEAVE...
I DON'T BELIEVE THIS...
WHY YOU... IT'S ALL YOUR FAULT, OHARA!!
NO, IT'S WHAT SHE REALLY WANTS, PUTLER! SHE'S JUST FICKLE!
LET'S GO SEE HER OFF TOGETHER...
GOOD-BYE, NATIVE LAND!
GOODBYE, YOU TWO!
GULP... SCARA... ??
ZUMMM
SCARA, WHERE EVER YOU GO, I HOPE YOU FIND HAPPINESS...

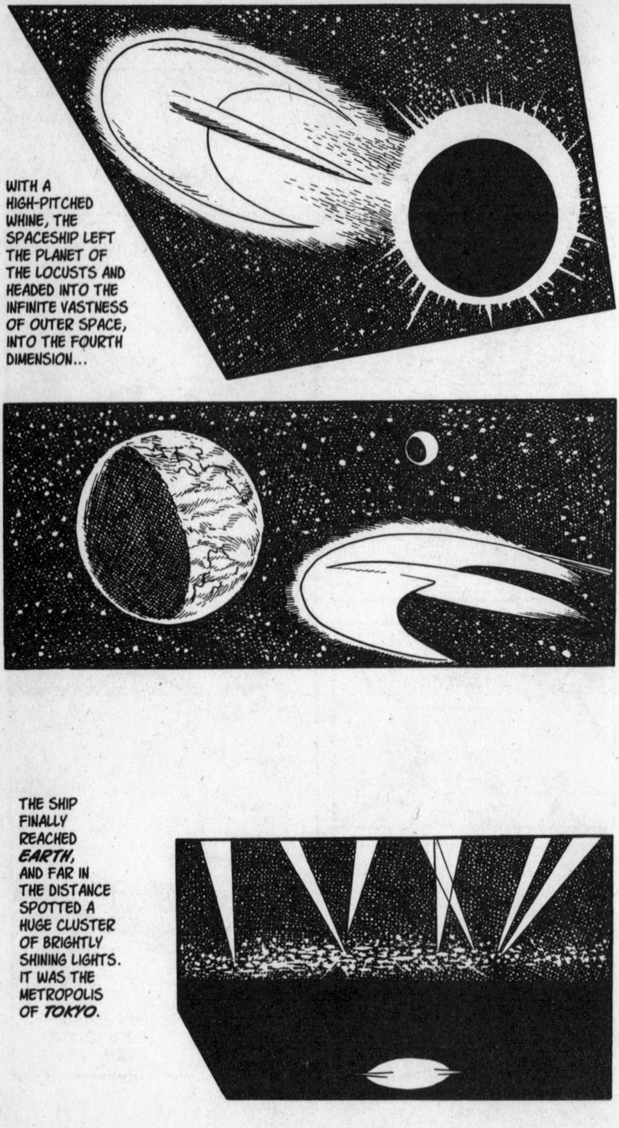
WITH A HIGH-PITCHED WHINE, THE SPACESHIP LEFT THE PLANET OF THE LOCUSTS AND HEADED INTO THE INFINITE VASTNESS OF OUTER SPACE, INTO THE FOURTH DIMENSION...
THE SHIP FINALLY REACHED *EARTH*, AND FAR IN THE DISTANCE SPOTTED A HUGE CLUSTER OF BRIGHTLY SHINING LIGHTS. IT WAS THE METROPOLIS OF *TOKYO*.

THE SPACESHIP PLUNGED INTO THE WATERS OF TOKYO BAY, BUT AS IT DID SO IT WAS *IRREPARABLY DAMAGED* BY THE FORCE OF THE IMPACT AND THE WATER PRESSURE.

SCARA, ONLY HALF-CONSCIOUS, PRESSED HER BODY AGAINST THE ESCAPE VALVE, AND JUST IN TIME MADE IT OUT OF THE SHIP INSIDE A GIANT AIR BUBBLE.

IT WAS THEN THAT THE HUGE EXPLOSION DESCRIBED AT THE BEGINNING OF THE STORY TOOK PLACE...

SO YOU SEE, MY SHIP'S BEEN DESTROYED, AND I'LL NEVER BE ABLE TO RETURN TO MY HOME PLANET.

NOT SO FAST... LET ME TALK TO PROFESSOR OCHANOMIZU ABOUT THIS.

HE'S THE HEAD OF THE MINISTRY OF SCIENCE.

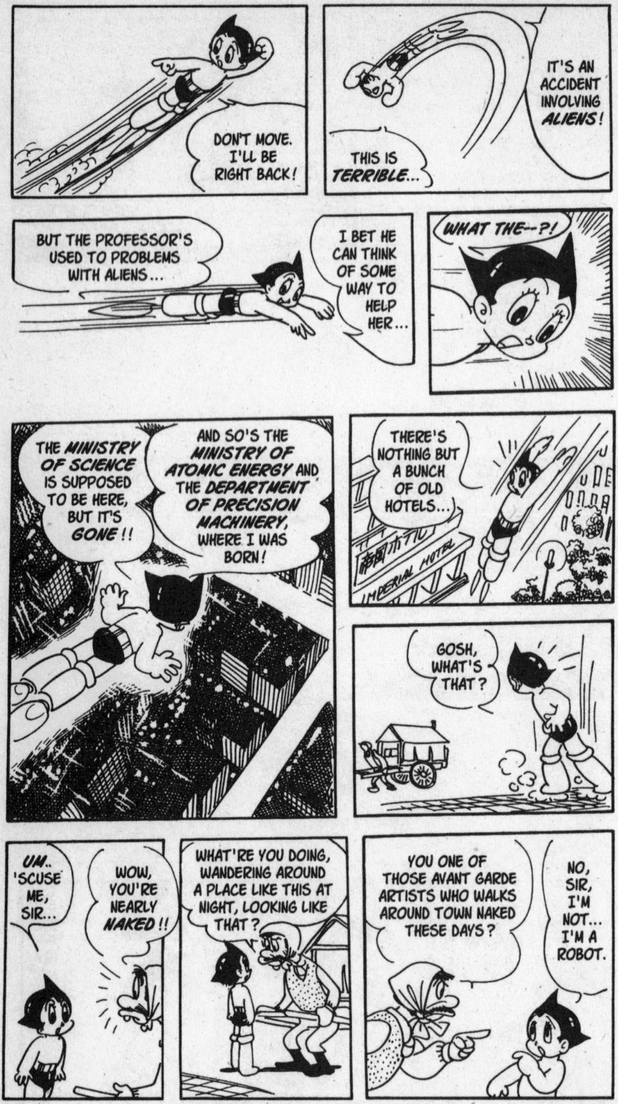

DON'T MOVE. I'LL BE RIGHT BACK!
THIS IS *TERRIBLE*...
IT'S AN ACCIDENT INVOLVING *ALIENS*!
BUT THE PROFESSOR'S USED TO PROBLEMS WITH ALIENS...
I BET HE CAN THINK OF SOME WAY TO HELP HER...
WHAT THE--?!
THE *MINISTRY OF SCIENCE* IS SUPPOSED TO BE HERE, BUT IT'S *GONE*!!
AND SO'S THE *MINISTRY OF ATOMIC ENERGY* AND THE *DEPARTMENT OF PRECISION MACHINERY*, WHERE I WAS BORN!
THERE'S NOTHING BUT A BUNCH OF OLD HOTELS...
帝国ホテル
IMPERIAL HOTEL
GOSH, WHAT'S THAT?
UM.. 'SCUSE ME, SIR...
WOW, YOU'RE NEARLY *NAKED*!!
WHAT'RE YOU DOING, WANDERING AROUND A PLACE LIKE THIS AT NIGHT, LOOKING LIKE THAT?
YOU ONE OF THOSE AVANT GARDE ARTISTS WHO WALKS AROUND TOWN NAKED THESE DAYS?
NO, SIR, I'M NOT... I'M A ROBOT.

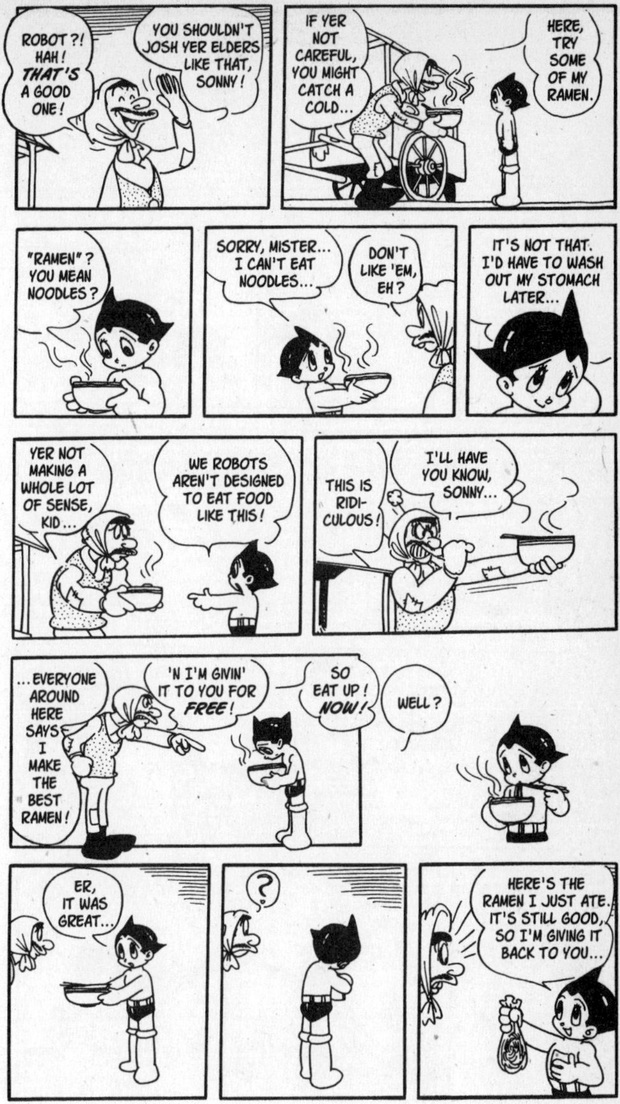
ROBOT?! HAH! THAT'S A GOOD ONE!
YOU SHOULDN'T JOSH YER ELDERS LIKE THAT, SONNY!
IF YER NOT CAREFUL, YOU MIGHT CATCH A COLD...
HERE, TRY SOME OF MY RAMEN.
"RAMEN"? YOU MEAN NOODLES?
SORRY, MISTER... I CAN'T EAT NOODLES...
DON'T LIKE 'EM, EH?
IT'S NOT THAT. I'D HAVE TO WASH OUT MY STOMACH LATER...
YER NOT MAKING A WHOLE LOT OF SENSE, KID...
WE ROBOTS AREN'T DESIGNED TO EAT FOOD LIKE THIS!
THIS IS RIDI-CULOUS!
I'LL HAVE YOU KNOW, SONNY...
...EVERYONE AROUND HERE SAYS I MAKE THE BEST RAMEN!
'N I'M GIVIN' IT TO YOU FOR FREE!
SO EAT UP! NOW!
WELL?
ER, IT WAS GREAT...
?
HERE'S THE RAMEN I JUST ATE. IT'S STILL GOOD, SO I'M GIVING IT BACK TO YOU...

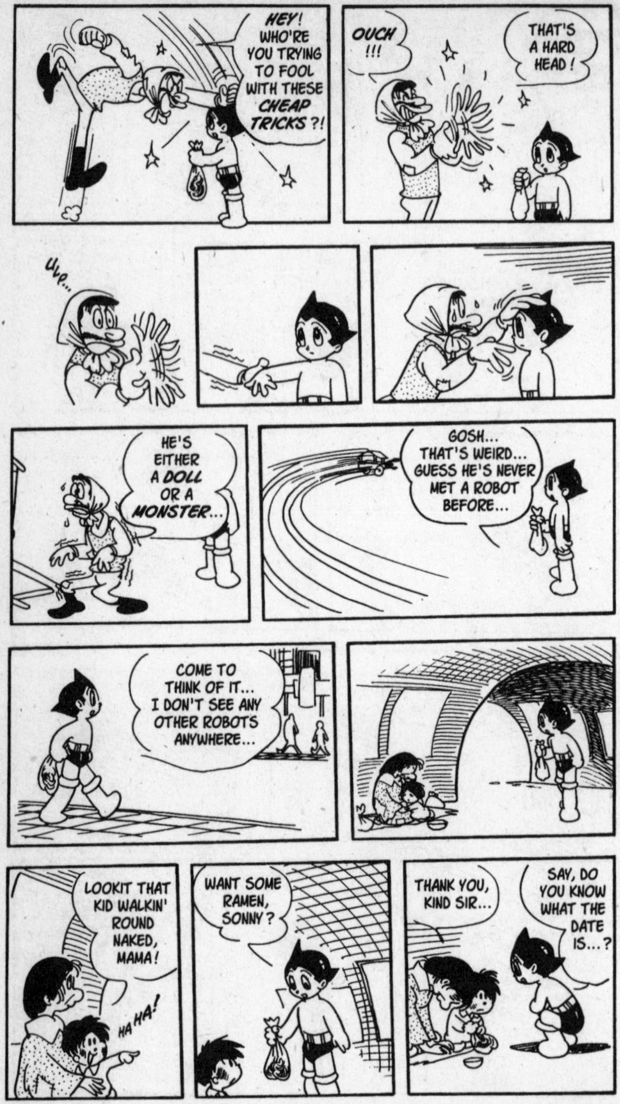
HEY! WHO'RE YOU TRYING TO FOOL WITH THESE CHEAP TRICKS?!
OUCH !!!
THAT'S A HARD HEAD!
UUP...
HE'S EITHER A DOLL OR A MONSTER...
GOSH... THAT'S WEIRD... GUESS HE'S NEVER MET A ROBOT BEFORE...
COME TO THINK OF IT... I DON'T SEE ANY OTHER ROBOTS ANYWHERE...
LOOKIT THAT KID WALKIN' ROUND NAKED, MAMA!
HA HA!
WANT SOME RAMEN, SONNY?
THANK YOU, KIND SIR...
SAY, DO YOU KNOW WHAT THE DATE IS...?

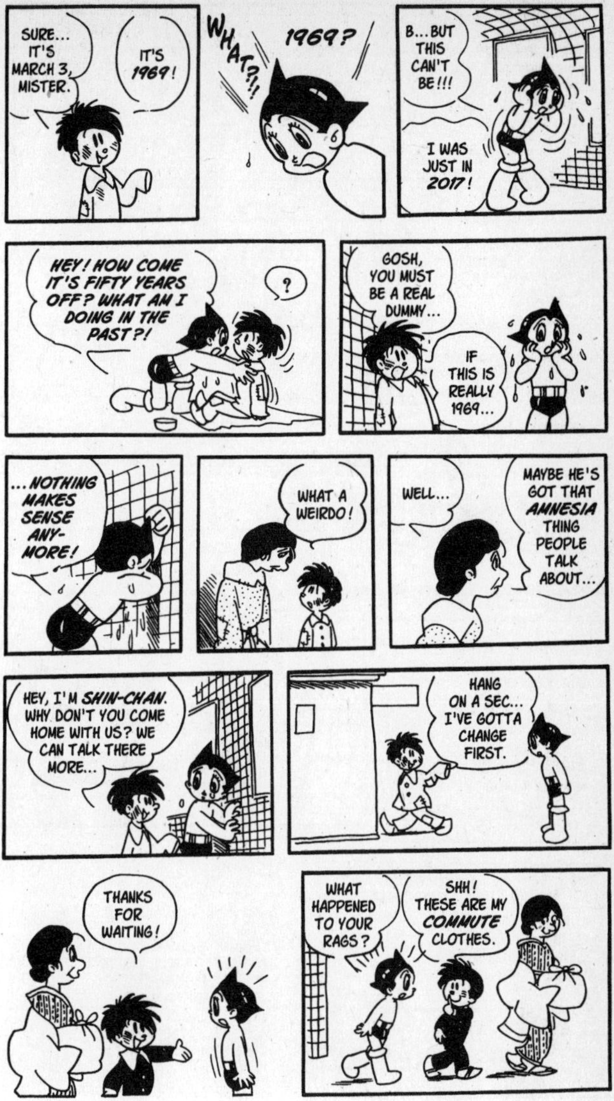
SURE... IT'S MARCH 3, MISTER.
IT'S 1969!
WHAT?!!
1969?
B...BUT THIS CAN'T BE!!!
I WAS JUST IN 2017!
HEY! HOW COME IT'S FIFTY YEARS OFF? WHAT AM I DOING IN THE PAST?!
?
GOSH, YOU MUST BE A REAL DUMMY...
IF THIS IS REALLY 1969...
...NOTHING MAKES SENSE ANY-MORE!
WHAT A WEIRDO!
WELL...
MAYBE HE'S GOT THAT AMNESIA THING PEOPLE TALK ABOUT...
HEY, I'M SHIN-CHAN. WHY DON'T YOU COME HOME WITH US? WE CAN TALK THERE MORE...
HANG ON A SEC... I'VE GOTTA CHANGE FIRST.
THANKS FOR WAITING!
WHAT HAPPENED TO YOUR RAGS?
SHH! THESE ARE MY COMMUTE CLOTHES.

ASTRO TRIED HARD TO FIGURE OUT WHAT WAS GOING ON. HE KNEW HE HAD BEEN IN 2017 BEFORE THE EXPLOSION. COULD HE POSSIBLY HAVE BEEN *BLOWN BACK* IN TIME TO 1969 BY ITS FORCE? HE DESPERATELY WANTED SOMEONE TO TELL HIM THE ANSWER.

HERE'S WHERE WE LIVE...

ASTRO ENTERED THE HOUSE AS INVITED BY THE BOY, AND HE COULD SCARCELY BELIEVE HIS EYES. THEY HAD BEEN BEGGING ON THE STREET, SO HE IMAGINED THEY LIVED IN A RUN-DOWN HOVEL...

BUT THEY HAD A FINE HOUSE WITH A GATE AND EVERYTHING. INSIDE, THEY HAD BIG CLOSETS AND DRESSERS AND A TV SET. IT WAS JUST LIKE THE HOUSES MIDDLE-CLASS SALARIED WORKERS LIVED IN...

THAT WAS MY DAD. HE WAS REALLY IMPORTANT!

"HAVE A SEAT! I KNOW YOU'RE SHOCKED, BUT IT REALLY IS OUR HOUSE. DAD BUILT IT AFTER THIRTY YEARS OF BEGGING ON THE STREETS AND SAVING HIS PENNIES. HE WAS THE CHAIRMAN OF THE NATIONAL HOMELESS FEDERATION."

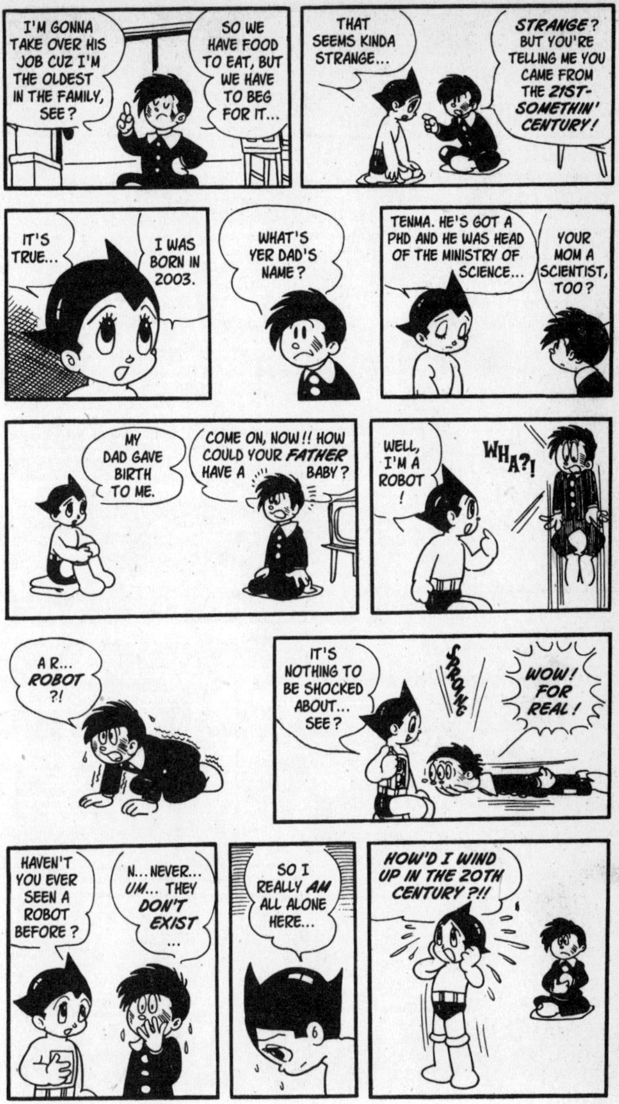
I'M GONNA TAKE OVER HIS JOB CUZ I'M THE OLDEST IN THE FAMILY, SEE?
SO WE HAVE FOOD TO EAT, BUT WE HAVE TO BEG FOR IT...
THAT SEEMS KINDA STRANGE...
STRANGE? BUT YOU'RE TELLING ME YOU CAME FROM THE 21ST-SOMETHIN' CENTURY!
IT'S TRUE...
I WAS BORN IN 2003.
WHAT'S YER DAD'S NAME?
TENMA. HE'S GOT A PHD AND HE WAS HEAD OF THE MINISTRY OF SCIENCE...
YOUR MOM A SCIENTIST, TOO?
MY DAD GAVE BIRTH TO ME.
COME ON, NOW!! HOW COULD YOUR FATHER HAVE A BABY?
WELL, I'M A ROBOT!
WHA?!
A R... ROBOT?!
IT'S NOTHING TO BE SHOCKED ABOUT... SEE?
SPRONG
WOW! FOR REAL!
HAVEN'T YOU EVER SEEN A ROBOT BEFORE?
N... NEVER... UM... THEY DON'T EXIST...
SO I REALLY AM ALL ALONE HERE...
HOW'D I WIND UP IN THE 20TH CENTURY?!!

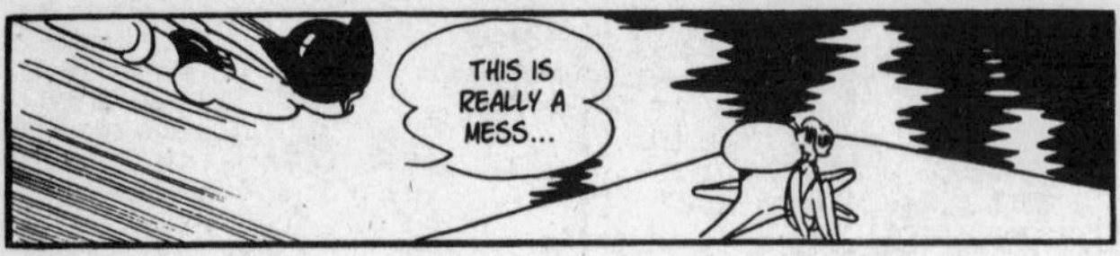
THIS IS REALLY A MESS...

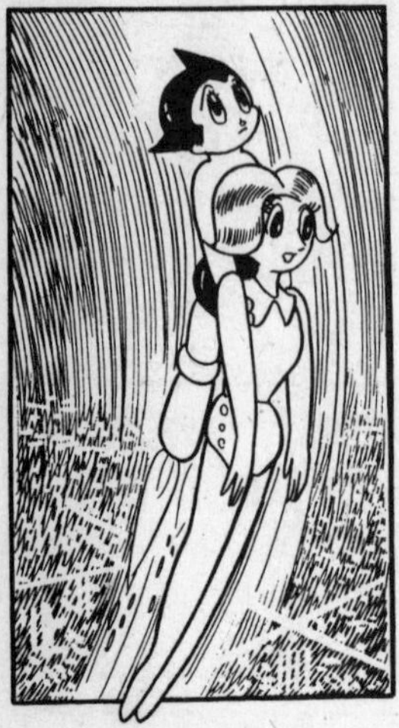

HAD ASTRO BEEN A HUMAN, HE PROBABLY WOULD HAVE FAINTED FROM THE SHOCK OF BEING IN THE WRONG TIME...

HE FLEW BACK TO THE BAY, PICKED UP SCARA, AND TOOK OFF AGAIN.

"WHERE ARE WE GOING?" SHE ASKED. "TO PROFESSOR OCHANOMIZU?"

"HE DOESN'T EXIST YET!" ASTRO REPLIED, SOUNDING AS THOUGH HE WOULD BURST INTO TEARS. "WE'RE GOING TO MY HOME."

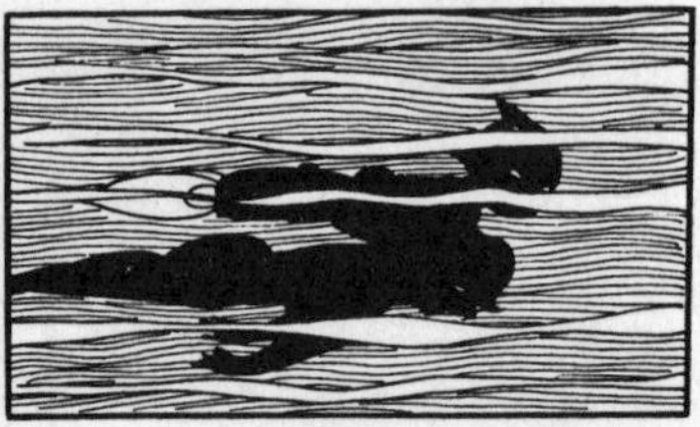

"TO YOUR HOME?" SCARA PERSISTED. "IS IT IN THIS CITY?"

"IT'S SUPPOSED TO BE," ASTRO REPLIED, FEELING TENSE JUST AS THEY LANDED.

THE SITE OF HIS OLD HOME WAS OVERGROWN WITH GRASS, AND THERE WAS NOT A SOUL AROUND. IT WAS A VACANT LOT, THE GROUND NEGLECTED AND EXPOSED...

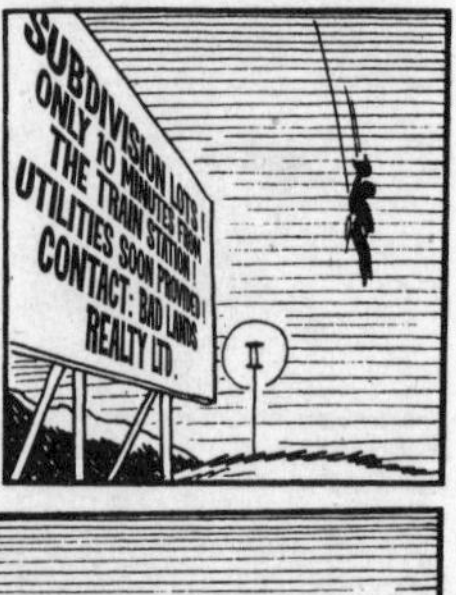
SUBDIVISION LOTS!
ONLY 10 MINUTES FROM THE TRAIN STATION!
UTILITIES SOON PROVIDED!
CONTACT: BAD LANDS REALTY LTD.

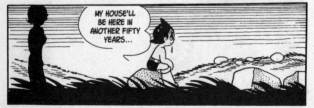

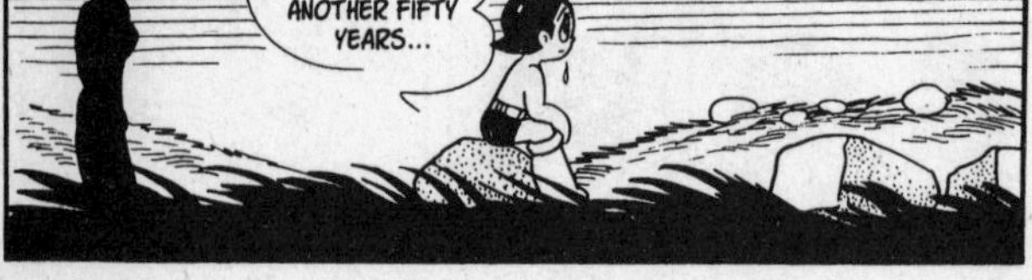
MY HOUSE'LL BE HERE IN ANOTHER FIFTY YEARS...

"IF I WAIT FIFTY YEARS, MY HOUSE'LL BE HERE, AND I CAN LIVE HAPPILY WITH MY MOM 'N DAD AND URAN AND COBALT. BUT LONG BEFORE THEN I'LL *RUN OUT OF ENERGY* AND TURN INTO *LIFELESS JUNK*... I'LL BE TAKEN TO THE DUMP OR CHOPPED UP FOR PARTS..."

TEARS FELL FROM ASTRO'S EYES. EVEN ROBOTS FEEL SADNESS, AND ASTRO HAD ARTIFICIAL TEAR DUCTS BUILT INTO HIS EYES, WITH WATER DESIGNED TO COME OUT OF THEM. SCARA CAME UP QUIETLY BEHIND HIM AND PUT HER ARMS ON HIS SHOULDERS...

YOU POOR ROBOT....

WHEN ASTRO COMPLAINED THAT HE COULDN'T UNDERSTAND WHAT HAD HAPPENED, SCARA REPLIED, "I DON'T KNOW WHY, ASTRO, BUT MAYBE IT WAS BECAUSE THERE WAS A TIME TRANSPORT DEVICE IN MY SPACE SHIP. WHEN IT EXPLODED, MAYBE WE WERE ACCIDENTALLY TOSSED INTO THE FOURTH DIMENSION. WE IMMEDIATELY CAME BACK TO THE SAME PLACE WE WERE IN, BUT MAYBE THE TIME WAS OFF BY FIFTY YEARS..."

43

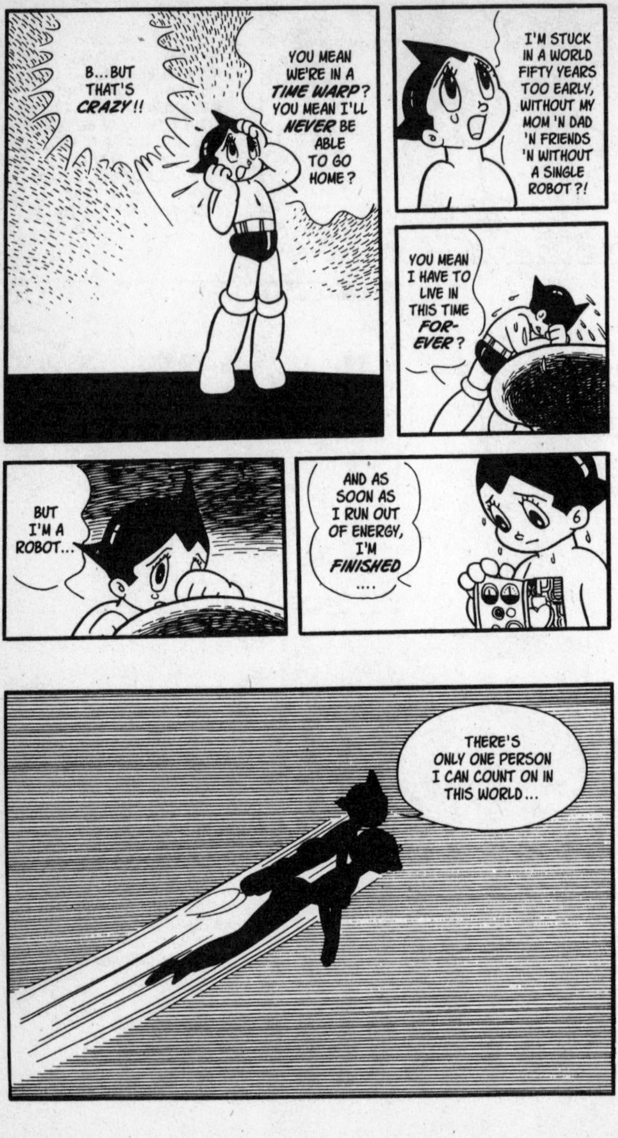
B...BUT THAT'S CRAZY!!
YOU MEAN WE'RE IN A TIME WARP? YOU MEAN I'LL NEVER BE ABLE TO GO HOME?
I'M STUCK IN A WORLD FIFTY YEARS TOO EARLY, WITHOUT MY MOM 'N DAD 'N FRIENDS 'N WITHOUT A SINGLE ROBOT?!
YOU MEAN I HAVE TO LIVE IN THIS TIME FOR-EVER?
BUT I'M A ROBOT...
AND AS SOON AS I RUN OUT OF ENERGY, I'M FINISHED ....
THERE'S ONLY ONE PERSON I CAN COUNT ON IN THIS WORLD...

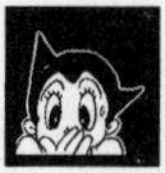

LIVING ON EARTH, 101

ASTRO'S FRIEND SHIN-CHAN WAS BUSY SORTING JUNK IN FRONT OF HIS HOUSE. HE ALSO WENT BY THE NICKNAME OF *"OVERPASS MANGA MAN,"* NOT BECAUSE HE WAS A CARTOON CHARACTER, BUT BECAUSE HE WAS ALWAYS SITTING UNDER THE OVERPASS READING COMIC BOOKS...

SHIN-CHAN WAS ASTONISHED WHEN ASTRO AND SCARA SUDDENLY LANDED IN FRONT OF HIM. "WHAT?" HE SAID, "YOU'RE STILL HERE? YOU MEAN YOU COULDN'T GO BACK TO THE FUTURE?"

"THAT'S RIGHT..."
ASTRO SADLY REPLIED.

"YOU POOR KID," SHIN-CHAN SAID, TRYING TO CONSOLE HIM. WHEN ASTRO EXPLAINED THAT HE WOULD HAVE TO TRY TO LIVE IN SHIN-CHAN'S WORLD, SHIN-CHAN TRIED TO ENCOURAGE HIM, TELLING HIM THAT IT WASN'T SUCH A BAD TIME AND THAT IT WAS IN FACT FAIRLY EASY TO MAKE ENDS MEET AS A BEGGAR. THEN, STARING AT SCARA, HE ASKED, "BUT WHO'S THE LADY WITH YOU?"

"BEFORE I EXPLAIN," ASTRO REPLIED, "DON'T YOU HAVE SOMETHING SHE COULD WEAR?"

"WHY NOT BUY HER SOME CLOTHES AT A STORE?"

"WELL, I CAN'T... AND THERE'S A REASON..."

"HM. ALL OUR CLOTHES HERE ARE IN TATTERS, BUT WE'VE GOT SOME CLOTH. MAYBE WE CAN MAKE HER SOMETHING... LET'S MEASURE HER..."

SCARA IMMEDIATELY GOT DOWN ON ALL FOURS. SHIN-CHAN DIDN'T KNOW WHAT TO MAKE OF IT.

WHAT'S WITH THE WEIRD POSE?

SCARA! DON'T DO THAT!

THAT'S WHAT EVERYONE DOES TO GET MEASURED BACK HOME...

BUT THAT'S FOR *LOCUST-PEOPLE*...

ON EARTH PEOPLE STAND UP!

WHAT'S THE DEAL WITH THIS LADY, ASTRO?

UM... SHE'S LIKE MY OLDER SISTER...

SO SHE'S A ROBOT, TOO?

WELL, I GOT HER DIMENSIONS.

BUT HOW COME SHE NEEDS CLOTHES IF SHE'S A ROBOT...?

I'LL GO FIND SOMEONE TO STITCH 'EM TOGETHER...

WAIT! I CAN SEW!

I CAN PUT SOMETHING TOGETHER WITH THIS INFORMATION...

REALLY? YOU KNOW HOW TO MAKE CLOTHES?

SURE. WE CUT THE CLOTH LIKE THIS...

SNIP SNIP SNIP

?

SNIP SNIP SNIP

B...BUT YOU'RE RUINING GOOD CLOTH!!

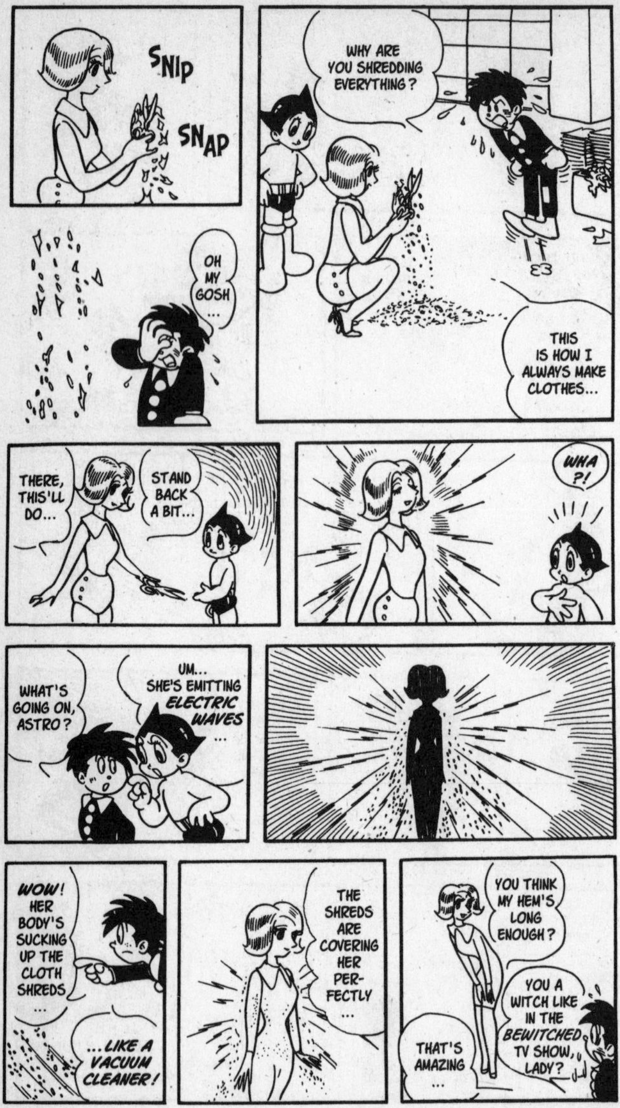
SNIP
SNAP
WHY ARE YOU SHREDDING EVERYTHING?
OH MY GOSH...
THIS IS HOW I ALWAYS MAKE CLOTHES...
THERE, THIS'LL DO...
STAND BACK A BIT...
WHA ?!
WHAT'S GOING ON, ASTRO?
UM... SHE'S EMITTING ELECTRIC WAVES...
WOW! HER BODY'S SUCKING UP THE CLOTH SHREDS...
...LIKE A VACUUM CLEANER!
THE SHREDS ARE COVERING HER PER-FECTLY...
YOU THINK MY HEM'S LONG ENOUGH?
YOU A WITCH LIKE IN THE BEWITCHED TV SHOW, LADY?
THAT'S AMAZING...

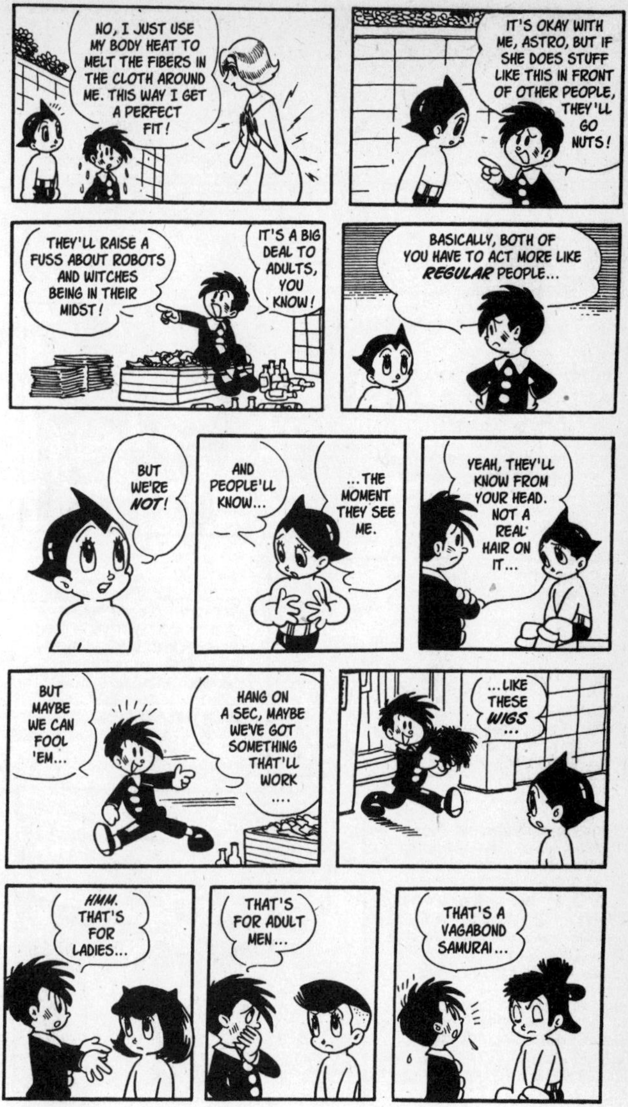
NO, I JUST USE MY BODY HEAT TO MELT THE FIBERS IN THE CLOTH AROUND ME. THIS WAY I GET A PERFECT FIT!
IT'S OKAY WITH ME, ASTRO, BUT IF SHE DOES STUFF LIKE THIS IN FRONT OF OTHER PEOPLE, THEY'LL GO NUTS!
THEY'LL RAISE A FUSS ABOUT ROBOTS AND WITCHES BEING IN THEIR MIDST!
IT'S A BIG DEAL TO ADULTS, YOU KNOW!
BASICALLY, BOTH OF YOU HAVE TO ACT MORE LIKE *REGULAR* PEOPLE...
BUT WE'RE *NOT*!
AND PEOPLE'LL KNOW...
...THE MOMENT THEY SEE ME.
YEAH, THEY'LL KNOW FROM YOUR HEAD. NOT A REAL HAIR ON IT...
BUT MAYBE WE CAN FOOL 'EM...
HANG ON A SEC, MAYBE WE'VE GOT SOMETHING THAT'LL WORK ....
...LIKE THESE *WIGS* ...
HMM. THAT'S FOR LADIES...
THAT'S FOR ADULT MEN...
THAT'S A VAGABOND SAMURAI...

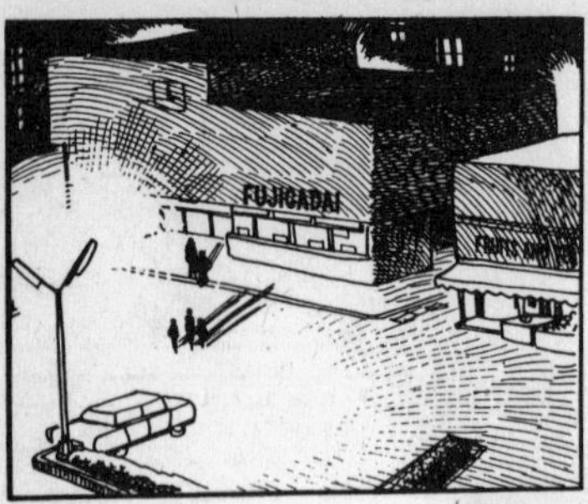
FUJIGADAI

THERE IS A SMALL TRAIN STATION CALLED FUJIGADAI, ABOUT AN HOUR'S CLICKETY-CLACK, CROWDED RIDE FROM THE CENTER OF TOKYO. IT'S IN THE OUTER SUBURBS, SO AT NIGHT THE SQUARE IN FRONT OF THE STATION IS QUITE DESERTED, BUT THIS IS WHERE ASTRO, SCARA, AND SHIN-CHAN NEXT SHOWED UP...

"I KNOW AN OLD GUY WHO RUNS AN APARTMENT BUILDING HERE," SAID SHIN-CHAN, "... AND YOU CAN PROB'LY LIVE IN IT."

"WHAT'S AN APARTMENT?" SCARA QUERIED. "IS IT LIKE A HOUSE?"

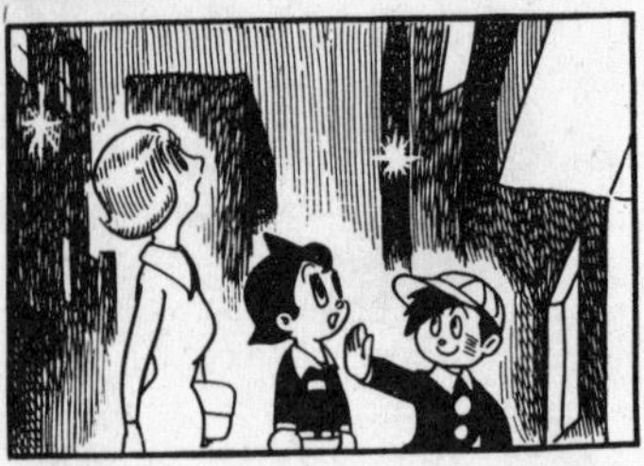

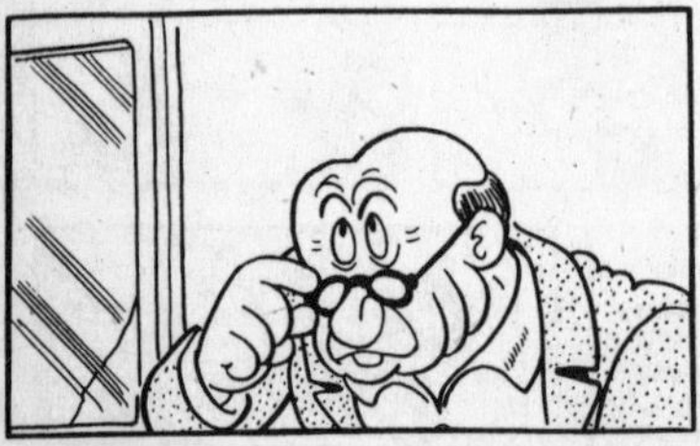

SHIN-CHAN COULDN'T BELIEVE THAT SCARA DIDN'T KNOW WHAT AN APARTMENT WAS. AS THEY MADE THEIR WAY THROUGH CROWDED BACKSTREETS, HE ADDED, "IT'S NOT VERY CLEAN, BUT IT'S REALLY CHEAP..."

THEY ARRIVED IN FRONT OF A RUN-DOWN APARTMENT BUILDING WITH A SIGN ON IT THAT SAID *NASUBI-SO*, OR "EGGPLANT PALACE." SHIN-CHAN YELLED OUT, "HEY, POPS!" WHEREUPON THE OWNER--A MIDDLE-AGED MAN WITH GLASSES SLIPPING OFF HIS NOSE--APPEARED AND SAID--

"YOU AGAIN, EH? I GOT THE PHONE CALL. SO THIS THE BROTHER AND SISTER YOU MENTIONED WHO'RE LOOKING FOR A PLACE TO LIVE, EH?"

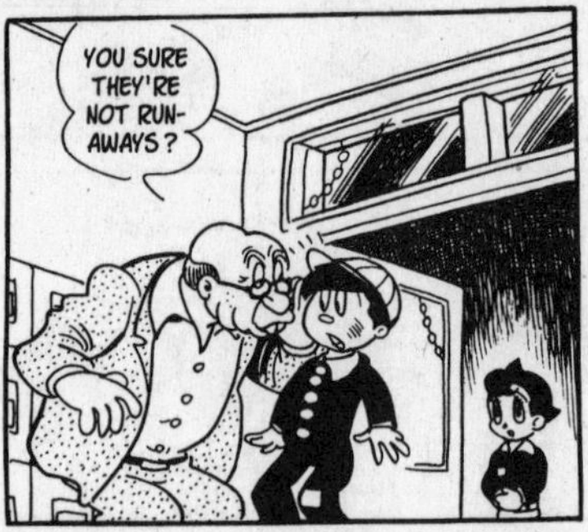
YOU SURE THEY'RE NOT RUN-AWAYS?

SHIN-CHAN ASKED IF THERE WERE ANY ROOMS AVAILABLE. THE MAN LOOKED AT SCARA SUSPICIOUSLY OUT OF THE CORNER OF HIS EYES, AND REPLIED...

"... WELL, YES, BUT WE ONLY RENT TO *TRUSTWORTHY* TENANTS..."

IT WAS EARLY SPRING, BUT COMING TO RENT A ROOM AT NIGHT, WITH NO COAT ON AND NO HANDBAG, WAS BOUND TO AROUSE SUSPICION.

THE TRIO FOLLOWED THE MAN UP THE BUILDING'S CREAKY STAIRS AND WATCHED AS HE OPENED ONE OF THE ROOMS WITH A KEY. BOASTING THAT "IT'S GOT GOOD SUNLIGHT," HE SHOWED THEM INSIDE. IT WAS A TINY, FOUR-AND-A-HALF TATAMI-MAT ROOM, THE STRAW MATS DISCOLORED FROM AGE AND COVERED WITH DUST.

SHIN-CHAN WHISPERED IN ASTRO'S EAR--

"THE OLD GUY USED TO BE A BEGGAR LIKE ME, BUT HE EARNED ENOUGH MONEY TO BUY THIS PLACE. HE SEEMS A LITTLE ODD, BUT DON'T WORRY, HE'S REALLY A GOOD FELLOW."

THINK SHE'S OKAY *UP HERE*?

"WELL, WHAT'S IT GONNA BE?" THE MANAGER ASKED THE TRIO. SCARA IMMEDIATELY GOT DOWN ON THE FLOOR MATS ON ALL FOURS. THE MANAGER LOOKED AT HER IN SHOCK, AND QUICKLY TOOK SHIN-CHAN ASIDE OUT OF THE ROOM AND WHISPERED, "MAYBE SHE'S DRUNK?"

"SO YOU WANT THE ROOM, RIGHT?"
SHIN-CHAN SAID TO ASTRO.

"SURE, WE'LL TAKE IT," ASTRO
ANSWERED.

"GOOD," SHIN-CHAN REPLIED. "I'LL
GO BACK HOME AND BRING YOU
STUFF YOU'LL NEED, LIKE AN OLD
FUTON, DESK, AND TEA KETTLE."

SHIN-CHAN AND THE OWNER THEN
PARTED FROM ASTRO AND SCARA.
ASTRO TURNED TO SCARA AND
COMMENTED, "GOSH, SHIN-CHAN
SURE IS A NICE GUY..."

"YES," SHE REPLIED, "FOR SUCH
A PRIMITIVE PERSON."

"WHAT DO YOU MEAN?" ASTRO SAID.

"WELL, HE LEADS SUCH A PRIMITIVE
LIFE," SAID SCARA. "LOOK AT THIS
ROOM. IT'S OKAY, I SUPPOSE, IF
YOU REALIZE IT'S WHERE PRIMITIVES
DWELL..."

ASTRO WAS UPSET BY THIS, AND
RETORTED, "WELL, I'M SURE THERE
ARE BETTER PLACES *SOME-
WHERE*..."

"LET'S GO THERE THEN," SAID SCARA.

"BUT WE'D PROBABLY NEED A LOT
MORE MONEY."

"MONEY?" SCARA WAS TAKEN ABACK.
"I DON'T HAVE ANY OF THAT!"

NEITHER DO I. WE'VE GOT TO GO TO WORK!

WE WHAT?

"WORK?" SCARA SAID. "ME?!
I DON'T WANT TO WORK. I
CAME HERE TO WALK AROUND IN
THE MOUNTAINS AND FIELDS, AND
SEE THE RIVERS, OCEANS, AND
FORESTS... I WANT TO ENJOY
MYSELF!"

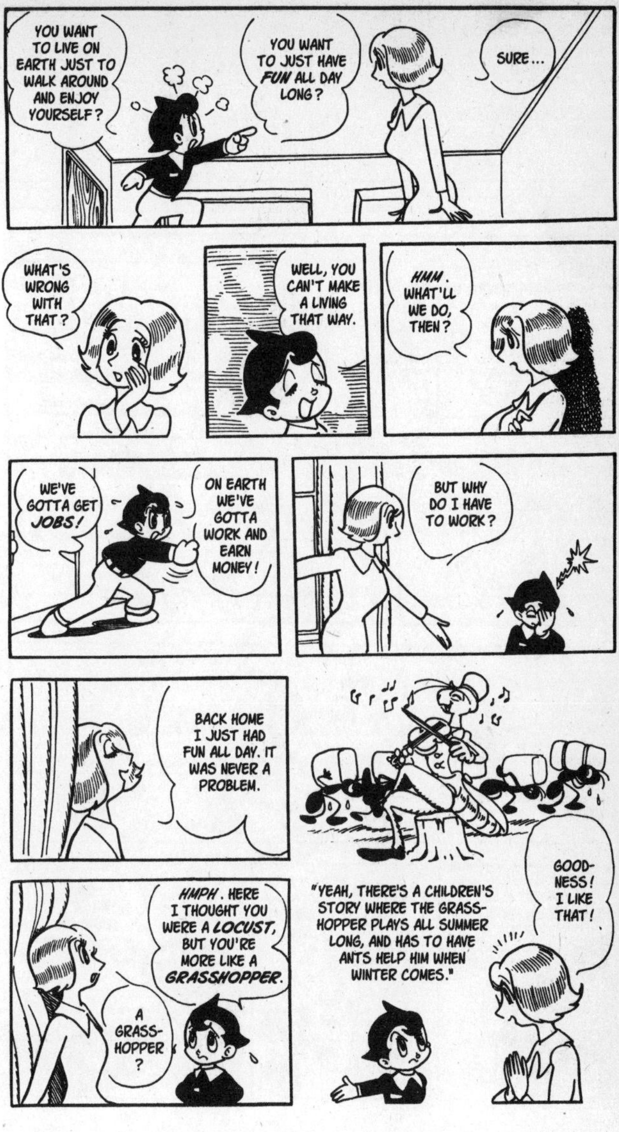
YOU WANT TO LIVE ON EARTH JUST TO WALK AROUND AND ENJOY YOURSELF?
YOU WANT TO JUST HAVE FUN ALL DAY LONG?
SURE...
WHAT'S WRONG WITH THAT?
WELL, YOU CAN'T MAKE A LIVING THAT WAY.
HMM. WHAT'LL WE DO, THEN?
WE'VE GOTTA GET JOBS!
ON EARTH WE'VE GOTTA WORK AND EARN MONEY!
BUT WHY DO I HAVE TO WORK?
BACK HOME I JUST HAD FUN ALL DAY. IT WAS NEVER A PROBLEM.
HMPH. HERE I THOUGHT YOU WERE A LOCUST, BUT YOU'RE MORE LIKE A GRASSHOPPER.
A GRASS-HOPPER?
"YEAH, THERE'S A CHILDREN'S STORY WHERE THE GRASS-HOPPER PLAYS ALL SUMMER LONG, AND HAS TO HAVE ANTS HELP HIM WHEN WINTER COMES."
GOOD-NESS! I LIKE THAT!

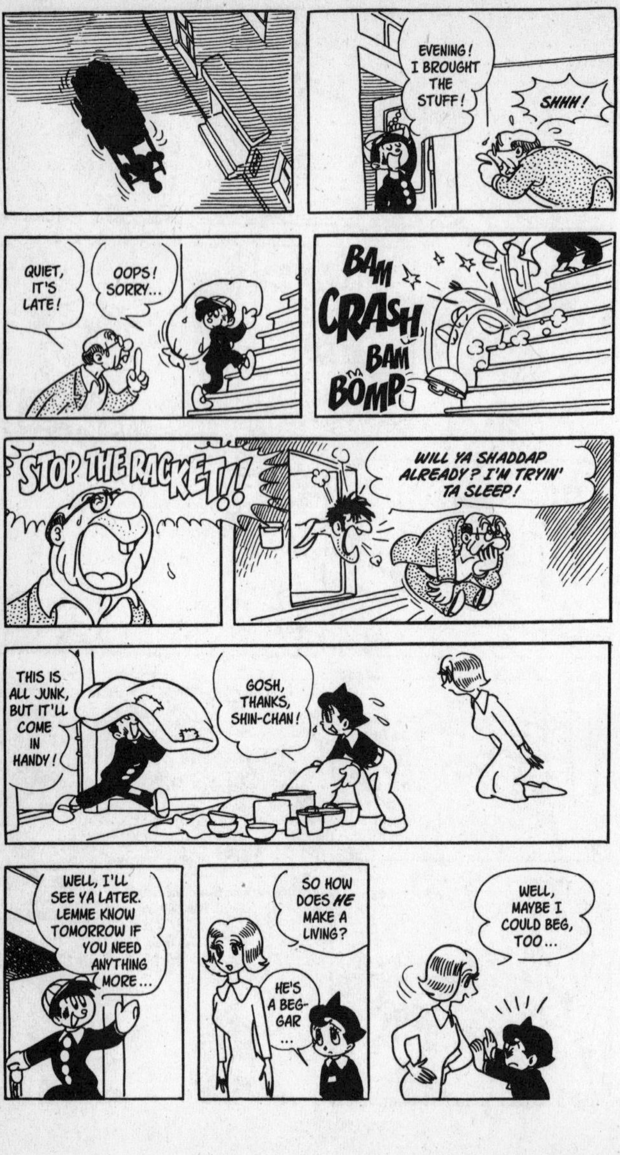
EVENING! I BROUGHT THE STUFF!
SHHH!
QUIET, IT'S LATE!
OOPS! SORRY...
BAM
CRASH
BAM
BOMP
STOP THE RACKET!!
WILL YA SHADDAP ALREADY? I'M TRYIN' TA SLEEP!
THIS IS ALL JUNK, BUT IT'LL COME IN HANDY!
GOSH, THANKS, SHIN-CHAN!
WELL, I'LL SEE YA LATER. LEMME KNOW TOMORROW IF YOU NEED ANYTHING MORE...
SO HOW DOES *HE* MAKE A LIVING?
HE'S A BEG-GAR ...
WELL, MAYBE I COULD BEG, TOO...

ASTRO AND SCARA CLOSED THE ROOM'S LACE CURTAINS, PULLED OUT THE FUTON, LAY DOWN, AND FELL SOUNDLY ASLEEP. THE LIGHT OF THE MOON SHOWN THROUGH THE WINDOW AND GENTLY ILLUMINATED THEIR FACES AS THEY DREAMED.

ASTRO WOKE AS DAWN APPROACHED. SCARA WAS STILL SLEEPING PEACEFULLY, BUT HE CHECKED HIS ENERGY LEVEL. HE REALIZED THAT IF HE WERE CAREFUL, HE MIGHT BE OKAY FOR THREE YEARS.

AFTER THINKING A WHILE, ASTRO SUDDENLY OPENED THE WINDOW AND FLEW UP INTO THE NIGHT SKY. UNLESS HE COULD MAKE SOME MONEY BY MORNING, HE KNEW THEY'D BE IN TROUBLE...

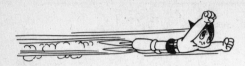

ANYWHERE
WILL DO...

ALL I NEED'S A GOOD VOLCANO...

YAY! THERE'S ONE!

WOW! IT'S REALLY ACTIVE!

WHEN VOLCANOES ARE FORMED...

...THE HEAT AND PRESSURE...

...CREATE DIAMONDS...

I LEARNED THAT IN SCHOOL...

THIS ISN'T WHAT I WANT...

DEVIL'S CAULDRON

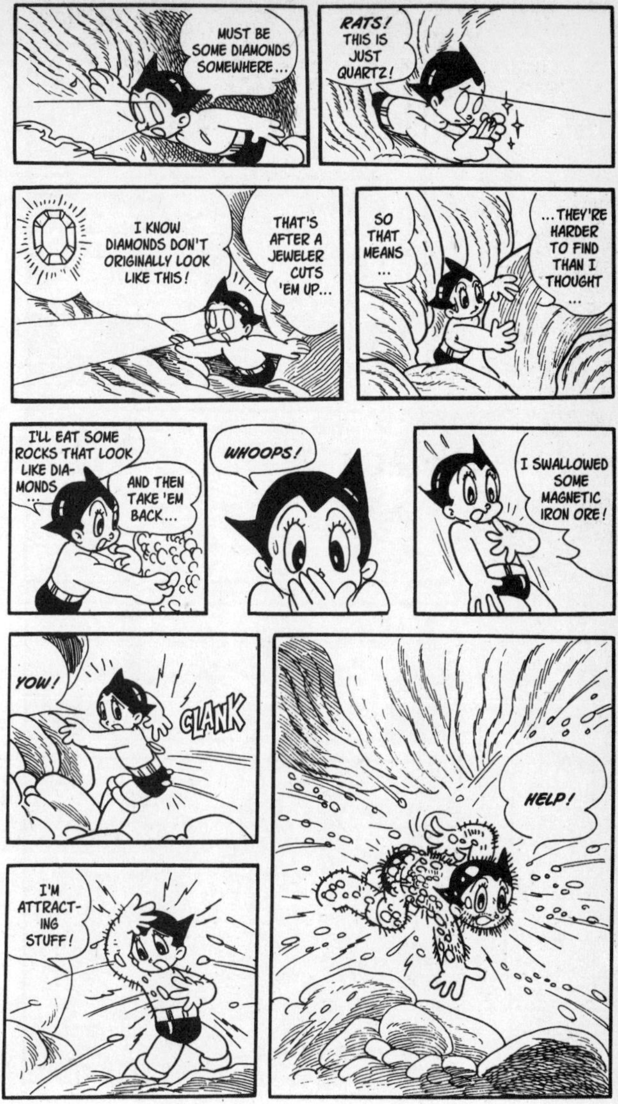
MUST BE SOME DIAMONDS SOMEWHERE...
RATS! THIS IS JUST QUARTZ!
I KNOW DIAMONDS DON'T ORIGINALLY LOOK LIKE THIS!
THAT'S AFTER A JEWELER CUTS 'EM UP...
SO THAT MEANS ...
...THEY'RE HARDER TO FIND THAN I THOUGHT ...
I'LL EAT SOME ROCKS THAT LOOK LIKE DIAMONDS ...
AND THEN TAKE 'EM BACK...
WHOOPS!
I SWALLOWED SOME MAGNETIC IRON ORE!
YOW!
CLANK
I'M ATTRACTING STUFF!
HELP!

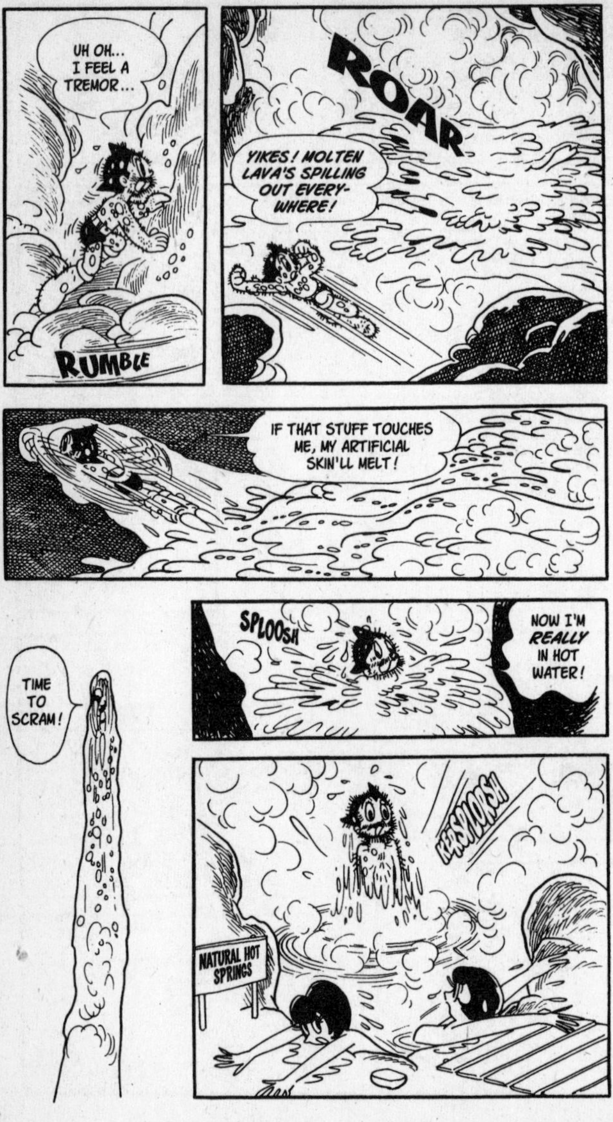
UH OH... I FEEL A TREMOR...
RUMBLE
ROAR
YIKES! MOLTEN LAVA'S SPILLING OUT EVERY-WHERE!
IF THAT STUFF TOUCHES ME, MY ARTIFICIAL SKIN'LL MELT!
TIME TO SCRAM!
SPLOOSH
NOW I'M *REALLY* IN HOT WATER!
KERSPLOOSH
NATURAL HOT SPRINGS

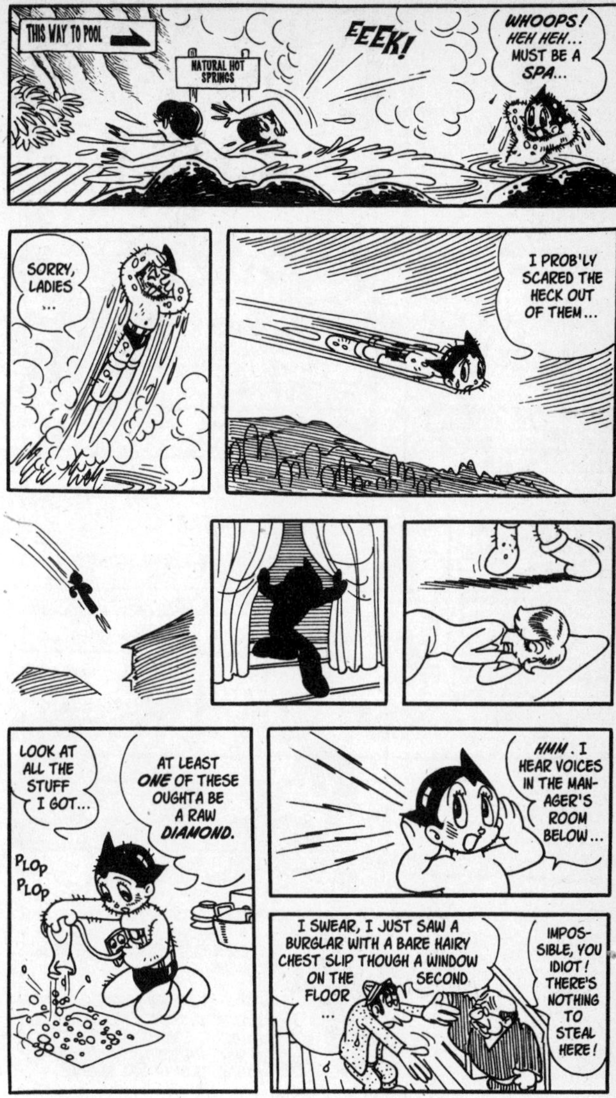
THIS WAY TO POOL
NATURAL HOT SPRINGS
EEEK!
WHOOPS! HEH HEH... MUST BE A SPA...
SORRY, LADIES ...
I PROB'LY SCARED THE HECK OUT OF THEM...
LOOK AT ALL THE STUFF I GOT...
AT LEAST ONE OF THESE OUGHTA BE A RAW DIAMOND.
PLOP PLOP
HMM. I HEAR VOICES IN THE MAN-AGER'S ROOM BELOW...
I SWEAR, I JUST SAW A BURGLAR WITH A BARE HAIRY CHEST SLIP THOUGH A WINDOW ON THE SECOND FLOOR ...
IMPOS-SIBLE, YOU IDIOT! THERE'S NOTHING TO STEAL HERE!

THE NEXT DAY ASTRO AND SCARA VISITED TOKYO'S GINZA DISTRICT. IN THE 20TH CENTURY IT WAS AN EXTRAORDINARILY BUSTLING PLACE, AND AS THE TWO OF THEM MADE THEIR WAY THROUGH THE CROWDS, THEY WERE AMAZED. FOR SCARA, IN PARTICULAR, EVERYTHING SEEMED NEW AND STRANGE.

"HERE, THIS IS THE PLACE, SCARA," SAID ASTRO.

"WHAT IS IT?"

"IT'S A JEWELRY STORE. I'VE GOT SOMETHING I WANT THEM TO BUY..."

"BUT THEY JUST HAVE A BUNCH OF WEIRD ROCKS ON DISPLAY..."

AN EMPLOYEE OF THE STORE CAME OUT, LOOKING VERY SERIOUS. HE STARED AT ASTRO, AND SAID, "WELL, WHAT CAN I DO FOR YOU?"

ASTRO SAID HESITANTLY, "UM... I, ER, WONDERED IF YOU COULD LOOK AT SOME OF THESE STONES I'VE BROUGHT..." AND THEN HE SPREAD THEM OUT ON THE STORE CASE.

THE STORE EMPLOYEE, WITH A LOOK OF DISDAIN, PICKED UP ONE OF THE STONES, STARED AT IT, AND THEN, WITH HIS VOICE SHAKING, SAID, "WHA-- WHAT HAVE WE GOT HERE?!"

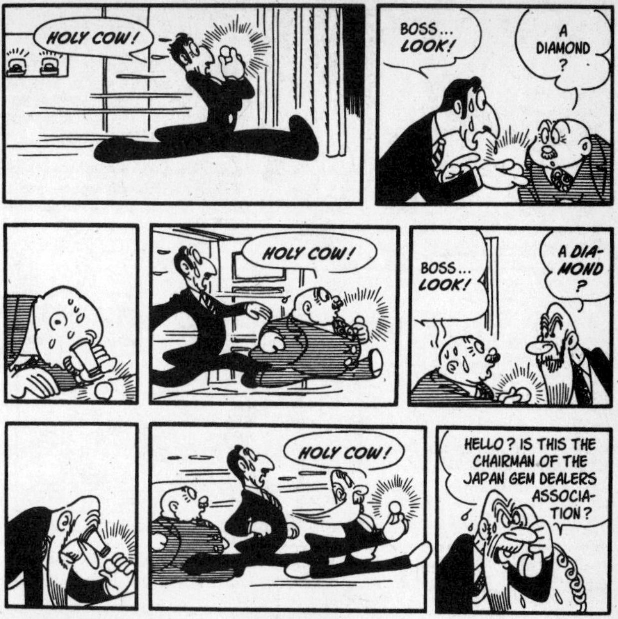
HOLY COW!
BOSS... LOOK!
A DIAMOND ?
HOLY COW!
BOSS... LOOK!
A DIA-MOND ?
HOLY COW!
HELLO ? IS THIS THE CHAIRMAN OF THE JAPAN GEM DEALERS ASSOCIA-TION ?

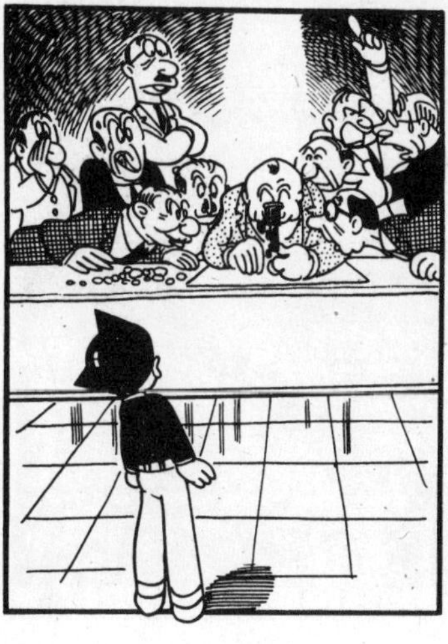

ASTRO COULDN'T STAND STILL ANY LONGER, SO HE BLURTED OUT, "SO WILL YOU BUY THEM, MISTER?"

"BUY? THESE ARE ***AMAZING,*** SONNY!"

"SO YOU'LL BUY THEM, RIGHT?"

"THERE'S NO WAY WE COULD BUY THEM..." ONE OF THE OTHER MEN SIGHED.

"THEN GIVE THEM BACK," ASTRO BEGGED. "I CAN TAKE THEM TO ANOTHER STORE!"

"SORRY, SONNY... ***NOBODY'S*** GOING TO BUY THESE..."

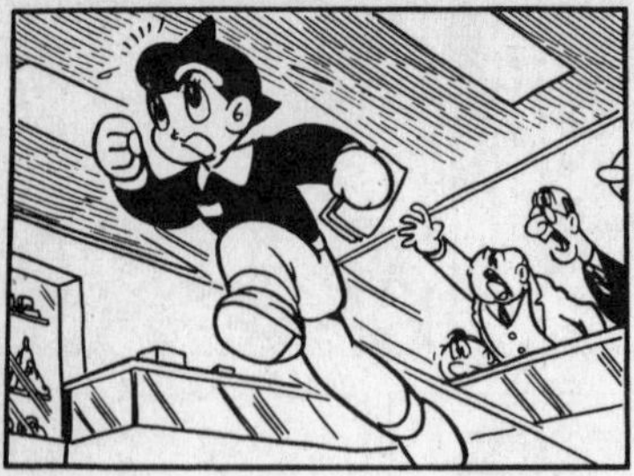

"THESE DIAMONDS ARE SO ***AMAZING*** THERE'S NO WAY WE COULD PRICE THEM. WE'RE GOING TO NEED SOME TIME TO CHECK THEM AND THEN ASK YOU THINGS, LIKE WHERE YOU FOUND THEM."

"BUT I'M IN A HURRY!" ASTRO PLEADED, "IF THEY'RE REALLY DIAMONDS, I NEED YOU TO TELL ME HOW MUCH THEY'RE WORTH!"

"I'D SAY YOU'VE GOT AT LEAST A ***MILLION YEN*** WORTH OF GEMS HERE, SONNY," ONE OF THE DEALERS SAID. "HERE, WE'LL GIVE YOU A LITTLE CASH AS A DOWNPAYMENT ..."

AS SOON AS HE WAS HANDED THE MONEY, ASTRO DASHED OUT OF THE STORE WITH SCARA.

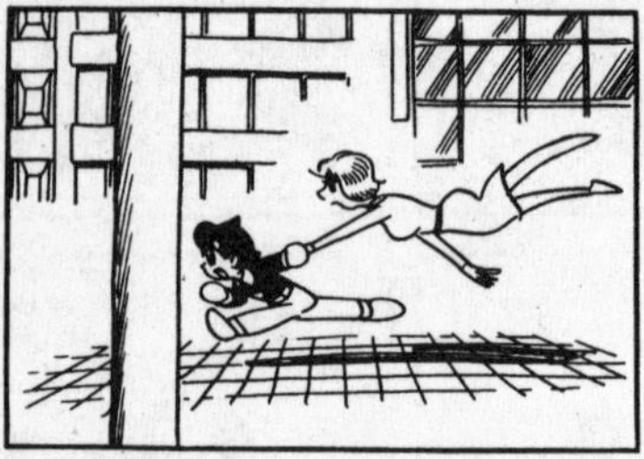

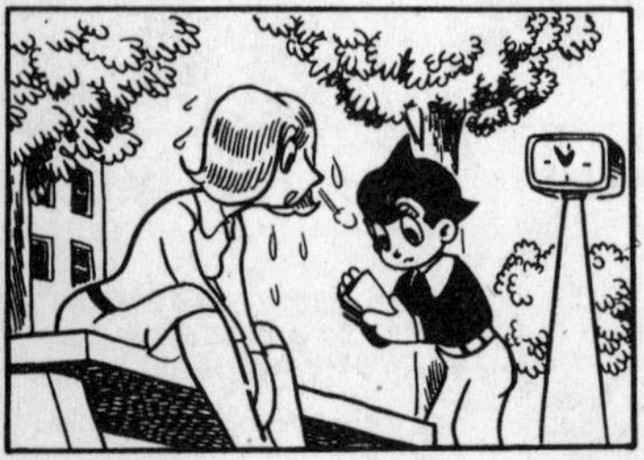

WITH THE GEM DEALERS CALLING OUT AFTER THEM TO WAIT, ASTRO AND SCARA RAN LIKE THE WIND TO A LITTLE LOCAL PARK. SCARA, OUT OF BREATH, SAT DOWN ON ONE OF THE BENCHES.

"GOSH, YOU REALLY SURPRISED ME, ASTRO," SHE GASPED.

"SORRY, BUT AT LEAST WE GOT SOME MONEY..."

"SO THAT'S WHAT YOU CALL MONEY?"

"YUP. YOU CAN BUY ANYTHING WITH IT. SO NOW WE CAN GO SHOPPING AT A DEPARTMENT STORE..."

AFTER ENTERING A STORE, ASTRO LED SCARA TO THE WOMEN'S WEAR SECTION, AND HAD HER BUY WHAT-EVER CLOTHES SHE WANTED.

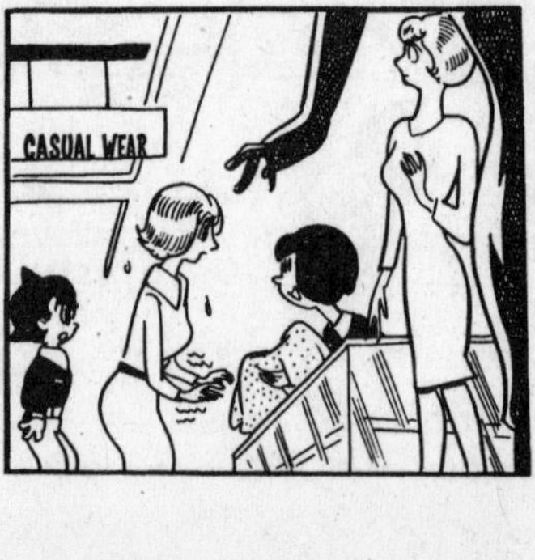
CASUAL WEAR

WHEN THE STORE EMPLOYEE ASKED SCARA WHAT SIZE SHE WANTED, SHE REPLIED, "SIZE?"

"YOU KNOW... YOUR MEASUREMENTS... YOUR HEIGHT, WAIST, BUST SIZE... THAT SORT OF THING..."

"BUST? WAIST?" SCARA WAS COMPLETELY CONFUSED.

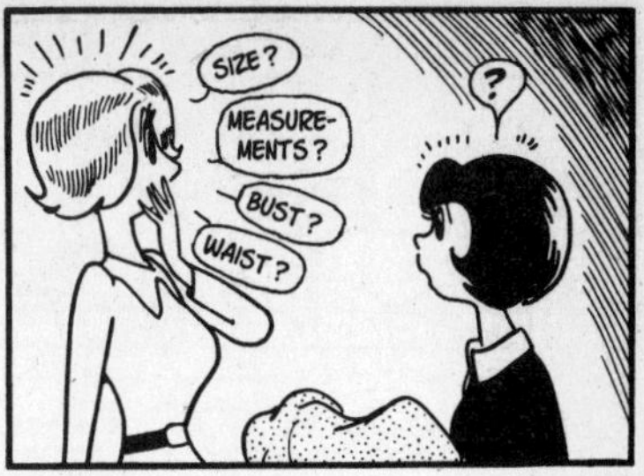
SIZE?
MEASURE-MENTS?
BUST?
WAIST?
?

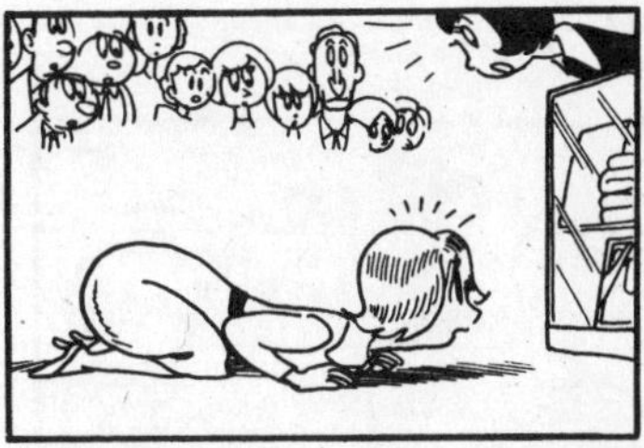

SCARA'S BEAUTIFUL BROW FURROWED. "I'M SORRY," SHE ANSWERED, "I'VE NO IDEA..."

WHEN THE EMPLOYEE OFFERED TO MEASURE SCARA, SHE SAW, TO HER SHOCK, THAT SCARA HAD ALREADY GOTTEN DOWN ON ALL FOURS ON THE FLOOR. "WHAT'S WRONG, MISS?" SHE ASKED, CONCERNED...

"WELL," SCARA REPLIED, "YOU WANTED TO MEASURE ME, SO I WAS JUST TRYING TO MAKE IT EASIER FOR YOU..."

ASTRO CAME OVER HER AND WHISPERED, "LISTEN, SCARA, YOU CAN'T ACT LIKE THAT HERE. WE'RE ON EARTH. DON'T DO THAT IN FRONT OF PEOPLE..."

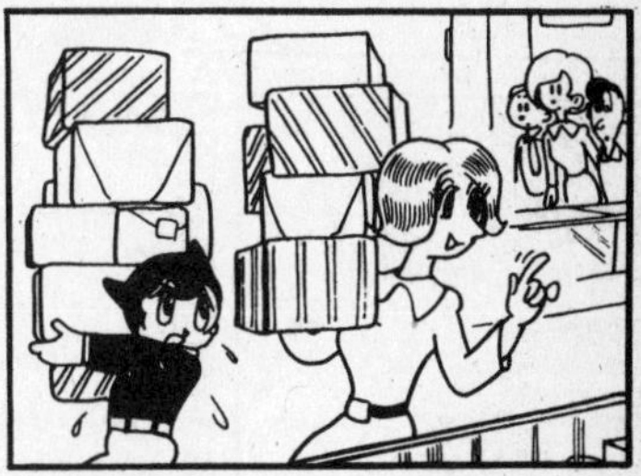

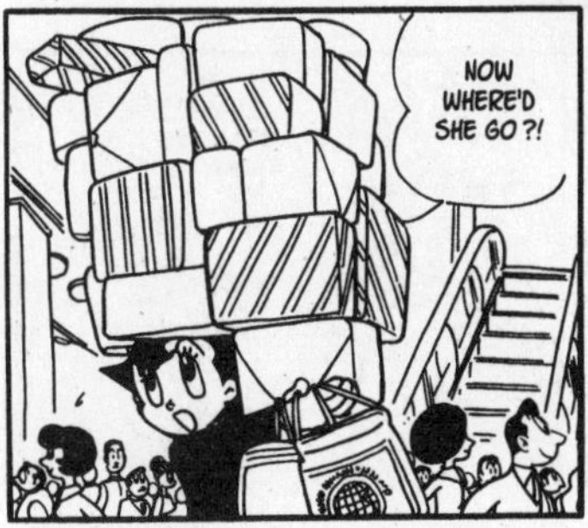
NOW WHERE'D SHE GO?!

AFTER MAKING THE ROUNDS OF THE STORE'S VARIOUS SECTIONS, SCARA BEGAN TO REALIZE HOW MUCH FUN SHOPPING COULD BE, AND STARTED EXCLAIMING, "I'LL TAKE ***THIS***... AND ***THIS***, TOO!"

ASTRO WAS AFRAID THINGS WERE GETTING OUT OF CONTROL, BUT WHEN HE NEXT LOOKED, HE COULDN'T SEE SCARA ANYWHERE.

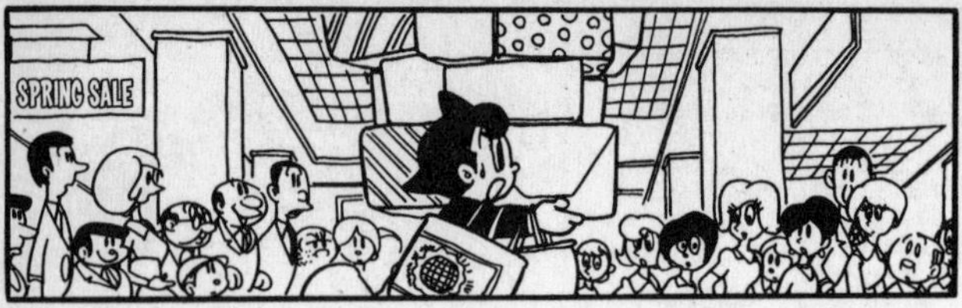
SPRING SALE

YELLING, ***"SCARA! WHERE ARE YOU?!"*** AND BALANCING A HUGE PILE OF HER PURCHASES, ASTRO SEARCHED ALL OVER FOR HER. "I WONDER IF SHE GOT LOST?"

TWO OF THREE PEOPLE CAME OVER TO ASK IF HE WAS ALL RIGHT, BUT HE JUST SAID, "*UM*... IT'S NOTHING..."

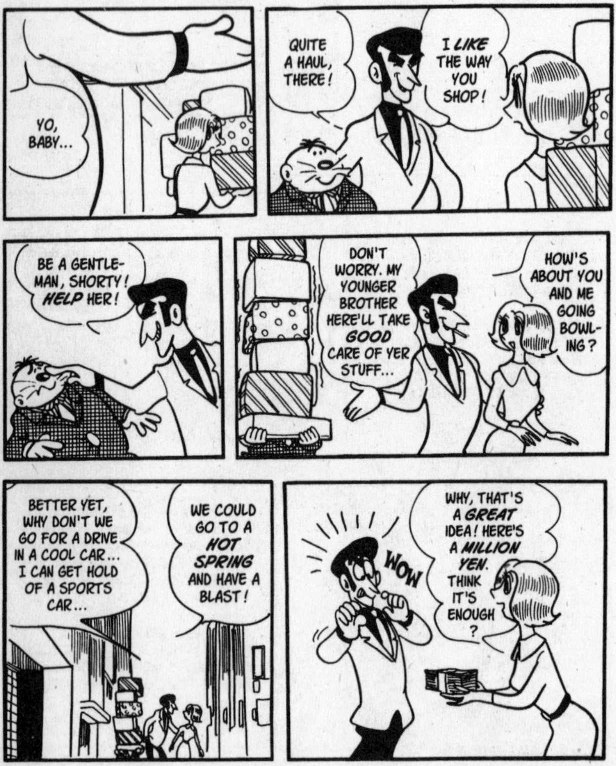
YO, BABY...
QUITE A HAUL, THERE!
I *LIKE* THE WAY YOU SHOP!
BE A GENTLEMAN, SHORTY! *HELP* HER!
DON'T WORRY. MY YOUNGER BROTHER HERE'LL TAKE *GOOD* CARE OF YER STUFF...
HOW'S ABOUT YOU AND ME GOING BOWLING?
BETTER YET, WHY DON'T WE GO FOR A DRIVE IN A COOL CAR... I CAN GET HOLD OF A SPORTS CAR...
WE COULD GO TO A *HOT SPRING* AND HAVE A BLAST!
WOW
WHY, THAT'S A *GREAT* IDEA! HERE'S A *MILLION YEN*. THINK IT'S ENOUGH?

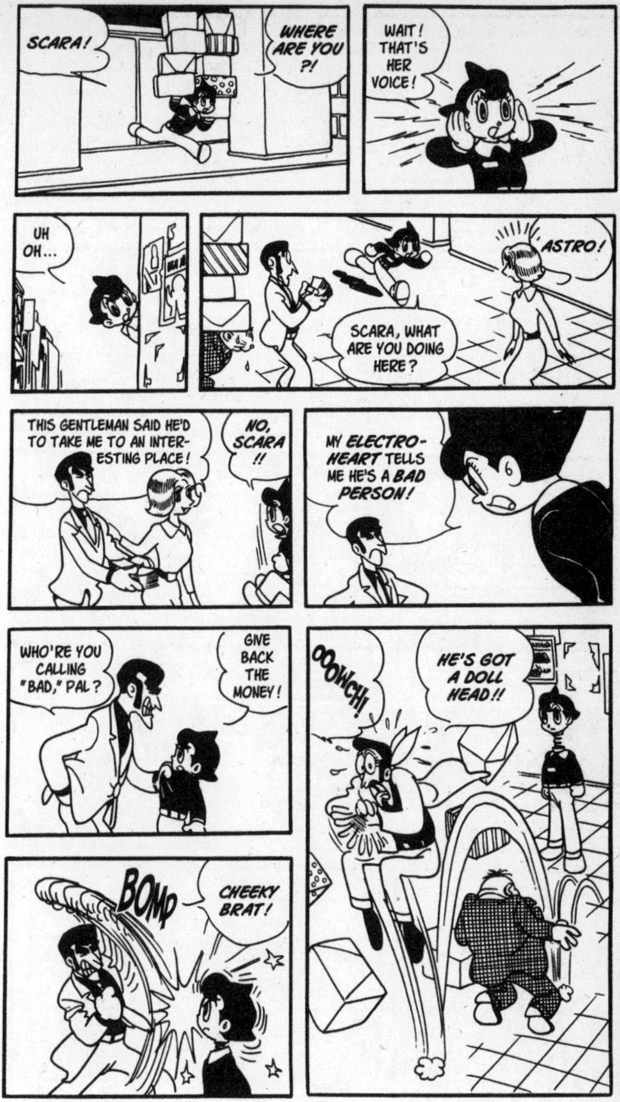
SCARA!
WHERE ARE YOU ?!
WAIT! THAT'S HER VOICE!
UH OH...
ASTRO!
SCARA, WHAT ARE YOU DOING HERE?
THIS GENTLEMAN SAID HE'D TO TAKE ME TO AN INTERESTING PLACE!
NO, SCARA !!
MY ELECTRO-HEART TELLS ME HE'S A BAD PERSON!
WHO'RE YOU CALLING "BAD," PAL?
GIVE BACK THE MONEY!
OOOWCH!
HE'S GOT A DOLL HEAD!!
BOMP
CHEEKY BRAT!

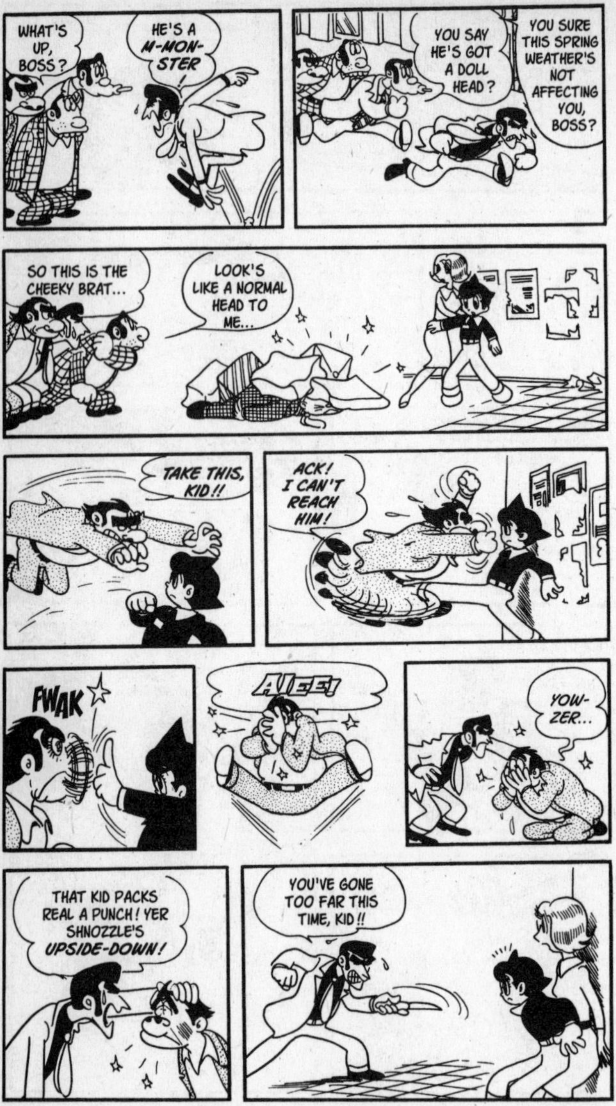
WHAT'S UP, BOSS?
HE'S A M-MONSTER!
YOU SAY HE'S GOT A DOLL HEAD?
YOU SURE THIS SPRING WEATHER'S NOT AFFECTING YOU, BOSS?
SO THIS IS THE CHEEKY BRAT...
LOOK'S LIKE A NORMAL HEAD TO ME...
TAKE THIS, KID!!
ACK! I CAN'T REACH HIM!
FWAK
AIEE!
YOW-ZER...
THAT KID PACKS REAL A PUNCH! YER SHNOZZLE'S UPSIDE-DOWN!
YOU'VE GONE TOO FAR THIS TIME, KID!!

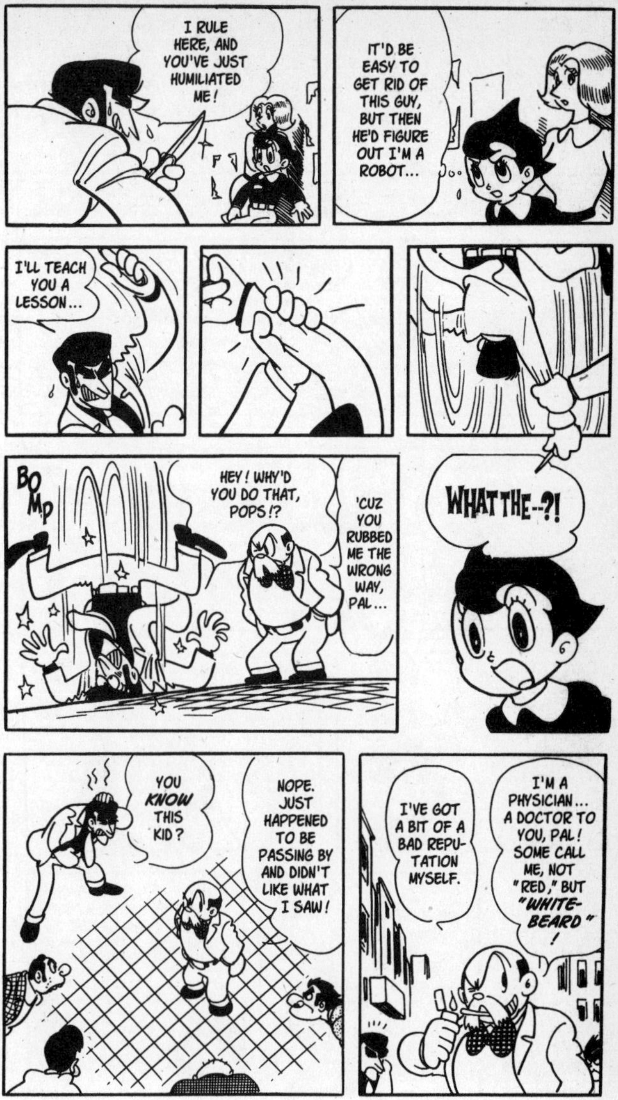
I RULE HERE, AND YOU'VE JUST HUMILIATED ME!
IT'D BE EASY TO GET RID OF THIS GUY, BUT THEN HE'D FIGURE OUT I'M A ROBOT...
I'LL TEACH YOU A LESSON...
BOMP
HEY! WHY'D YOU DO THAT, POPS!?
'CUZ YOU RUBBED ME THE WRONG WAY, PAL...
WHAT THE--?!
YOU KNOW THIS KID?
NOPE. JUST HAPPENED TO BE PASSING BY AND DIDN'T LIKE WHAT I SAW!
I'VE GOT A BIT OF A BAD REPUTATION MYSELF.
I'M A PHYSICIAN... A DOCTOR TO YOU, PAL! SOME CALL ME, NOT "RED," BUT "WHITE-BEARD"!

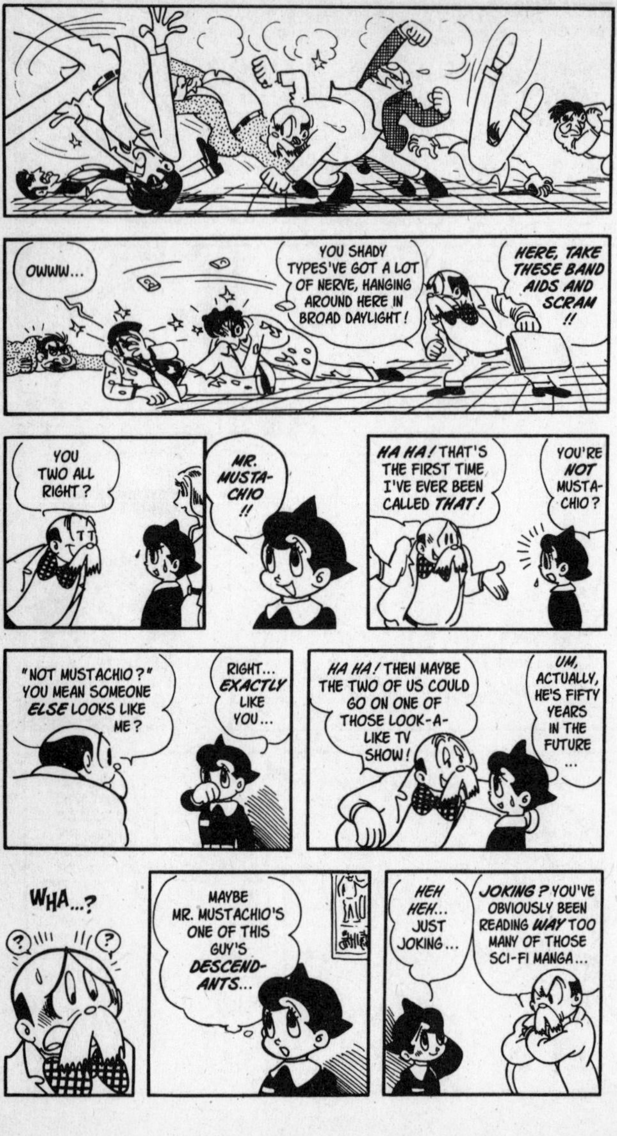
OWWW...
YOU SHADY TYPES'VE GOT A LOT OF NERVE, HANGING AROUND HERE IN BROAD DAYLIGHT!
HERE, TAKE THESE BAND AIDS AND SCRAM!!
YOU TWO ALL RIGHT?
MR. MUSTACHIO!!
HA HA! THAT'S THE FIRST TIME I'VE EVER BEEN CALLED THAT!
YOU'RE NOT MUSTACHIO?
"NOT MUSTACHIO?" YOU MEAN SOMEONE ELSE LOOKS LIKE ME?
RIGHT... EXACTLY LIKE YOU...
HA HA! THEN MAYBE THE TWO OF US COULD GO ON ONE OF THOSE LOOK-A-LIKE TV SHOW!
UM, ACTUALLY, HE'S FIFTY YEARS IN THE FUTURE...
WHA...?
MAYBE MR. MUSTACHIO'S ONE OF THIS GUY'S DESCENDANTS...
HEH HEH... JUST JOKING...
JOKING? YOU'VE OBVIOUSLY BEEN READING WAY TOO MANY OF THOSE SCI-FI MANGA...

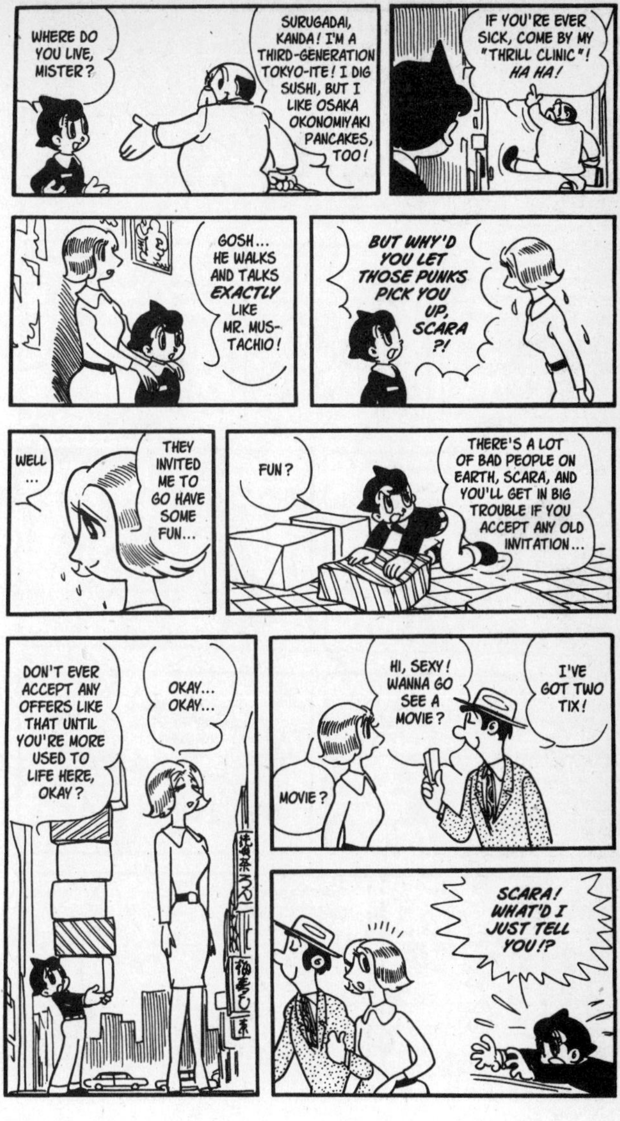
WHERE DO YOU LIVE, MISTER?
SURUGADAI, KANDA! I'M A THIRD-GENERATION TOKYO-ITE! I DIG SUSHI, BUT I LIKE OSAKA OKONOMIYAKI PANCAKES, TOO!
IF YOU'RE EVER SICK, COME BY MY "THRILL CLINIC"! HA HA!
GOSH... HE WALKS AND TALKS EXACTLY LIKE MR. MUSTACHIO!
BUT WHY'D YOU LET THOSE PUNKS PICK YOU UP, SCARA?!
WELL...
THEY INVITED ME TO GO HAVE SOME FUN...
FUN?
THERE'S A LOT OF BAD PEOPLE ON EARTH, SCARA, AND YOU'LL GET IN BIG TROUBLE IF YOU ACCEPT ANY OLD INVITATION...
DON'T EVER ACCEPT ANY OFFERS LIKE THAT UNTIL YOU'RE MORE USED TO LIFE HERE, OKAY?
OKAY... OKAY...
HI, SEXY! WANNA GO SEE A MOVIE?
I'VE GOT TWO TIX!
MOVIE?
SCARA! WHAT'D I JUST TELL YOU!?

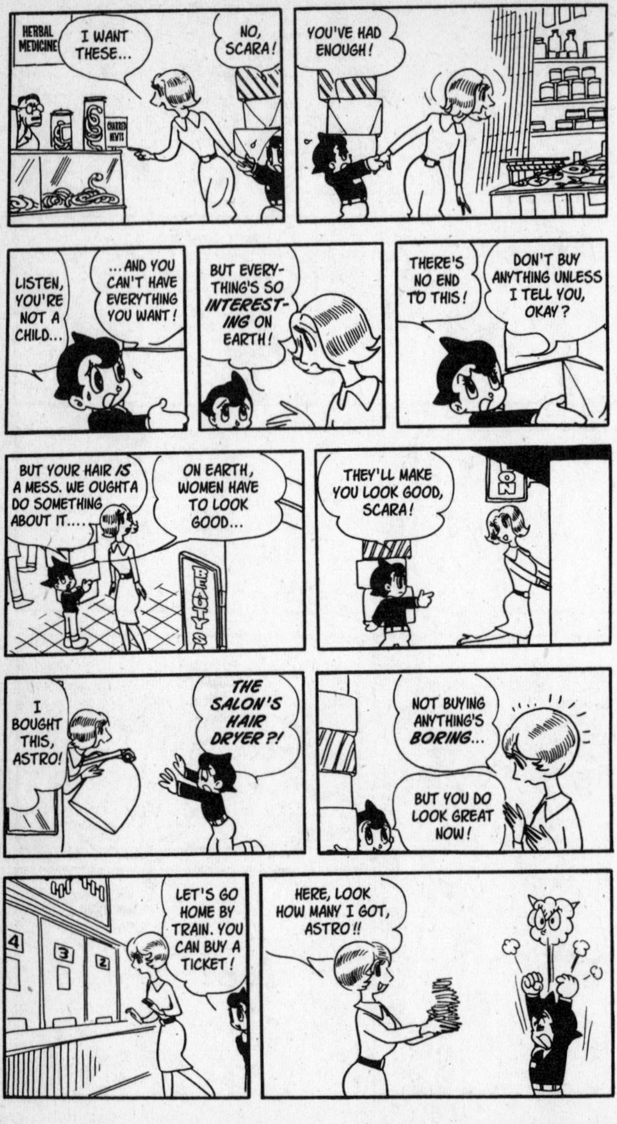
HERBAL MEDICINE
I WANT THESE...
CHARRED NEWTS
NO, SCARA!
YOU'VE HAD ENOUGH!
LISTEN, YOU'RE NOT A CHILD...
...AND YOU CAN'T HAVE EVERYTHING YOU WANT!
BUT EVERYTHING'S SO *INTERESTING* ON EARTH!
THERE'S NO END TO THIS!
DON'T BUY ANYTHING UNLESS I TELL YOU, OKAY?
BUT YOUR HAIR *IS* A MESS. WE OUGHTA DO SOMETHING ABOUT IT....
ON EARTH, WOMEN HAVE TO LOOK GOOD...
THEY'LL MAKE YOU LOOK GOOD, SCARA!
I BOUGHT THIS, ASTRO!
THE SALON'S HAIR DRYER?!
NOT BUYING ANYTHING'S *BORING*...
BUT YOU DO LOOK GREAT NOW!
LET'S GO HOME BY TRAIN. YOU CAN BUY A TICKET!
HERE, LOOK HOW MANY I GOT, ASTRO!!

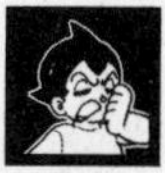

THE BIRTH OF NEVA #2

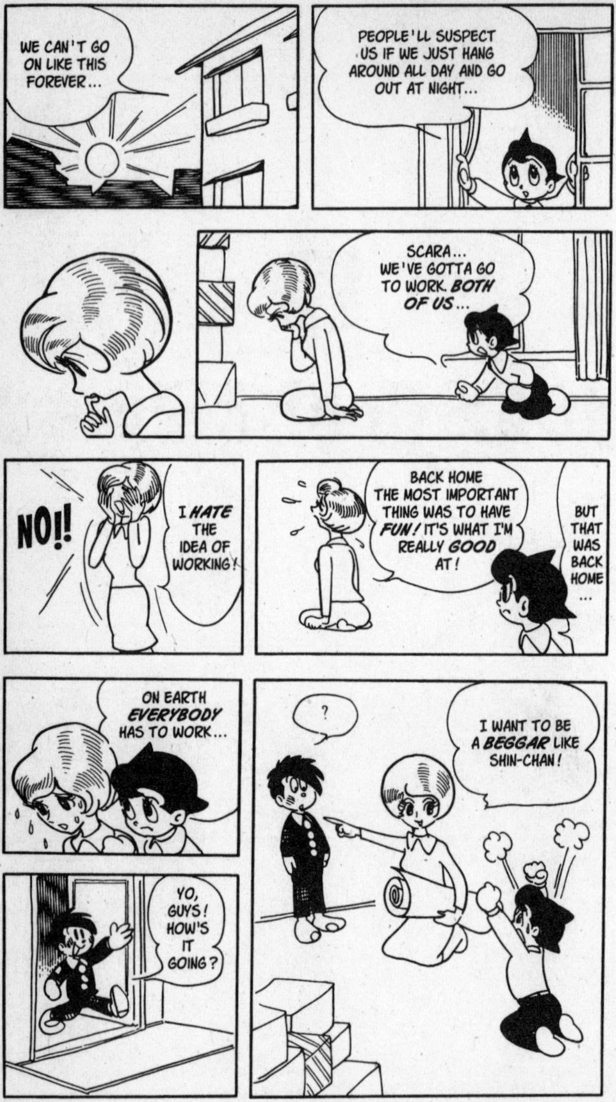
WE CAN'T GO ON LIKE THIS FOREVER...
PEOPLE'LL SUSPECT US IF WE JUST HANG AROUND ALL DAY AND GO OUT AT NIGHT...
SCARA... WE'VE GOTTA GO TO WORK BOTH OF US...
NO!!
I HATE THE IDEA OF WORKING!
BACK HOME THE MOST IMPORTANT THING WAS TO HAVE FUN! IT'S WHAT I'M REALLY GOOD AT!
BUT THAT WAS BACK HOME...
ON EARTH EVERYBODY HAS TO WORK...
YO, GUYS! HOW'S IT GOING?
?
I WANT TO BE A BEGGAR LIKE SHIN-CHAN!

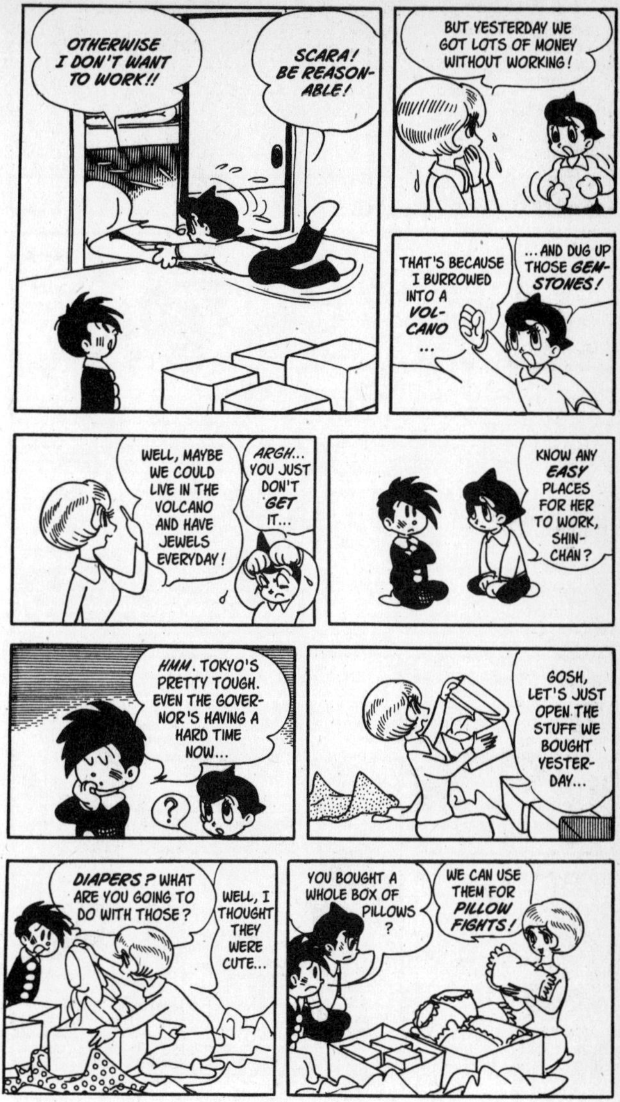
OTHERWISE I DON'T WANT TO WORK!!
SCARA! BE REASONABLE!
BUT YESTERDAY WE GOT LOTS OF MONEY WITHOUT WORKING!
THAT'S BECAUSE I BURROWED INTO A VOLCANO ...
...AND DUG UP THOSE GEMSTONES!
WELL, MAYBE WE COULD LIVE IN THE VOLCANO AND HAVE JEWELS EVERYDAY!
ARGH... YOU JUST DON'T GET IT...
KNOW ANY EASY PLACES FOR HER TO WORK, SHIN-CHAN?
HMM. TOKYO'S PRETTY TOUGH. EVEN THE GOVERNOR'S HAVING A HARD TIME NOW...
?
GOSH, LET'S JUST OPEN THE STUFF WE BOUGHT YESTERDAY...
DIAPERS? WHAT ARE YOU GOING TO DO WITH THOSE?
WELL, I THOUGHT THEY WERE CUTE...
YOU BOUGHT A WHOLE BOX OF PILLOWS?
WE CAN USE THEM FOR PILLOW FIGHTS!

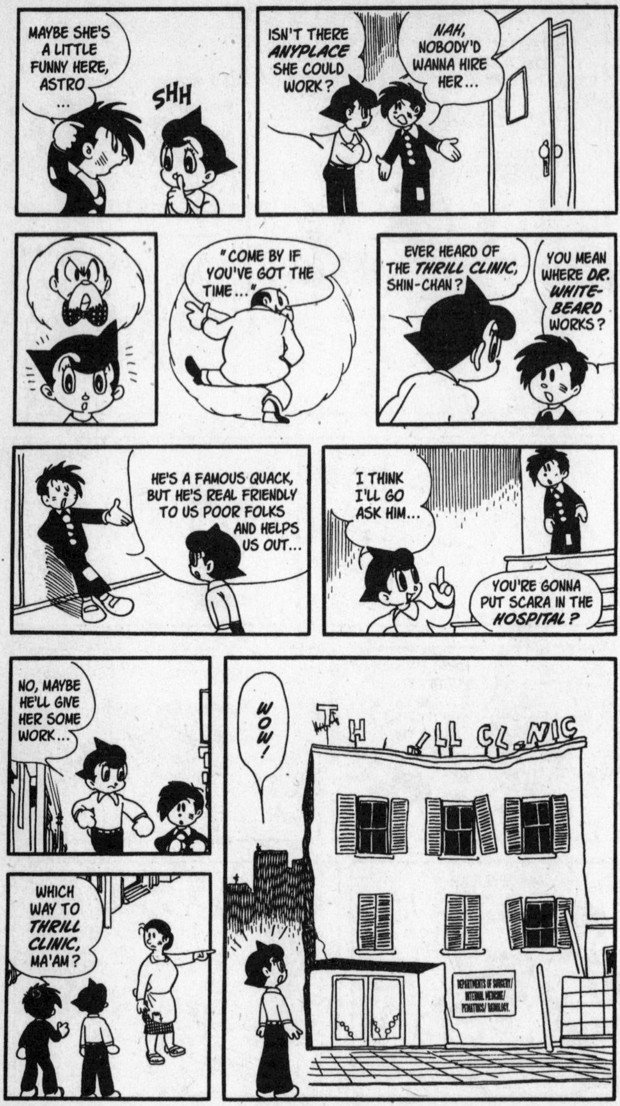
MAYBE SHE'S A LITTLE FUNNY HERE, ASTRO ...
SHH
ISN'T THERE *ANYPLACE* SHE COULD WORK?
NAH, NOBODY'D WANNA HIRE HER...
"COME BY IF YOU'VE GOT THE TIME..."
EVER HEARD OF THE *THRILL CLINIC,* SHIN-CHAN?
YOU MEAN WHERE *DR. WHITE-BEARD* WORKS?
HE'S A FAMOUS QUACK, BUT HE'S REAL FRIENDLY TO US POOR FOLKS AND HELPS US OUT...
I THINK I'LL GO ASK HIM...
YOU'RE GONNA PUT SCARA IN THE *HOSPITAL?*
NO, MAYBE HE'LL GIVE HER SOME WORK...
WHICH WAY TO *THRILL CLINIC,* MA'AM?
WOW!
DEPARTMENTS OF SURGERY/ INTERNAL MEDICINE/ PEDIATRICS/ RADIOLOGY.

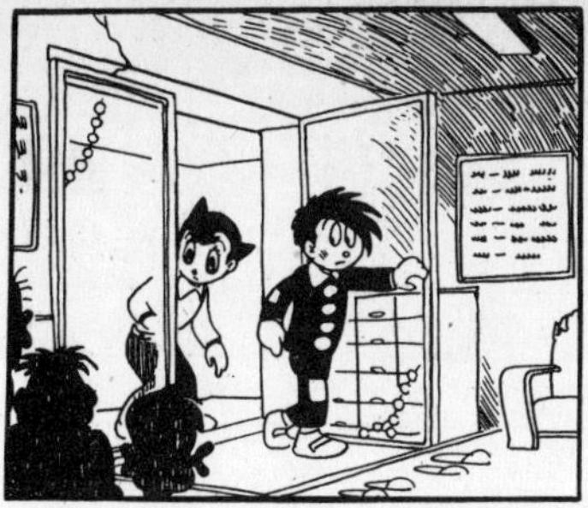

SHIN-CHAN AND ASTRO GINGERLY OPENED THE DOOR AND ENTERED A DARK WAITING ROOM. THE PATIENTS THERE WERE ALL SHABBILY DRESSED, AND THEY STARED AT THE BOYS.

"*UM*... WE'D LIKE TO MEET DR. WHITEBEARD," SHIN-CHAN SAID TO THE RECEPTION NURSE.

"THIS YOUR FIRST TIME HERE FOR A CHECKUP?" SHE ASKED.

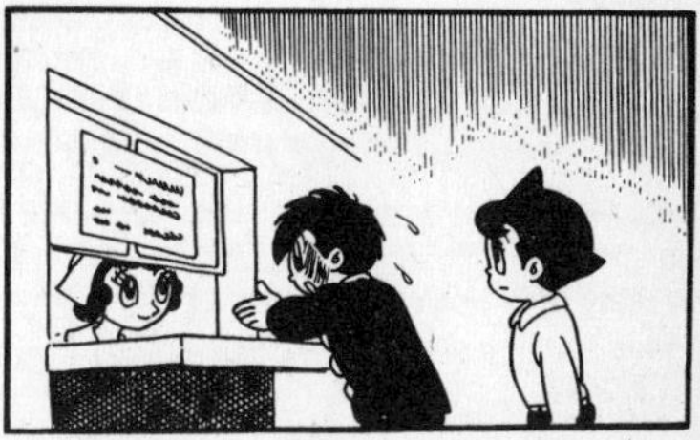

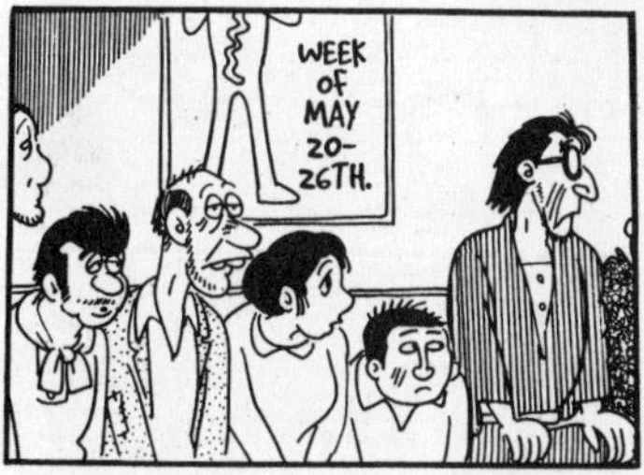
WEEK OF MAY 20-26TH.

"*UM,* ACTUALLY, WE'RE NOT HERE FOR THAT. HE ASKED US TO STOP BY, AND WE NEED TO TALK TO HIM ABOUT SOMETHING..."

"OPEN THE DOOR THERE, THEN, AND GO DOWN ONE FLIGHT OF STAIRS TO THE BASEMENT, AND WAIT IN THE THIRD ROOM ON THE RIGHT..."

ASTRO AND SHIN-CHAN DID AS TOLD, BUT AT THE BOTTOM OF THE STAIRS THERE WAS A STRANGE UNDERGROUND PASSAGEWAY AND A HUMMING NOISE THAT SOUNDED AS IF IT WERE COMING FROM MACHINES...

"SOMETHING'S WEIRD ABOUT THIS PLACE," ASTRO SAID.

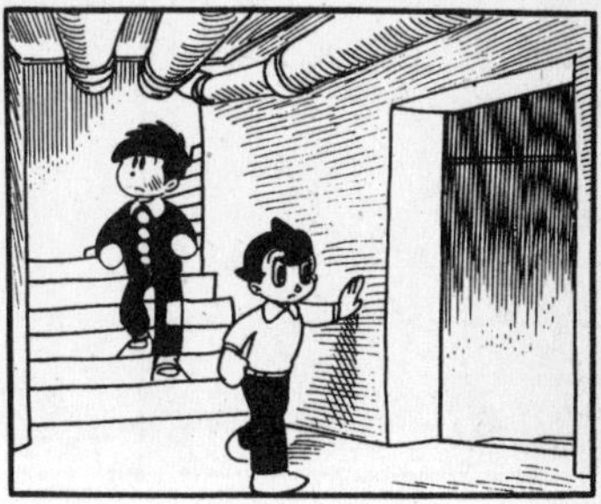

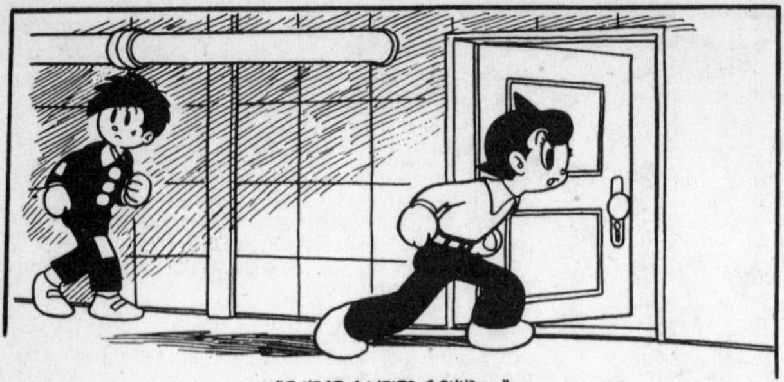

"I HEAR A WEIRD SOUND..."

"MAYBE IT'S FROM A MOTOR? NO, WAIT A SEC, MAYBE IT'S FROM A RADIO RECEIVER..."

"MAYBE IT'S COMING FROM THIS ROOM HERE..."

"BUT THIS IS SUPPOSED TO BE A WAITING ROOM!"

THE PAIR ENTERED THE ROOM WHERE THE NURSE HAD INSTRUCTED THEM TO WAIT, AND SAT DOWN ON A SOFA.

"YOU KNOW, ASTRO," SHIN-CHAN COMMENTED, "AFTER SEEING ALL THOSE POOR PEOPLE UPSTAIRS, I WONDER HOW THIS CLINIC CAN STAY IN BUSINESS...

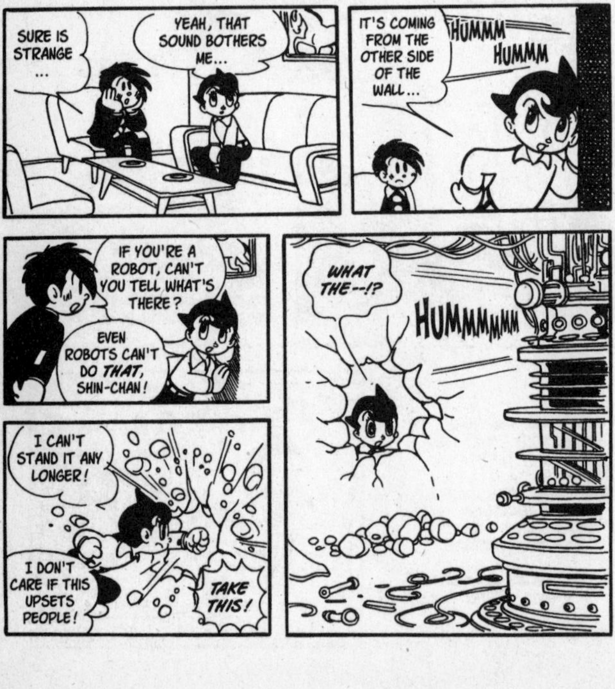
SURE IS STRANGE ...
YEAH, THAT SOUND BOTHERS ME...
IT'S COMING FROM THE OTHER SIDE OF THE WALL...
HUMMM
HUMMM
IF YOU'RE A ROBOT, CAN'T YOU TELL WHAT'S THERE?
EVEN ROBOTS CAN'T DO *THAT*, SHIN-CHAN!
I CAN'T STAND IT ANY LONGER!
I DON'T CARE IF THIS UPSETS PEOPLE!
TAKE THIS!
WHAT THE--!?
HUMMMMMM

ALL SORTS OF MACHINES IN THE ROOM WERE CREATING THE HUMMING NOISE, RIGHT IN FRONT OF HIM. THEN, HE REALIZED WITH SHOCK: "HEY! THERE'S A *ROBOT* HERE! IT'S A CRUDE, OLD FASHIONED MODEL, BUT IT'S A *ROBOT!*"

IT'S A ROBOT!

"WOW! IT'S GREAT TO SEE A ROBOT, EVEN IF IT IS AN ANTIQUE! IT'S LIKE MEETING AN OLD FRIEND!" ASTRO PUT HIS HANDS ON THE ROBOT AND STROKED IT, AND TEARS WELLED IN HIS EYES.

WHILE ASTRO WAS LOOKING AT ANOTHER MACHINE AND THINKING IT MUST BE THE CONTROLLER, SHIN-CHAN CAME IN LOOKING UPSET AND SAID, "WATCH OUT, ASTRO! I HEAR FOOTSTEPS!"

SOME-ONE'S COMING!

"WE BETTER GET BACK IN THE OTHER ROOM!" SO SAYING, THE PAIR JUMPED BACK THROUGH THE HOLE IN THE WALL.

"WHAT'LL WE DO ABOUT THE HOLE?" THEY WONDERED.

"WE COULD SEAL IT UP," SHIN-CHAN SAID, BUT ASTRO DIDN'T THINK THAT WOULD WORK.

ON SHIN-CHAN'S SUGGESTION ASTRO DECIDED TO BLOCK THE HOLE WITH THE WAITING ROOM'S COFFEE TABLE, PROPPING IT UP AGAINST THE WALL. BUT THEN HE HEARD A SCREAM FROM THE OTHER SIDE OF THE WALL...

SOMEONE STARTED POUNDING ANGRILY ON THE TABLE FROM THE OTHER SIDE, YELLING, "WHO'S THERE?! WHO'S BEEN IN HERE? WHO'S ON THE OTHER SIDE OF THIS HOLE?! REMOVE THAT TABLE!!"

SHIN-CHAN, TERRIFIED, BEGGED ASTRO NOT TO LET GO OF THE TABLE. FROM THE OTHER SIDE THE A VOICE SCREAMED, "BURGLAR! BURGLAR!" AND IT ECHOED DOWN THE BASEMENT PASSAGEWAY.

THEN DR. WHITEBEARD SUDDENLY ENTERED THE ROOM, YELLING "BURGLAR?! WHERE?! WHERE'D HE GO?"

SOMEBODY SAY BURGLAR?!

"OUT OF THE WAY!" THE DOCTOR SAID. "WHO PUT THIS TABLE UP AGAINST THE WALL?! WHAT? WHO MADE THIS HOLE?!"

THEN, FROM THE OTHER SIDE OF THE WALL, A VOICE SAID, "IT'S A BURGLAR, WHITEBEARD!"

TURNING TO ASTRO AND SHIN-CHAN, DR. WHITE BEARD SAID, "DON'T TELL ME *YOU BOYS* MADE THIS HOLE? EH?!"

I BET *YOU* DID IT, DIDN'T YOU?! WHY?!

ASTRO WAS SO SURPRISED HE COULDN'T ANSWER, BUT THE DOCTOR PERSISTED, ASKING HOW HE COULD HAVE DONE IT, GIVEN THE WALL'S THICKNESS.

THEN, SUDDENLY, A MAN MASKED IN A WHITE SHEET POKED HIS FACE OUT FROM THE HOLE...

"LOOKS LIKE THE BURGLAR LEFT WITHOUT TAKING ANYTHING," THE MASKED MAN SAID.

"BUT I DIDN'T SEE ANYONE IN THE HALLWAY, AND THESE TWO BOYS ARE THE ONLY ONES IN THIS ROOM," THE DOCTOR REPLIED.

STARING AT THE BOYS WITH A REPROVING LOOK, THE MASKED MAN ASKED, "BUT WHO ELSE COULD HAVE SMASHED THIS HOLE?"

SHIN-CHAN SUDDENLY CAME FORWARD AND ANNOUNCED, "IT WAS THAT *ROBOT* IN THE NEXT ROOM! I *SAW* HIM!" HE WAS MAKING IT UP, OF COURSE, BUT THE MASKED MAN WAS SUDDENLY TAKEN ABACK.

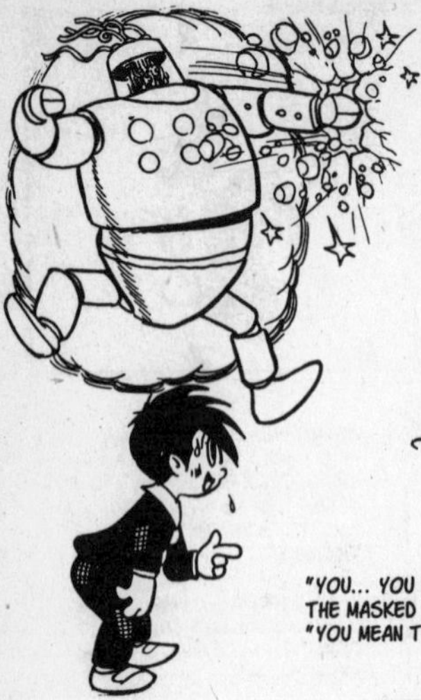

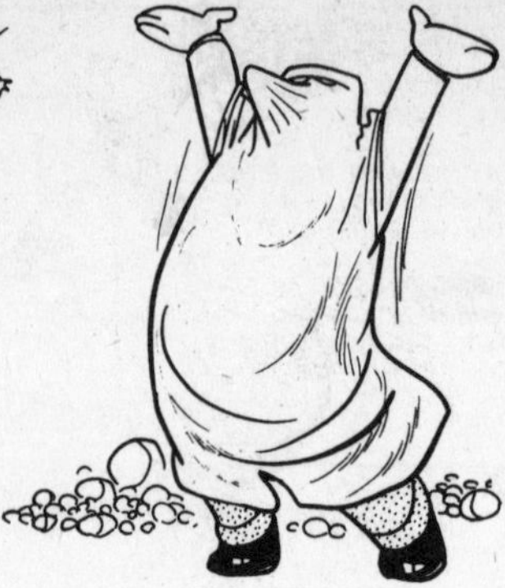

"YOU... YOU REALLY SAW THE ***ROBOT*** DO THAT?" THE MASKED MAN ASKED, SUDDENLY APPEARING HAPPY. "YOU MEAN THE ROBOT REALLY ***MOVED***?"

WITH A "HALLELUJAH!" HE RAISED BOTH HANDS OVER HIS HEAD AND SHOUTED, "***NEVA #1*** MOVED ON HIS OWN AND SMASHED THE WALL? HE'S A SUCCESS! MY ROBOT ***WORKS***!" AND THEN HE CLIMBED BACK THROUGH THE HOLE INTO THE OTHER ROOM.

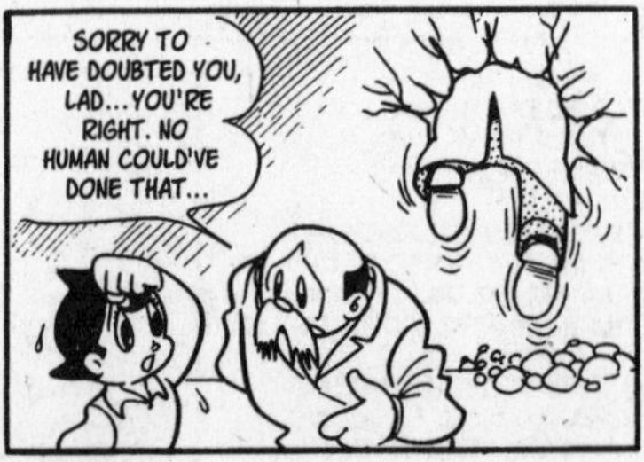
SORRY TO HAVE DOUBTED YOU, LAD...YOU'RE RIGHT. NO HUMAN COULD'VE DONE THAT...

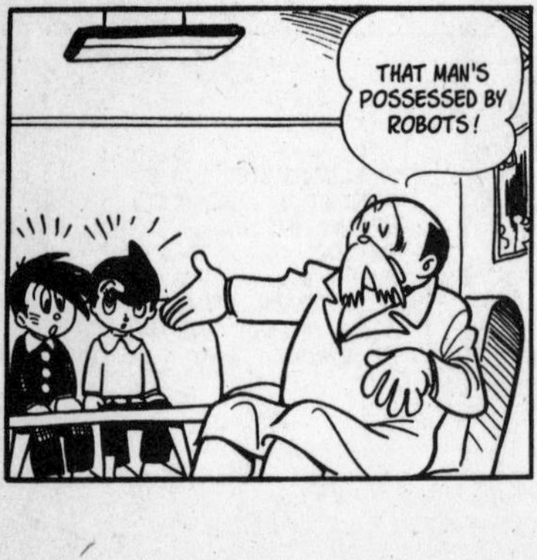
THAT MAN'S POSSESSED BY ROBOTS!

THE DOCTOR SIGHED AND APOLOGIZED TO THE BOYS, ESPECIALLY ASTRO. "HE'S AN INVENTOR, SEE? FOR YEARS HE'S BEEN TRYING TO BUILD A ROBOT CALLED ***NEVA #1***... HE'S PUT HIS BODY AND SOUL INTO IT..."

ASTRO AND SHIN-CHAN EXCHANGED PUZZLED LOOKS.

"HOW COME HE'S WEARING THAT WEIRD MASKED SMOCK?" THE BOYS ASKED.

"WELL," THE DOCTOR REPLIED WITH A SIGH, "IT'S APPARENTLY TO WARD OFF *RADIATION*. HE'S USING *ATOMIC ENERGY*, SEE, AND HE'S GOTTEN IN THE HABIT OF WEARING IT... YOU KNOW, I'VE NEVER MET ANYONE WHO'S INVENTED SO MANY THINGS. NOT MANY PEOPLE KNOW ABOUT IT, OF COURSE, BUT HE'S PROBABLY UP THERE WITH THOMAS EDISON. ALMOST ALL HIS INVENTIONS ARE BOUGHT BY THE UNITED STATES OR EUROPEAN NATIONS,

SO HE'S ACTUALLY BETTER KNOWN OVERSEAS. BUT THE MAN'S GOT NO SENSE OF MONEY, AND HE DOESN'T EVEN KNOW WHAT TO DO WITH ALL THE CASH THE AMERICANS KEEP SENDING HIM..."

"HE BUYS A FEW PARTS ONCE IN A WHILE, OF COURSE, BUT HE JUST LEAVES THE REST LYING AROUND. WHY, I'VE EVEN FISHED PERFECTLY GOOD DOLLAR BILLS OUT OF THE *TRASH CAN*! I DON'T WANT HIS MONEY TO GO TO WASTE, SO WE BUILT THIS HOSPITAL WITH IT, AND I USE IT TO TREAT PEOPLE WHO DON'T HAVE ANY. THAT'S WHAT THIS PLACE IS ALL ABOUT, SEE?"

OKAY, NEVA! MOVE FOR ME! LEMMEE SEE YOU MOVE!!

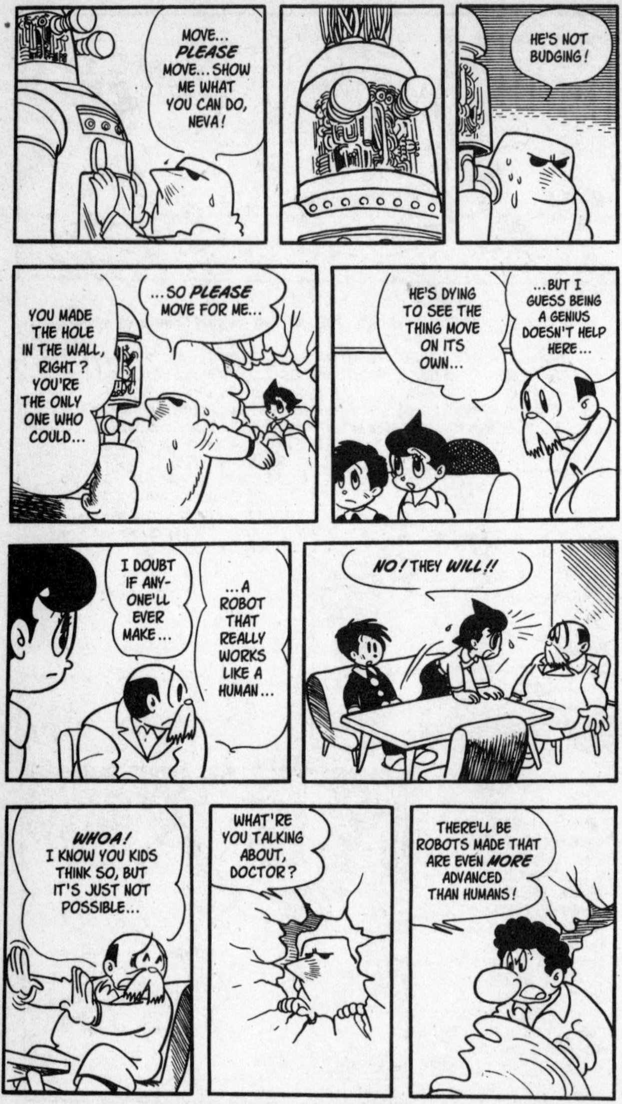
MOVE... ***PLEASE*** MOVE... SHOW ME WHAT YOU CAN DO, NEVA!
HE'S NOT BUDGING!
YOU MADE THE HOLE IN THE WALL, RIGHT? YOU'RE THE ONLY ONE WHO COULD...
...SO ***PLEASE*** MOVE FOR ME...
HE'S DYING TO SEE THE THING MOVE ON ITS OWN...
...BUT I GUESS BEING A GENIUS DOESN'T HELP HERE...
I DOUBT IF ANY-ONE'LL EVER MAKE...
...A ROBOT THAT REALLY WORKS LIKE A HUMAN...
NO! THEY ***WILL!!***
WHOA! I KNOW YOU KIDS THINK SO, BUT IT'S JUST NOT POSSIBLE...
WHAT'RE YOU TALKING ABOUT, DOCTOR?
THERE'LL BE ROBOTS MADE THAT ARE EVEN ***MORE*** ADVANCED THAN HUMANS!

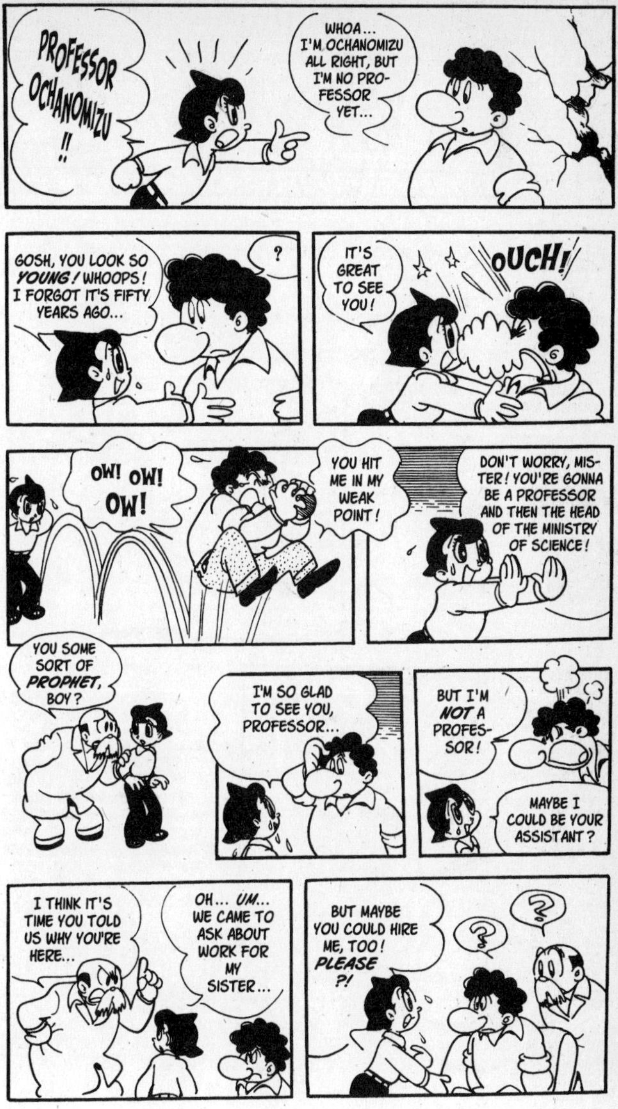
PROFESSOR OCHANOMIZU !!
WHOA... I'M OCHANOMIZU ALL RIGHT, BUT I'M NO PROFESSOR YET...
GOSH, YOU LOOK SO YOUNG! WHOOPS! I FORGOT IT'S FIFTY YEARS AGO...
?
IT'S GREAT TO SEE YOU!
OUCH!
OW! OW! OW!
YOU HIT ME IN MY WEAK POINT!
DON'T WORRY, MISTER! YOU'RE GONNA BE A PROFESSOR AND THEN THE HEAD OF THE MINISTRY OF SCIENCE!
YOU SOME SORT OF PROPHET, BOY?
I'M SO GLAD TO SEE YOU, PROFESSOR...
BUT I'M NOT A PROFESSOR!
MAYBE I COULD BE YOUR ASSISTANT?
I THINK IT'S TIME YOU TOLD US WHY YOU'RE HERE...
OH... UM... WE CAME TO ASK ABOUT WORK FOR MY SISTER...
BUT MAYBE YOU COULD HIRE ME, TOO! PLEASE?!
?
?

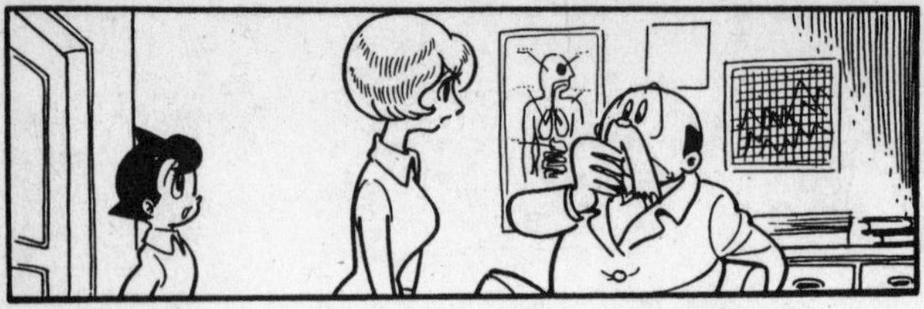

THE NEXT DAY ASTRO TOOK SCARA TO THE THRILL CLINIC, AND INTRODUCED HER TO DR. WHITEBEARD.

"SO YOU'RE THE ONE HE WAS TALKING ABOUT, EH?" THE DOCTOR COMMENTED. "AND, YOU WANT TO WORK AS A NURSE AT MY CLINIC?"

"*ER, YES...* AND I'D DO MY VERY BEST," SCARA REPLIED.

"GOOD. BUT YOU'LL HAVE TO TAKE COURSES AT NURSING SCHOOL. YOU HAVE TO PASS AN EXAM IN ORDER TO WORK AS A NURSE..."

"I HAVE TO GO TO SCHOOL? THAT SOUNDS LIKE AN INTERESTING PLACE. I'LL GO ANYWHERE, TO SCHOOL, EVEN TO THE POLICE!"

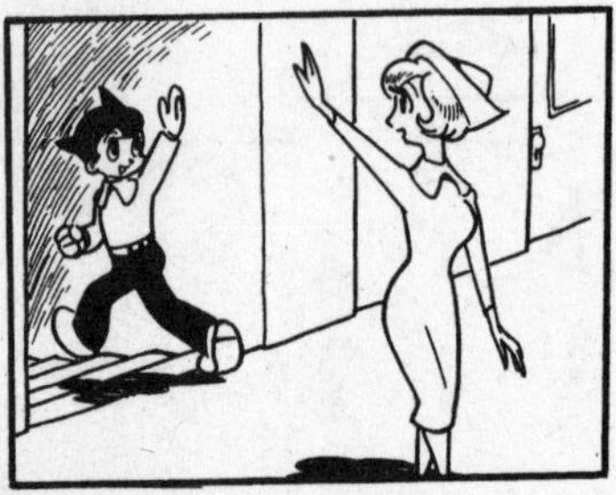

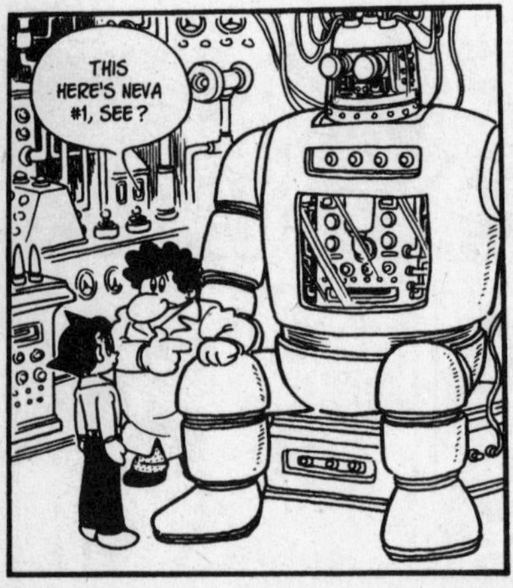
THIS HERE'S NEVA #1, SEE?

"WELL," WHITEBEARD REPLIED, "NO NEED FOR YOU TO GO TO THE ***POLICE***, BUT YOU WILL HAVE TO STUDY HARD. OH, AND ASTRO... THAT WAS THE NAME WASN'T IT? YOU CAN START WORK AS OCHANOMIZU'S ASSISTANT FROM TODAY IF YOU WANT. FEEL FREE TO GO JOIN HIM IN HIS LAB DOWN IN THE BASEMENT."

ASTRO TURNED TO SCARA. "THIS WORKED OUT GREAT, DIDN'T IT?" HE SAID. "I'LL SEE YOU LATER! LET'S BOTH DO OUR BEST!"

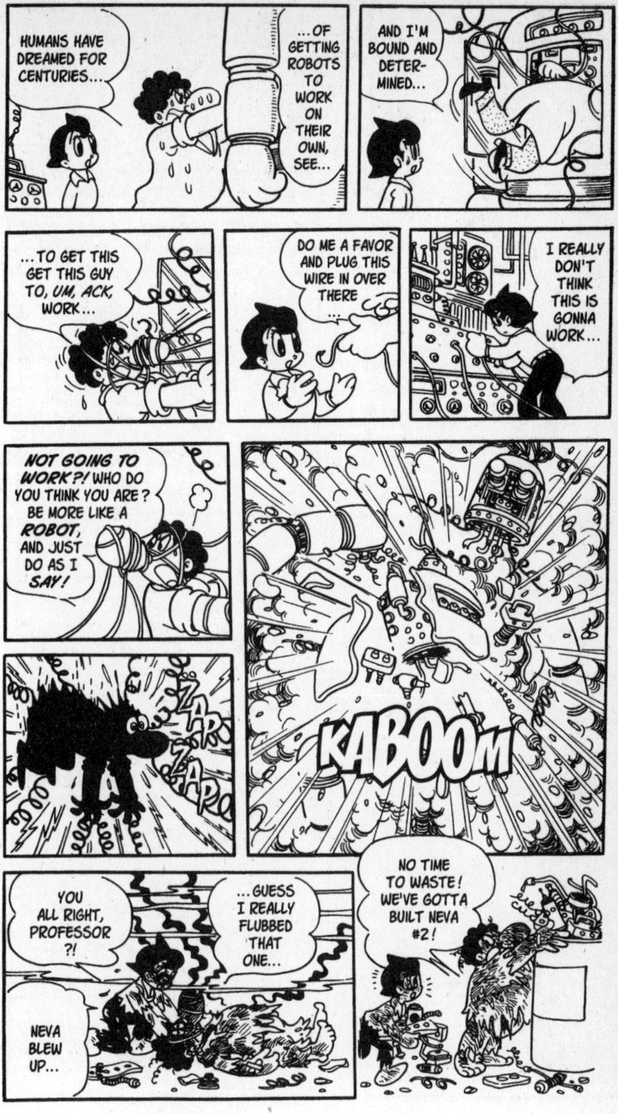
HUMANS HAVE DREAMED FOR CENTURIES...
...OF GETTING ROBOTS TO WORK ON THEIR OWN, SEE...
AND I'M BOUND AND DETERMINED...
...TO GET THIS GET THIS GUY TO, UM, ACK, WORK...
DO ME A FAVOR AND PLUG THIS WIRE IN OVER THERE ...
I REALLY DON'T THINK THIS IS GONNA WORK...
NOT GOING TO WORK?! WHO DO YOU THINK YOU ARE? BE MORE LIKE A ROBOT, AND JUST DO AS I SAY!
ZAP
ZAP
KABOOM
YOU ALL RIGHT, PROFESSOR ?!
...GUESS I REALLY FLUBBED THAT ONE...
NEVA BLEW UP...
NO TIME TO WASTE! WE'VE GOTTA BUILT NEVA #2!

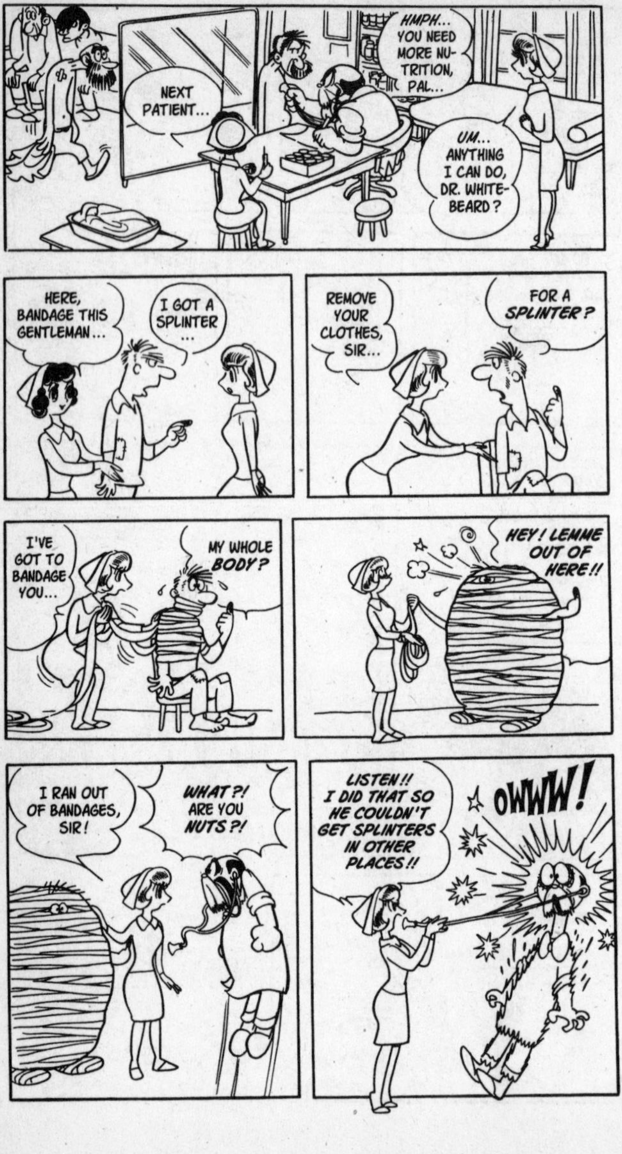

NEXT PATIENT...
HMPH... YOU NEED MORE NU-TRITION, PAL...
UM... ANYTHING I CAN DO, DR. WHITE-BEARD?
HERE, BANDAGE THIS GENTLEMAN...
I GOT A SPLINTER ...
REMOVE YOUR CLOTHES, SIR...
FOR A SPLINTER?
I'VE GOT TO BANDAGE YOU...
MY WHOLE BODY?
HEY! LEMME OUT OF HERE!!
I RAN OUT OF BANDAGES, SIR!
WHAT?! ARE YOU NUTS?!
LISTEN!! I DID THAT SO HE COULDN'T GET SPLINTERS IN OTHER PLACES!!
OWWW!

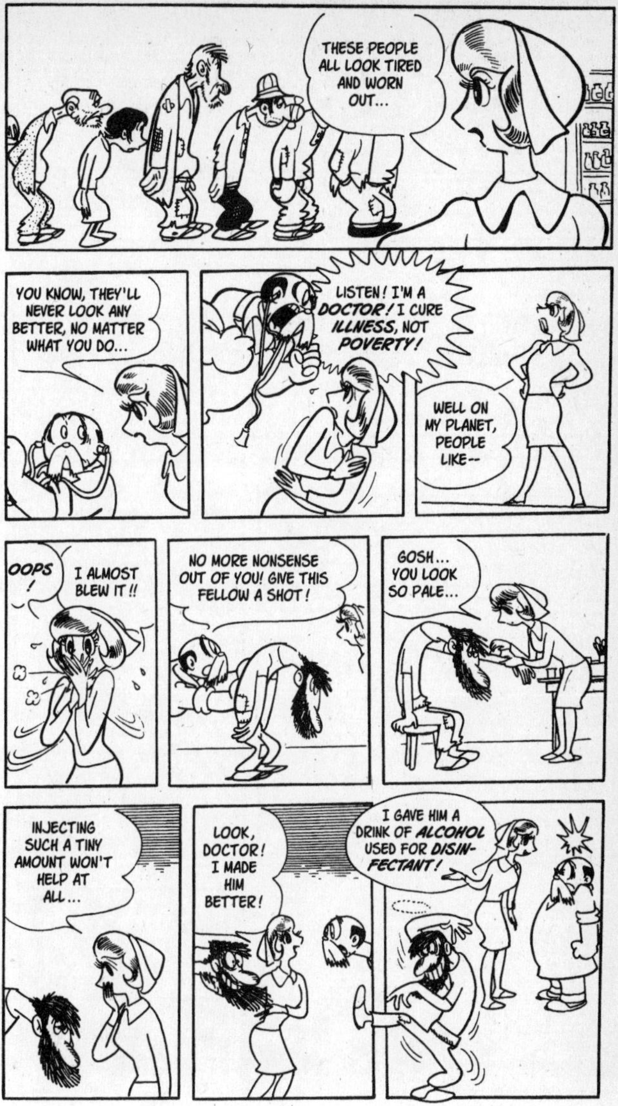
THESE PEOPLE ALL LOOK TIRED AND WORN OUT...
YOU KNOW, THEY'LL NEVER LOOK ANY BETTER, NO MATTER WHAT YOU DO...
LISTEN! I'M A DOCTOR! I CURE ILLNESS, NOT POVERTY!
WELL ON MY PLANET, PEOPLE LIKE--
OOPS!
I ALMOST BLEW IT!!
NO MORE NONSENSE OUT OF YOU! GIVE THIS FELLOW A SHOT!
GOSH... YOU LOOK SO PALE...
INJECTING SUCH A TINY AMOUNT WON'T HELP AT ALL...
LOOK, DOCTOR! I MADE HIM BETTER!
I GAVE HIM A DRINK OF ALCOHOL USED FOR DISIN-FECTANT!

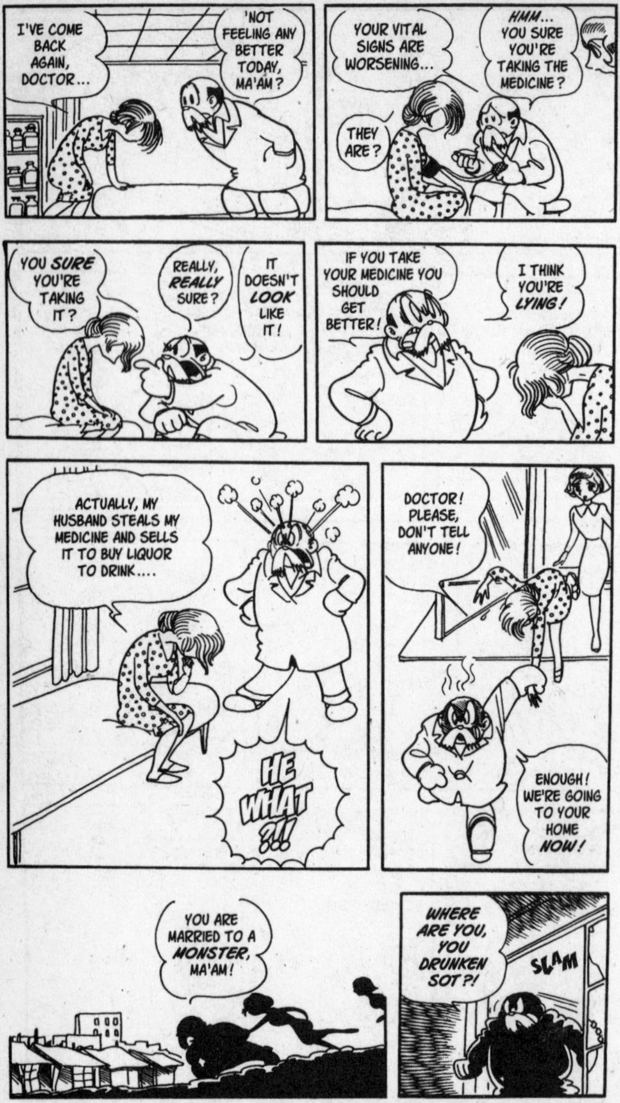
I'VE COME BACK AGAIN, DOCTOR...
'NOT FEELING ANY BETTER TODAY, MA'AM?
YOUR VITAL SIGNS ARE WORSENING...
HMM... YOU SURE YOU'RE TAKING THE MEDICINE?
THEY ARE?
YOU SURE YOU'RE TAKING IT?
REALLY, REALLY SURE?
IT DOESN'T LOOK LIKE IT!
IF YOU TAKE YOUR MEDICINE YOU SHOULD GET BETTER!
I THINK YOU'RE LYING!
ACTUALLY, MY HUSBAND STEALS MY MEDICINE AND SELLS IT TO BUY LIQUOR TO DRINK....
HE WHAT ?!!
DOCTOR! PLEASE, DON'T TELL ANYONE!
ENOUGH! WE'RE GOING TO YOUR HOME NOW!
YOU ARE MARRIED TO A MONSTER, MA'AM!
WHERE ARE YOU, YOU DRUNKEN SOT?!
SLAM

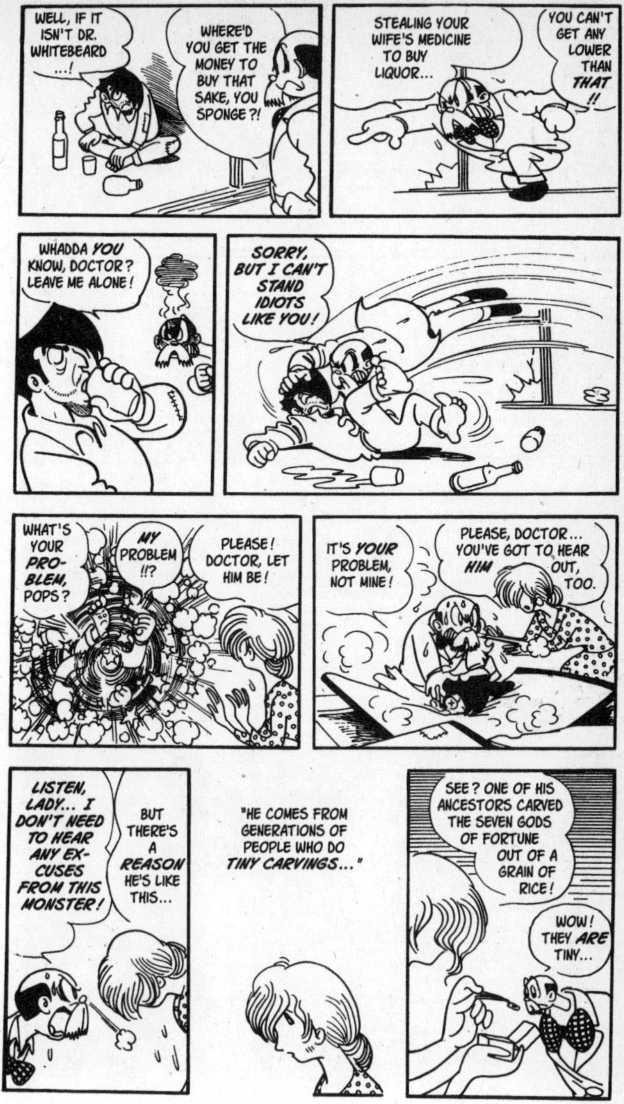
WELL, IF IT ISN'T DR. WHITEBEARD ...!
WHERE'D YOU GET THE MONEY TO BUY THAT SAKE, YOU SPONGE?!
STEALING YOUR WIFE'S MEDICINE TO BUY LIQUOR...
YOU CAN'T GET ANY LOWER THAN *THAT*!!
WHADDA *YOU* KNOW, DOCTOR? LEAVE ME ALONE!
SORRY, BUT I CAN'T STAND IDIOTS LIKE YOU!
WHAT'S YOUR *PROBLEM*, POPS?
MY PROBLEM!!?
PLEASE! DOCTOR, LET HIM BE!
IT'S *YOUR* PROBLEM, NOT MINE!
PLEASE, DOCTOR... YOU'VE GOT TO HEAR *HIM* OUT, TOO.
LISTEN, LADY... I DON'T NEED TO HEAR ANY EXCUSES FROM THIS MONSTER!
BUT THERE'S A *REASON* HE'S LIKE THIS...
"HE COMES FROM GENERATIONS OF PEOPLE WHO DO *TINY CARVINGS...*"
SEE? ONE OF HIS ANCESTORS CARVED THE SEVEN GODS OF FORTUNE OUT OF A GRAIN OF RICE!
WOW! THEY *ARE* TINY...

"MY HUSBAND PRIDED HIMSELF ON BEING ONE OF THE TOP MINIATURE CARVERS IN ALL JAPAN."

100 FLEAS CARVED FROM ERASER SHAVING

1 MILLIMETER-DIAMETER BELL

SCENES OF MERCY CARVED FROM MATCH STICK

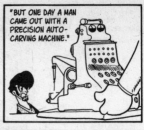

"BUT ONE DAY A MAN CAME OUT WITH A PRECISION AUTO-CARVING MACHINE."

"IT COULD CARVE ANYTHING, RIGHT BEFORE YOUR EYES."

HMPH. NO MACHINE'S GONNA OUT-CARVE ME!

I COME FROM A LONG LINE OF SKILLED CRAFTSMEN! I'M THE BEST CARVER IN ALL JAPAN!

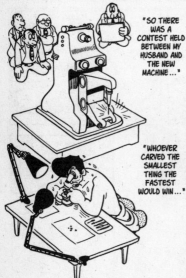

"SO THERE WAS A CONTEST HELD BETWEEN MY HUSBAND AND THE NEW MACHINE..."

"WHOEVER CARVED THE SMALLEST THING THE FASTEST WOULD WIN..."

AND THE MACHINE WINS!

B... BUT...

THE MACHINE'S CARVING IS THE BEST!

I HATE TECHNOLOGY! I LOST TO A MACHINE!!

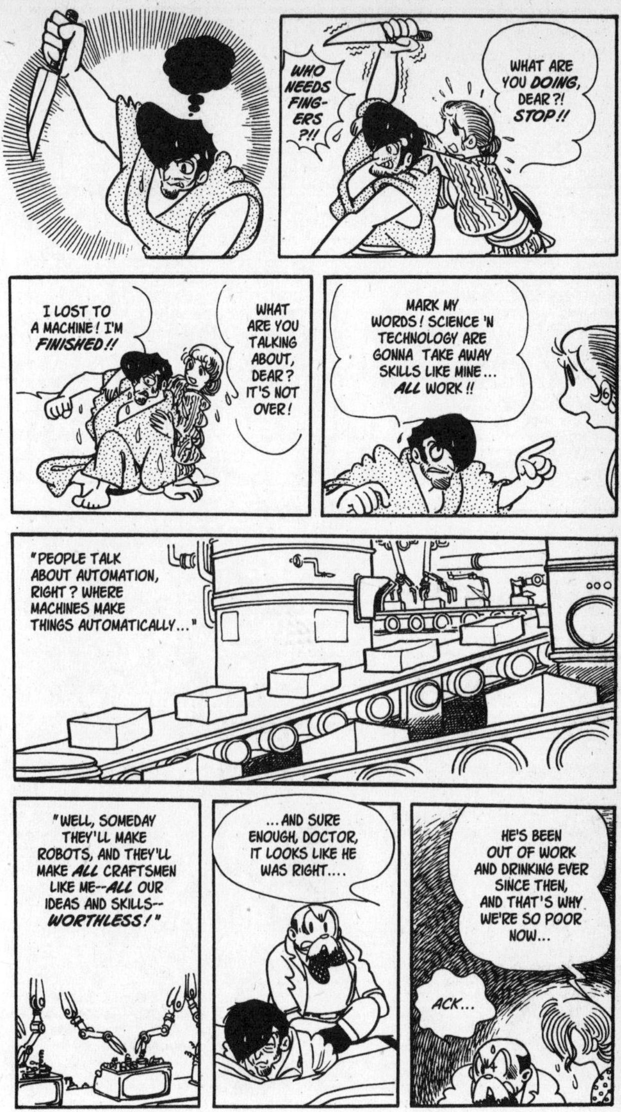
WHO NEEDS FING- ERS ?!!
WHAT ARE YOU DOING, DEAR?! STOP!!
I LOST TO A MACHINE! I'M FINISHED!!
WHAT ARE YOU TALKING ABOUT, DEAR? IT'S NOT OVER!
MARK MY WORDS! SCIENCE 'N TECHNOLOGY ARE GONNA TAKE AWAY SKILLS LIKE MINE... ALL WORK!!
"PEOPLE TALK ABOUT AUTOMATION, RIGHT? WHERE MACHINES MAKE THINGS AUTOMATICALLY..."
"WELL, SOMEDAY THEY'LL MAKE ROBOTS, AND THEY'LL MAKE ALL CRAFTSMEN LIKE ME--ALL OUR IDEAS AND SKILLS-- WORTHLESS!"
...AND SURE ENOUGH, DOCTOR, IT LOOKS LIKE HE WAS RIGHT....
HE'S BEEN OUT OF WORK AND DRINKING EVER SINCE THEN, AND THAT'S WHY WE'RE SO POOR NOW...
ACK...

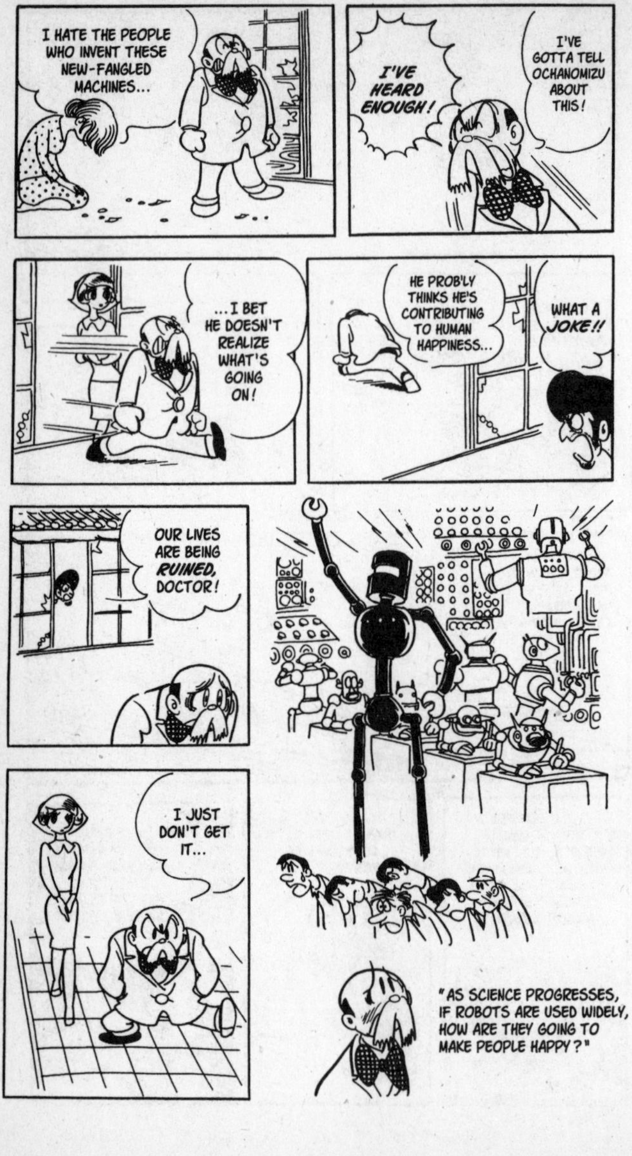
I HATE THE PEOPLE WHO INVENT THESE NEW-FANGLED MACHINES...
I'VE HEARD ENOUGH!
I'VE GOTTA TELL OCHANOMIZU ABOUT THIS!
...I BET HE DOESN'T REALIZE WHAT'S GOING ON!
HE PROB'LY THINKS HE'S CONTRIBUTING TO HUMAN HAPPINESS...
WHAT A JOKE!!
OUR LIVES ARE BEING RUINED, DOCTOR!
I JUST DON'T GET IT...
"AS SCIENCE PROGRESSES, IF ROBOTS ARE USED WIDELY, HOW ARE THEY GOING TO MAKE PEOPLE HAPPY?"

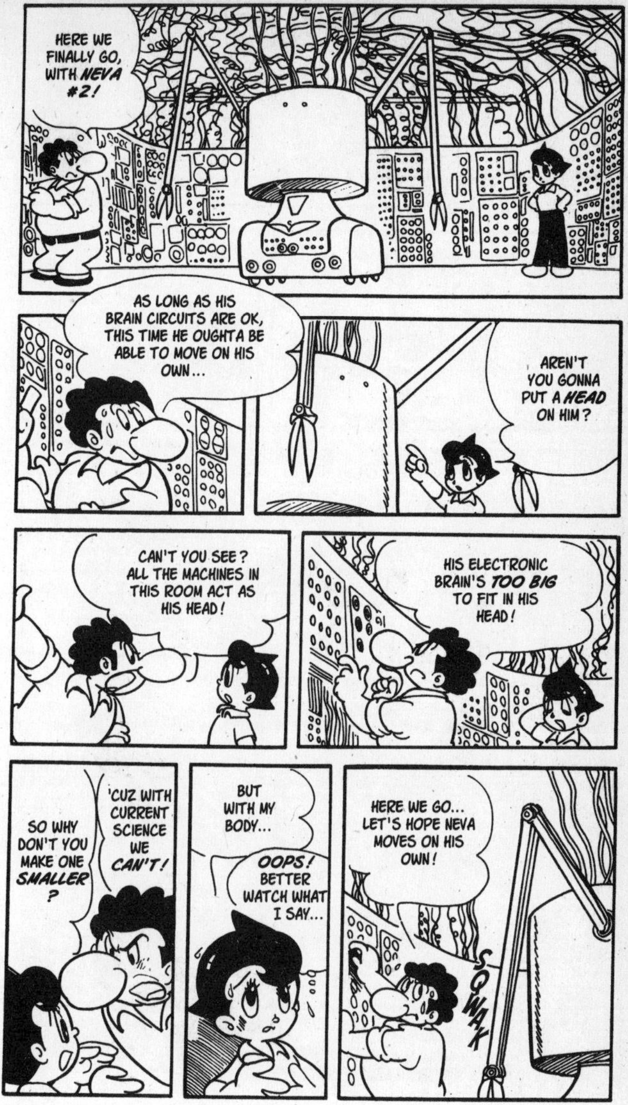

HERE WE FINALLY GO, WITH NEVA #2!
AS LONG AS HIS BRAIN CIRCUITS ARE OK, THIS TIME HE OUGHTA BE ABLE TO MOVE ON HIS OWN...
AREN'T YOU GONNA PUT A HEAD ON HIM?
CAN'T YOU SEE? ALL THE MACHINES IN THIS ROOM ACT AS HIS HEAD!
HIS ELECTRONIC BRAIN'S TOO BIG TO FIT IN HIS HEAD!
SO WHY DON'T YOU MAKE ONE SMALLER?
'CUZ WITH CURRENT SCIENCE WE CAN'T!
BUT WITH MY BODY...
OOPS! BETTER WATCH WHAT I SAY...
HERE WE GO... LET'S HOPE NEVA MOVES ON HIS OWN!
SQWAK

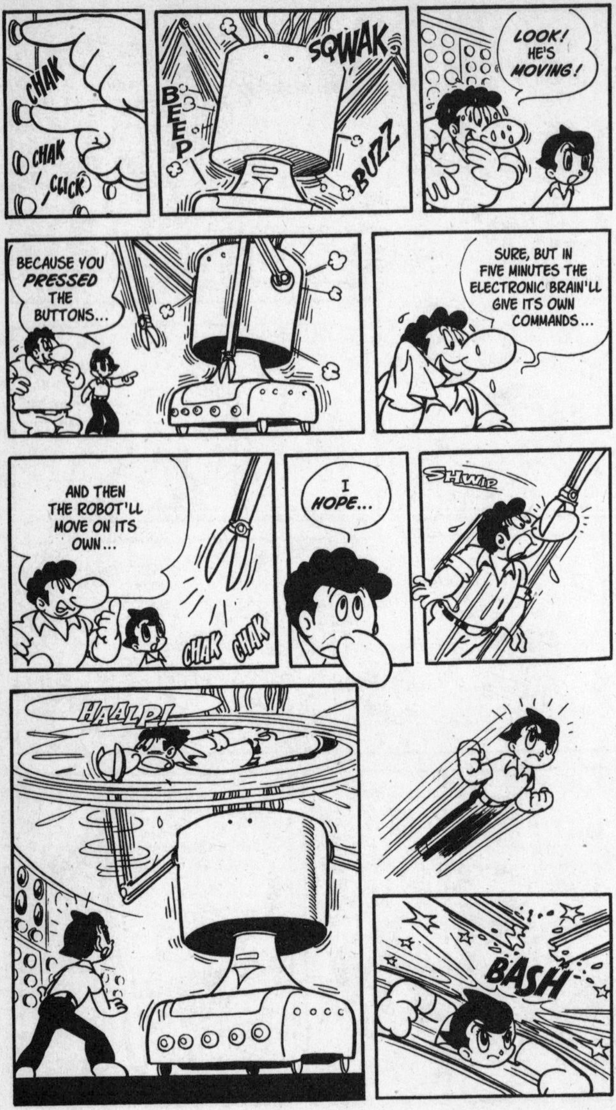
CHAK
CHAK
CLICK
SQWAK
BEEP
BUZZ
LOOK! HE'S MOVING!
BECAUSE YOU PRESSED THE BUTTONS...
SURE, BUT IN FIVE MINUTES THE ELECTRONIC BRAIN'LL GIVE ITS OWN COMMANDS...
AND THEN THE ROBOT'LL MOVE ON ITS OWN...
CHAK CHAK
I HOPE...
SHWIP
HAALP!
BASH

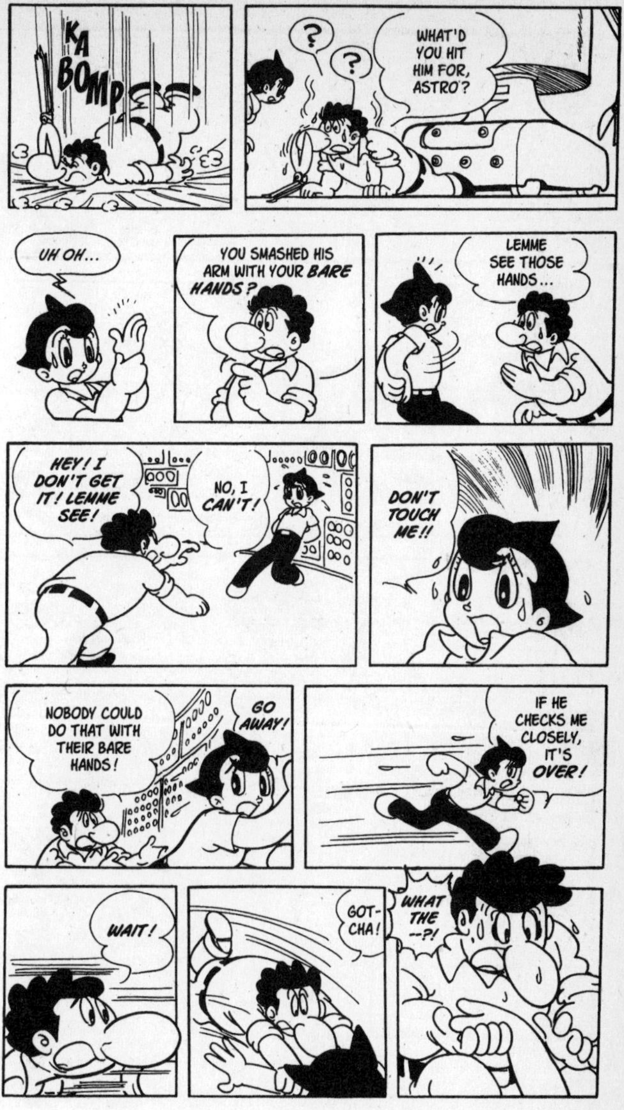
KA BOMP
?
?
WHAT'D YOU HIT HIM FOR, ASTRO?
UH OH...
YOU SMASHED HIS ARM WITH YOUR BARE HANDS?
LEMME SEE THOSE HANDS...
HEY! I DON'T GET IT! LEMME SEE!
NO, I CAN'T!
DON'T TOUCH ME!!
NOBODY COULD DO THAT WITH THEIR BARE HANDS!
GO AWAY!
IF HE CHECKS ME CLOSELY, IT'S OVER!
WAIT!
GOT-CHA!
WHAT THE --?!

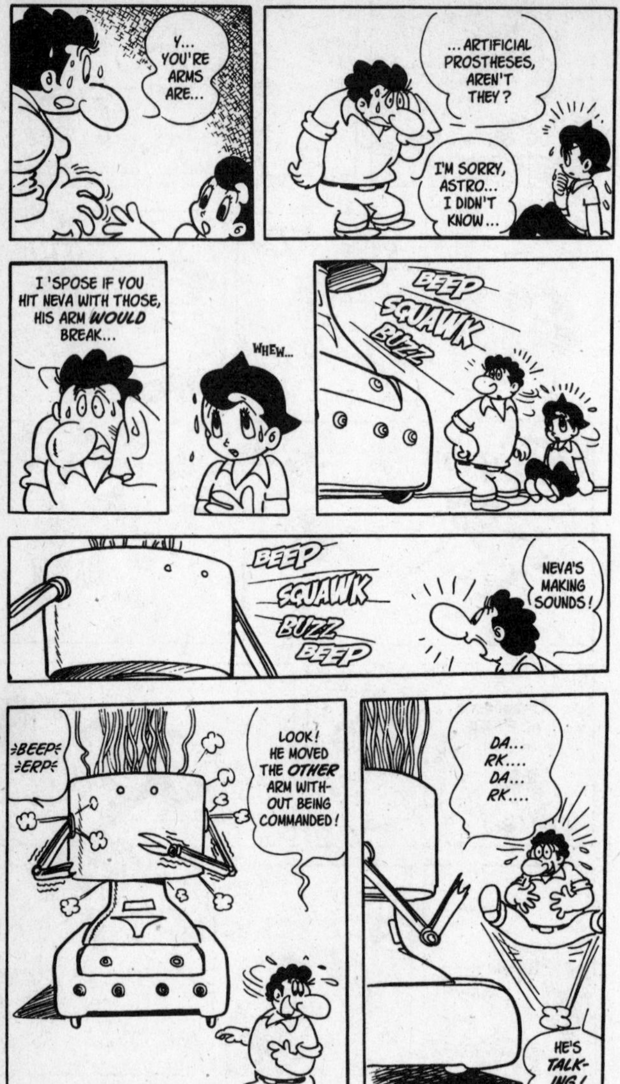
Y... YOU'RE ARMS ARE...
...ARTIFICIAL PROSTHESES, AREN'T THEY?
I'M SORRY, ASTRO... I DIDN'T KNOW...
I 'SPOSE IF YOU HIT NEVA WITH THOSE, HIS ARM WOULD BREAK...
WHEW...
BEEP
SQUAWK
BUZZ
BEEP
SQUAWK
BUZZ
BEEP
NEVA'S MAKING SOUNDS!
BEEP
ERP
LOOK! HE MOVED THE OTHER ARM WITH-OUT BEING COMMANDED!
DA... RK.... DA... RK....
HE'S TALK-ING!

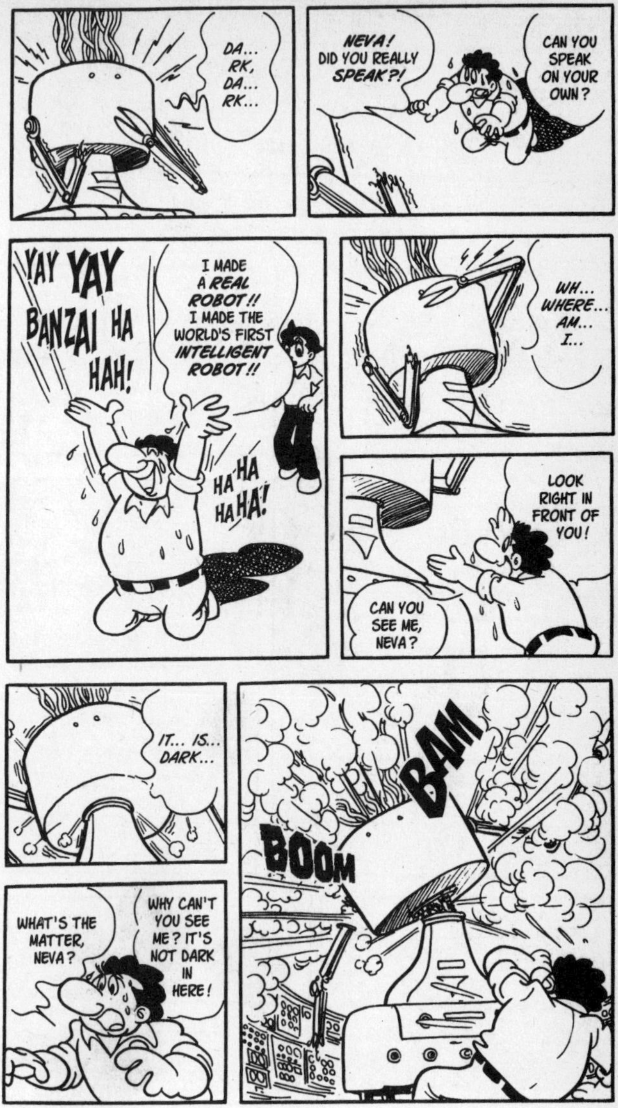
DA... RK, DA... RK...
NEVA! DID YOU REALLY SPEAK?!
CAN YOU SPEAK ON YOUR OWN?
YAY YAY BANZAI HA HAH!
I MADE A REAL ROBOT!! I MADE THE WORLD'S FIRST INTELLIGENT ROBOT!!
HA HA HA HA!
WH... WHERE... AM... I...
LOOK RIGHT IN FRONT OF YOU!
CAN YOU SEE ME, NEVA?
IT... IS... DARK...
WHAT'S THE MATTER, NEVA?
WHY CAN'T YOU SEE ME? IT'S NOT DARK IN HERE!
BAM
BOOM

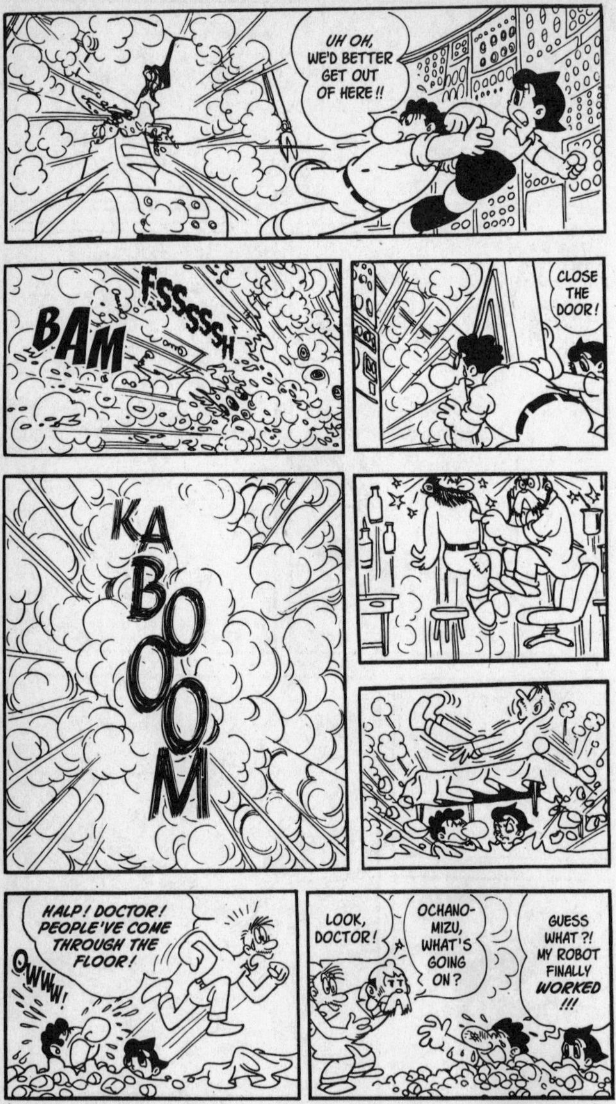
UH OH, WE'D BETTER GET OUT OF HERE!!
BAM
FSSSSSSH
CLOSE THE DOOR!
KABOOOOM
HALP! DOCTOR! PEOPLE'VE COME THROUGH THE FLOOR!
OWWW!
LOOK, DOCTOR!
OCHANO-MIZU, WHAT'S GOING ON?
GUESS WHAT?! MY ROBOT FINALLY WORKED!!!

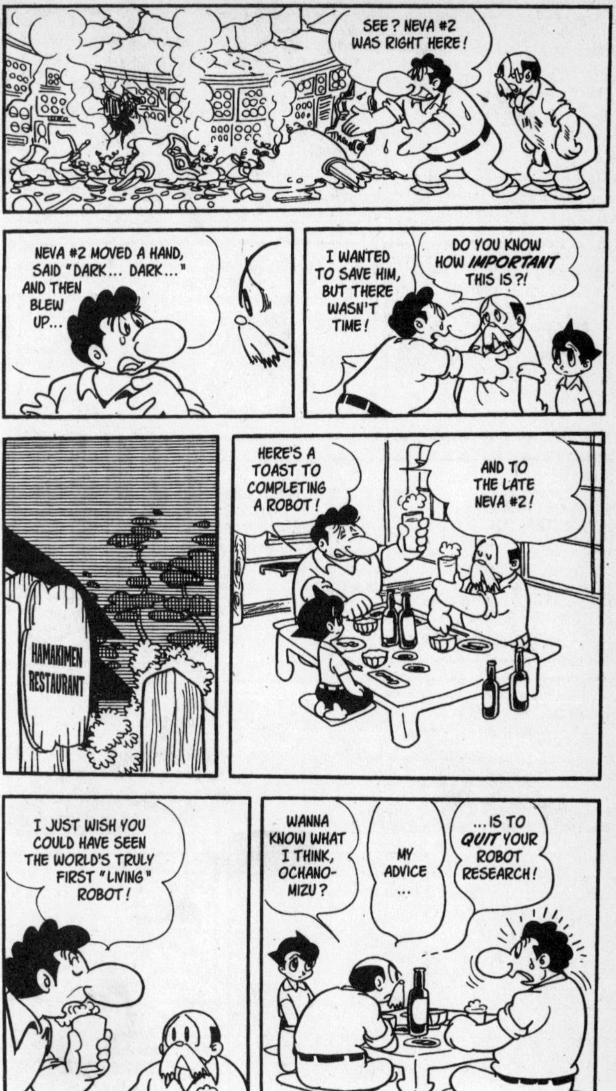
SEE? NEVA #2 WAS RIGHT HERE!
NEVA #2 MOVED A HAND, SAID "DARK... DARK..." AND THEN BLEW UP...
I WANTED TO SAVE HIM, BUT THERE WASN'T TIME!
DO YOU KNOW HOW *IMPORTANT* THIS IS?!
HAMAKIMEN RESTAURANT
HERE'S A TOAST TO COMPLETING A ROBOT!
AND TO THE LATE NEVA #2!
I JUST WISH YOU COULD HAVE SEEN THE WORLD'S TRULY FIRST "LIVING" ROBOT!
WANNA KNOW WHAT I THINK, OCHANO-MIZU?
MY ADVICE ...
...IS TO *QUIT* YOUR ROBOT RESEARCH!

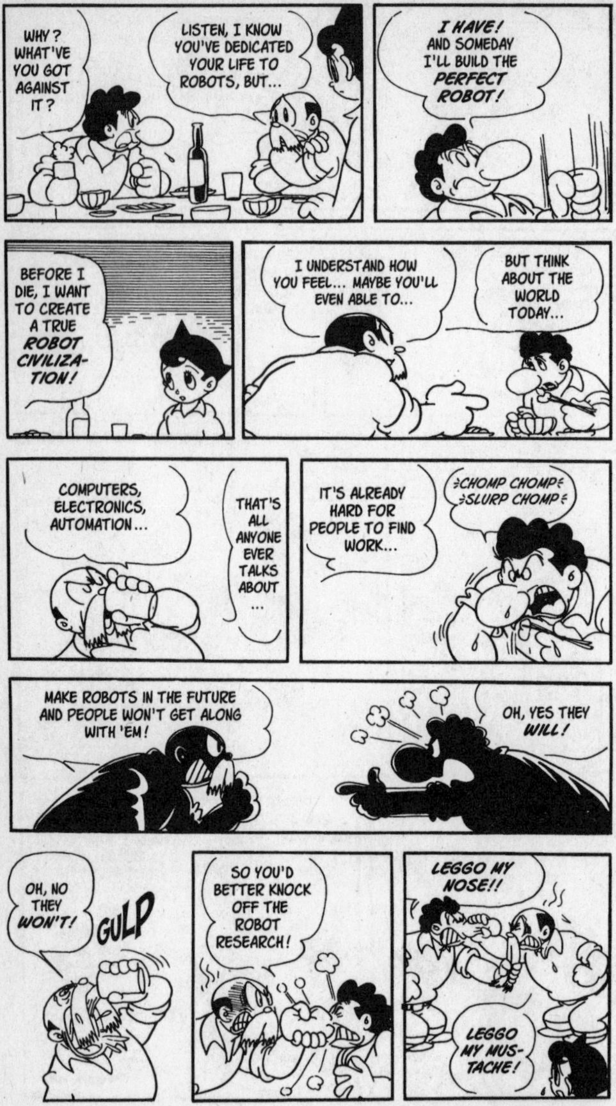
WHY? WHAT'VE YOU GOT AGAINST IT?
LISTEN, I KNOW YOU'VE DEDICATED YOUR LIFE TO ROBOTS, BUT...
I HAVE! AND SOMEDAY I'LL BUILD THE PERFECT ROBOT!
BEFORE I DIE, I WANT TO CREATE A TRUE ROBOT CIVILIZATION!
I UNDERSTAND HOW YOU FEEL... MAYBE YOU'LL EVEN ABLE TO...
BUT THINK ABOUT THE WORLD TODAY...
COMPUTERS, ELECTRONICS, AUTOMATION...
THAT'S ALL ANYONE EVER TALKS ABOUT ...
IT'S ALREADY HARD FOR PEOPLE TO FIND WORK...
CHOMP CHOMP SLURP CHOMP
MAKE ROBOTS IN THE FUTURE AND PEOPLE WON'T GET ALONG WITH 'EM!
OH, YES THEY WILL!
OH, NO THEY WON'T!
GULP
SO YOU'D BETTER KNOCK OFF THE ROBOT RESEARCH!
LEGGO MY NOSE!!
LEGGO MY MUSTACHE!

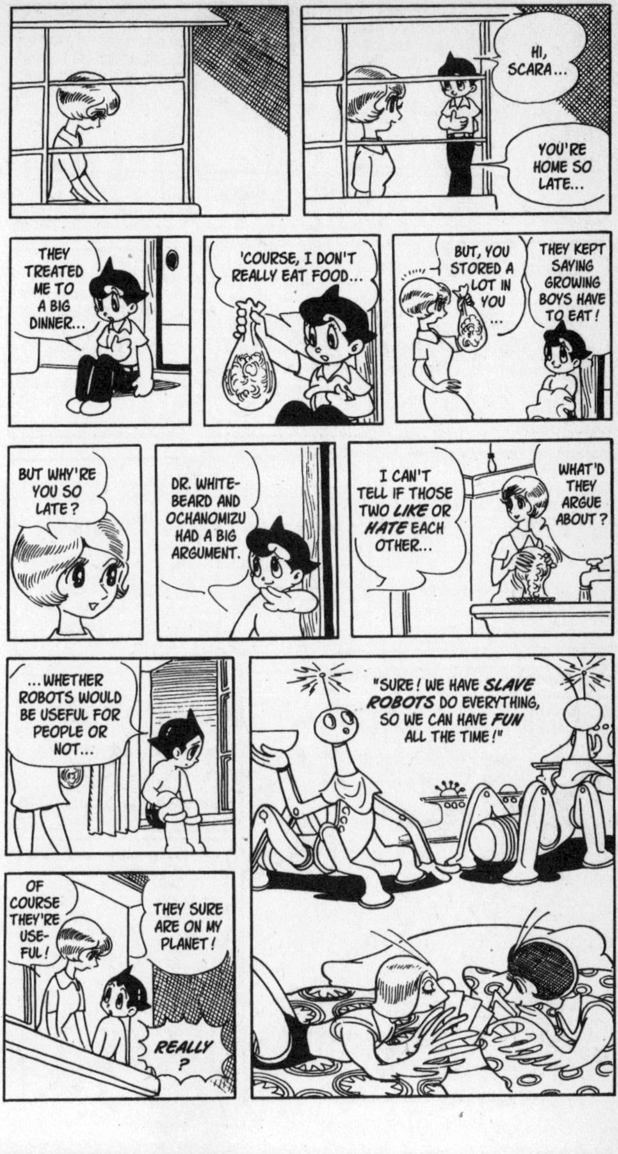
HI, SCARA...
YOU'RE HOME SO LATE...
THEY TREATED ME TO A BIG DINNER...
'COURSE, I DON'T REALLY EAT FOOD...
BUT, YOU STORED A LOT IN YOU ...
THEY KEPT SAYING GROWING BOYS HAVE TO EAT!
BUT WHY'RE YOU SO LATE?
DR. WHITE-BEARD AND OCHANOMIZU HAD A BIG ARGUMENT.
I CAN'T TELL IF THOSE TWO LIKE OR HATE EACH OTHER...
WHAT'D THEY ARGUE ABOUT?
...WHETHER ROBOTS WOULD BE USEFUL FOR PEOPLE OR NOT...
"SURE! WE HAVE SLAVE ROBOTS DO EVERYTHING, SO WE CAN HAVE FUN ALL THE TIME!"
OF COURSE THEY'RE USE-FUL!
THEY SURE ARE ON MY PLANET!
REALLY?

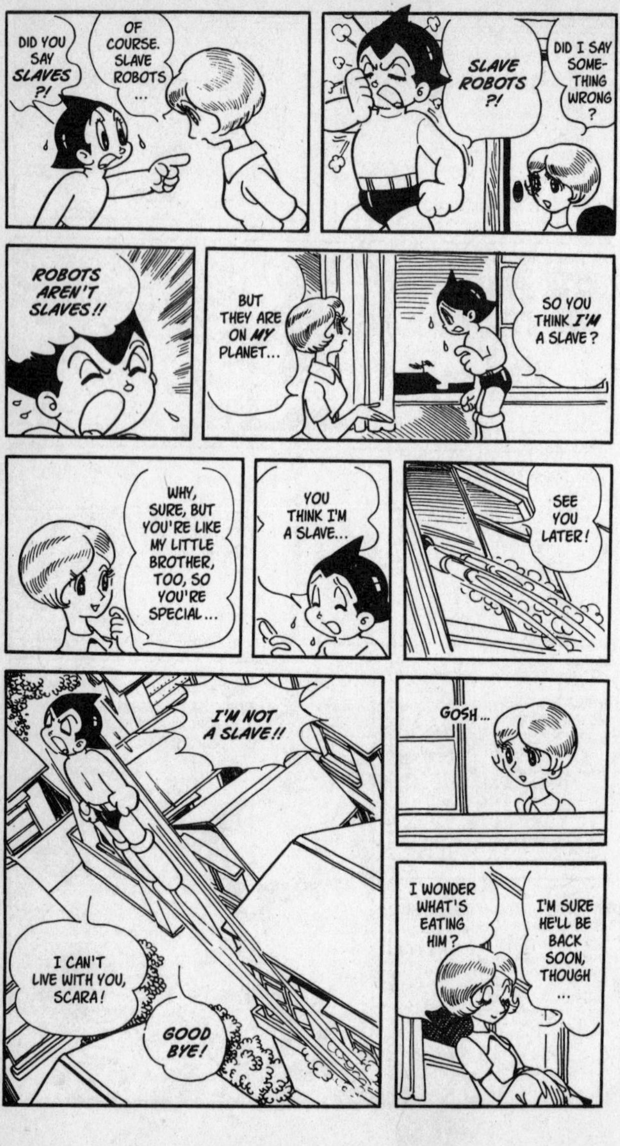
DID YOU SAY SLAVES ?!
OF COURSE. SLAVE ROBOTS ...
SLAVE ROBOTS ?!
DID I SAY SOME-THING WRONG ?
ROBOTS AREN'T SLAVES !!
BUT THEY ARE ON MY PLANET...
SO YOU THINK I'M A SLAVE ?
WHY, SURE, BUT YOU'RE LIKE MY LITTLE BROTHER, TOO, SO YOU'RE SPECIAL...
YOU THINK I'M A SLAVE...
SEE YOU LATER!
I'M NOT A SLAVE !!
I CAN'T LIVE WITH YOU, SCARA!
GOOD BYE!
GOSH...
I WONDER WHAT'S EATING HIM ?
I'M SURE HE'LL BE BACK SOON, THOUGH ...

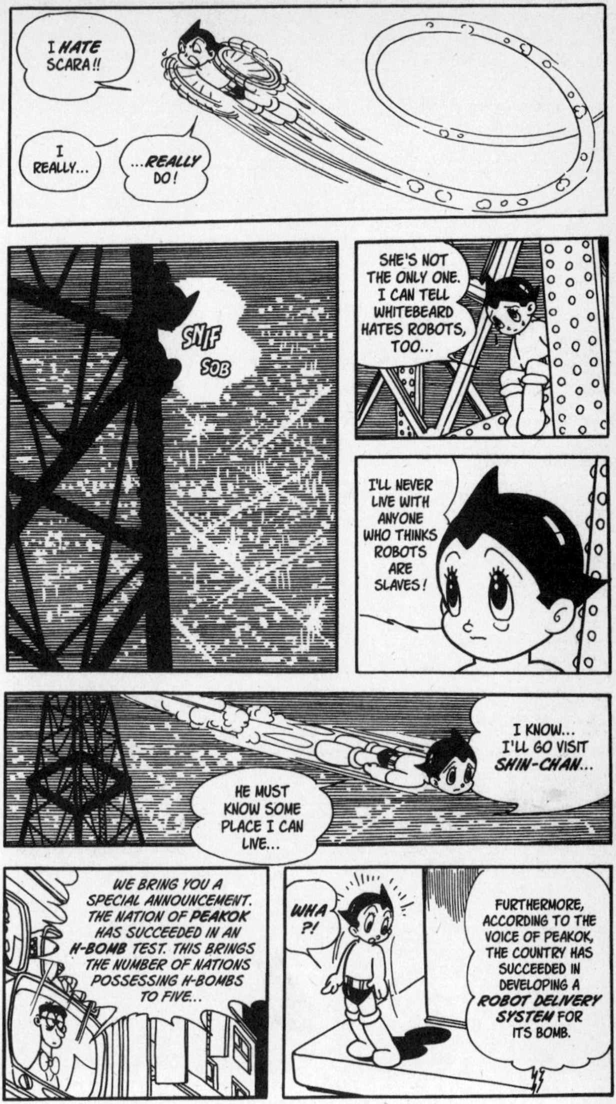
I HATE SCARA!!
I REALLY...
...REALLY DO!
SNIF
SOB
SHE'S NOT THE ONLY ONE. I CAN TELL WHITEBEARD HATES ROBOTS, TOO...
I'LL NEVER LIVE WITH ANYONE WHO THINKS ROBOTS ARE SLAVES!
I KNOW... I'LL GO VISIT SHIN-CHAN...
HE MUST KNOW SOME PLACE I CAN LIVE...
WE BRING YOU A SPECIAL ANNOUNCEMENT. THE NATION OF PEAKOK HAS SUCCEEDED IN AN H-BOMB TEST. THIS BRINGS THE NUMBER OF NATIONS POSSESSING H-BOMBS TO FIVE...
WHA?!
FURTHERMORE, ACCORDING TO THE VOICE OF PEAKOK, THE COUNTRY HAS SUCCEEDED IN DEVELOPING A ROBOT DELIVERY SYSTEM FOR ITS BOMB.

BARO, THE ROBOT

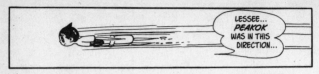

LESSEE... *PEAKOK* WAS IN THIS DIRECTION...

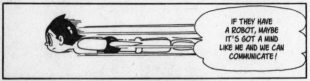

IF THEY HAVE A ROBOT, MAYBE IT'S GOT A MIND LIKE ME AND WE CAN COMMUNICATE!

FINALLY, AFTER ALL THAT OCEAN, LAND... WITH LIGHTS! MUST BE PEAKOK!

SWALLOWS SWIRL IN THE EVENING SKY! TRA LA TRA LA LA!

WHAT THE--?! A VISITOR FROM OUTER SPACE?!

UH-OH...

WHAT'S THIS ?!

I DIDN'T KNOW THERE WAS A *STATUE* THERE...

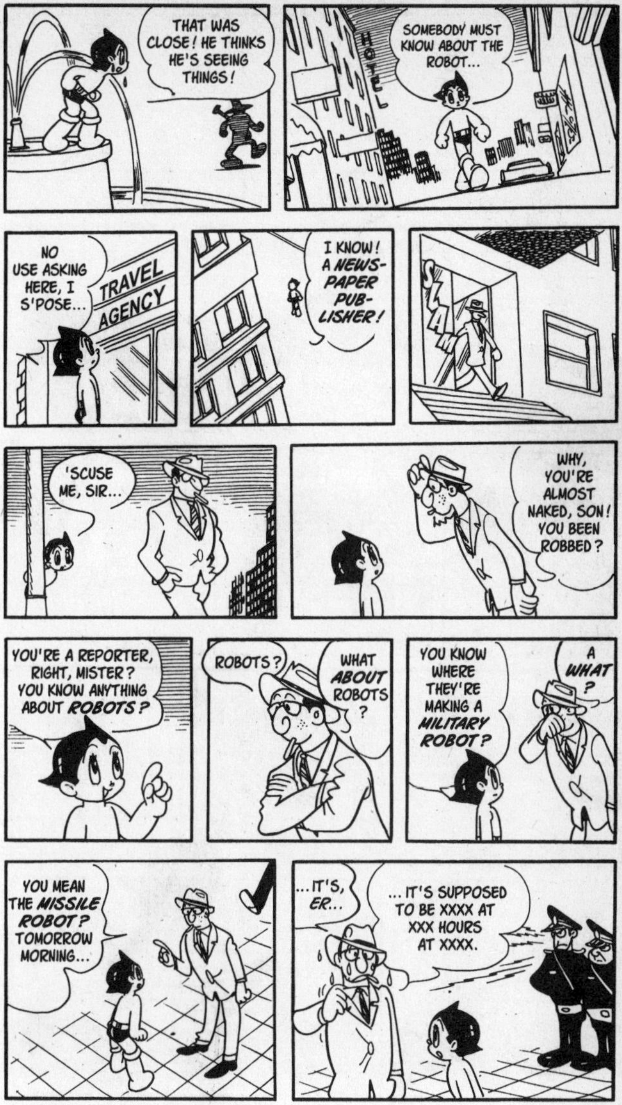
THAT WAS CLOSE! HE THINKS HE'S SEEING THINGS!
SOMEBODY MUST KNOW ABOUT THE ROBOT...
HOTEL
NO USE ASKING HERE, I S'POSE...
TRAVEL AGENCY
I KNOW! A NEWS-PAPER PUB-LISHER!
'SCUSE ME, SIR...
WHY, YOU'RE ALMOST NAKED, SON! YOU BEEN ROBBED?
YOU'RE A REPORTER, RIGHT, MISTER? YOU KNOW ANYTHING ABOUT ROBOTS?
ROBOTS?
WHAT ABOUT ROBOTS?
YOU KNOW WHERE THEY'RE MAKING A MILITARY ROBOT?
A WHAT?
YOU MEAN THE MISSILE ROBOT? TOMORROW MORNING...
...IT'S, ER...
...IT'S SUPPOSED TO BE XXXX AT XXX HOURS AT XXXX.

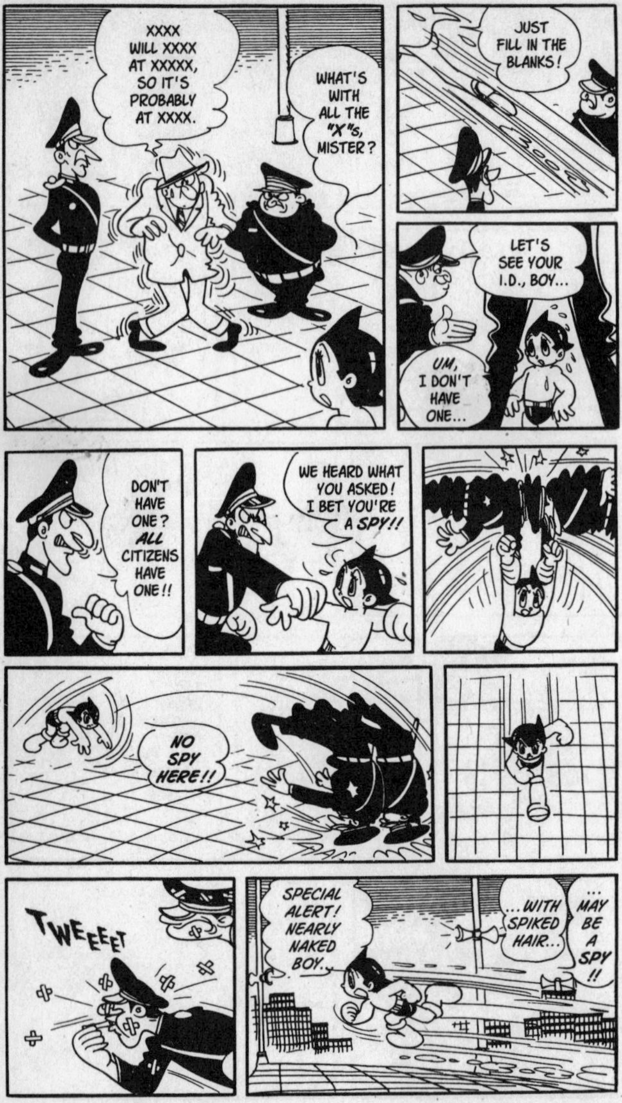
XXXX WILL XXXX AT XXXXX, SO IT'S PROBABLY AT XXXX.
WHAT'S WITH ALL THE "X"s, MISTER?
JUST FILL IN THE BLANKS!
LET'S SEE YOUR I.D., BOY...
UM, I DON'T HAVE ONE...
DON'T HAVE ONE? ALL CITIZENS HAVE ONE!!
WE HEARD WHAT YOU ASKED! I BET YOU'RE A SPY!!
NO SPY HERE!!
TWEEEET
SPECIAL ALERT! NEARLY NAKED BOY...
...WITH SPIKED HAIR...
...MAY BE A SPY!!

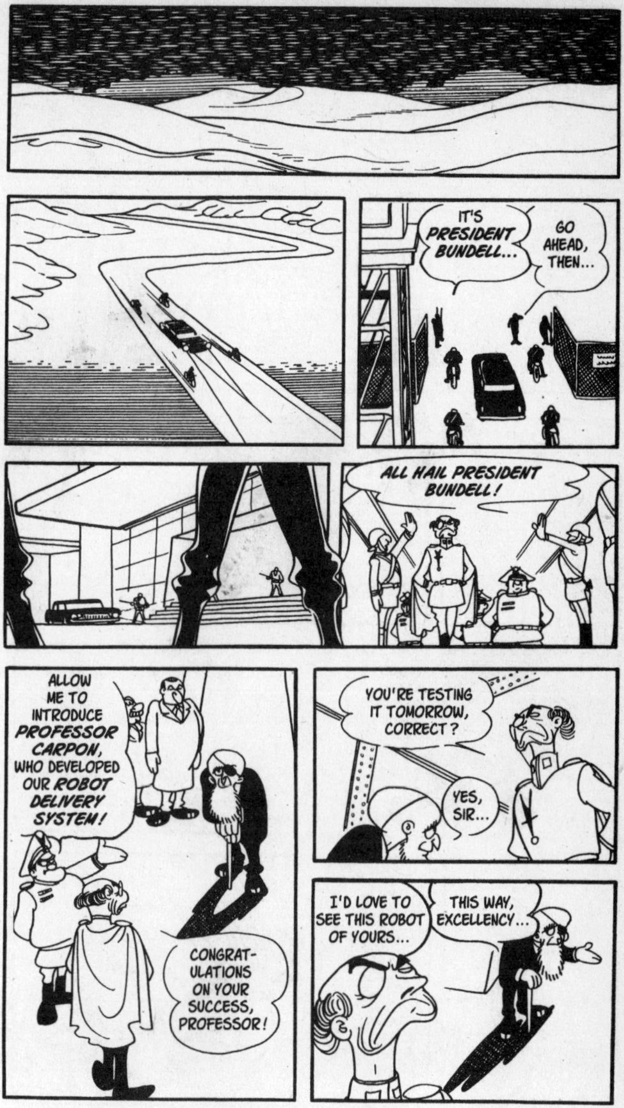
IT'S PRESIDENT BUNDELL...
GO AHEAD, THEN...
ALL HAIL PRESIDENT BUNDELL!
ALLOW ME TO INTRODUCE PROFESSOR CARPON, WHO DEVELOPED OUR ROBOT DELIVERY SYSTEM!
CONGRAT-ULATIONS ON YOUR SUCCESS, PROFESSOR!
YOU'RE TESTING IT TOMORROW, CORRECT?
YES, SIR...
I'D LOVE TO SEE THIS ROBOT OF YOURS...
THIS WAY, EXCELLENCY...

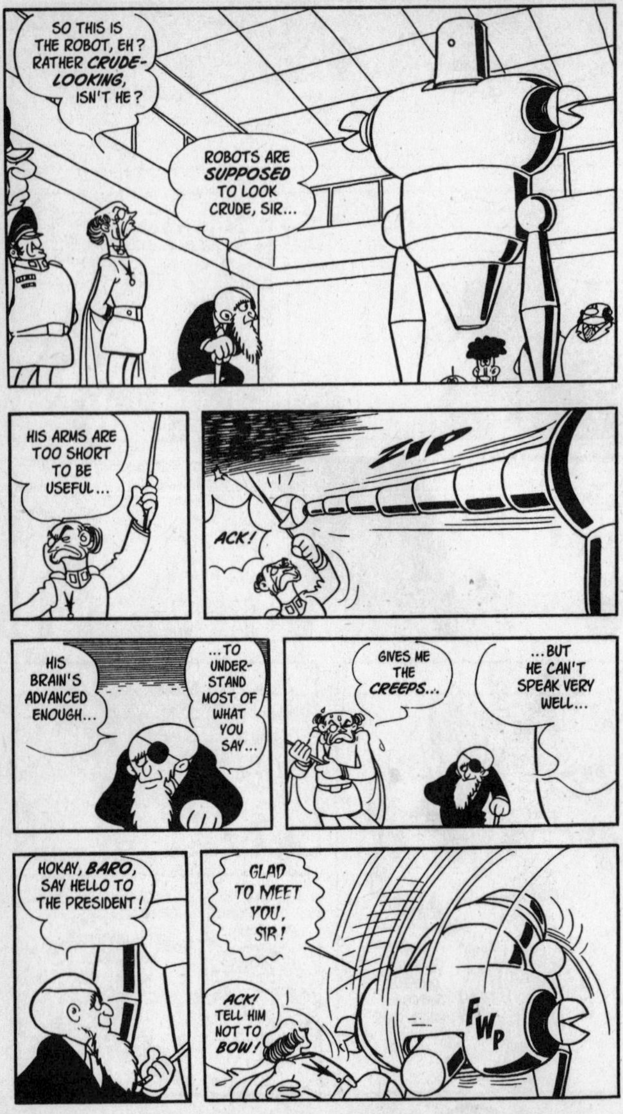
SO THIS IS THE ROBOT, EH? RATHER CRUDE-LOOKING, ISN'T HE?
ROBOTS ARE SUPPOSED TO LOOK CRUDE, SIR...
HIS ARMS ARE TOO SHORT TO BE USEFUL...
ZIP
ACK!
HIS BRAIN'S ADVANCED ENOUGH...
...TO UNDER-STAND MOST OF WHAT YOU SAY...
GIVES ME THE CREEPS...
...BUT HE CAN'T SPEAK VERY WELL...
HOKAY, BARO, SAY HELLO TO THE PRESIDENT!
GLAD TO MEET YOU, SIR!
ACK! TELL HIM NOT TO BOW!
FWP

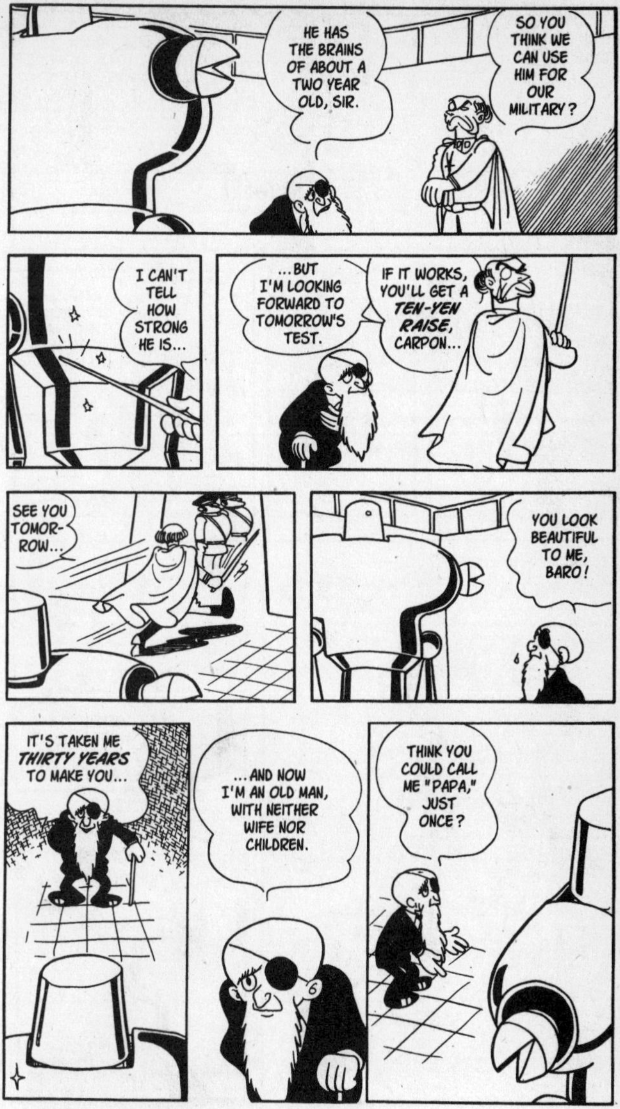
HE HAS THE BRAINS OF ABOUT A TWO YEAR OLD, SIR.
SO YOU THINK WE CAN USE HIM FOR OUR MILITARY?
I CAN'T TELL HOW STRONG HE IS...
...BUT I'M LOOKING FORWARD TO TOMORROW'S TEST.
IF IT WORKS, YOU'LL GET A *TEN-YEN RAISE*, CARPON...
SEE YOU TOMOR-ROW...
YOU LOOK BEAUTIFUL TO ME, BARO!
IT'S TAKEN ME *THIRTY YEARS* TO MAKE YOU...
...AND NOW I'M AN OLD MAN, WITH NEITHER WIFE NOR CHILDREN.
THINK YOU COULD CALL ME "PAPA," JUST ONCE?

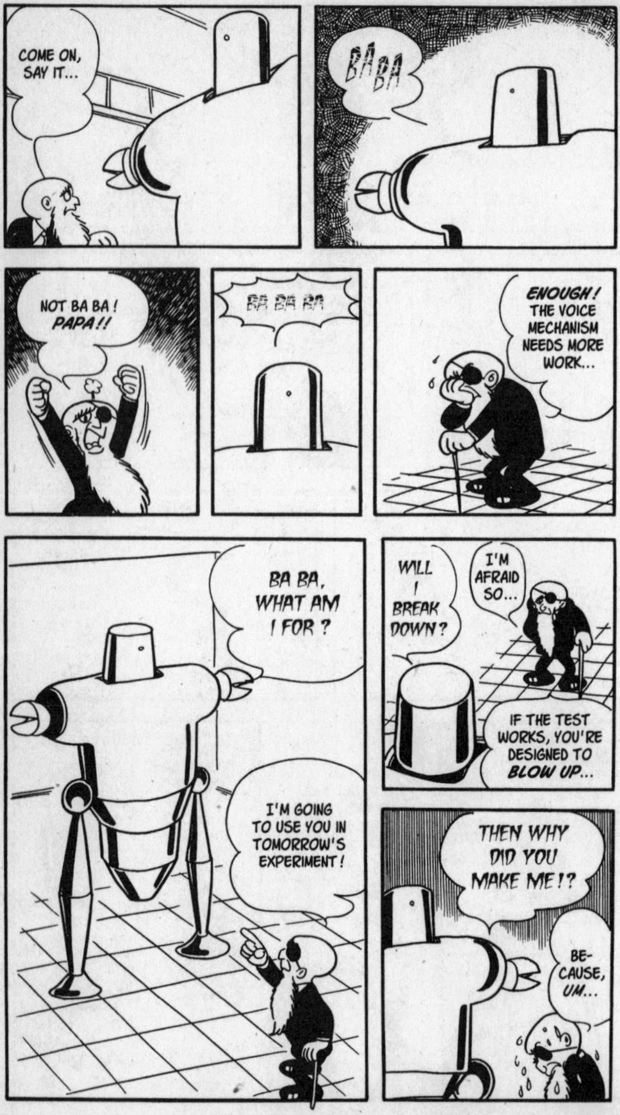
COME ON, SAY IT...
BABA
NOT BA BA ! PAPA!!
BA BA BA
ENOUGH! THE VOICE MECHANISM NEEDS MORE WORK...
BA BA, WHAT AM I FOR ?
I'M GOING TO USE YOU IN TOMORROW'S EXPERIMENT !
WILL I BREAK DOWN?
I'M AFRAID SO...
IF THE TEST WORKS, YOU'RE DESIGNED TO BLOW UP...
THEN WHY DID YOU MAKE ME!?
BE-CAUSE, UM...

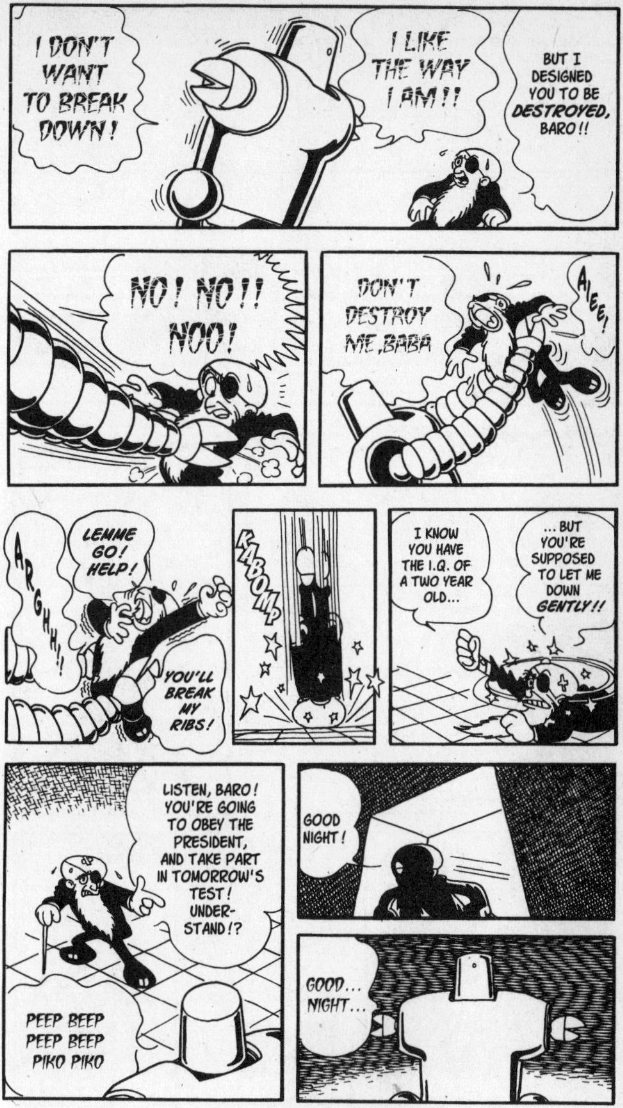
I DON'T WANT TO BREAK DOWN!
I LIKE THE WAY I AM!!
BUT I DESIGNED YOU TO BE DESTROYED, BARO!!
NO! NO!! NOO!
DON'T DESTROY ME, BABA
AIEEE!
ARGHH!!
LEMME GO! HELP!
YOU'LL BREAK MY RIBS!
KABOMP
I KNOW YOU HAVE THE I.Q. OF A TWO YEAR OLD...
... BUT YOU'RE SUPPOSED TO LET ME DOWN GENTLY!!
LISTEN, BARO! YOU'RE GOING TO OBEY THE PRESIDENT, AND TAKE PART IN TOMORROW'S TEST! UNDER-STAND!?
PEEP BEEP PEEP BEEP PIKO PIKO
GOOD NIGHT!
GOOD... NIGHT...

EARLY TO BED AND EARLY TO RISE. TOMORROW IT'S *GOOD-BYE TO BARO...*

I DON'T WANT TO DIE...

DON'T KILL ME, PAPA! WHY DID YOU CREATE ME?

ARGH! I CAN'T GET HIS VOICE OUT OF MY HEAD!

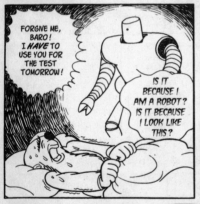

FORGIVE ME, BARO! I *HAVE* TO USE YOU FOR THE TEST TOMORROW!

IS IT BECAUSE I AM A ROBOT? IS IT BECAUSE I LOOK LIKE THIS?

WHAT IF I LOOKED LIKE THIS?

I'M ONLY TWO YEARS OLD!

NO! NO!

WOULD YOU STILL *KILL* ME, PAPA?

MY BEAUTIFUL SON! NO ONE COULD THINK OF KILLING YOU!

ARGH!! I WAS WRONG! ROBOTS AND HUMANS REALLY *ARE* THE SAME!!

WHA?!

I MUST'VE BEEN DREAM- ING!

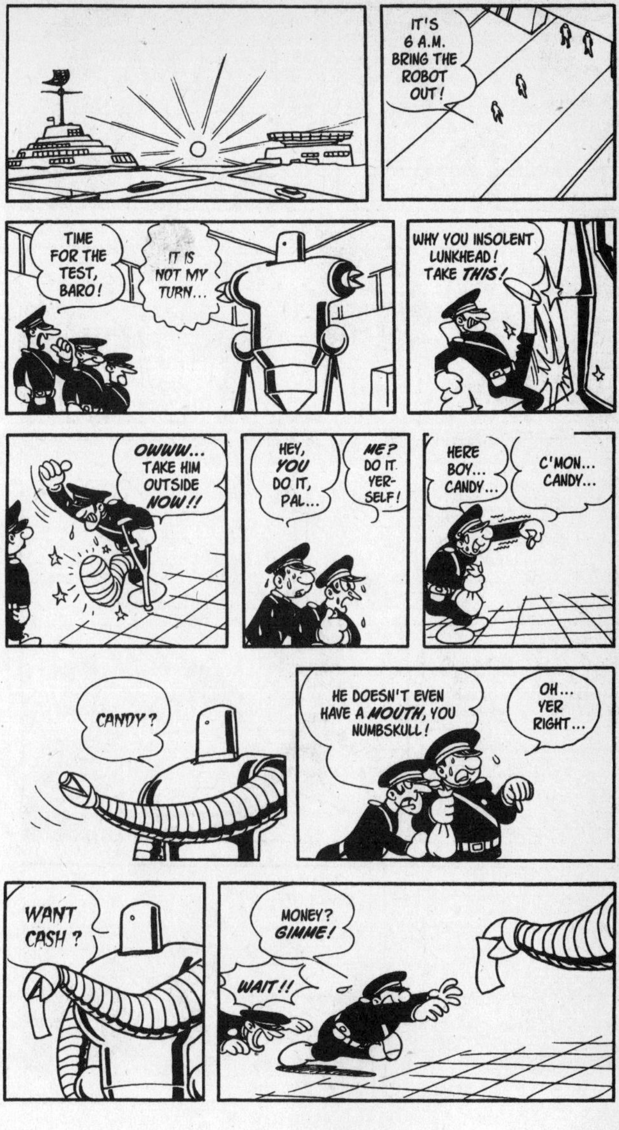
IT'S 6 A.M. BRING THE ROBOT OUT!
TIME FOR THE TEST, BARO!
IT IS NOT MY TURN...
WHY YOU INSOLENT LUNKHEAD! TAKE THIS!
OWWW... TAKE HIM OUTSIDE NOW!!
HEY, YOU DO IT, PAL...
ME? DO IT YER-SELF!
HERE BOY... CANDY...
C'MON... CANDY...
CANDY?
HE DOESN'T EVEN HAVE A MOUTH, YOU NUMBSKULL!
OH... YER RIGHT...
WANT CASH?
MONEY? GIMME!
WAIT!!

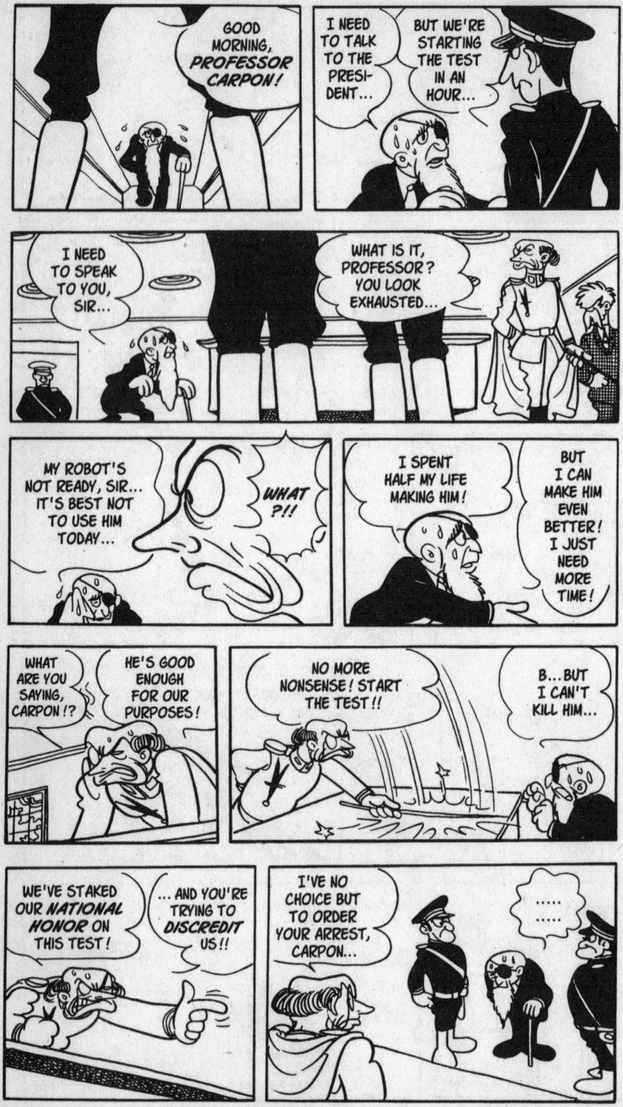
GOOD MORNING, PROFESSOR CARPON!
I NEED TO TALK TO THE PRESI- DENT...
BUT WE'RE STARTING THE TEST IN AN HOUR...
I NEED TO SPEAK TO YOU, SIR...
WHAT IS IT, PROFESSOR? YOU LOOK EXHAUSTED...
MY ROBOT'S NOT READY, SIR... IT'S BEST NOT TO USE HIM TODAY...
WHAT ?!!
I SPENT HALF MY LIFE MAKING HIM!
BUT I CAN MAKE HIM EVEN BETTER! I JUST NEED MORE TIME!
WHAT ARE YOU SAYING, CARPON!?
HE'S GOOD ENOUGH FOR OUR PURPOSES!
NO MORE NONSENSE! START THE TEST!!
B...BUT I CAN'T KILL HIM...
WE'VE STAKED OUR NATIONAL HONOR ON THIS TEST!
... AND YOU'RE TRYING TO DISCREDIT US!!
I'VE NO CHOICE BUT TO ORDER YOUR ARREST, CARPON...
.....
.....

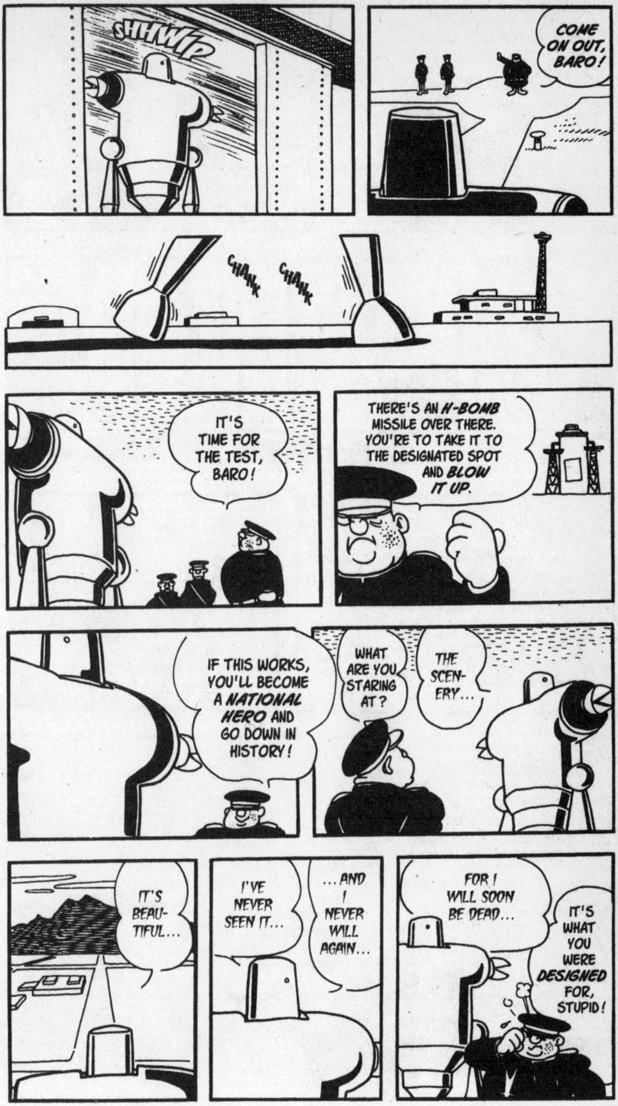
SHHWIP
COME ON OUT, BARO!
CHANK
CHANK
IT'S TIME FOR THE TEST, BARO!
THERE'S AN H-BOMB MISSILE OVER THERE. YOU'RE TO TAKE IT TO THE DESIGNATED SPOT AND BLOW IT UP.
IF THIS WORKS, YOU'LL BECOME A NATIONAL HERO AND GO DOWN IN HISTORY!
WHAT ARE YOU STARING AT?
THE SCEN-ERY...
IT'S BEAU-TIFUL...
I'VE NEVER SEEN IT...
...AND I NEVER WILL AGAIN...
FOR I WILL SOON BE DEAD...
IT'S WHAT YOU WERE DESIGNED FOR, STUPID!

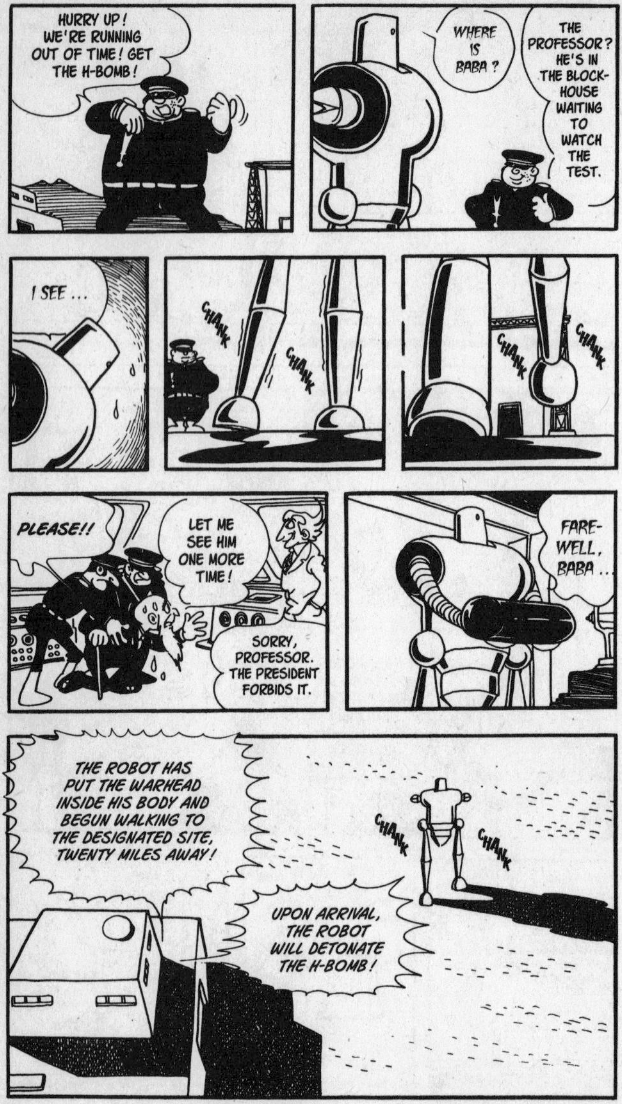
HURRY UP! WE'RE RUNNING OUT OF TIME! GET THE H-BOMB!
WHERE IS BABA?
THE PROFESSOR? HE'S IN THE BLOCK-HOUSE WAITING TO WATCH THE TEST.
I SEE...
CHANK
CHANK
CHANK
CHANK
PLEASE!!
LET ME SEE HIM ONE MORE TIME!
SORRY, PROFESSOR. THE PRESIDENT FORBIDS IT.
FARE-WELL, BABA...
THE ROBOT HAS PUT THE WARHEAD INSIDE HIS BODY AND BEGUN WALKING TO THE DESIGNATED SITE, TWENTY MILES AWAY!
CHANK
CHANK
UPON ARRIVAL, THE ROBOT WILL DETONATE THE H-BOMB!

CHANK
CHANK

HE SHOULD REACH THE SITE IN TWO HOURS...

AND THEN HE BLOWS UP!

GENTLEMEN! THE EXPERIMENT OF THE CENTURY'S ABOUT TO START!

WITH THIS, PEAKOK WILL BECOME THE WORLD'S MOST POWERFUL NATION!

WE'LL MASS PRODUCE THESE ROBOTS AND BE ABLE TO SEND THEM ANYWHERE!

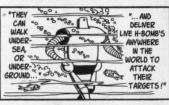

"THEY CAN WALK UNDER-SEA, OR UNDER-GROUND..."

"...AND DELIVER LIVE H-BOMB'S ANYWHERE IN THE WORLD TO ATTACK THEIR TARGETS!"

CHANK
CHANK

KOOSH

HI, ARE YOU THE H-BOMB ROBOT?

119

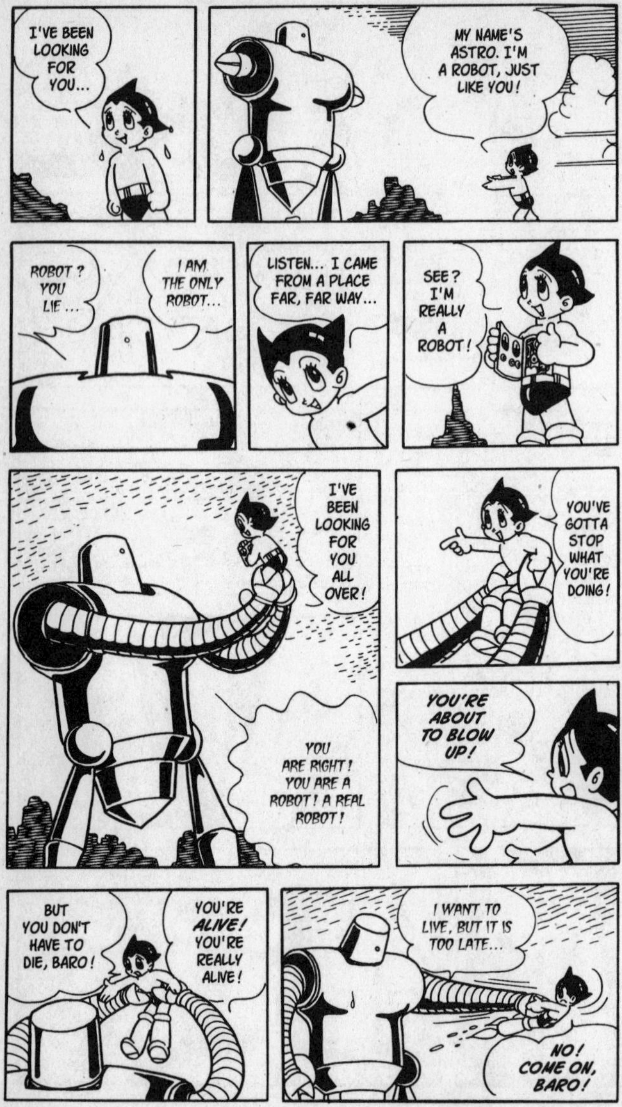
I'VE BEEN LOOKING FOR YOU...
MY NAME'S ASTRO. I'M A ROBOT, JUST LIKE YOU!
ROBOT? YOU LIE...
I AM THE ONLY ROBOT...
LISTEN... I CAME FROM A PLACE FAR, FAR WAY...
SEE? I'M REALLY A ROBOT!
I'VE BEEN LOOKING FOR YOU ALL OVER!
YOU ARE RIGHT! YOU ARE A ROBOT! A REAL ROBOT!
YOU'VE GOTTA STOP WHAT YOU'RE DOING!
YOU'RE ABOUT TO BLOW UP!
BUT YOU DON'T HAVE TO DIE, BARO!
YOU'RE ALIVE! YOU'RE REALLY ALIVE!
I WANT TO LIVE, BUT IT IS TOO LATE...
NO! COME ON, BARO!

NO! IT IS NO USE! I HAVE A JOB TO DO!

BUT YOUR JOB'S NOT TO BLOW UP AN H-BOMB! ROBOTS AREN'T SUPPOSED TO BECOME MURDERERS!

BESIDES... I'D BE LONELY...

I NEED A *ROBOT FRIEND*, BARO...

FRIEND?

YEAH! WE CAN BE FRIENDS AND ESCAPE TOGETHER...

WE CAN TAKE THIS H-BOMB CAPSULE OUTA HERE, VERY CAREFULLY...

...THEN SMASH IT AND BURY IT IN THE SAND.

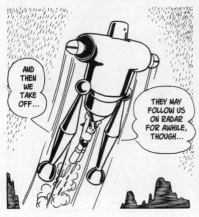

AND THEN WE TAKE OFF...

THEY MAY FOLLOW US ON RADAR FOR AWHILE, THOUGH...

THE SKY! I AM FLYING!

WE'VE GOTTA HURRY AND HIDE IN THE MOUNTAINS!

121

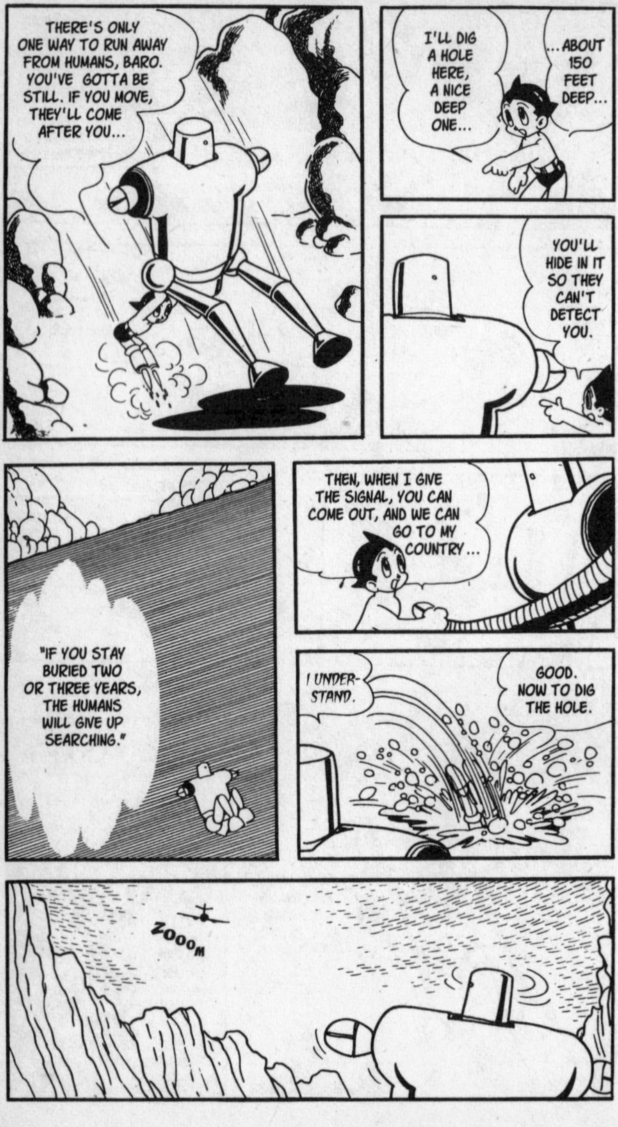
THERE'S ONLY ONE WAY TO RUN AWAY FROM HUMANS, BARO. YOU'VE GOTTA BE STILL. IF YOU MOVE, THEY'LL COME AFTER YOU...
I'LL DIG A HOLE HERE, A NICE DEEP ONE...
...ABOUT 150 FEET DEEP...
YOU'LL HIDE IN IT SO THEY CAN'T DETECT YOU.
"IF YOU STAY BURIED TWO OR THREE YEARS, THE HUMANS WILL GIVE UP SEARCHING."
THEN, WHEN I GIVE THE SIGNAL, YOU CAN COME OUT, AND WE CAN GO TO MY COUNTRY...
I UNDER-STAND.
GOOD. NOW TO DIG THE HOLE.
ZOOOM

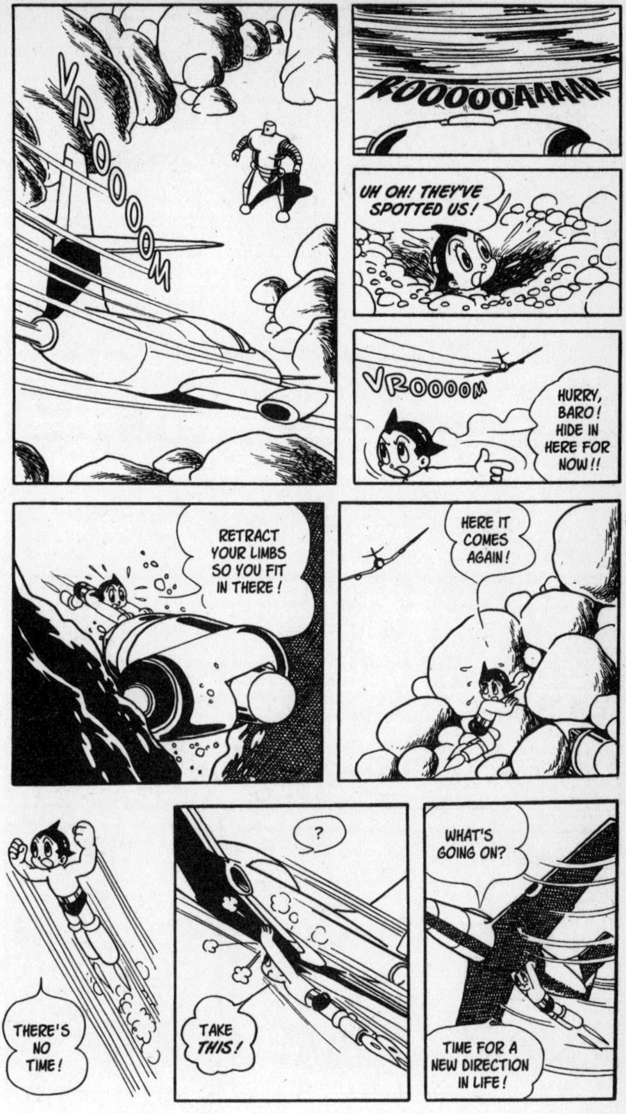
VROOOOM
ROOOOOAAAAR
UH OH! THEY'VE SPOTTED US!
VROOOOM
HURRY, BARO! HIDE IN HERE FOR NOW!!
RETRACT YOUR LIMBS SO YOU FIT IN THERE!
HERE IT COMES AGAIN!
THERE'S NO TIME!
?
TAKE THIS!
WHAT'S GOING ON?
TIME FOR A NEW DIRECTION IN LIFE!

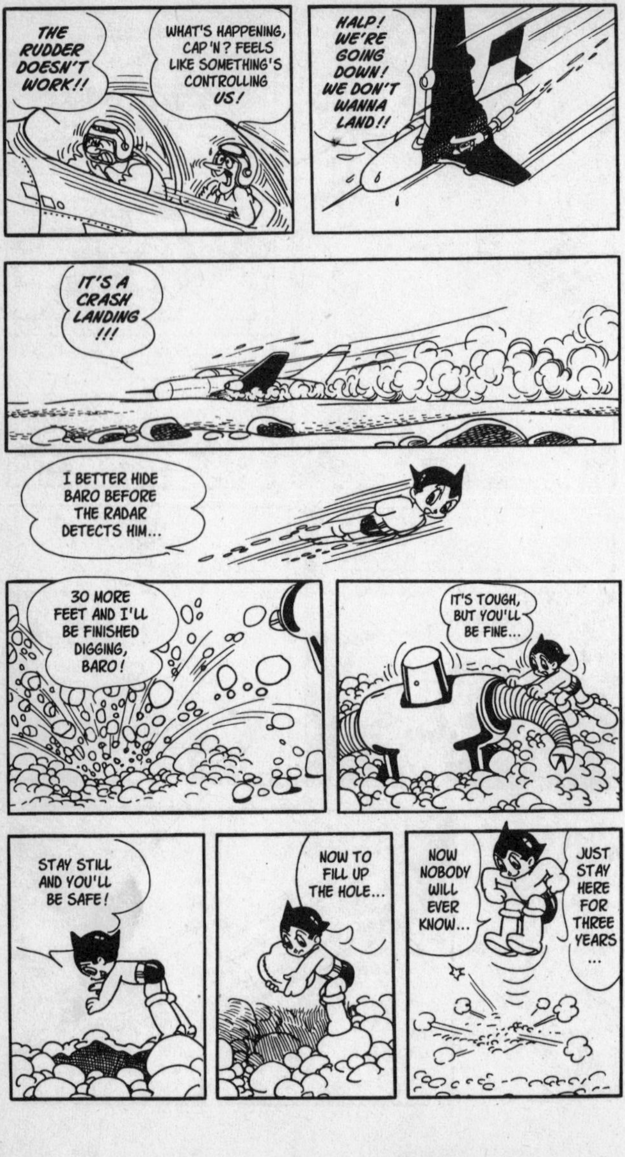
THE RUDDER DOESN'T WORK!!
WHAT'S HAPPENING, CAP'N? FEELS LIKE SOMETHING'S CONTROLLING US!
HALP! WE'RE GOING DOWN! WE DON'T WANNA LAND!!
IT'S A CRASH LANDING !!!
I BETTER HIDE BARO BEFORE THE RADAR DETECTS HIM...
30 MORE FEET AND I'LL BE FINISHED DIGGING, BARO!
IT'S TOUGH, BUT YOU'LL BE FINE...
STAY STILL AND YOU'LL BE SAFE!
NOW TO FILL UP THE HOLE...
NOW NOBODY WILL EVER KNOW...
JUST STAY HERE FOR THREE YEARS ...

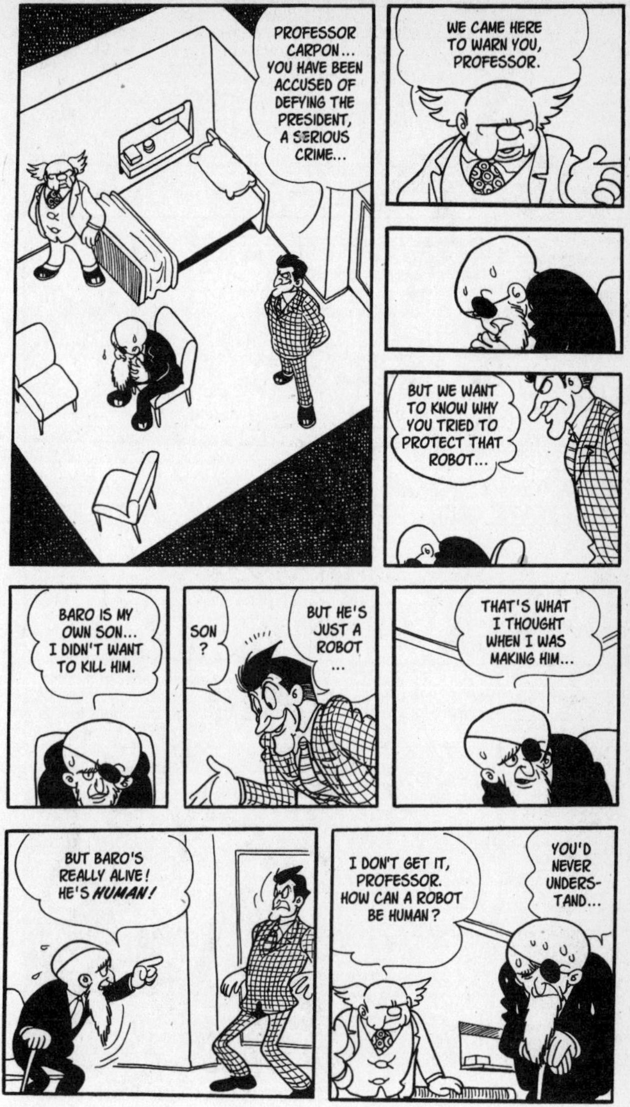
PROFESSOR CARPON... YOU HAVE BEEN ACCUSED OF DEFYING THE PRESIDENT, A SERIOUS CRIME...
WE CAME HERE TO WARN YOU, PROFESSOR.
BUT WE WANT TO KNOW WHY YOU TRIED TO PROTECT THAT ROBOT...
BARO IS MY OWN SON... I DIDN'T WANT TO KILL HIM.
SON ?
BUT HE'S JUST A ROBOT ...
THAT'S WHAT I THOUGHT WHEN I WAS MAKING HIM...
BUT BARO'S REALLY ALIVE! HE'S HUMAN!
I DON'T GET IT, PROFESSOR. HOW CAN A ROBOT BE HUMAN?
YOU'D NEVER UNDERS-TAND...

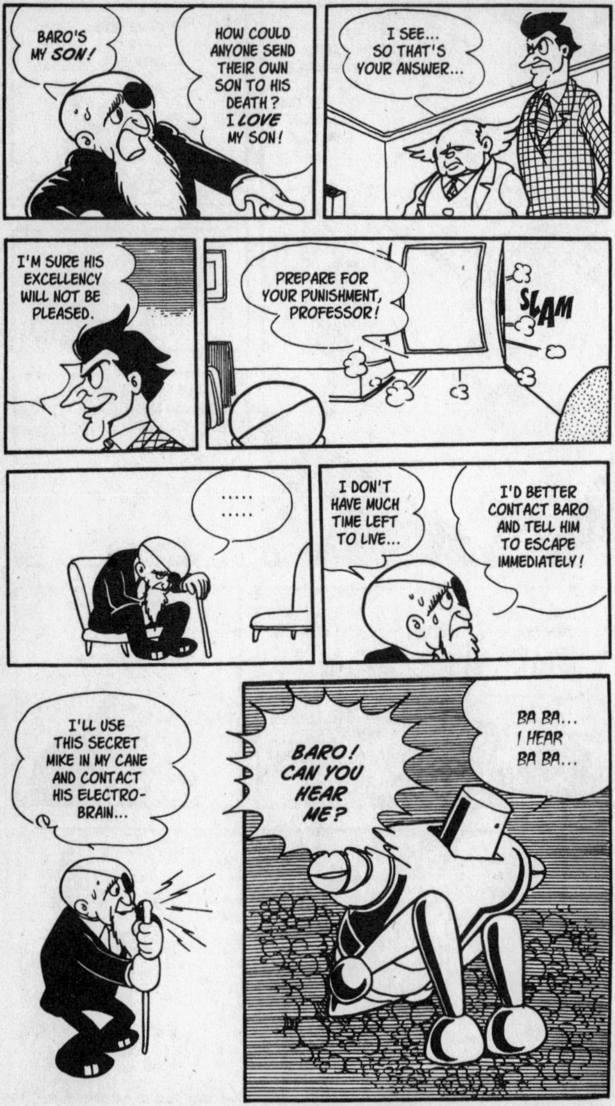
BARO'S MY SON!
HOW COULD ANYONE SEND THEIR OWN SON TO HIS DEATH? I LOVE MY SON!
I SEE... SO THAT'S YOUR ANSWER...
I'M SURE HIS EXCELLENCY WILL NOT BE PLEASED.
PREPARE FOR YOUR PUNISHMENT, PROFESSOR!
SLAM
.....
.....
I DON'T HAVE MUCH TIME LEFT TO LIVE...
I'D BETTER CONTACT BARO AND TELL HIM TO ESCAPE IMMEDIATELY!
I'LL USE THIS SECRET MIKE IN MY CANE AND CONTACT HIS ELECTRO-BRAIN...
BARO! CAN YOU HEAR ME?
BA BA... I HEAR BA BA...

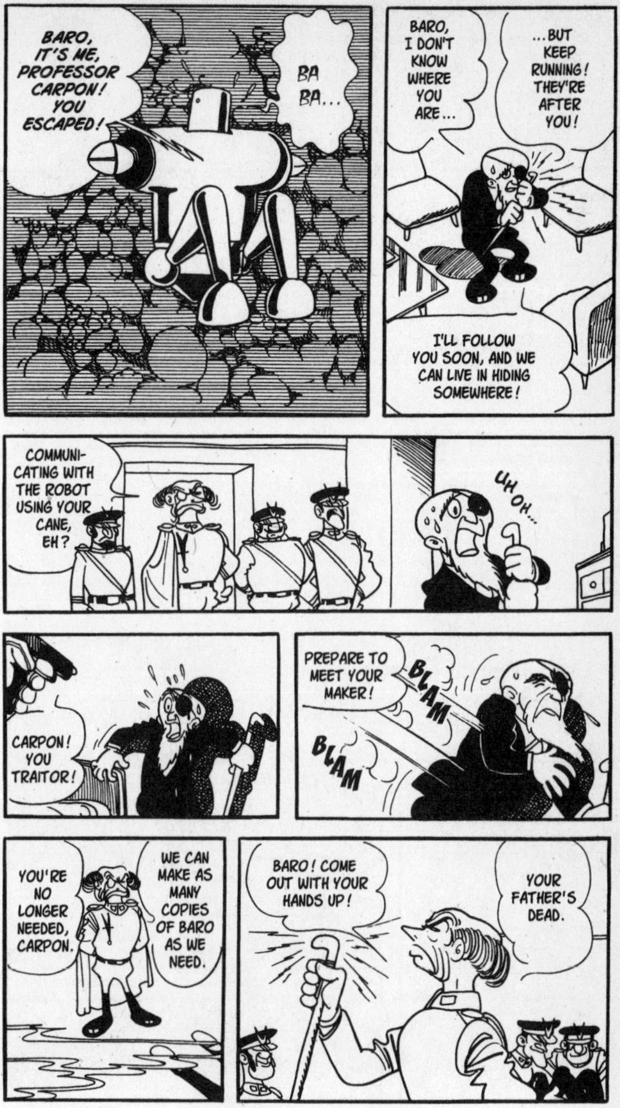
BARO, IT'S ME, PROFESSOR CARPON! YOU ESCAPED!
BA BA...
BARO, I DON'T KNOW WHERE YOU ARE...
...BUT KEEP RUNNING! THEY'RE AFTER YOU!
I'LL FOLLOW YOU SOON, AND WE CAN LIVE IN HIDING SOMEWHERE!
COMMUNICATING WITH THE ROBOT USING YOUR CANE, EH?
UH OH...
CARPON! YOU TRAITOR!
PREPARE TO MEET YOUR MAKER!
BLAM
BLAM
YOU'RE NO LONGER NEEDED, CARPON.
WE CAN MAKE AS MANY COPIES OF BARO AS WE NEED.
BARO! COME OUT WITH YOUR HANDS UP!
YOUR FATHER'S DEAD.

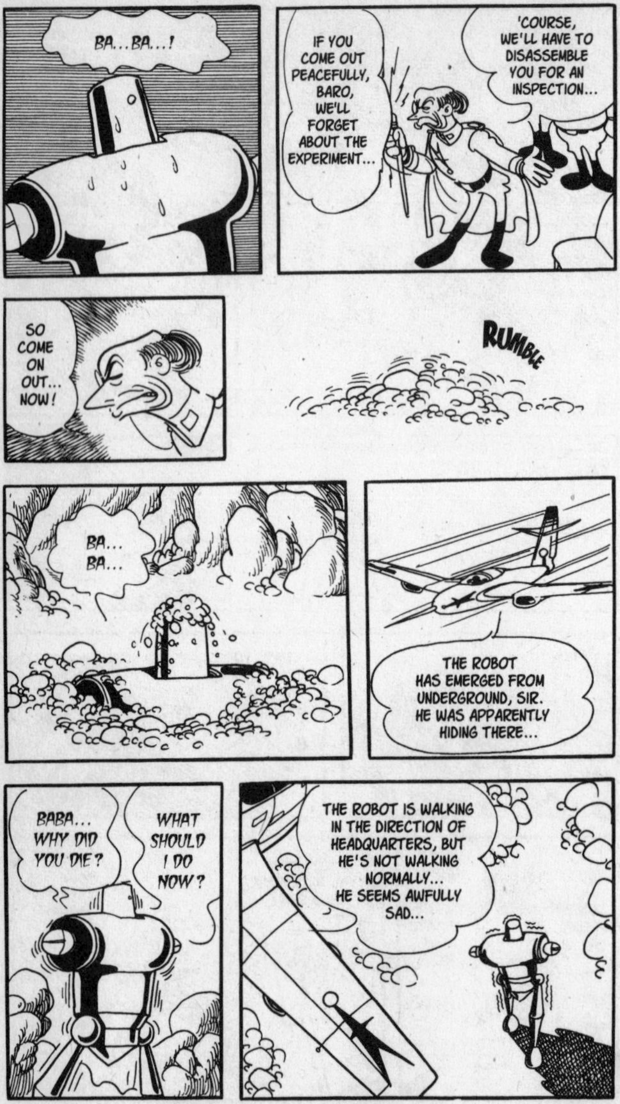
BA...BA...!
IF YOU COME OUT PEACEFULLY, BARO, WE'LL FORGET ABOUT THE EXPERIMENT...
'COURSE, WE'LL HAVE TO DISASSEMBLE YOU FOR AN INSPECTION...
SO COME ON OUT... NOW!
RUMBLE
BA... BA...
THE ROBOT HAS EMERGED FROM UNDERGROUND, SIR. HE WAS APPARENTLY HIDING THERE...
BABA... WHY DID YOU DIE?
WHAT SHOULD I DO NOW?
THE ROBOT IS WALKING IN THE DIRECTION OF HEADQUARTERS, BUT HE'S NOT WALKING NORMALLY... HE SEEMS AWFULLY SAD...

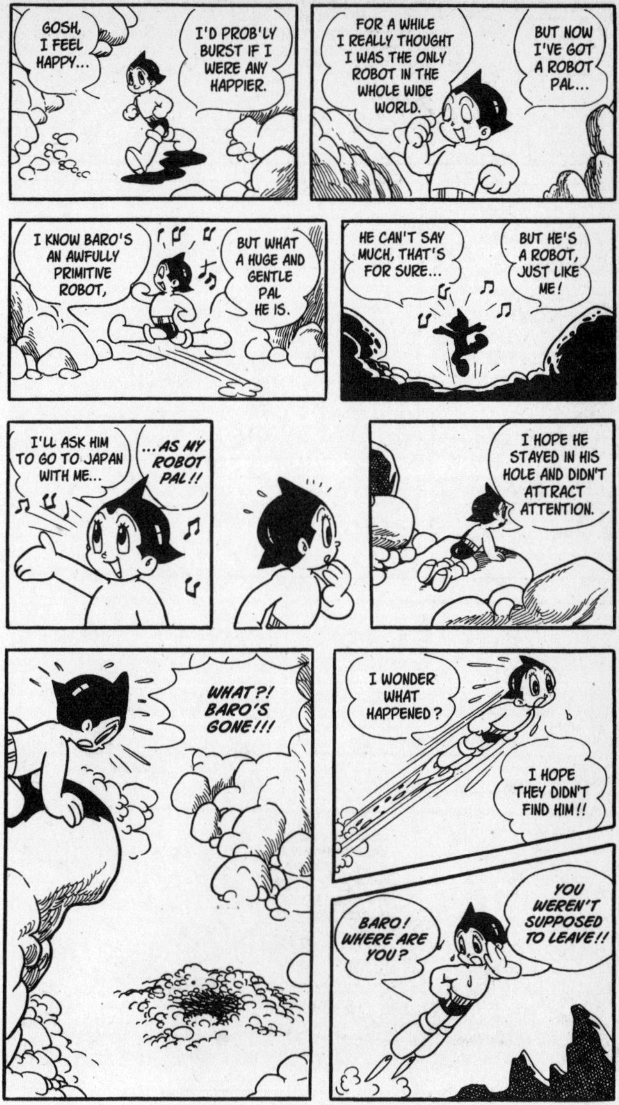
GOSH, I FEEL HAPPY...
I'D PROB'LY BURST IF I WERE ANY HAPPIER.
FOR A WHILE I REALLY THOUGHT I WAS THE ONLY ROBOT IN THE WHOLE WIDE WORLD.
BUT NOW I'VE GOT A ROBOT PAL...
I KNOW BARO'S AN AWFULLY PRIMITIVE ROBOT,
BUT WHAT A HUGE AND GENTLE PAL HE IS.
HE CAN'T SAY MUCH, THAT'S FOR SURE...
BUT HE'S A ROBOT, JUST LIKE ME!
I'LL ASK HIM TO GO TO JAPAN WITH ME...
...AS MY ROBOT PAL!!
I HOPE HE STAYED IN HIS HOLE AND DIDN'T ATTRACT ATTENTION.
WHAT?! BARO'S GONE!!!
I WONDER WHAT HAPPENED?
I HOPE THEY DIDN'T FIND HIM!!
BARO! WHERE ARE YOU?
YOU WEREN'T SUPPOSED TO LEAVE!!

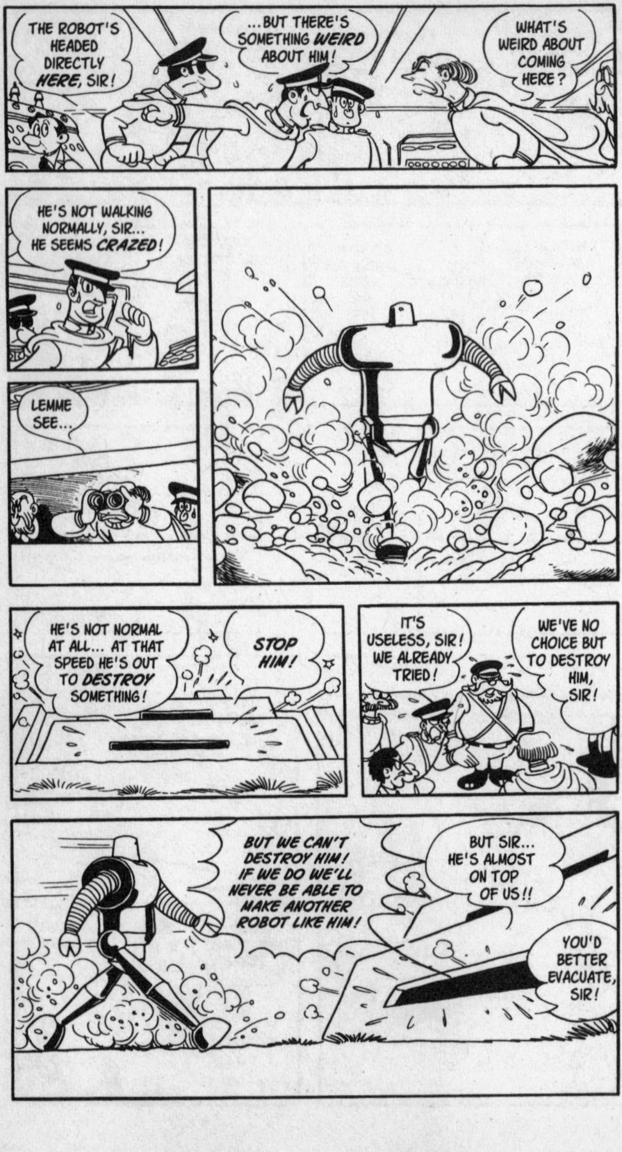
THE ROBOT'S HEADED DIRECTLY *HERE*, SIR!
...BUT THERE'S SOMETHING *WEIRD* ABOUT HIM!
WHAT'S WEIRD ABOUT COMING HERE?
HE'S NOT WALKING NORMALLY, SIR... HE SEEMS *CRAZED*!
LEMME SEE...
HE'S NOT NORMAL AT ALL... AT THAT SPEED HE'S OUT TO *DESTROY* SOMETHING!
STOP HIM!
IT'S USELESS, SIR! WE ALREADY TRIED!
WE'VE NO CHOICE BUT TO DESTROY HIM, SIR!
BUT WE CAN'T DESTROY HIM! IF WE DO WE'LL NEVER BE ABLE TO MAKE ANOTHER ROBOT LIKE HIM!
BUT SIR... HE'S ALMOST ON TOP OF US!!
YOU'D BETTER EVACUATE, SIR!

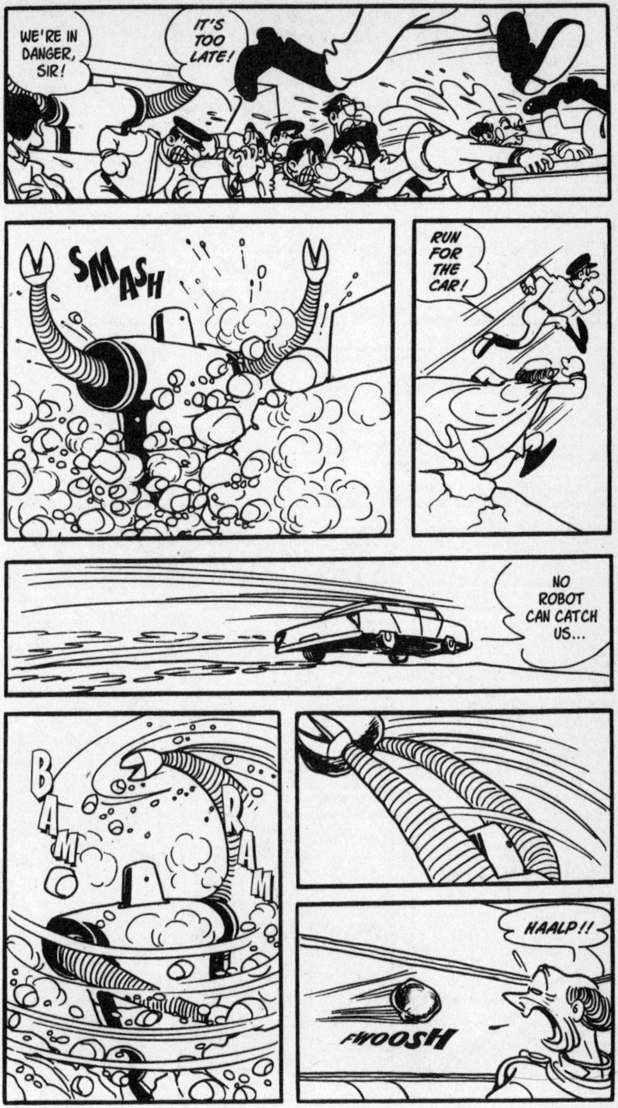
WE'RE IN DANGER, SIR!
IT'S TOO LATE!
SMASH
RUN FOR THE CAR!
NO ROBOT CAN CATCH US...
BAM
RAM
HAALP!!
FWOOSH

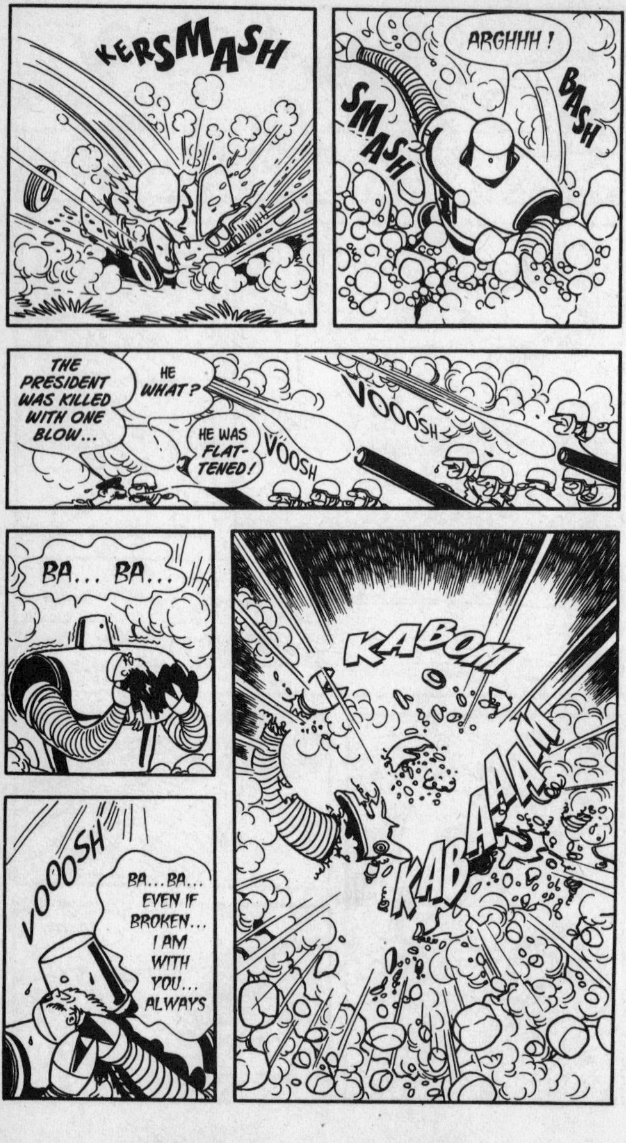
KERSMASH
ARGHHH !
SMASH
BASH
THE PRESIDENT WAS KILLED WITH ONE BLOW...
HE WHAT?
HE WAS FLAT-TENED!
VOOSH
VOOOSH
BA... BA...
VOOOSH
BA...BA... EVEN IF BROKEN... I AM WITH YOU... ALWAYS
KABOM
KABAAAAM

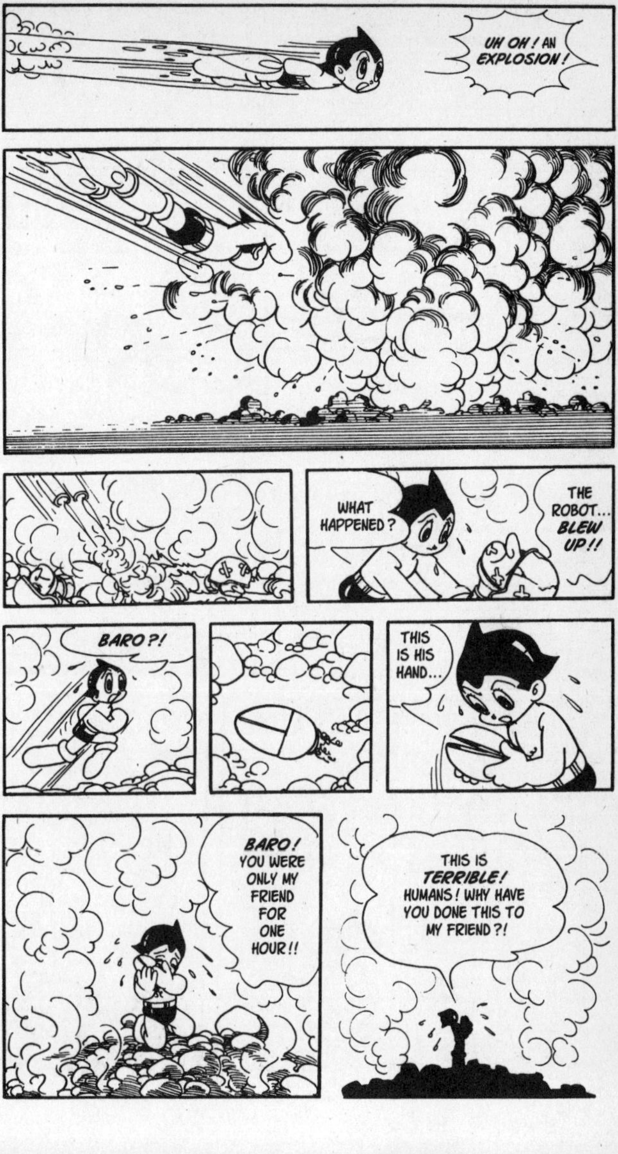
UH OH! AN EXPLOSION!
WHAT HAPPENED?
THE ROBOT... BLEW UP!!
BARO?!
THIS IS HIS HAND...
BARO! YOU WERE ONLY MY FRIEND FOR ONE HOUR!!
THIS IS TERRIBLE! HUMANS! WHY HAVE YOU DONE THIS TO MY FRIEND?!

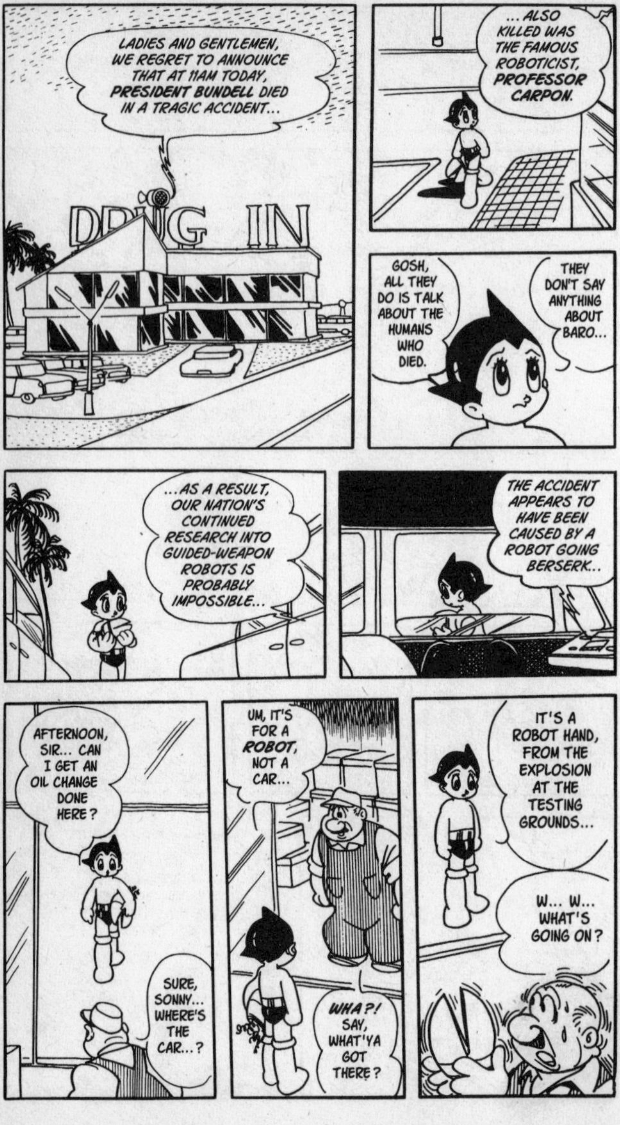
LADIES AND GENTLEMEN, WE REGRET TO ANNOUNCE THAT AT 11AM TODAY, PRESIDENT BUNDELL DIED IN A TRAGIC ACCIDENT...
DRUG IN
... ALSO KILLED WAS THE FAMOUS ROBOTICIST, PROFESSOR CARPON.
GOSH, ALL THEY DO IS TALK ABOUT THE HUMANS WHO DIED.
THEY DON'T SAY ANYTHING ABOUT BARO...
...AS A RESULT, OUR NATION'S CONTINUED RESEARCH INTO GUIDED-WEAPON ROBOTS IS PROBABLY IMPOSSIBLE...
THE ACCIDENT APPEARS TO HAVE BEEN CAUSED BY A ROBOT GOING BERSERK...
AFTERNOON, SIR... CAN I GET AN OIL CHANGE DONE HERE?
SURE, SONNY... WHERE'S THE CAR...?
UM, IT'S FOR A ROBOT, NOT A CAR...
WHA?! SAY, WHAT'YA GOT THERE?
IT'S A ROBOT HAND, FROM THE EXPLOSION AT THE TESTING GROUNDS...
W... W... WHAT'S GOING ON?

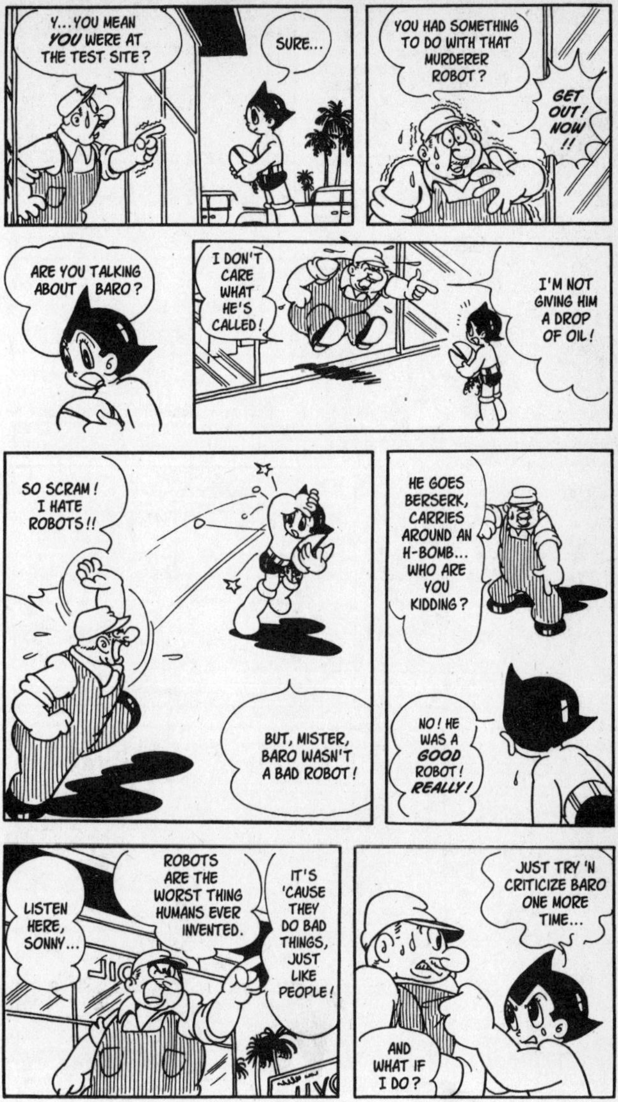
Y...YOU MEAN YOU WERE AT THE TEST SITE?
SURE...
YOU HAD SOMETHING TO DO WITH THAT MURDERER ROBOT?
GET OUT! NOW!!
ARE YOU TALKING ABOUT BARO?
I DON'T CARE WHAT HE'S CALLED!
I'M NOT GIVING HIM A DROP OF OIL!
SO SCRAM! I HATE ROBOTS!!
BUT, MISTER, BARO WASN'T A BAD ROBOT!
HE GOES BERSERK, CARRIES AROUND AN H-BOMB... WHO ARE YOU KIDDING?
NO! HE WAS A GOOD ROBOT! REALLY!
LISTEN HERE, SONNY...
ROBOTS ARE THE WORST THING HUMANS EVER INVENTED.
IT'S 'CAUSE THEY DO BAD THINGS, JUST LIKE PEOPLE!
JUST TRY 'N CRITICIZE BARO ONE MORE TIME...
AND WHAT IF I DO?

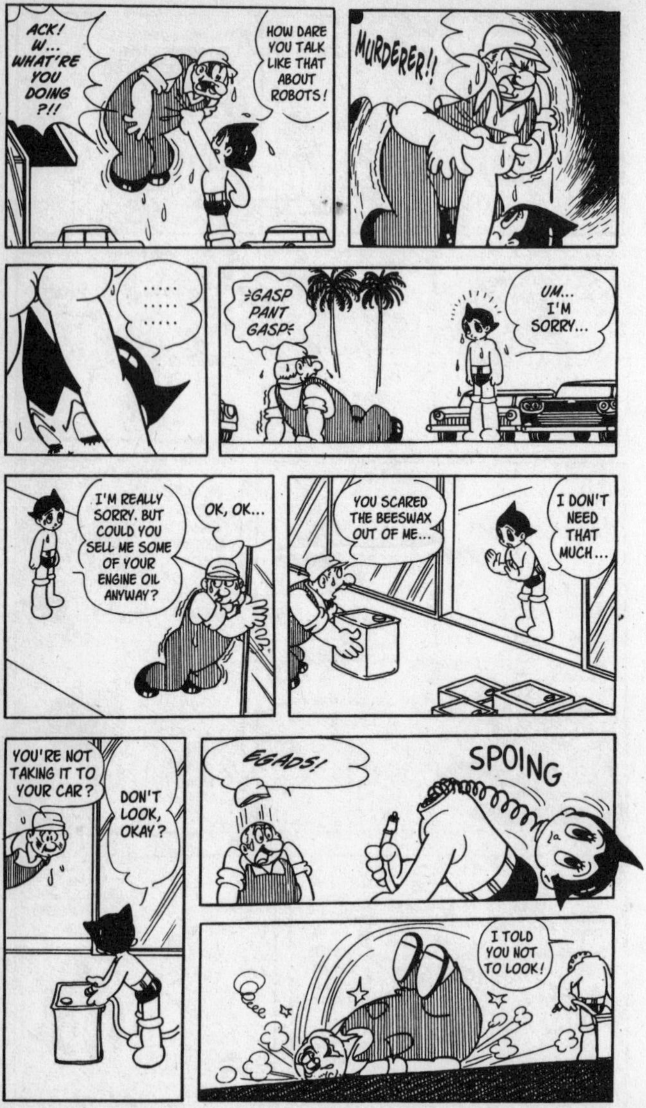
ACK! W... WHAT'RE YOU DOING ?!!
HOW DARE YOU TALK LIKE THAT ABOUT ROBOTS!
MURDERER!!
......
......
......
GASP PANT GASP
UM... I'M SORRY...
I'M REALLY SORRY. BUT COULD YOU SELL ME SOME OF YOUR ENGINE OIL ANYWAY?
OK, OK...
YOU SCARED THE BEESWAX OUT OF ME...
I DON'T NEED THAT MUCH...
YOU'RE NOT TAKING IT TO YOUR CAR?
DON'T LOOK, OKAY?
EGADS!
SPOING
I TOLD YOU NOT TO LOOK!

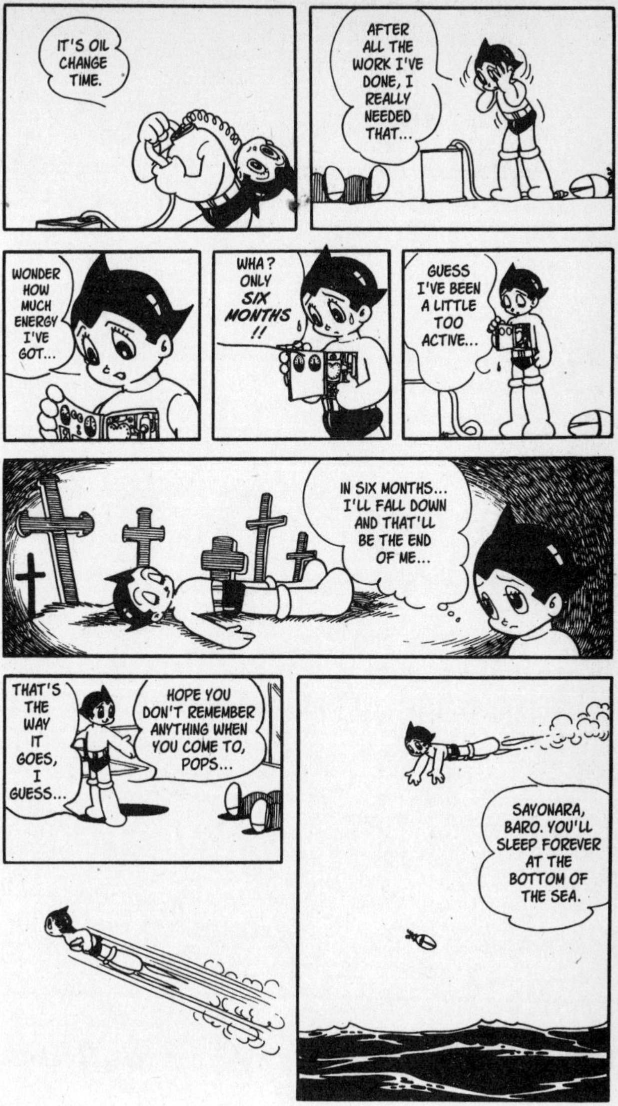
IT'S OIL CHANGE TIME.
AFTER ALL THE WORK I'VE DONE, I REALLY NEEDED THAT...
WONDER HOW MUCH ENERGY I'VE GOT...
WHA? ONLY SIX MONTHS !!
GUESS I'VE BEEN A LITTLE TOO ACTIVE...
IN SIX MONTHS... I'LL FALL DOWN AND THAT'LL BE THE END OF ME...
THAT'S THE WAY IT GOES, I GUESS...
HOPE YOU DON'T REMEMBER ANYTHING WHEN YOU COME TO, POPS...
SAYONARA, BARO. YOU'LL SLEEP FOREVER AT THE BOTTOM OF THE SEA.

SCARA DISAPPEARS

UP TO THIS POINT THE FOCUS OF THIS STORY HAS BEEN ON ASTRO, BUT NOW WE RETURN TO SCARA. WHEN MORNING CAME, SHE OPENED THE CURTAINS OF HER APARTMENT WINDOW AND STARED OUT OVER TOKYO'S SEA OF ROOFS, WATCHING THE CITY COME ALIVE.

"WHAT A DIRTY AND DUSTY PLACE," SHE SAID TO HERSELF. "THIS IS RIDICULOUS. I CAME HERE TO SEE EARTH'S BEAUTIFUL NATURAL SCENERY, AND HERE I AM STUCK INDOORS..."

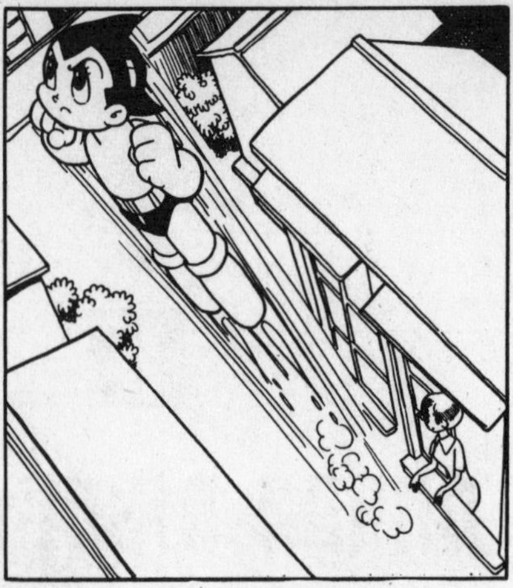

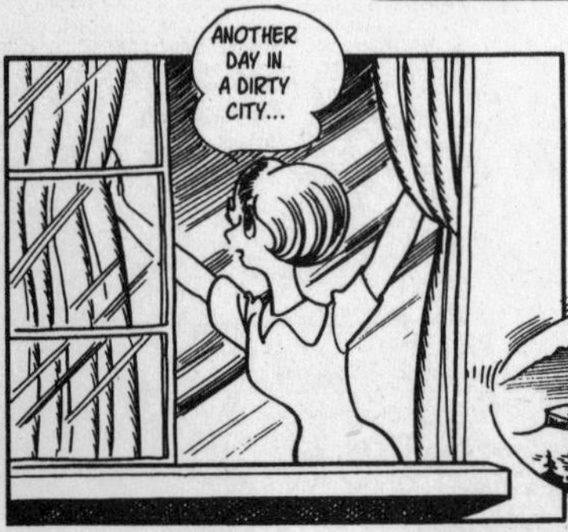
ANOTHER DAY IN A DIRTY CITY...

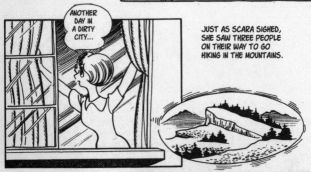

JUST AS SCARA SIGHED, SHE SAW THREE PEOPLE ON THEIR WAY TO GO HIKING IN THE MOUNTAINS.

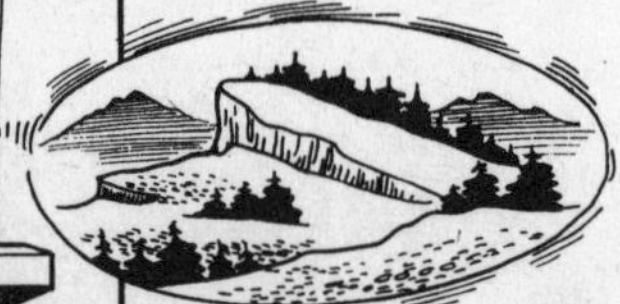

"HI, WHERE ARE YOU GOING?" SHE CALLED OUT, AS IF SHE KNEW THEM WELL. "TO THE MOUNTAINS? CAN I COME, TOO?"

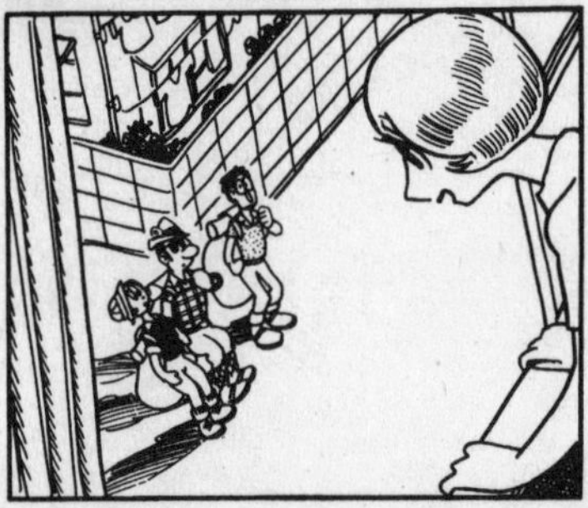

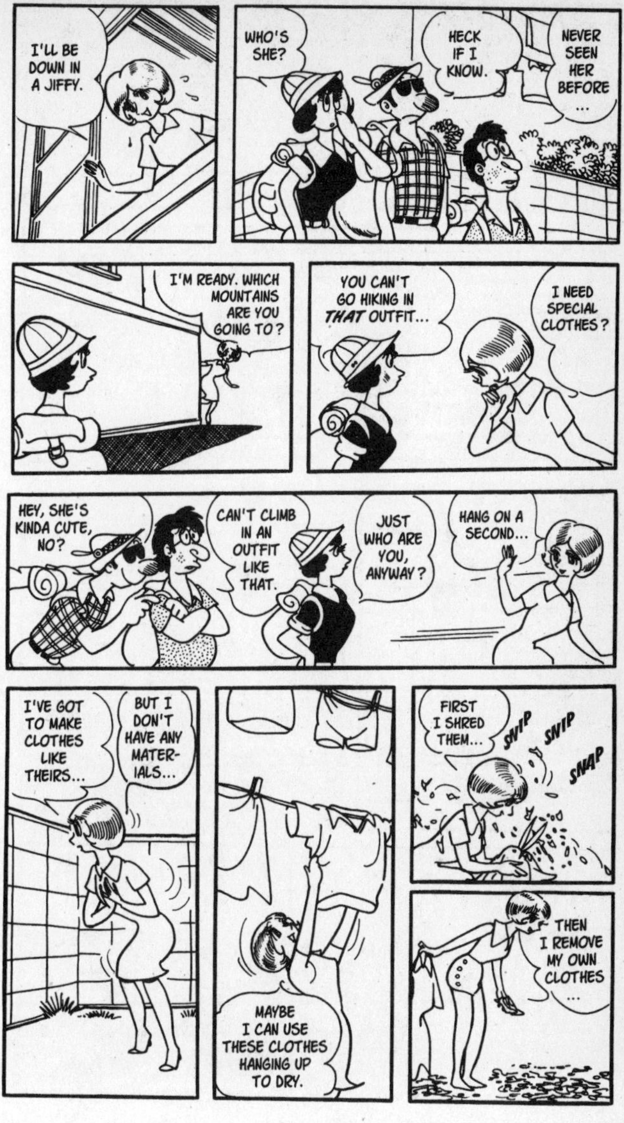
I'LL BE DOWN IN A JIFFY.
WHO'S SHE?
HECK IF I KNOW.
NEVER SEEN HER BEFORE ...
I'M READY. WHICH MOUNTAINS ARE YOU GOING TO?
YOU CAN'T GO HIKING IN *THAT* OUTFIT...
I NEED SPECIAL CLOTHES?
HEY, SHE'S KINDA CUTE, NO?
CAN'T CLIMB IN AN OUTFIT LIKE THAT.
JUST WHO ARE YOU, ANYWAY?
HANG ON A SECOND...
I'VE GOT TO MAKE CLOTHES LIKE THEIRS...
BUT I DON'T HAVE ANY MATER-IALS...
MAYBE I CAN USE THESE CLOTHES HANGING UP TO DRY.
FIRST I SHRED THEM...
SNIP
SNIP
SNAP
THEN I REMOVE MY OWN CLOTHES ...

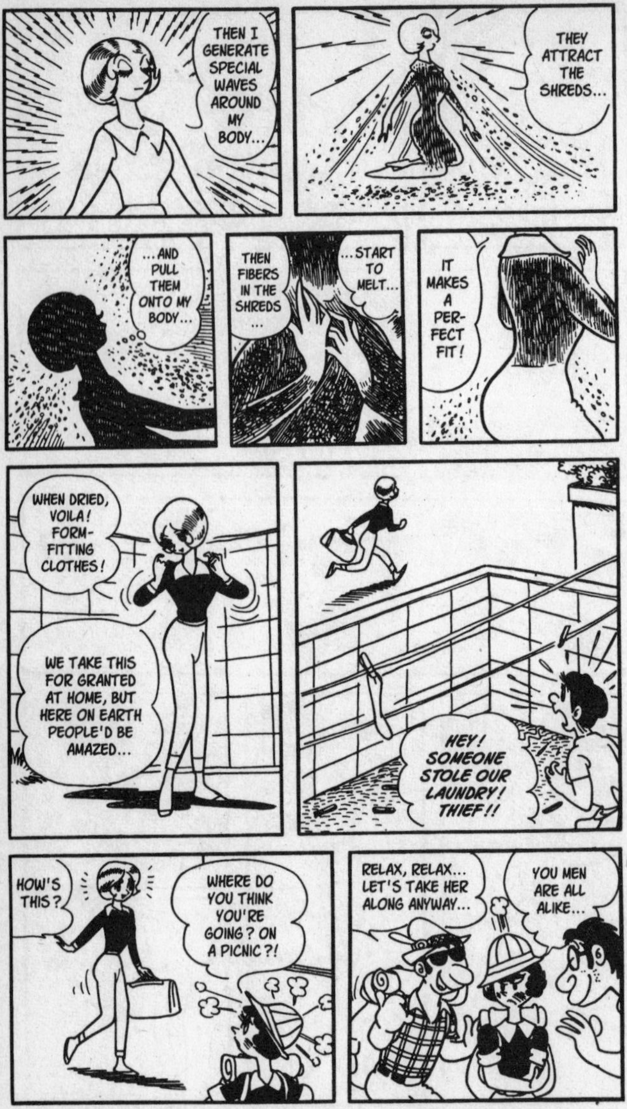
THEN I GENERATE SPECIAL WAVES AROUND MY BODY...
THEY ATTRACT THE SHREDS...
...AND PULL THEM ONTO MY BODY...
THEN FIBERS IN THE SHREDS ...
...START TO MELT...
IT MAKES A PERFECT FIT!
WHEN DRIED, VOILA! FORM-FITTING CLOTHES!
WE TAKE THIS FOR GRANTED AT HOME, BUT HERE ON EARTH PEOPLE'D BE AMAZED...
HEY! SOMEONE STOLE OUR LAUNDRY! THIEF!!
HOW'S THIS?
WHERE DO YOU THINK YOU'RE GOING? ON A PICNIC?!
RELAX, RELAX... LET'S TAKE HER ALONG ANYWAY...
YOU MEN ARE ALL ALIKE...

THROUGH THE FORCE OF HER PERSONALITY, SCARA GOT THE GROUP TO TAKE HER WITH THEM. THE TRAIN LEFT TOKYO AND ZOOMED THROUGH COUNTRY FIELDS ON ITS WAY TO THE MOUNTAINS.

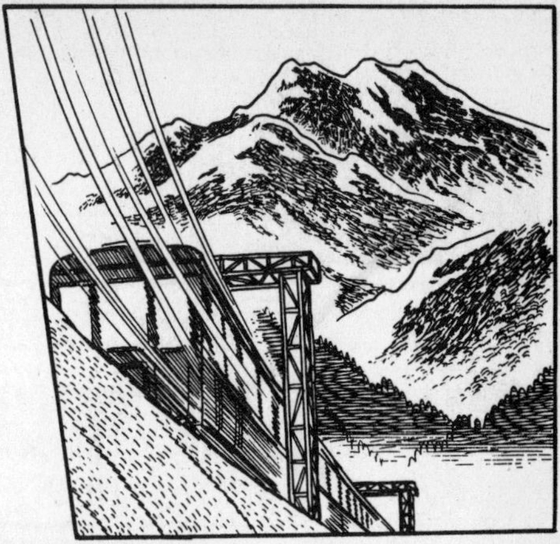

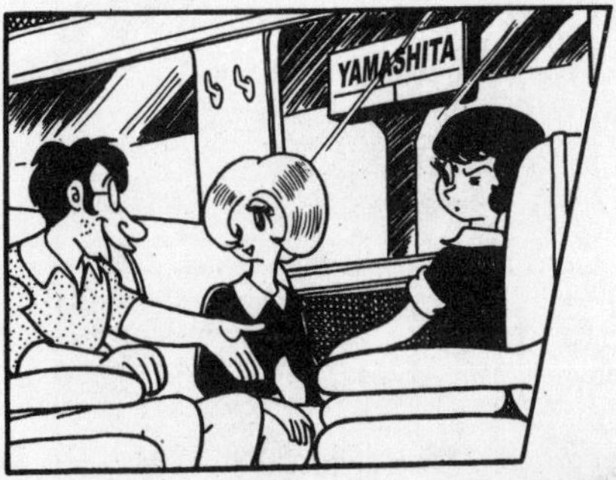
YAMASHITA

SCARA WAS ENTRANCED BY THE GREEN FIELDS AND FORESTS ALL AROUND HER. IT WAS WHAT SHE HAD ALWAYS DREAMED OF SEEING. THE TWO MEN AT FIRST THOUGHT SCARA'S REACTION WAS A LITTLE OVER-BLOWN, BUT THEN THEY STARTED TO ENJOY HER PRESENCE AND TO TEASE HER IN A FRIENDLY FASHION.

"THIS YOUR FIRST TIME OUTSIDE OF TOKYO?"

"YES. I'VE NEVER SEEN MOUNTAINS BEFORE..."

"YOU'RE KIDDING! DIDN'T YOU EVER GO ON FIELD TRIPS IN SCHOOL?!"

"WHAT'S A FIELD TRIP?"

"OH, COME ON... YOU MUST BE PULLING OUR LEGS..."

"PULLING YOUR LEGS?"

JUST THEN A BOY WITH A BUTTERFLY NET AND A LITTLE INSECT CAGE WALKED DOWN THE AISLE...

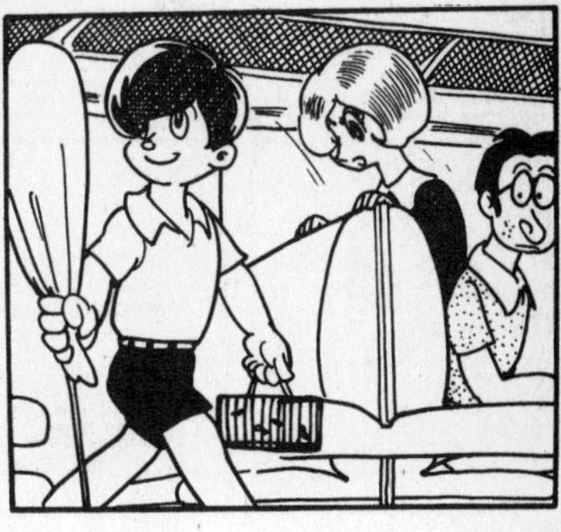

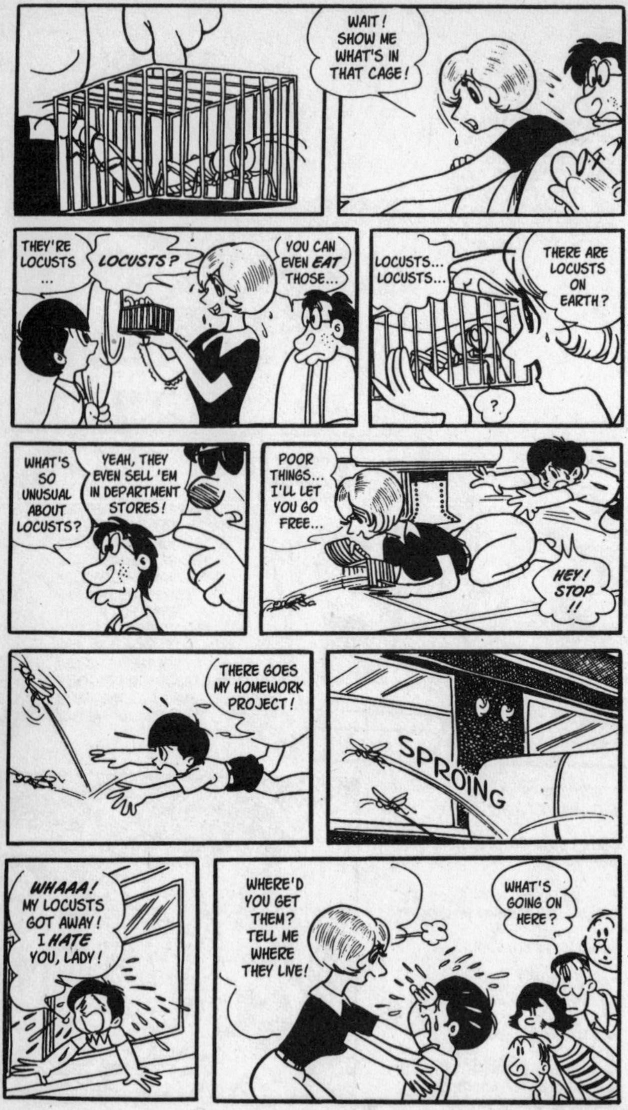
WAIT! SHOW ME WHAT'S IN THAT CAGE!
THEY'RE LOCUSTS ...
LOCUSTS?
YOU CAN EVEN EAT THOSE...
LOCUSTS... LOCUSTS...
THERE ARE LOCUSTS ON EARTH?
?
WHAT'S SO UNUSUAL ABOUT LOCUSTS?
YEAH, THEY EVEN SELL 'EM IN DEPARTMENT STORES!
POOR THINGS... I'LL LET YOU GO FREE...
HEY! STOP !!
THERE GOES MY HOMEWORK PROJECT!
SPROING
WHAAA! MY LOCUSTS GOT AWAY! I HATE YOU, LADY!
WHERE'D YOU GET THEM? TELL ME WHERE THEY LIVE!
WHAT'S GOING ON HERE?

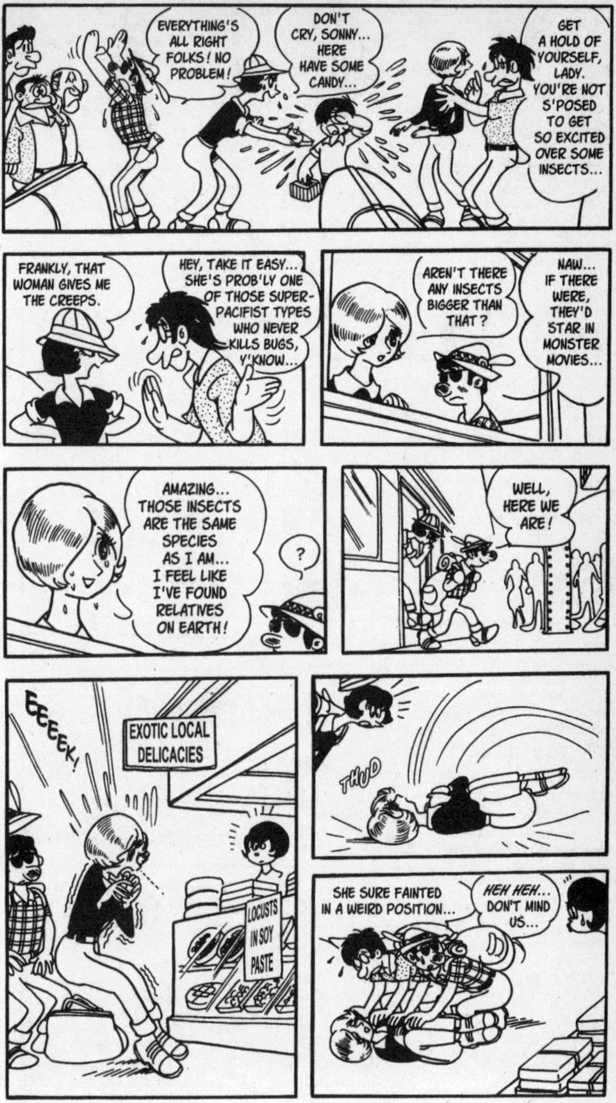
EVERYTHING'S ALL RIGHT FOLKS! NO PROBLEM!
DON'T CRY, SONNY... HERE HAVE SOME CANDY...
GET A HOLD OF YOURSELF, LADY. YOU'RE NOT S'POSED TO GET SO EXCITED OVER SOME INSECTS...
FRANKLY, THAT WOMAN GIVES ME THE CREEPS.
HEY, TAKE IT EASY... SHE'S PROB'LY ONE OF THOSE SUPER-PACIFIST TYPES WHO NEVER KILLS BUGS, Y'KNOW...
AREN'T THERE ANY INSECTS BIGGER THAN THAT?
NAW... IF THERE WERE, THEY'D STAR IN MONSTER MOVIES...
AMAZING... THOSE INSECTS ARE THE SAME SPECIES AS I AM... I FEEL LIKE I'VE FOUND RELATIVES ON EARTH!
?
WELL, HERE WE ARE!
EEEEK!
EXOTIC LOCAL DELICACIES
LOCUSTS IN SOY PASTE
THUD
SHE SURE FAINTED IN A WEIRD POSITION...
HEH HEH... DON'T MIND US...

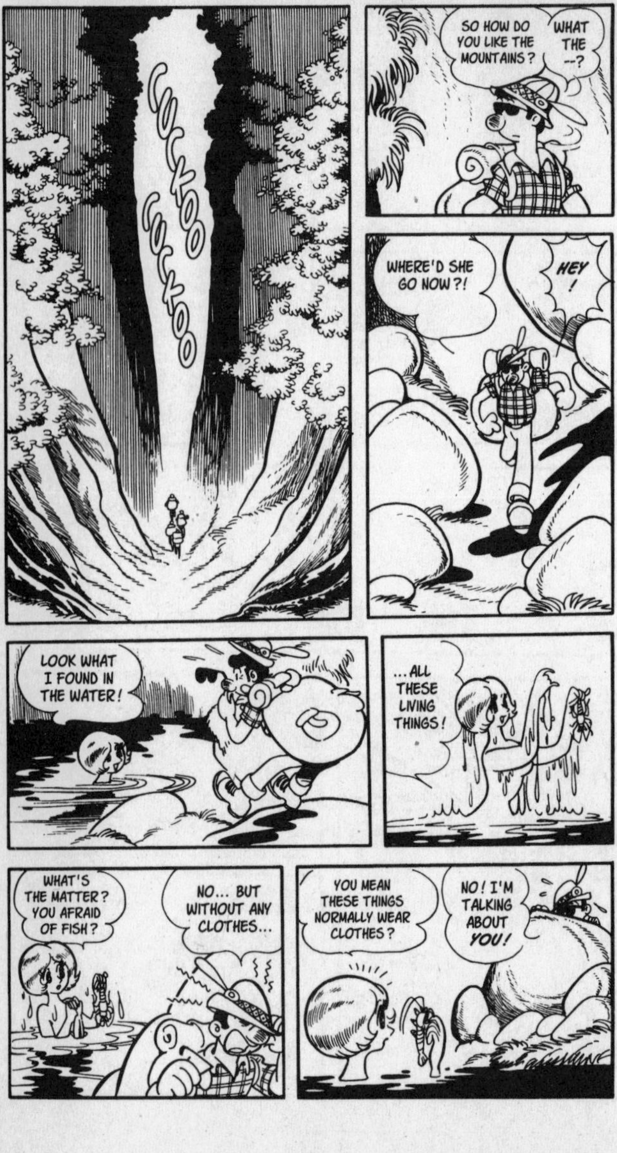
CUCKOO CUCKOO
SO HOW DO YOU LIKE THE MOUNTAINS?
WHAT THE --?
WHERE'D SHE GO NOW?!
HEY!
LOOK WHAT I FOUND IN THE WATER!
...ALL THESE LIVING THINGS!
WHAT'S THE MATTER? YOU AFRAID OF FISH?
NO... BUT WITHOUT ANY CLOTHES...
YOU MEAN THESE THINGS NORMALLY WEAR CLOTHES?
NO! I'M TALKING ABOUT YOU!

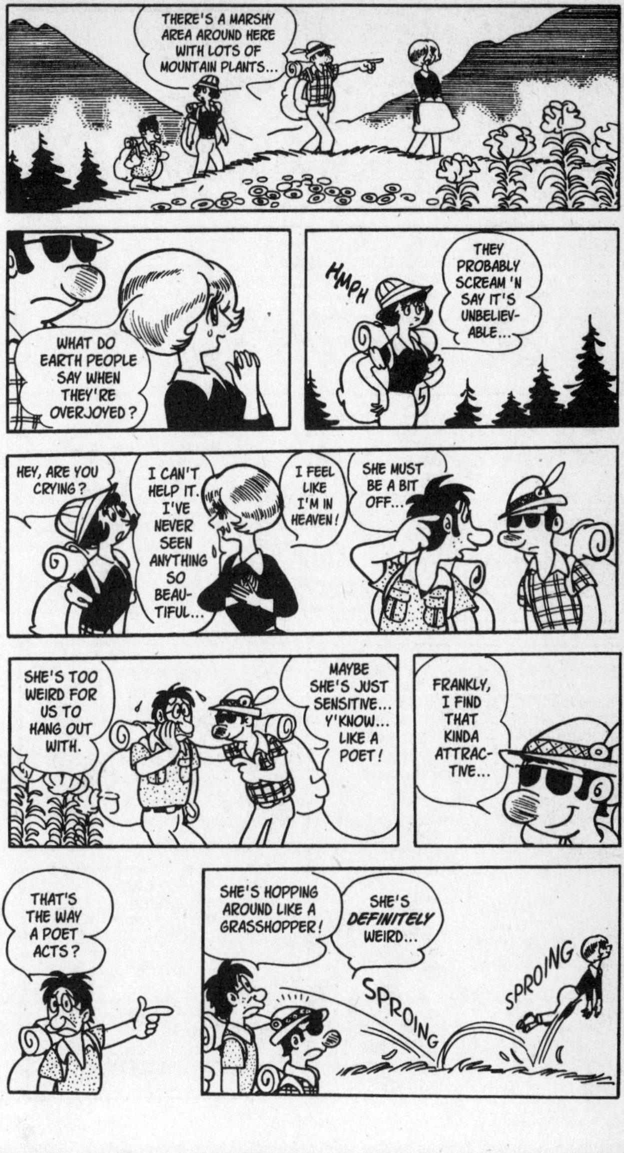
THERE'S A MARSHY AREA AROUND HERE WITH LOTS OF MOUNTAIN PLANTS...
WHAT DO EARTH PEOPLE SAY WHEN THEY'RE OVERJOYED?
HMPH
THEY PROBABLY SCREAM 'N SAY IT'S UNBELIEV-ABLE...
HEY, ARE YOU CRYING?
I CAN'T HELP IT. I'VE NEVER SEEN ANYTHING SO BEAU-TIFUL...
I FEEL LIKE I'M IN HEAVEN!
SHE MUST BE A BIT OFF...
SHE'S TOO WEIRD FOR US TO HANG OUT WITH.
MAYBE SHE'S JUST SENSITIVE... Y'KNOW... LIKE A POET!
FRANKLY, I FIND THAT KINDA ATTRAC-TIVE...
THAT'S THE WAY A POET ACTS?
SHE'S HOPPING AROUND LIKE A GRASSHOPPER!
SHE'S *DEFINITELY* WEIRD...
SPROING
SPROING

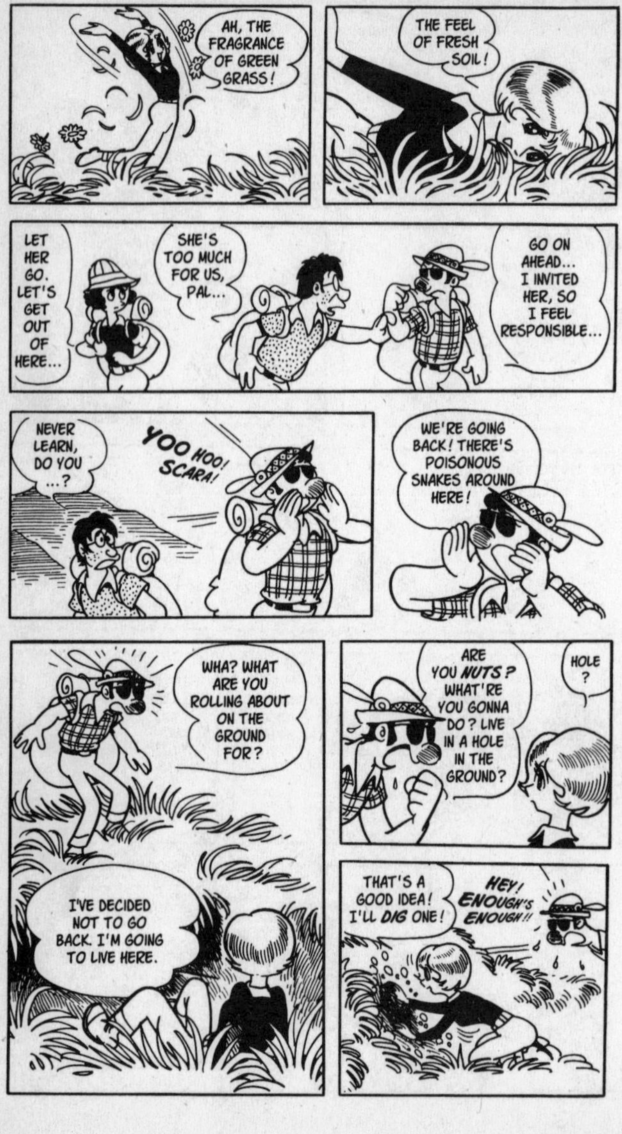
AH, THE FRAGRANCE OF GREEN GRASS!
THE FEEL OF FRESH SOIL!
LET HER GO. LET'S GET OUT OF HERE...
SHE'S TOO MUCH FOR US, PAL...
GO ON AHEAD... I INVITED HER, SO I FEEL RESPONSIBLE...
NEVER LEARN, DO YOU ...?
YOO HOO! SCARA!
WE'RE GOING BACK! THERE'S POISONOUS SNAKES AROUND HERE!
WHA? WHAT ARE YOU ROLLING ABOUT ON THE GROUND FOR?
I'VE DECIDED NOT TO GO BACK. I'M GOING TO LIVE HERE.
ARE YOU NUTS? WHAT'RE YOU GONNA DO? LIVE IN A HOLE IN THE GROUND?
HOLE?
THAT'S A GOOD IDEA! I'LL DIG ONE!
HEY! ENOUGH'S ENOUGH!!

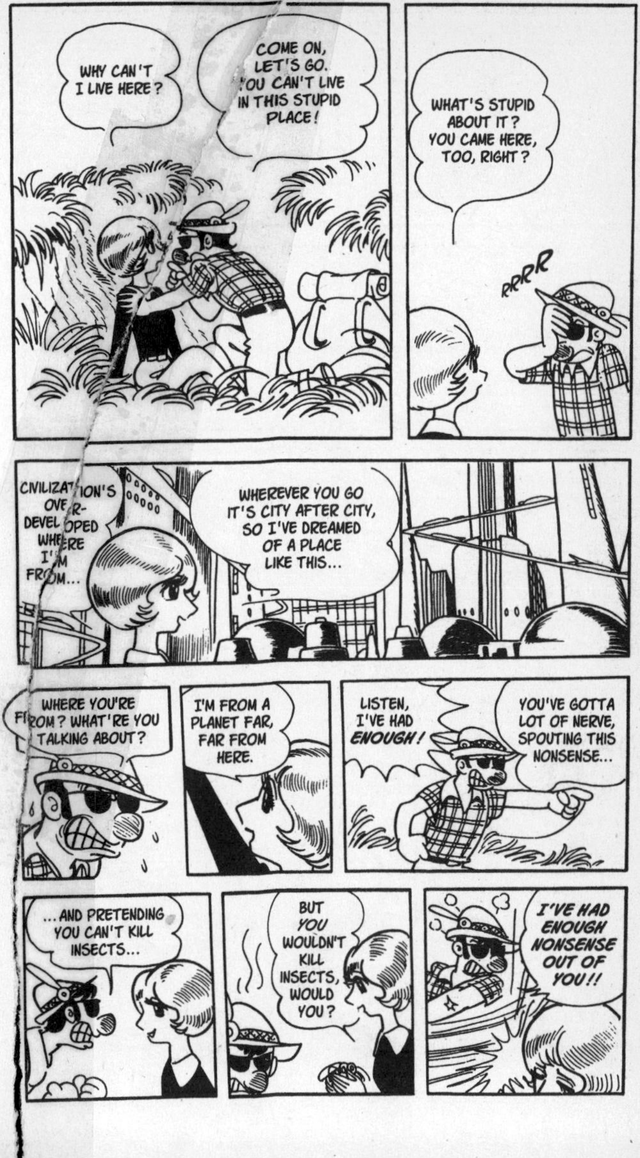
WHY CAN'T I LIVE HERE?
COME ON, LET'S GO. YOU CAN'T LIVE IN THIS STUPID PLACE!
WHAT'S STUPID ABOUT IT? YOU CAME HERE, TOO, RIGHT?
RRRR
CIVILIZATION'S OVER-DEVELOPED WHERE I'M FROM...
WHEREVER YOU GO IT'S CITY AFTER CITY, SO I'VE DREAMED OF A PLACE LIKE THIS...
WHERE YOU'RE FROM? WHAT'RE YOU TALKING ABOUT?
I'M FROM A PLANET FAR, FAR FROM HERE.
LISTEN, I'VE HAD *ENOUGH!*
YOU'VE GOTTA LOT OF NERVE, SPOUTING THIS NONSENSE...
...AND PRETENDING YOU CAN'T KILL INSECTS...
BUT *YOU* WOULDN'T KILL INSECTS, WOULD YOU?
I'VE HAD ENOUGH NONSENSE OUT OF YOU!!

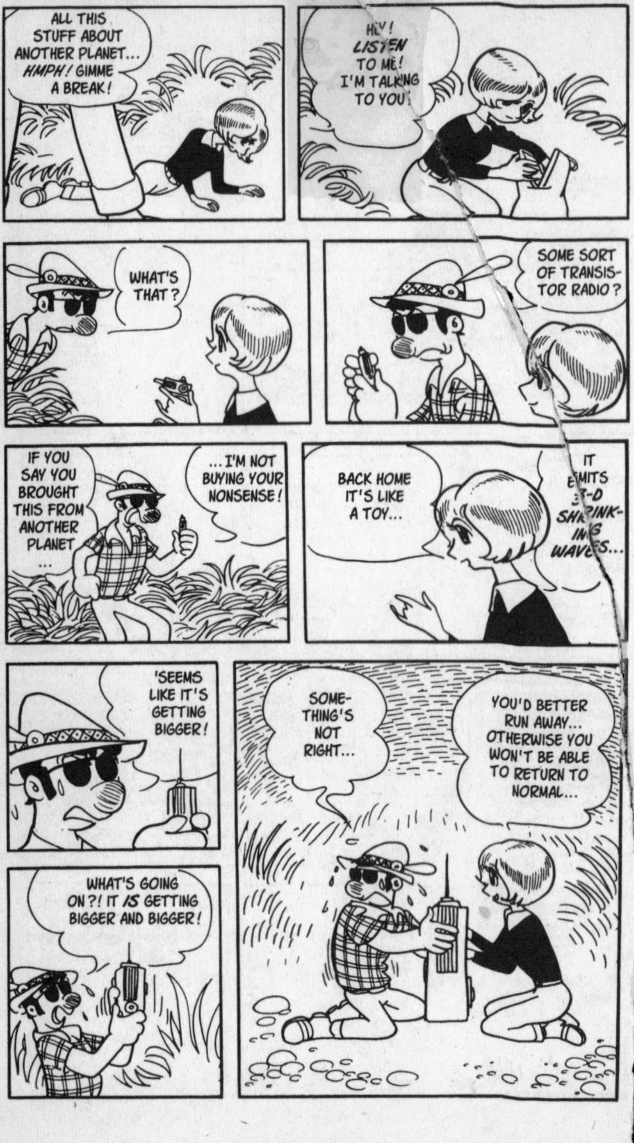
ALL THIS STUFF ABOUT ANOTHER PLANET... HMPH! GIMME A BREAK!
HEY! LISTEN TO ME! I'M TALKING TO YOU!
WHAT'S THAT?
SOME SORT OF TRANSIS-TOR RADIO?
IF YOU SAY YOU BROUGHT THIS FROM ANOTHER PLANET ...
... I'M NOT BUYING YOUR NONSENSE!
BACK HOME IT'S LIKE A TOY...
IT EMITS 3-D SHRINK-ING WAVES...
'SEEMS LIKE IT'S GETTING BIGGER!
WHAT'S GOING ON?! IT IS GETTING BIGGER AND BIGGER!
SOME-THING'S NOT RIGHT...
YOU'D BETTER RUN AWAY... OTHERWISE YOU WON'T BE ABLE TO RETURN TO NORMAL...

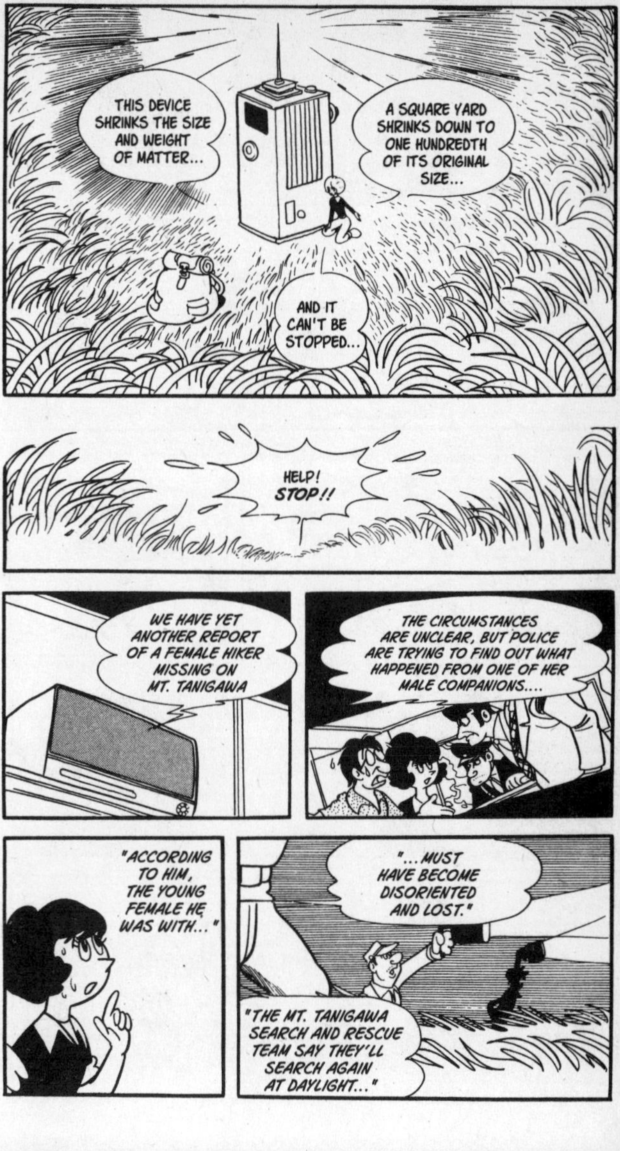

THIS DEVICE SHRINKS THE SIZE AND WEIGHT OF MATTER...
A SQUARE YARD SHRINKS DOWN TO ONE HUNDREDTH OF ITS ORIGINAL SIZE...
AND IT CAN'T BE STOPPED...
HELP! STOP!!
WE HAVE YET ANOTHER REPORT OF A FEMALE HIKER MISSING ON MT. TANIGAWA
THE CIRCUMSTANCES ARE UNCLEAR, BUT POLICE ARE TRYING TO FIND OUT WHAT HAPPENED FROM ONE OF HER MALE COMPANIONS....
"ACCORDING TO HIM, THE YOUNG FEMALE HE WAS WITH..."
"...MUST HAVE BECOME DISORIENTED AND LOST."
"THE MT. TANIGAWA SEARCH AND RESCUE TEAM SAY THEY'LL SEARCH AGAIN AT DAYLIGHT..."

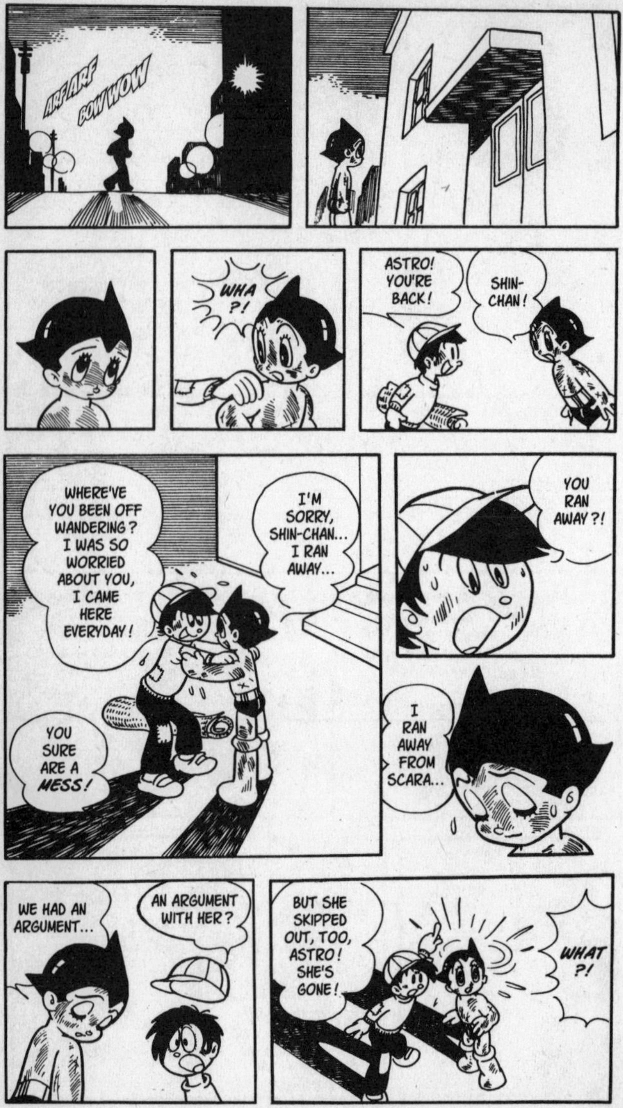
ARF ARF
BOW WOW
WHA ?!
ASTRO! YOU'RE BACK!
SHIN-CHAN!
WHERE'VE YOU BEEN OFF WANDERING? I WAS SO WORRIED ABOUT YOU, I CAME HERE EVERYDAY!
I'M SORRY, SHIN-CHAN... I RAN AWAY...
YOU SURE ARE A MESS!
YOU RAN AWAY?!
I RAN AWAY FROM SCARA...
WE HAD AN ARGUMENT...
AN ARGUMENT WITH HER?
BUT SHE SKIPPED OUT, TOO, ASTRO! SHE'S GONE!
WHAT ?!

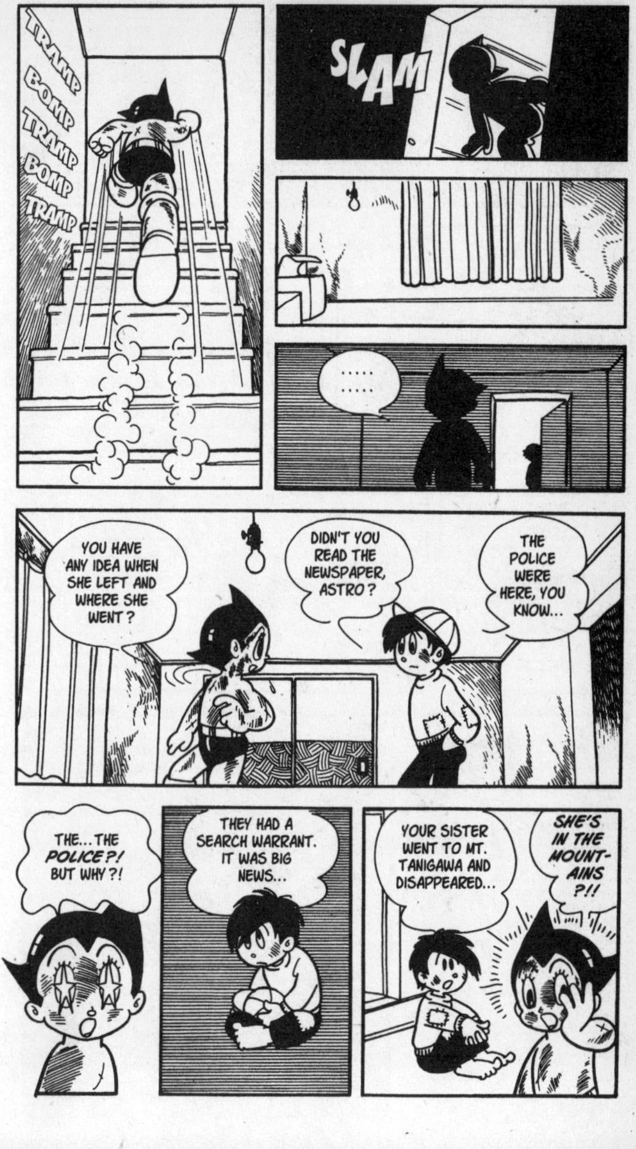
TRAMP BOMP TRAMP BOMP TRAMP
SLAM
.....
.....
YOU HAVE ANY IDEA WHEN SHE LEFT AND WHERE SHE WENT?
DIDN'T YOU READ THE NEWSPAPER, ASTRO?
THE POLICE WERE HERE, YOU KNOW...
THE... THE POLICE?! BUT WHY?!
THEY HAD A SEARCH WARRANT. IT WAS BIG NEWS...
YOUR SISTER WENT TO MT. TANIGAWA AND DISAPPEARED...
SHE'S IN THE MOUNT-AINS?!!

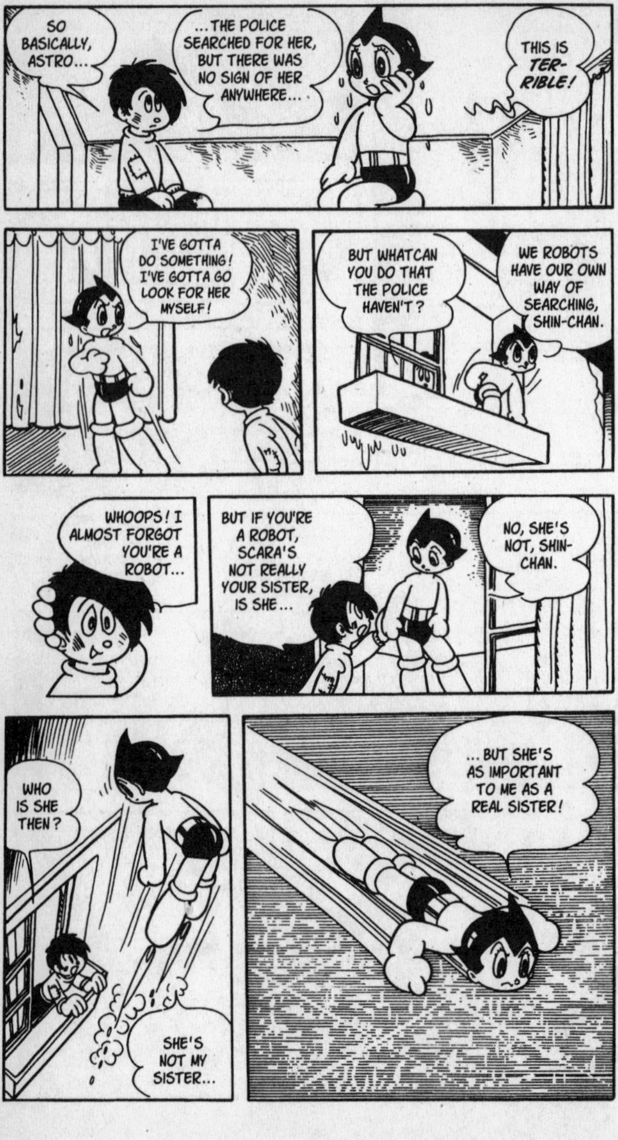
SO BASICALLY, ASTRO...
...THE POLICE SEARCHED FOR HER, BUT THERE WAS NO SIGN OF HER ANYWHERE...
THIS IS TERRIBLE!
I'VE GOTTA DO SOMETHING! I'VE GOTTA GO LOOK FOR HER MYSELF!
BUT WHATCAN YOU DO THAT THE POLICE HAVEN'T?
WE ROBOTS HAVE OUR OWN WAY OF SEARCHING, SHIN-CHAN.
WHOOPS! I ALMOST FORGOT YOU'RE A ROBOT...
BUT IF YOU'RE A ROBOT, SCARA'S NOT REALLY YOUR SISTER, IS SHE...
NO, SHE'S NOT, SHIN-CHAN.
WHO IS SHE THEN?
SHE'S NOT MY SISTER...
...BUT SHE'S AS IMPORTANT TO ME AS A REAL SISTER!

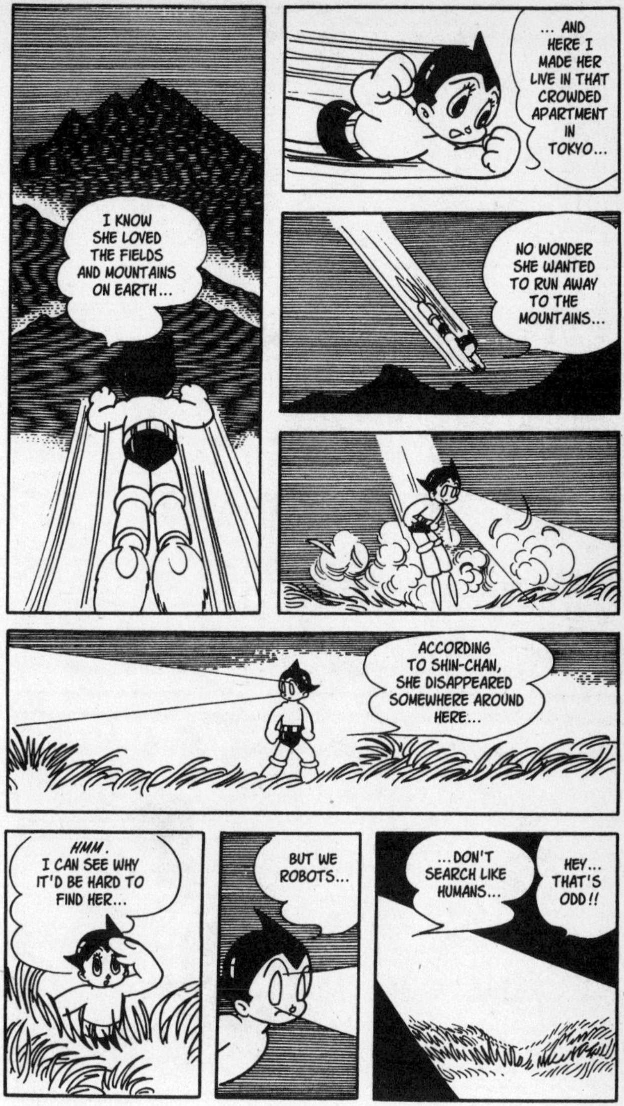

I KNOW SHE LOVED THE FIELDS AND MOUNTAINS ON EARTH...
... AND HERE I MADE HER LIVE IN THAT CROWDED APARTMENT IN TOKYO...
NO WONDER SHE WANTED TO RUN AWAY TO THE MOUNTAINS...
ACCORDING TO SHIN-CHAN, SHE DISAPPEARED SOMEWHERE AROUND HERE...
HMM. I CAN SEE WHY IT'D BE HARD TO FIND HER...
BUT WE ROBOTS...
...DON'T SEARCH LIKE HUMANS...
HEY... THAT'S ODD!!

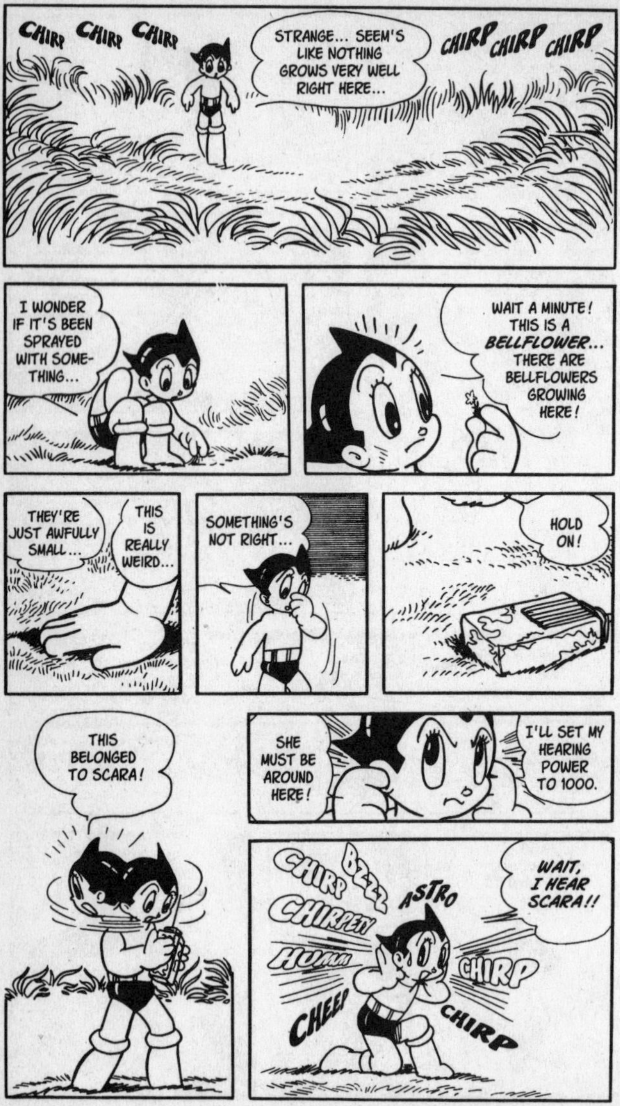
CHIRP CHIRP CHIRP
STRANGE... SEEM'S LIKE NOTHING GROWS VERY WELL RIGHT HERE...
CHIRP CHIRP CHIRP
I WONDER IF IT'S BEEN SPRAYED WITH SOME-THING...
WAIT A MINUTE! THIS IS A BELLFLOWER... THERE ARE BELLFLOWERS GROWING HERE!
THEY'RE JUST AWFULLY SMALL...
THIS IS REALLY WEIRD...
SOMETHING'S NOT RIGHT...
HOLD ON!
THIS BELONGED TO SCARA!
SHE MUST BE AROUND HERE!
I'LL SET MY HEARING POWER TO 1000.
CHIRP
BZZZ
CHIRPETY
ASTRO
HUMM
CHEEP
CHIRP
CHIRP
WAIT, I HEAR SCARA!!

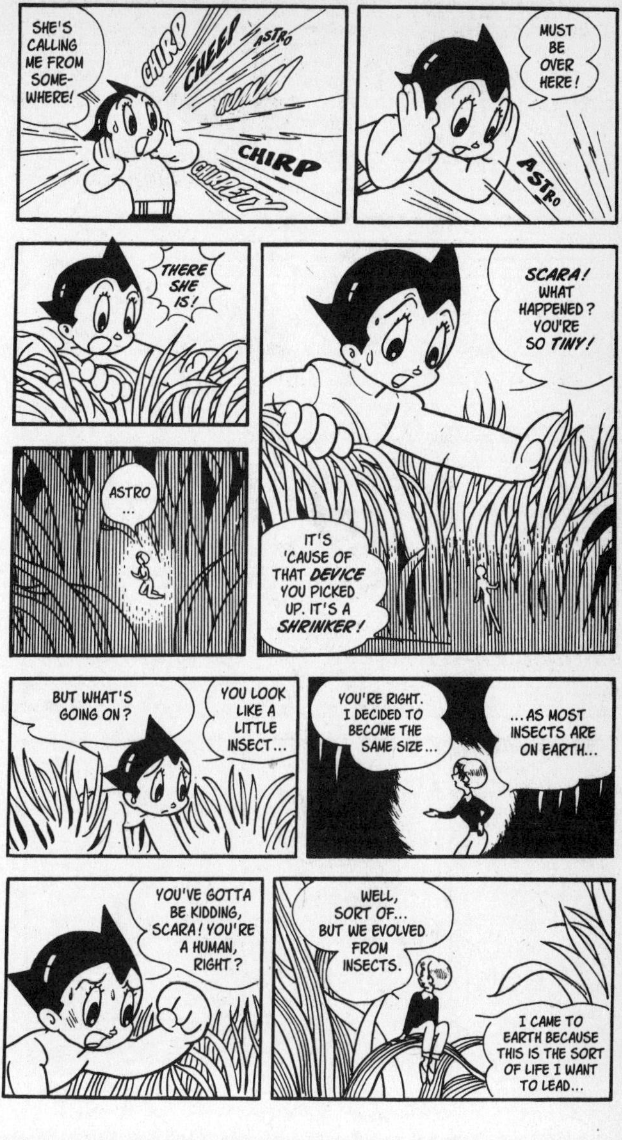
SHE'S CALLING ME FROM SOME-WHERE!
CHIRP
CHEEP
ASTRO
CHIRP
CHIRPETY
MUST BE OVER HERE!
ASTRO
THERE SHE IS!
SCARA! WHAT HAPPENED? YOU'RE SO TINY!
ASTRO ...
IT'S 'CAUSE OF THAT DEVICE YOU PICKED UP. IT'S A SHRINKER!
BUT WHAT'S GOING ON?
YOU LOOK LIKE A LITTLE INSECT...
YOU'RE RIGHT. I DECIDED TO BECOME THE SAME SIZE...
...AS MOST INSECTS ARE ON EARTH...
YOU'VE GOTTA BE KIDDING, SCARA! YOU'RE A HUMAN, RIGHT?
WELL, SORT OF... BUT WE EVOLVED FROM INSECTS.
I CAME TO EARTH BECAUSE THIS IS THE SORT OF LIFE I WANT TO LEAD...

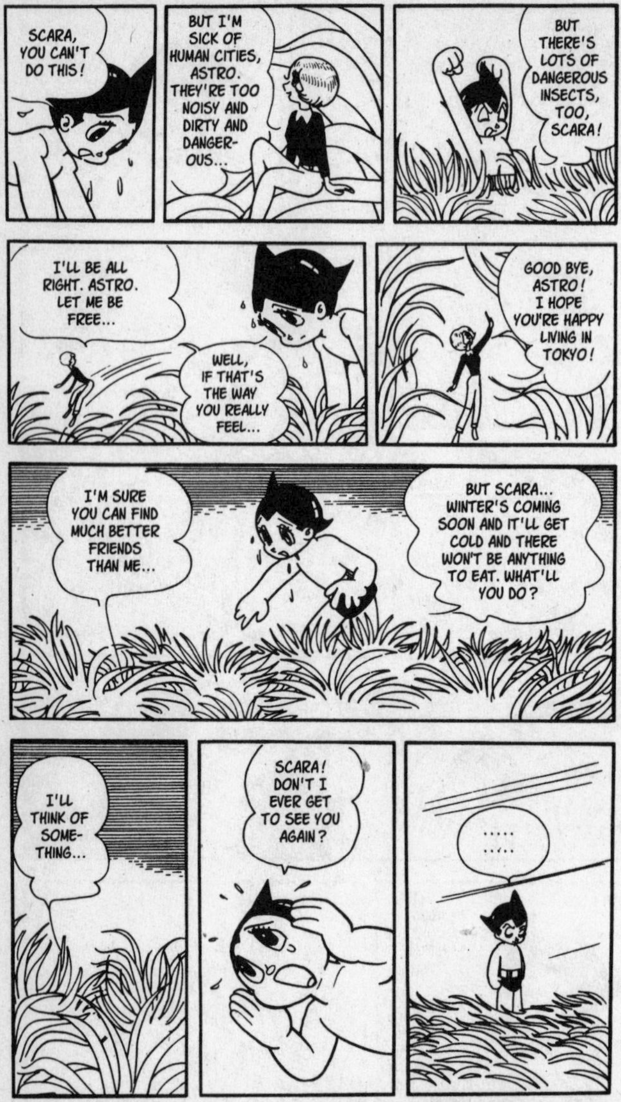
SCARA, YOU CAN'T DO THIS!
BUT I'M SICK OF HUMAN CITIES, ASTRO. THEY'RE TOO NOISY AND DIRTY AND DANGER-OUS...
BUT THERE'S LOTS OF DANGEROUS INSECTS, TOO, SCARA!
I'LL BE ALL RIGHT. ASTRO. LET ME BE FREE...
WELL, IF THAT'S THE WAY YOU REALLY FEEL...
GOOD BYE, ASTRO! I HOPE YOU'RE HAPPY LIVING IN TOKYO!
I'M SURE YOU CAN FIND MUCH BETTER FRIENDS THAN ME...
BUT SCARA... WINTER'S COMING SOON AND IT'LL GET COLD AND THERE WON'T BE ANYTHING TO EAT. WHAT'LL YOU DO?
I'LL THINK OF SOME-THING...
SCARA! DON'T I EVER GET TO SEE YOU AGAIN?
....

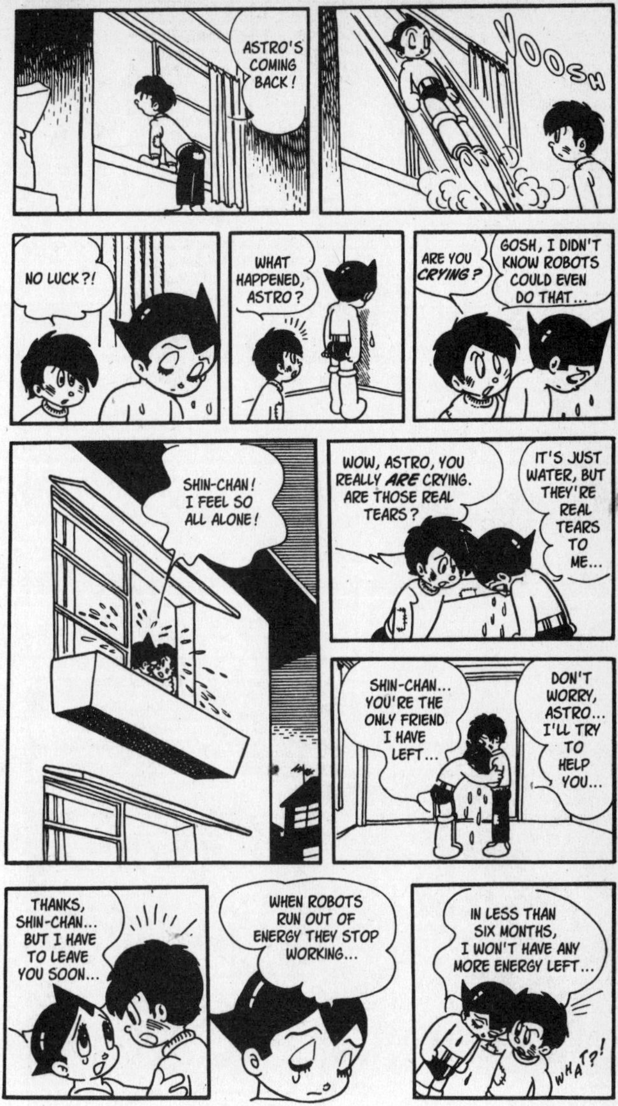
ASTRO'S COMING BACK!
VOOOSH
NO LUCK?!
WHAT HAPPENED, ASTRO?
ARE YOU CRYING?
GOSH, I DIDN'T KNOW ROBOTS COULD EVEN DO THAT...
SHIN-CHAN! I FEEL SO ALL ALONE!
WOW, ASTRO, YOU REALLY ARE CRYING. ARE THOSE REAL TEARS?
IT'S JUST WATER, BUT THEY'RE REAL TEARS TO ME...
SHIN-CHAN... YOU'RE THE ONLY FRIEND I HAVE LEFT...
DON'T WORRY, ASTRO... I'LL TRY TO HELP YOU...
THANKS, SHIN-CHAN... BUT I HAVE TO LEAVE YOU SOON...
WHEN ROBOTS RUN OUT OF ENERGY THEY STOP WORKING...
IN LESS THAN SIX MONTHS, I WON'T HAVE ANY MORE ENERGY LEFT...
WHAT?!

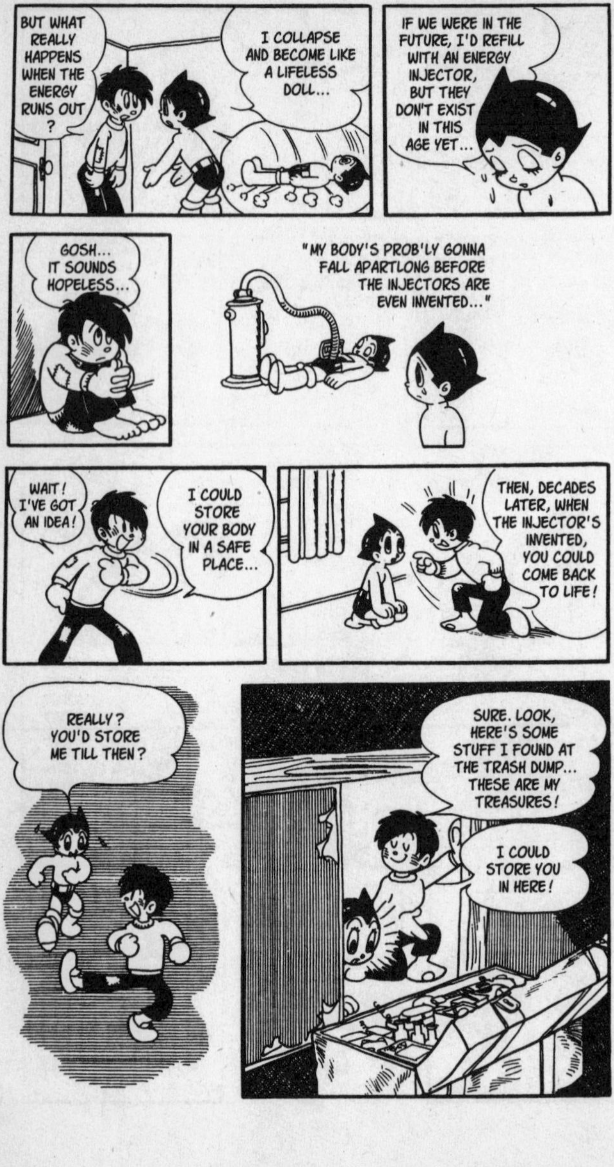
BUT WHAT REALLY HAPPENS WHEN THE ENERGY RUNS OUT ?
I COLLAPSE AND BECOME LIKE A LIFELESS DOLL...
IF WE WERE IN THE FUTURE, I'D REFILL WITH AN ENERGY INJECTOR, BUT THEY DON'T EXIST IN THIS AGE YET...
GOSH... IT SOUNDS HOPELESS...
"MY BODY'S PROB'LY GONNA FALL APARTLONG BEFORE THE INJECTORS ARE EVEN INVENTED..."
WAIT! I'VE GOT AN IDEA!
I COULD STORE YOUR BODY IN A SAFE PLACE...
THEN, DECADES LATER, WHEN THE INJECTOR'S INVENTED, YOU COULD COME BACK TO LIFE!
REALLY? YOU'D STORE ME TILL THEN?
SURE. LOOK, HERE'S SOME STUFF I FOUND AT THE TRASH DUMP... THESE ARE MY TREASURES!
I COULD STORE YOU IN HERE!

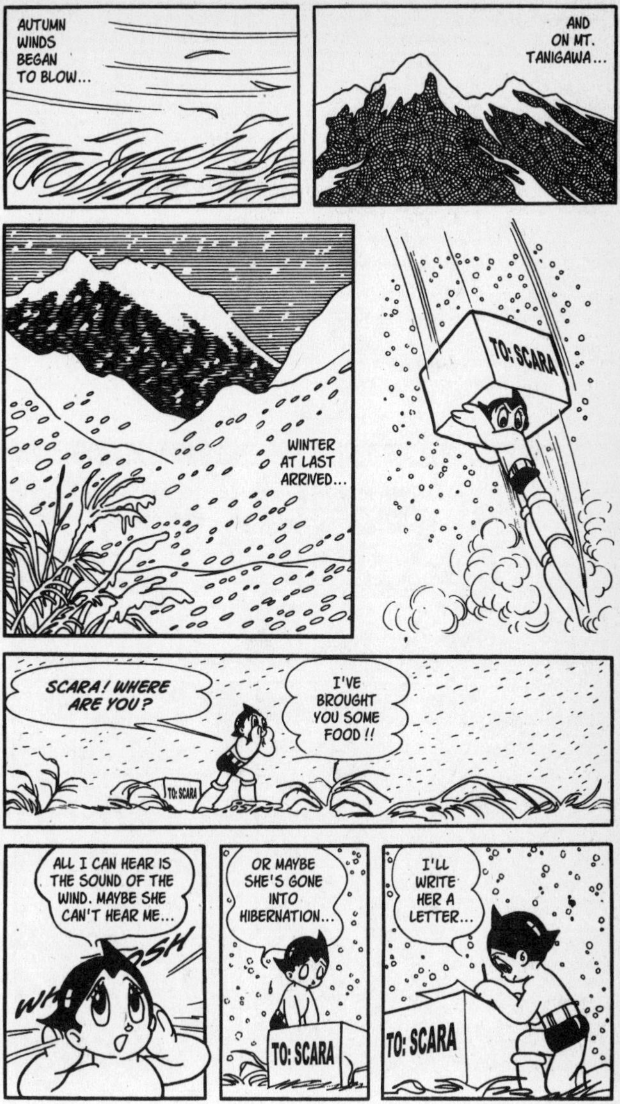
AUTUMN WINDS BEGAN TO BLOW...
AND ON MT. TANIGAWA...
WINTER AT LAST ARRIVED...
TO: SCARA
SCARA! WHERE ARE YOU?
I'VE BROUGHT YOU SOME FOOD!!
TO: SCARA
ALL I CAN HEAR IS THE SOUND OF THE WIND. MAYBE SHE CAN'T HEAR ME...
OR MAYBE SHE'S GONE INTO HIBERNATION...
TO: SCARA
I'LL WRITE HER A LETTER...
TO: SCARA

Dear Scara,

I'm leaving some food here for you.
it should last you through the winter,
and help you make it till spring.
I'm going to run out of energy before then,
so I might never see you again .
I wish the best for you always.
be careful not to get caught by insect
collectors in the summer and sold
at a department store.

Sayonara

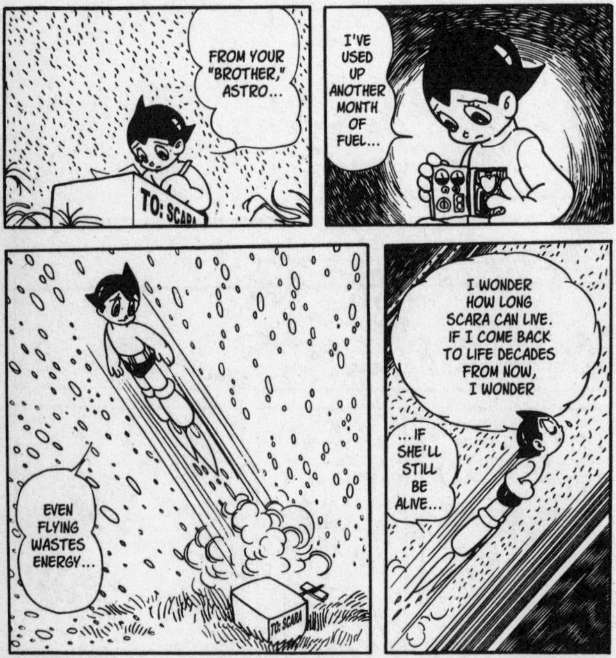

FROM YOUR "BROTHER," ASTRO...
I'VE USED UP ANOTHER MONTH OF FUEL...
EVEN FLYING WASTES ENERGY...
TO: SCARA
I WONDER HOW LONG SCARA CAN LIVE. IF I COME BACK TO LIFE DECADES FROM NOW, I WONDER
...IF SHE'LL STILL BE ALIVE...

THE ENERGY TUBE

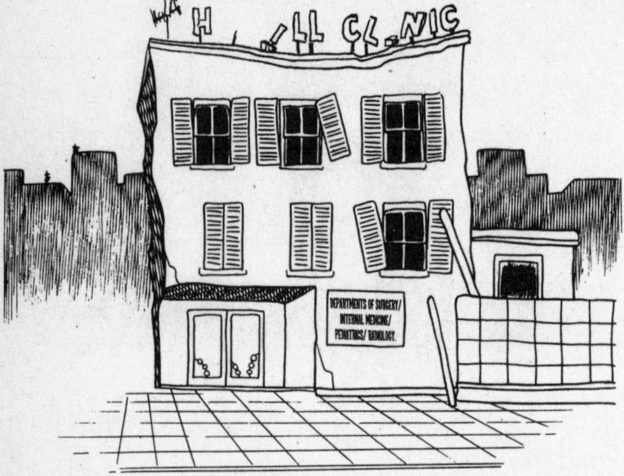
DEPARTMENTS OF SURGERY/ INTERNAL MEDICINE/ PEDIATRICS/ RADIOLOGY.

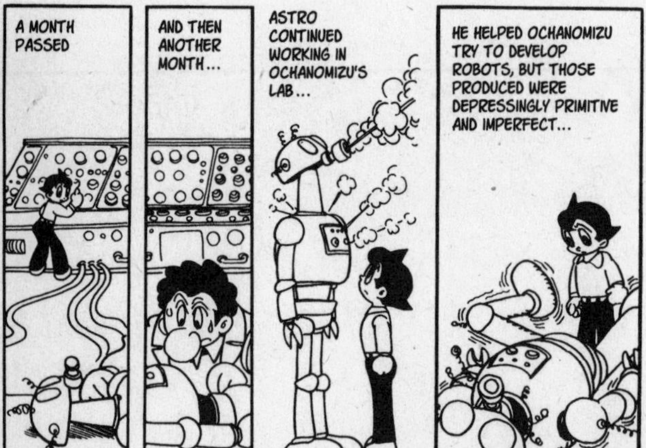
A MONTH PASSED
AND THEN ANOTHER MONTH...
ASTRO CONTINUED WORKING IN OCHANOMIZU'S LAB...
HE HELPED OCHANOMIZU TRY TO DEVELOP ROBOTS, BUT THOSE PRODUCED WERE DEPRESSINGLY PRIMITIVE AND IMPERFECT...

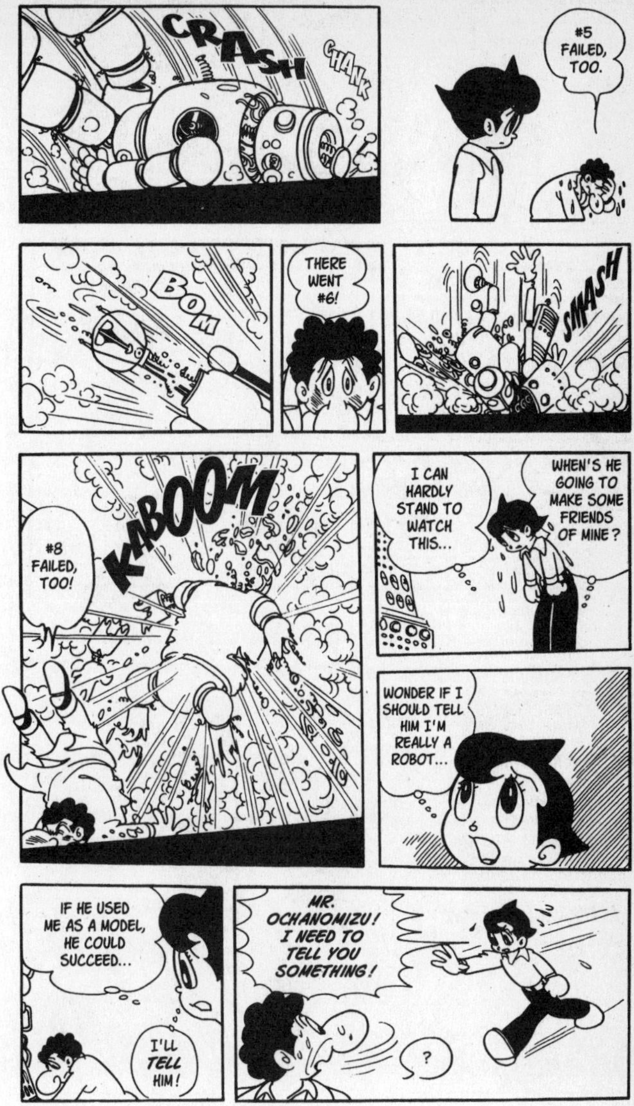
CRASH
CHANK
#5 FAILED, TOO.
BOM
THERE WENT #6!
SMASH
KABOOM
#8 FAILED, TOO!
I CAN HARDLY STAND TO WATCH THIS...
WHEN'S HE GOING TO MAKE SOME FRIENDS OF MINE?
WONDER IF I SHOULD TELL HIM I'M REALLY A ROBOT...
IF HE USED ME AS A MODEL, HE COULD SUCCEED...
I'LL TELL HIM!
MR. OCHANOMIZU! I NEED TO TELL YOU SOMETHING!
?

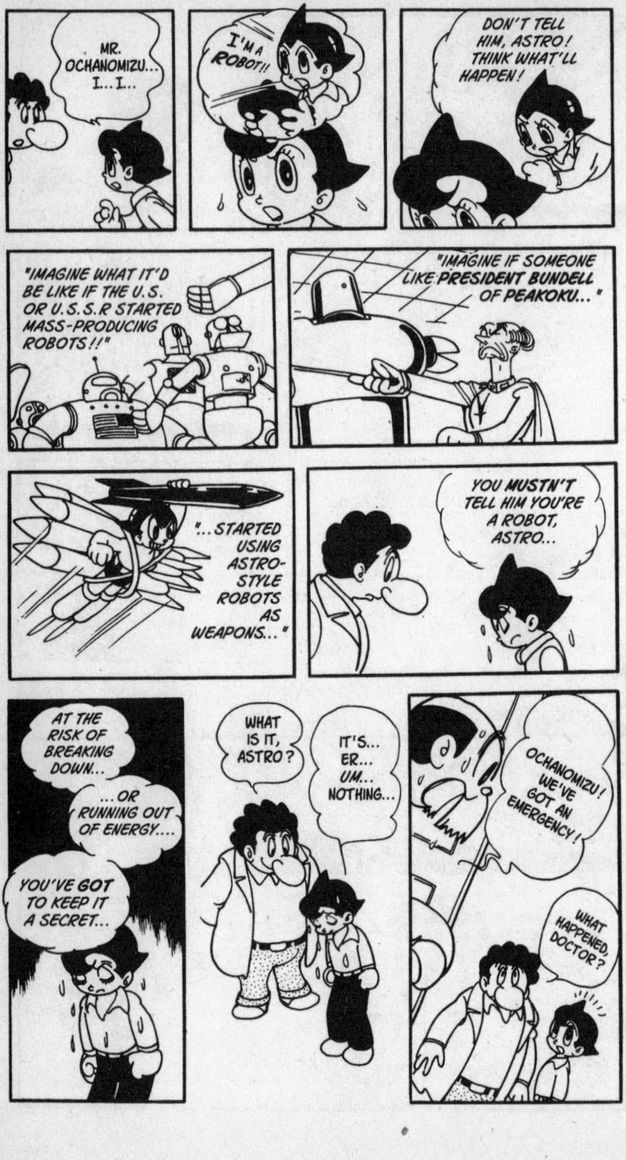
MR. OCHANOMIZU... I... I...
I'M A ROBOT!!
DON'T TELL HIM, ASTRO! THINK WHAT'LL HAPPEN!
"IMAGINE WHAT IT'D BE LIKE IF THE U.S. OR U.S.S.R STARTED MASS-PRODUCING ROBOTS!!"
"IMAGINE IF SOMEONE LIKE PRESIDENT BUNDELL OF PEAKOKU..."
"...STARTED USING ASTRO-STYLE ROBOTS AS WEAPONS..."
YOU MUSTN'T TELL HIM YOU'RE A ROBOT, ASTRO...
AT THE RISK OF BREAKING DOWN...
...OR RUNNING OUT OF ENERGY....
YOU'VE GOT TO KEEP IT A SECRET...
WHAT IS IT, ASTRO?
IT'S... ER... UM... NOTHING...
OCHANOMIZU! WE'VE GOT AN EMERGENCY!
WHAT HAPPENED, DOCTOR?

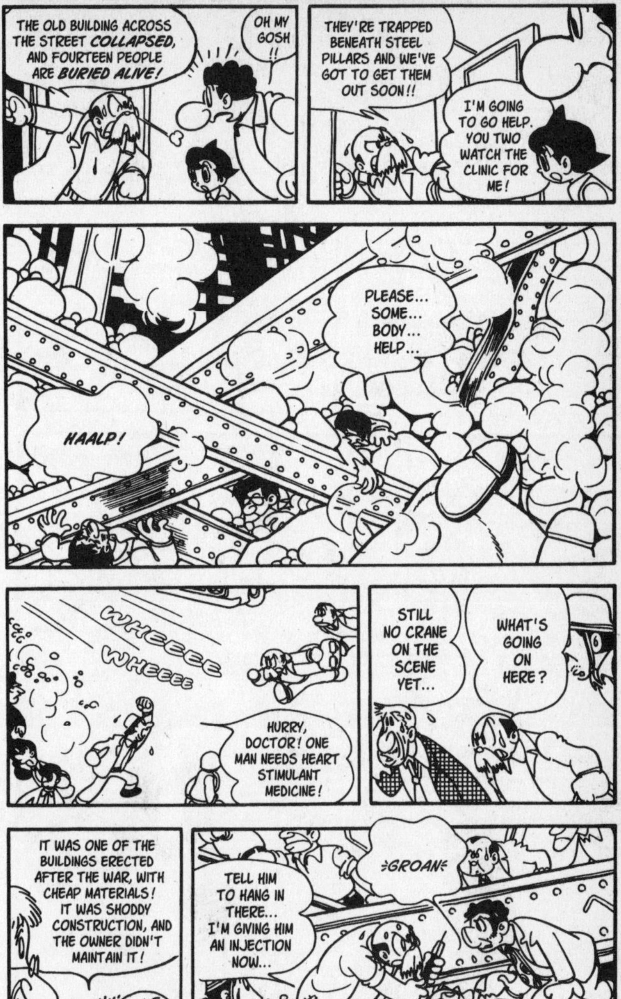

THE OLD BUILDING ACROSS THE STREET COLLAPSED, AND FOURTEEN PEOPLE ARE BURIED ALIVE!
OH MY GOSH !!
THEY'RE TRAPPED BENEATH STEEL PILLARS AND WE'VE GOT TO GET THEM OUT SOON!!
I'M GOING TO GO HELP. YOU TWO WATCH THE CLINIC FOR ME!
PLEASE... SOME... BODY... HELP...
HAALP!
WHEEEE
WHEEEE
HURRY, DOCTOR! ONE MAN NEEDS HEART STIMULANT MEDICINE!
STILL NO CRANE ON THE SCENE YET...
WHAT'S GOING ON HERE?
IT WAS ONE OF THE BUILDINGS ERECTED AFTER THE WAR, WITH CHEAP MATERIALS! IT WAS SHODDY CONSTRUCTION, AND THE OWNER DIDN'T MAINTAIN IT!
HMPH...
GROAN
TELL HIM TO HANG IN THERE... I'M GIVING HIM AN INJECTION NOW...
BE BRAVE, SIR, BE BRAVE...

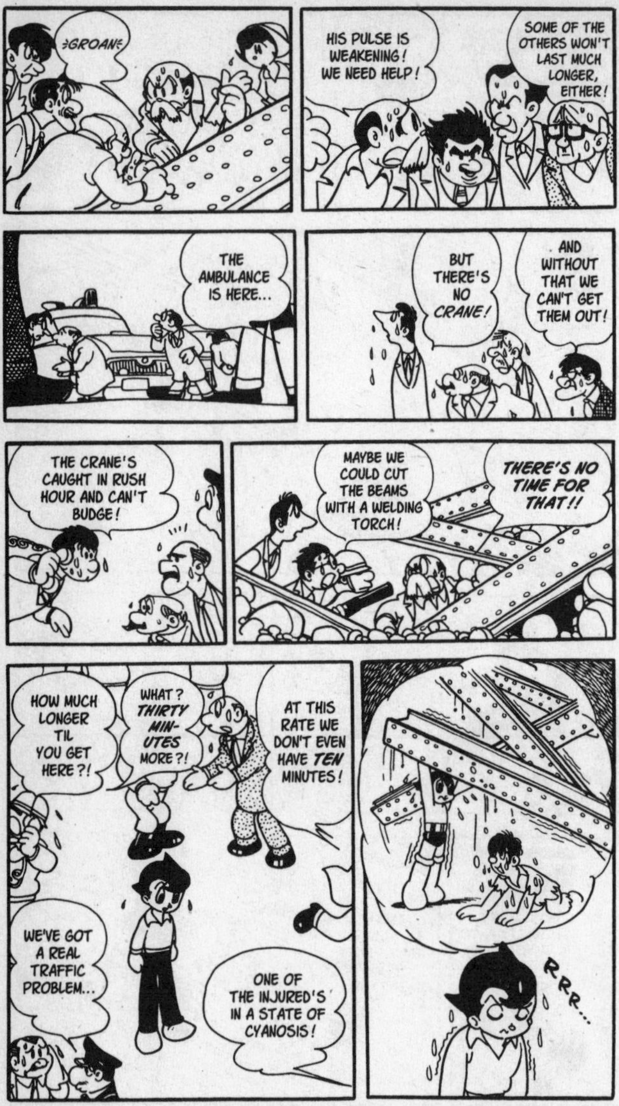
GROAN
HIS PULSE IS WEAKENING! WE NEED HELP!
SOME OF THE OTHERS WON'T LAST MUCH LONGER, EITHER!
THE AMBULANCE IS HERE...
BUT THERE'S NO CRANE!
AND WITHOUT THAT WE CAN'T GET THEM OUT!
THE CRANE'S CAUGHT IN RUSH HOUR AND CAN'T BUDGE!
MAYBE WE COULD CUT THE BEAMS WITH A WELDING TORCH!
THERE'S NO TIME FOR THAT!!
HOW MUCH LONGER TIL YOU GET HERE?!
WHAT? THIRTY MIN-UTES MORE?!
AT THIS RATE WE DON'T EVEN HAVE TEN MINUTES!
WE'VE GOT A REAL TRAFFIC PROBLEM...
ONE OF THE INJURED'S IN A STATE OF CYANOSIS!
RRR...

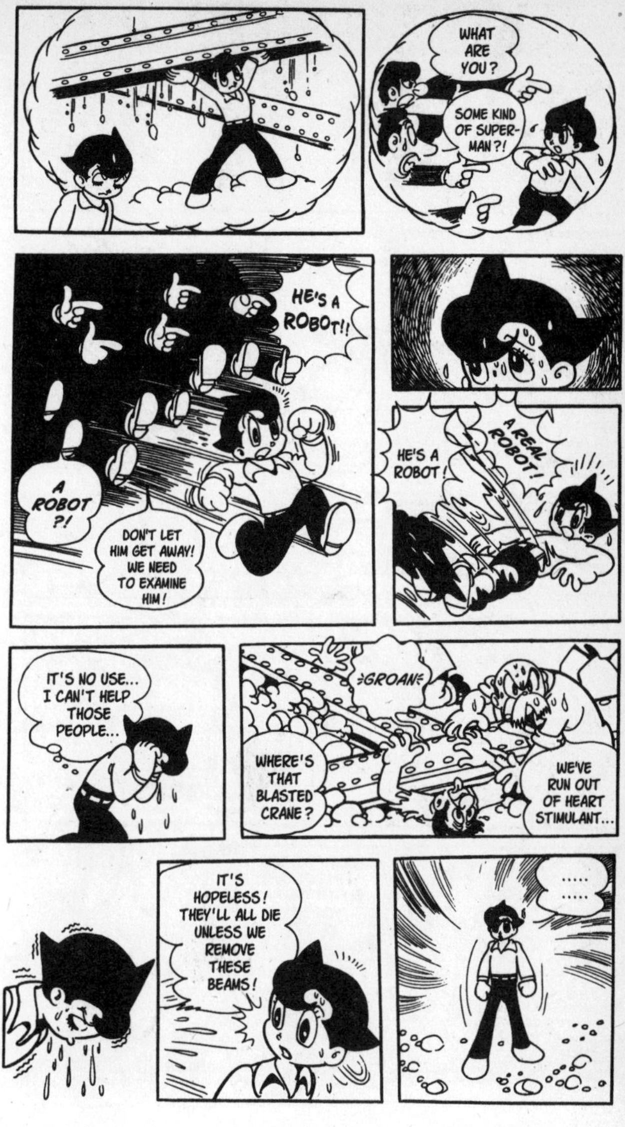
WHAT ARE YOU?
SOME KIND OF SUPER-MAN?!
HE'S A ROBOT!!
A ROBOT ?!
DON'T LET HIM GET AWAY! WE NEED TO EXAMINE HIM!
HE'S A ROBOT!
A REAL ROBOT!
IT'S NO USE... I CAN'T HELP THOSE PEOPLE...
GROAN
WHERE'S THAT BLASTED CRANE?
WE'VE RUN OUT OF HEART STIMULANT...
IT'S HOPELESS! THEY'LL ALL DIE UNLESS WE REMOVE THESE BEAMS!
....

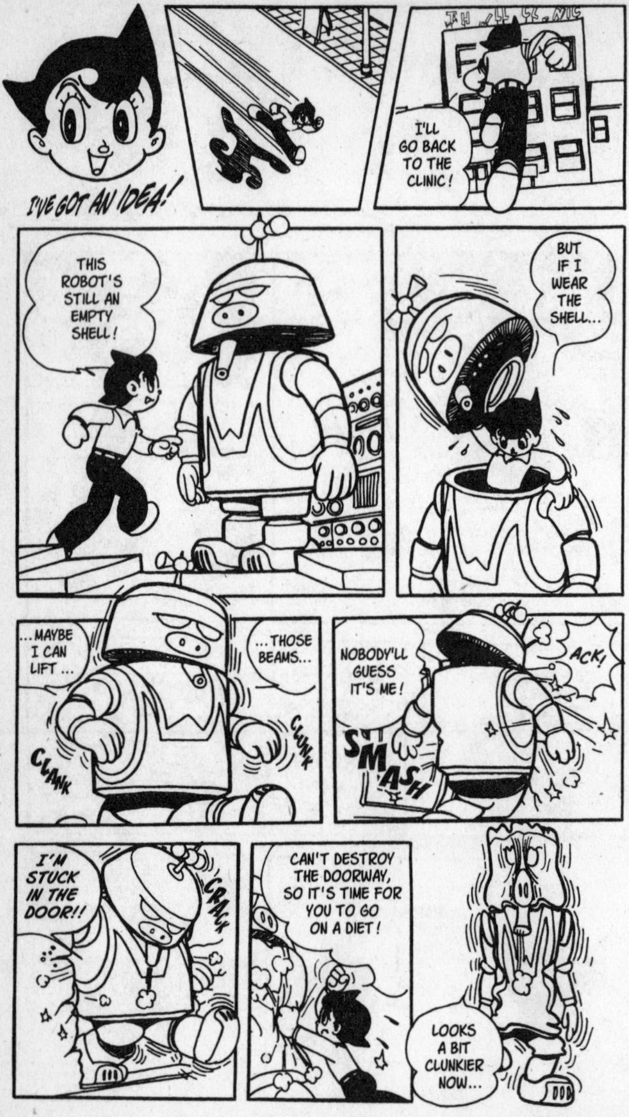
I'VE GOT AN IDEA!
I'LL GO BACK TO THE CLINIC!
THIS ROBOT'S STILL AN EMPTY SHELL!
BUT IF I WEAR THE SHELL...
...MAYBE I CAN LIFT ...
...THOSE BEAMS...
CLUNK
CLANK
NOBODY'LL GUESS IT'S ME!
ACK!
SMASH
I'M STUCK IN THE DOOR!!
CRACK
CAN'T DESTROY THE DOORWAY, SO IT'S TIME FOR YOU TO GO ON A DIET!
LOOKS A BIT CLUNKIER NOW...

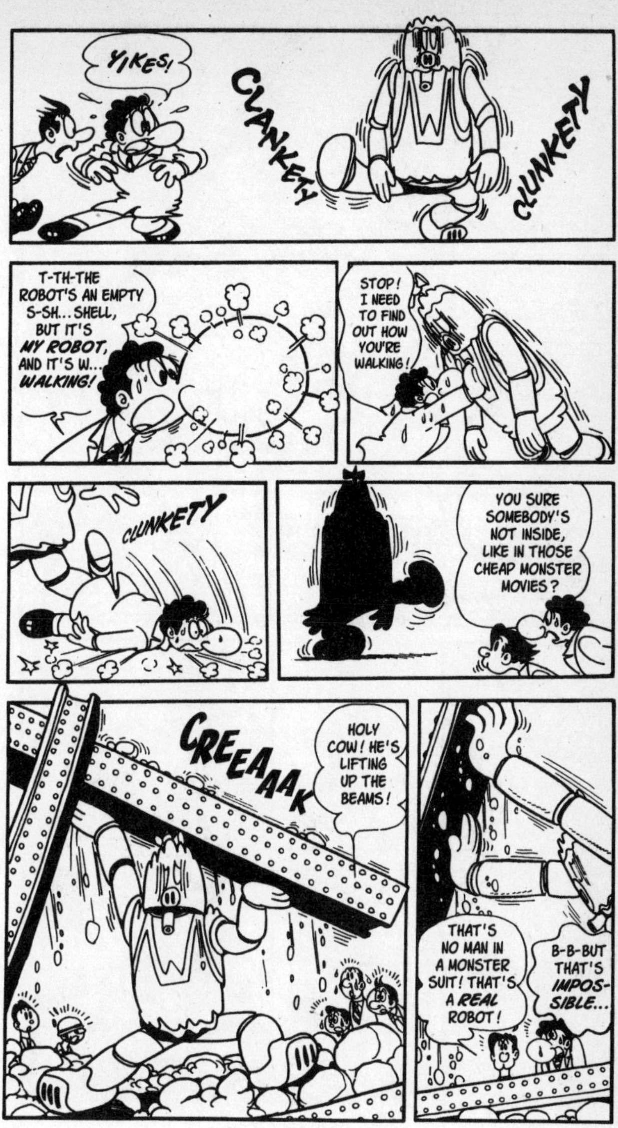
YIKES!
CLANKETY
CLUNKETY
T-TH-THE ROBOT'S AN EMPTY S-SH... SHELL, BUT IT'S MY ROBOT, AND IT'S W... WALKING!
STOP! I NEED TO FIND OUT HOW YOU'RE WALKING!
CLUNKETY
YOU SURE SOMEBODY'S NOT INSIDE, LIKE IN THOSE CHEAP MONSTER MOVIES?
CREEAAAK
HOLY COW! HE'S LIFTING UP THE BEAMS!
THAT'S NO MAN IN A MONSTER SUIT! THAT'S A REAL ROBOT!
B-B-BUT THAT'S IMPOSSIBLE...

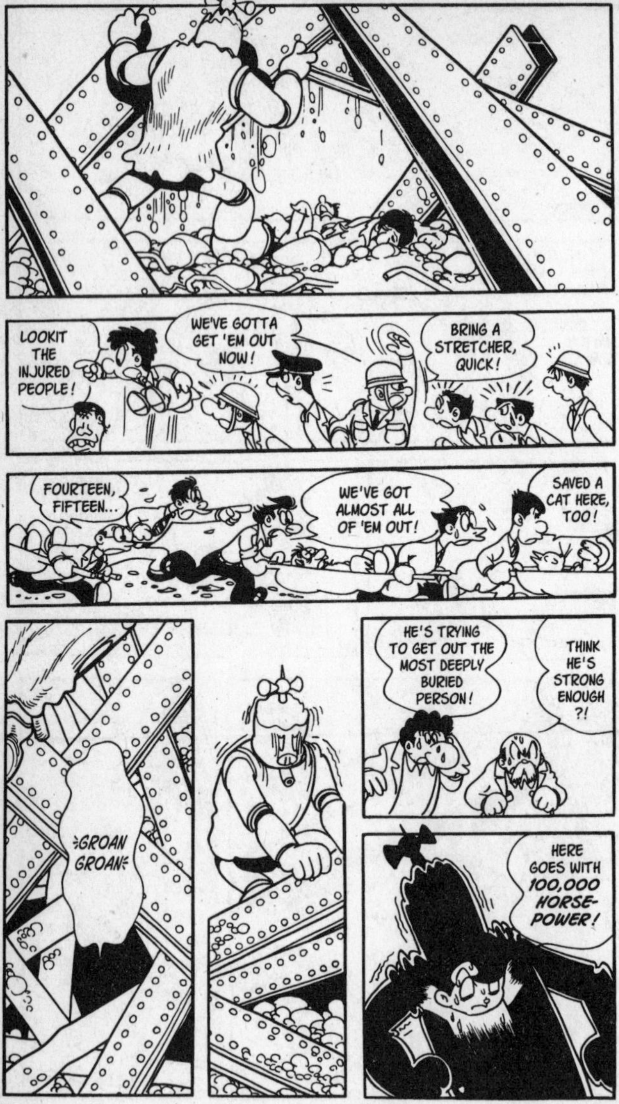
LOOKIT THE INJURED PEOPLE!
WE'VE GOTTA GET 'EM OUT NOW!
BRING A STRETCHER, QUICK!
FOURTEEN, FIFTEEN...
WE'VE GOT ALMOST ALL OF 'EM OUT!
SAVED A CAT HERE, TOO!
GROAN GROAN
HE'S TRYING TO GET OUT THE MOST DEEPLY BURIED PERSON!
THINK HE'S STRONG ENOUGH ?!
HERE GOES WITH 100,000 HORSE-POWER!

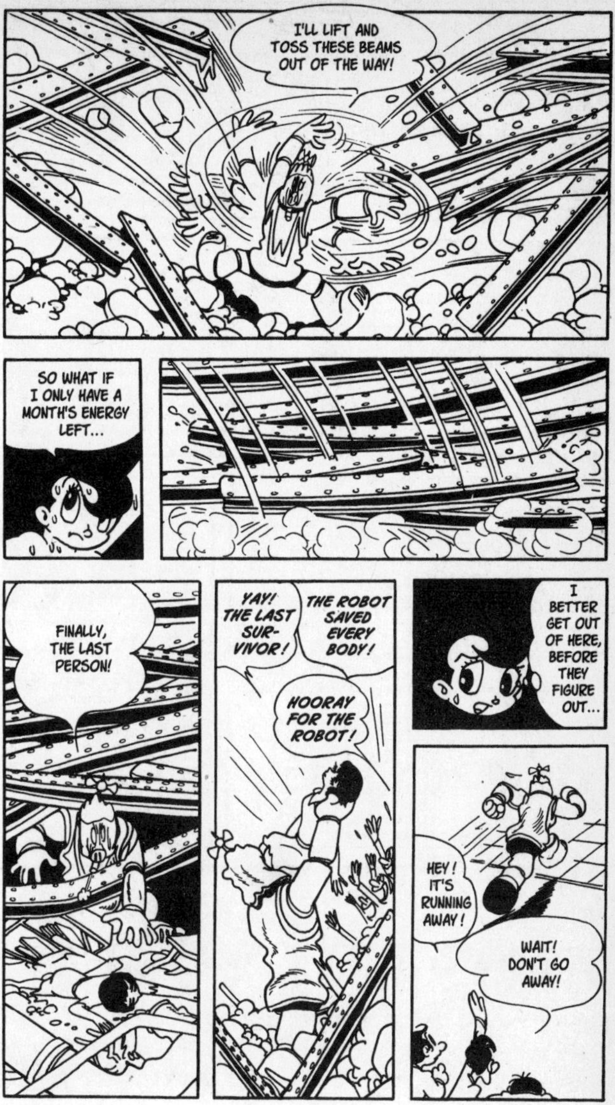

I'LL LIFT AND TOSS THESE BEAMS OUT OF THE WAY!
SO WHAT IF I ONLY HAVE A MONTH'S ENERGY LEFT...
FINALLY, THE LAST PERSON!
YAY! THE LAST SUR-VIVOR!
THE ROBOT SAVED EVERY BODY!
HOORAY FOR THE ROBOT!
I BETTER GET OUT OF HERE, BEFORE THEY FIGURE OUT...
HEY! IT'S RUNNING AWAY!
WAIT! DON'T GO AWAY!

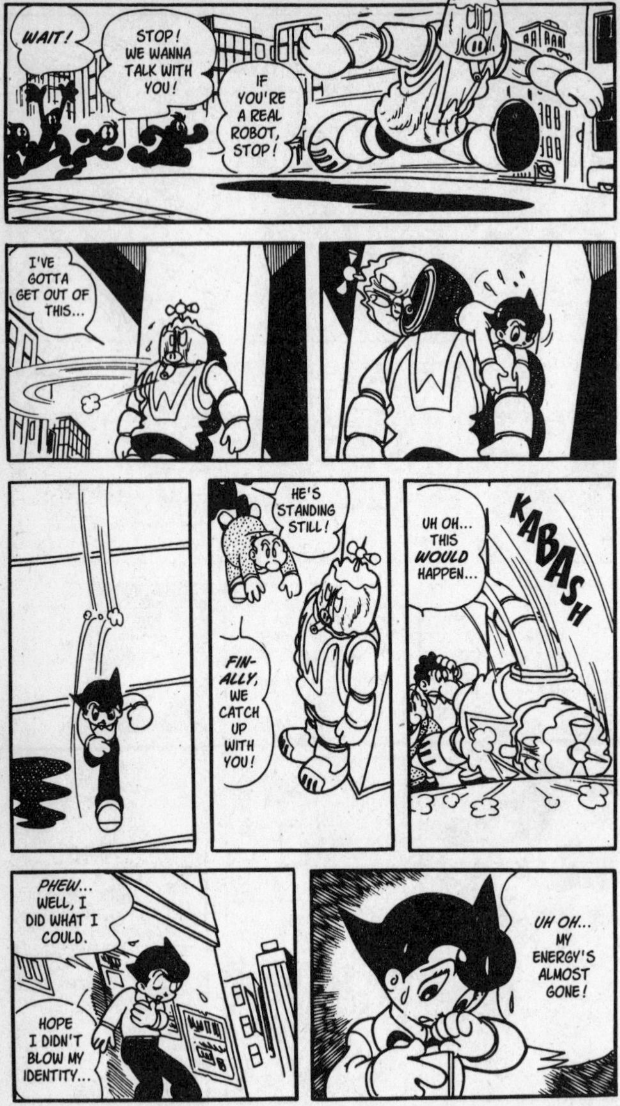

WAIT!
STOP! WE WANNA TALK WITH YOU!
IF YOU'RE A REAL ROBOT, STOP!
I'VE GOTTA GET OUT OF THIS...
HE'S STANDING STILL!
FIN-ALLY, WE CATCH UP WITH YOU!
UH OH... THIS WOULD HAPPEN...
KABASH
PHEW... WELL, I DID WHAT I COULD.
HOPE I DIDN'T BLOW MY IDENTITY...
UH OH... MY ENERGY'S ALMOST GONE!

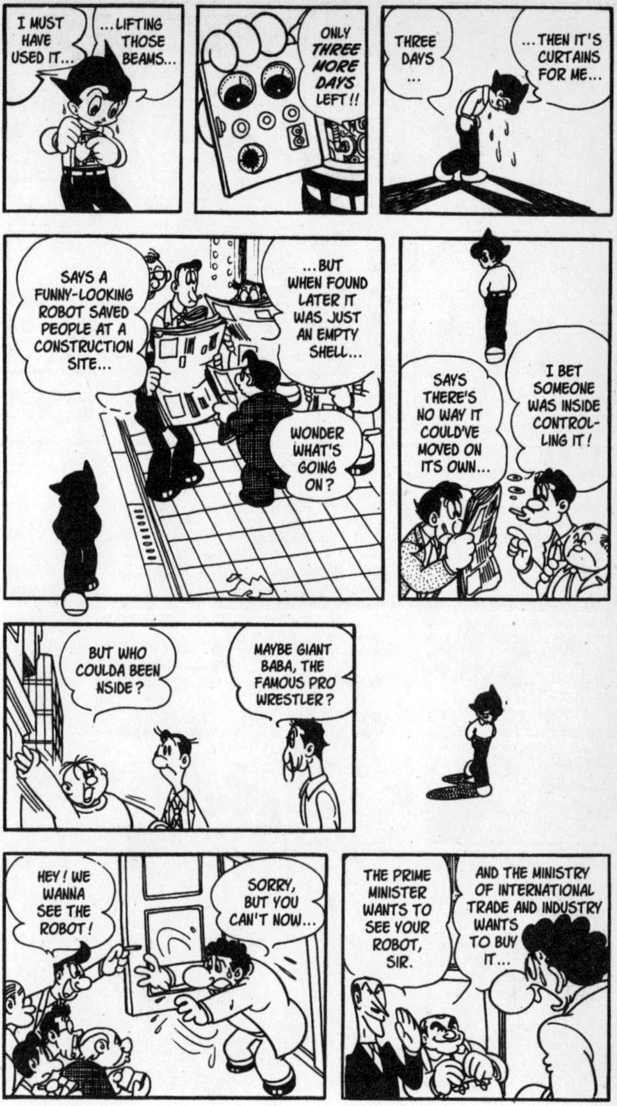
I MUST HAVE USED IT...
...LIFTING THOSE BEAMS...
ONLY THREE MORE DAYS LEFT!!
THREE DAYS ...
...THEN IT'S CURTAINS FOR ME...
SAYS A FUNNY-LOOKING ROBOT SAVED PEOPLE AT A CONSTRUCTION SITE...
...BUT WHEN FOUND LATER IT WAS JUST AN EMPTY SHELL...
WONDER WHAT'S GOING ON?
SAYS THERE'S NO WAY IT COULD'VE MOVED ON ITS OWN...
I BET SOMEONE WAS INSIDE CONTROL-LING IT!
BUT WHO COULDA BEEN NSIDE?
MAYBE GIANT BABA, THE FAMOUS PRO WRESTLER?
HEY! WE WANNA SEE THE ROBOT!
SORRY, BUT YOU CAN'T NOW...
THE PRIME MINISTER WANTS TO SEE YOUR ROBOT, SIR.
AND THE MINISTRY OF INTERNATIONAL TRADE AND INDUSTRY WANTS TO BUY IT...

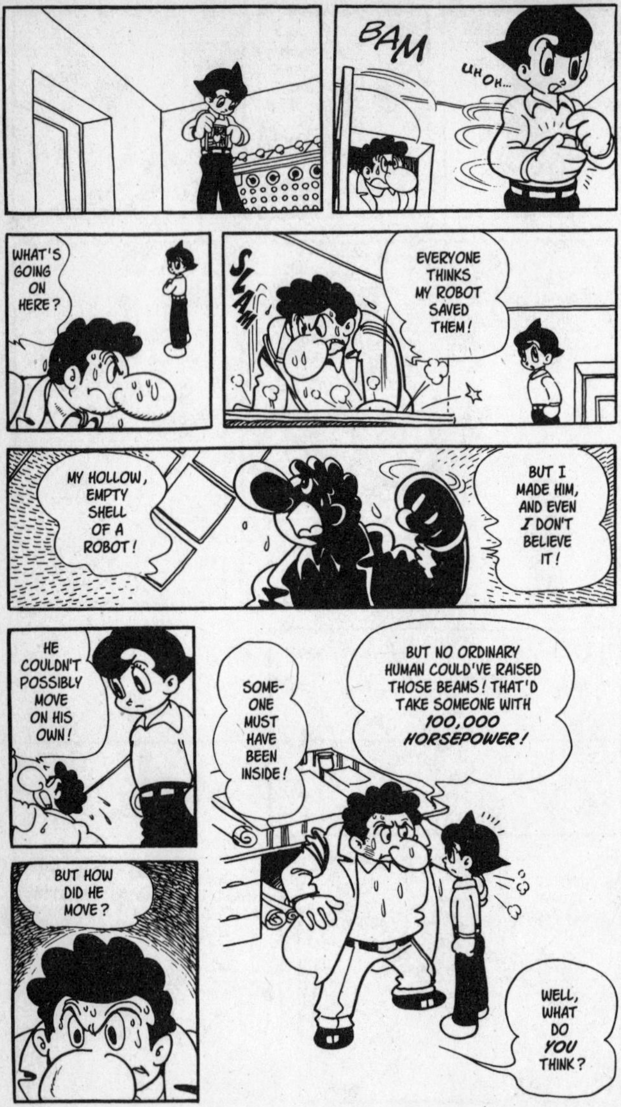
BAM
UH OH...
WHAT'S GOING ON HERE?
SLAM
EVERYONE THINKS MY ROBOT SAVED THEM!
MY HOLLOW, EMPTY SHELL OF A ROBOT!
BUT I MADE HIM, AND EVEN *I* DON'T BELIEVE IT!
HE COULDN'T POSSIBLY MOVE ON HIS OWN!
BUT HOW DID HE MOVE?
SOME-ONE MUST HAVE BEEN INSIDE!
BUT NO ORDINARY HUMAN COULD'VE RAISED THOSE BEAMS! THAT'D TAKE SOMEONE WITH ***100,000 HORSEPOWER!***
WELL, WHAT DO ***YOU*** THINK?

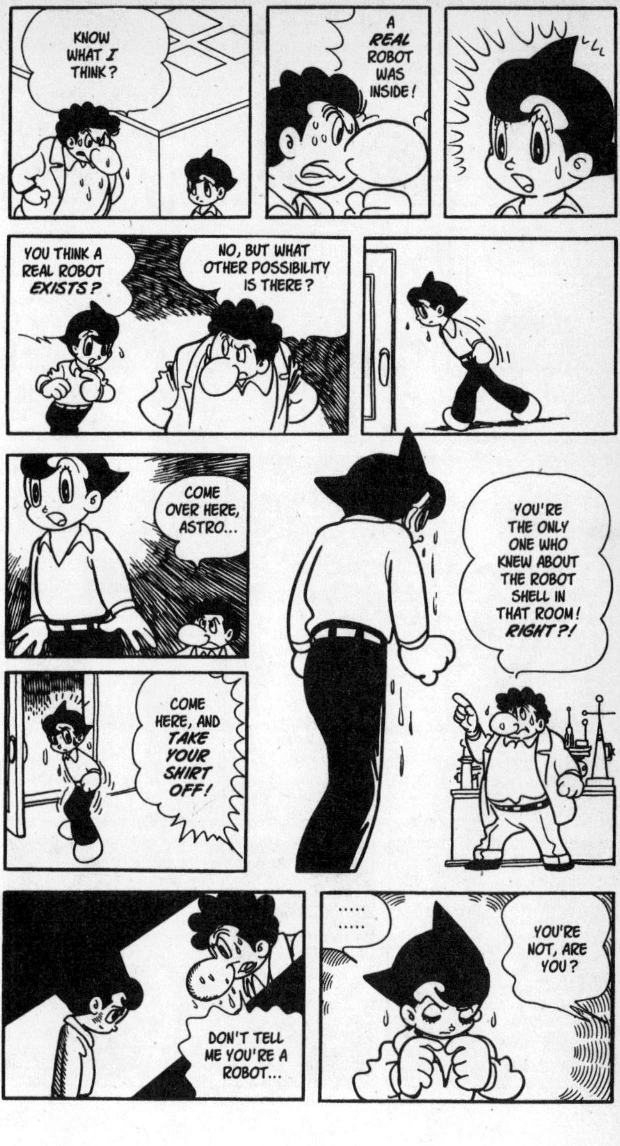
KNOW WHAT *I* THINK?
A *REAL* ROBOT WAS INSIDE!
YOU THINK A REAL ROBOT *EXISTS?*
NO, BUT WHAT OTHER POSSIBILITY IS THERE?
COME OVER HERE, ASTRO...
COME HERE, AND *TAKE YOUR SHIRT OFF!*
YOU'RE THE ONLY ONE WHO KNEW ABOUT THE ROBOT SHELL IN THAT ROOM! *RIGHT?!*
DON'T TELL ME YOU'RE A ROBOT...
.....
.....
YOU'RE NOT, ARE YOU?

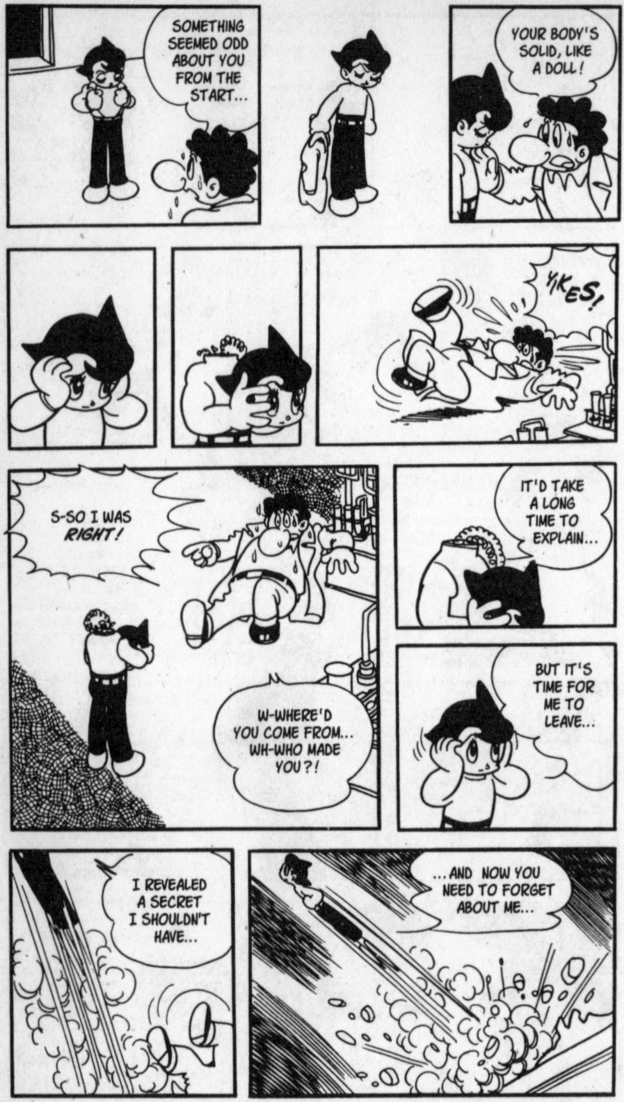
SOMETHING SEEMED ODD ABOUT YOU FROM THE START...
YOUR BODY'S SOLID, LIKE A DOLL!
YIKES!
S-SO I WAS *RIGHT!*
W-WHERE'D YOU COME FROM... WH-WHO MADE YOU?!
IT'D TAKE A LONG TIME TO EXPLAIN...
BUT IT'S TIME FOR ME TO LEAVE...
I REVEALED A SECRET I SHOULDN'T HAVE...
...AND NOW YOU NEED TO FORGET ABOUT ME...

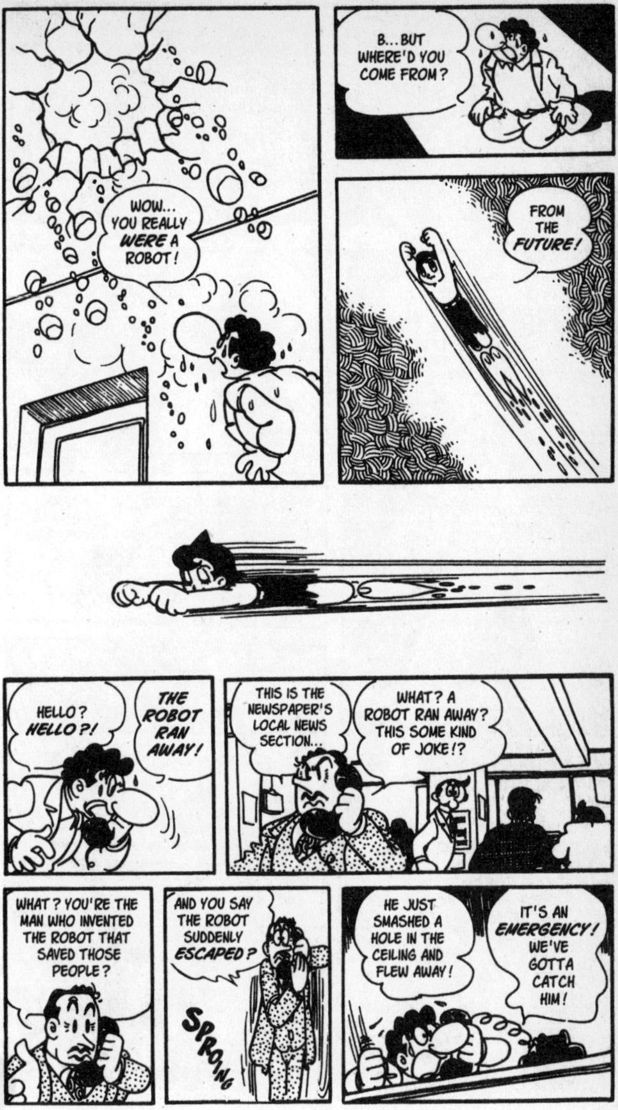
WOW... YOU REALLY *WERE* A ROBOT!
B...BUT WHERE'D YOU COME FROM?
FROM THE *FUTURE!*
HELLO? *HELLO?!*
THE ROBOT RAN AWAY!
THIS IS THE NEWSPAPER'S LOCAL NEWS SECTION...
WHAT? A ROBOT RAN AWAY? THIS SOME KIND OF JOKE!?
WHAT? YOU'RE THE MAN WHO INVENTED THE ROBOT THAT SAVED THOSE PEOPLE?
AND YOU SAY THE ROBOT SUDDENLY *ESCAPED?*
SPROING
HE JUST SMASHED A HOLE IN THE CEILING AND FLEW AWAY!
IT'S AN *EMERGENCY!* WE'VE GOTTA CATCH HIM!

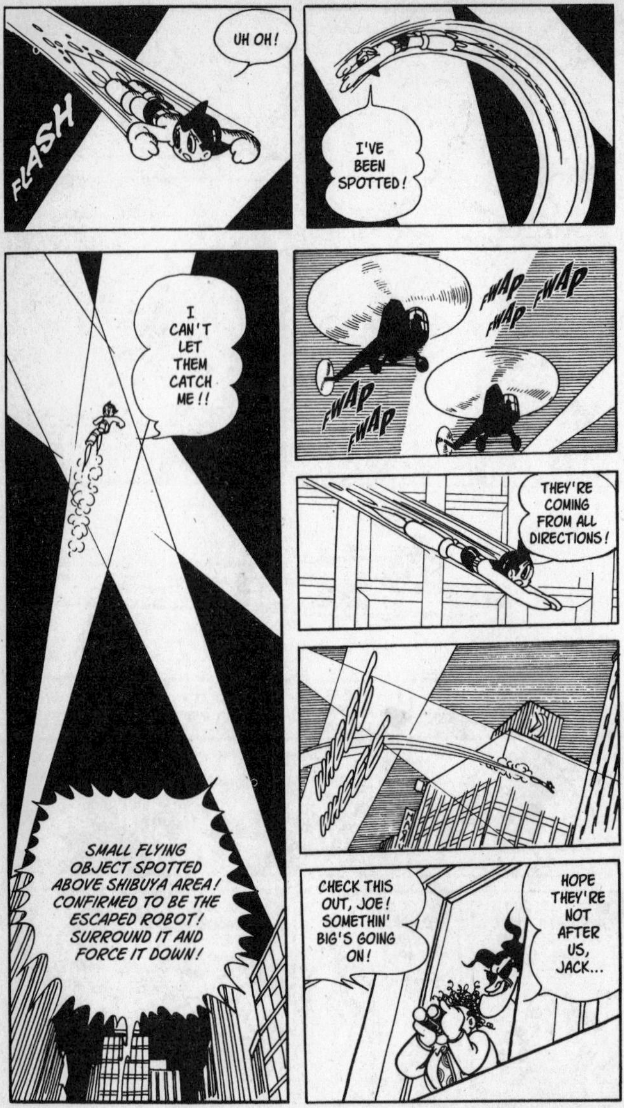
UH OH!
FLASH
I'VE BEEN SPOTTED!
I CAN'T LET THEM CATCH ME!!
SMALL FLYING OBJECT SPOTTED ABOVE SHIBUYA AREA! CONFIRMED TO BE THE ESCAPED ROBOT! SURROUND IT AND FORCE IT DOWN!
FWAP FWAP FWAP
FWAP FWAP
THEY'RE COMING FROM ALL DIRECTIONS!
CHECK THIS OUT, JOE! SOMETHIN' BIG'S GOING ON!
HOPE THEY'RE NOT AFTER US, JACK...

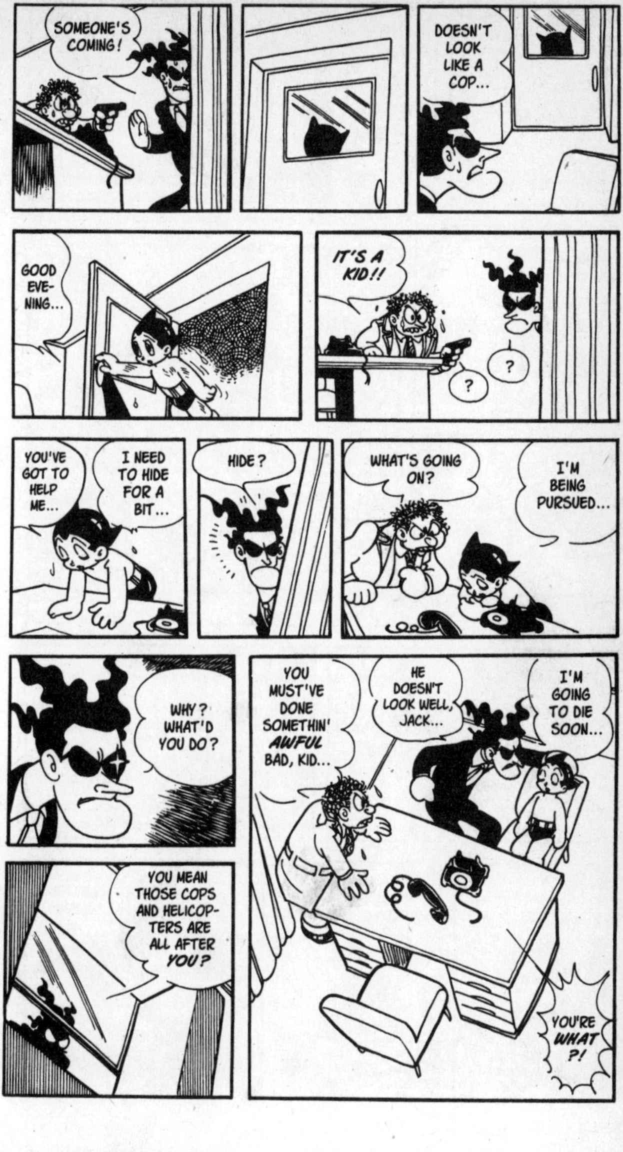
SOMEONE'S COMING!
DOESN'T LOOK LIKE A COP...
GOOD EVE-NING...
IT'S A KID!!
?
?
YOU'VE GOT TO HELP ME...
I NEED TO HIDE FOR A BIT...
HIDE?
WHAT'S GOING ON?
I'M BEING PURSUED...
WHY? WHAT'D YOU DO?
YOU MEAN THOSE COPS AND HELICOP-TERS ARE ALL AFTER YOU?
YOU MUST'VE DONE SOMETHIN' AWFUL BAD, KID...
HE DOESN'T LOOK WELL, JACK...
I'M GOING TO DIE SOON...
YOU'RE WHAT?!

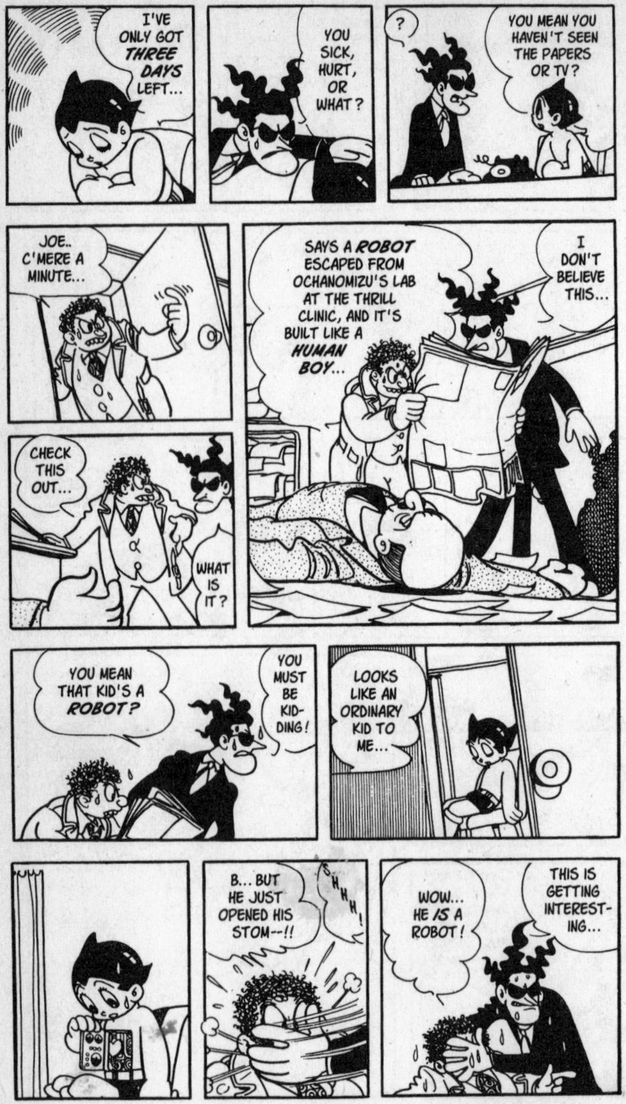
I'VE ONLY GOT THREE DAYS LEFT...
YOU SICK, HURT, OR WHAT?
?
YOU MEAN YOU HAVEN'T SEEN THE PAPERS OR TV?
JOE.. C'MERE A MINUTE...
CHECK THIS OUT...
WHAT IS IT?
SAYS A ROBOT ESCAPED FROM OCHANOMIZU'S LAB AT THE THRILL CLINIC, AND IT'S BUILT LIKE A HUMAN BOY...
I DON'T BELIEVE THIS...
YOU MEAN THAT KID'S A ROBOT?
YOU MUST BE KID-DING!
LOOKS LIKE AN ORDINARY KID TO ME...
B... BUT HE JUST OPENED HIS STOM--!!
SHHH!
WOW... HE IS A ROBOT!
THIS IS GETTING INTEREST-ING...

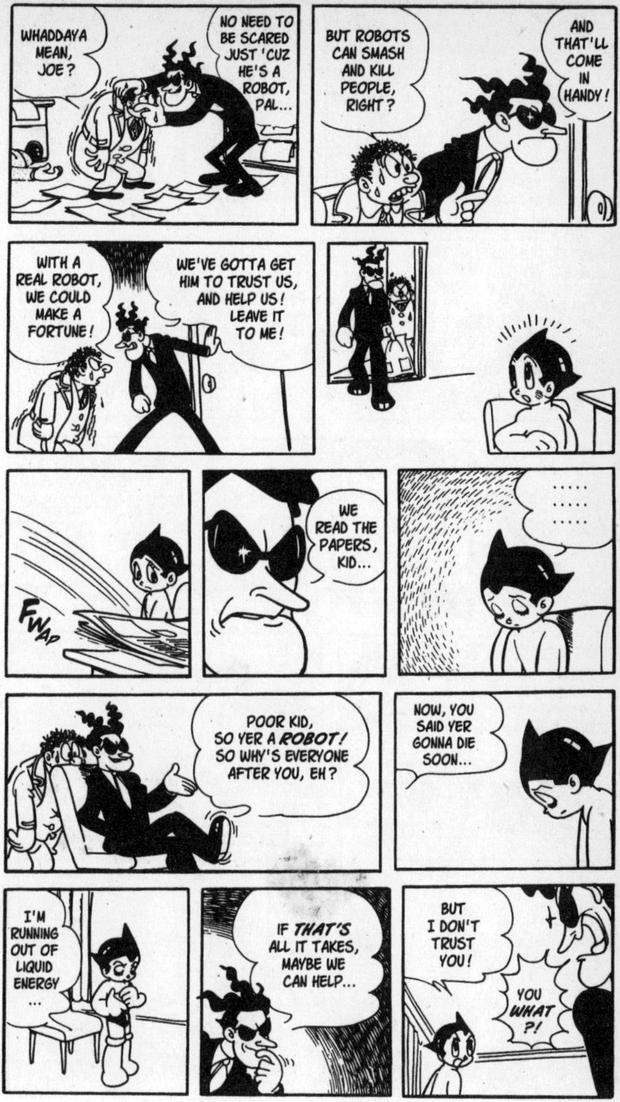
WHADDAYA MEAN, JOE?
NO NEED TO BE SCARED JUST 'CUZ HE'S A ROBOT, PAL...
BUT ROBOTS CAN SMASH AND KILL PEOPLE, RIGHT?
AND THAT'LL COME IN HANDY!
WITH A REAL ROBOT, WE COULD MAKE A FORTUNE!
WE'VE GOTTA GET HIM TO TRUST US, AND HELP US! LEAVE IT TO ME!
FWAP
WE READ THE PAPERS, KID...
....
POOR KID, SO YER A ROBOT! SO WHY'S EVERYONE AFTER YOU, EH?
NOW, YOU SAID YER GONNA DIE SOON...
I'M RUNNING OUT OF LIQUID ENERGY ...
IF THAT'S ALL IT TAKES, MAYBE WE CAN HELP...
BUT I DON'T TRUST YOU!
YOU WHAT?!

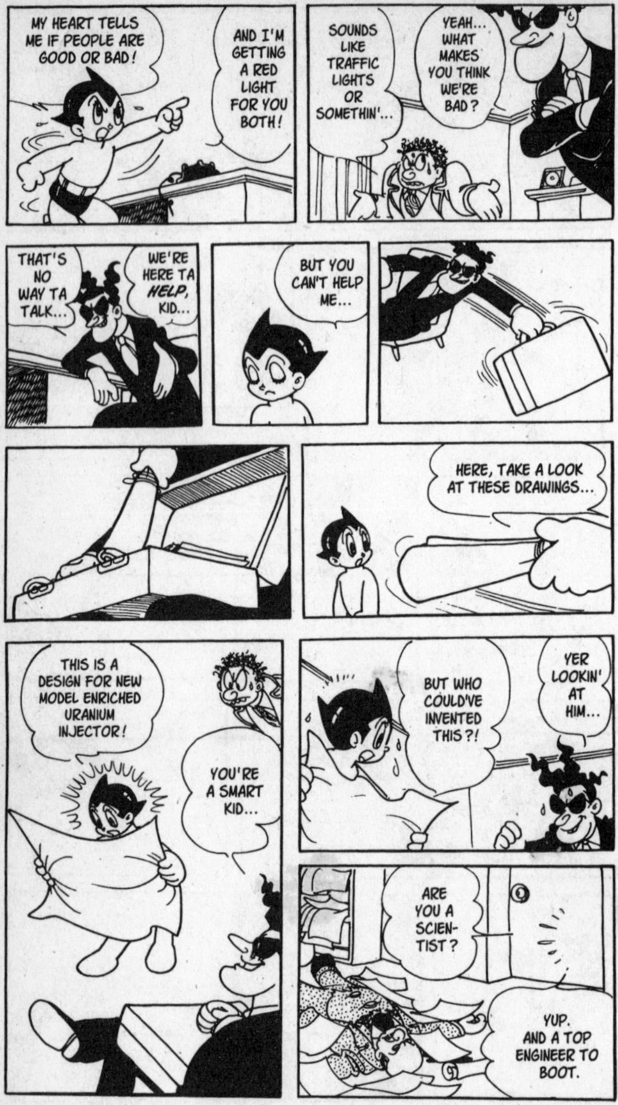
MY HEART TELLS ME IF PEOPLE ARE GOOD OR BAD!
AND I'M GETTING A RED LIGHT FOR YOU BOTH!
SOUNDS LIKE TRAFFIC LIGHTS OR SOMETHIN'...
YEAH... WHAT MAKES YOU THINK WE'RE BAD?
THAT'S NO WAY TA TALK...
WE'RE HERE TA *HELP*, KID...
BUT YOU CAN'T HELP ME...
HERE, TAKE A LOOK AT THESE DRAWINGS...
THIS IS A DESIGN FOR NEW MODEL ENRICHED URANIUM INJECTOR!
YOU'RE A SMART KID...
BUT WHO COULD'VE INVENTED THIS?!
YER LOOKIN' AT HIM...
ARE YOU A SCIENTIST?
YUP. AND A TOP ENGINEER TO BOOT.

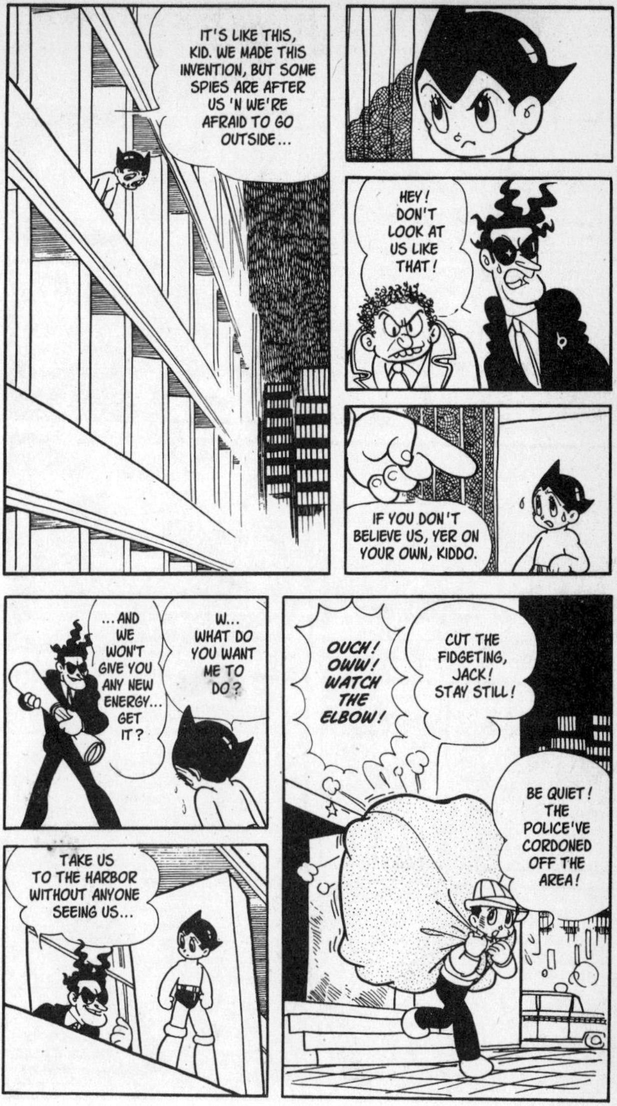

IT'S LIKE THIS, KID. WE MADE THIS INVENTION, BUT SOME SPIES ARE AFTER US 'N WE'RE AFRAID TO GO OUTSIDE...
HEY! DON'T LOOK AT US LIKE THAT!
IF YOU DON'T BELIEVE US, YER ON YOUR OWN, KIDDO.
...AND WE WON'T GIVE YOU ANY NEW ENERGY... GET IT?
W... WHAT DO YOU WANT ME TO DO?
TAKE US TO THE HARBOR WITHOUT ANYONE SEEING US...
OUCH! OWW! WATCH THE ELBOW!
CUT THE FIDGETING, JACK! STAY STILL!
BE QUIET! THE POLICE'VE CORDONED OFF THE AREA!

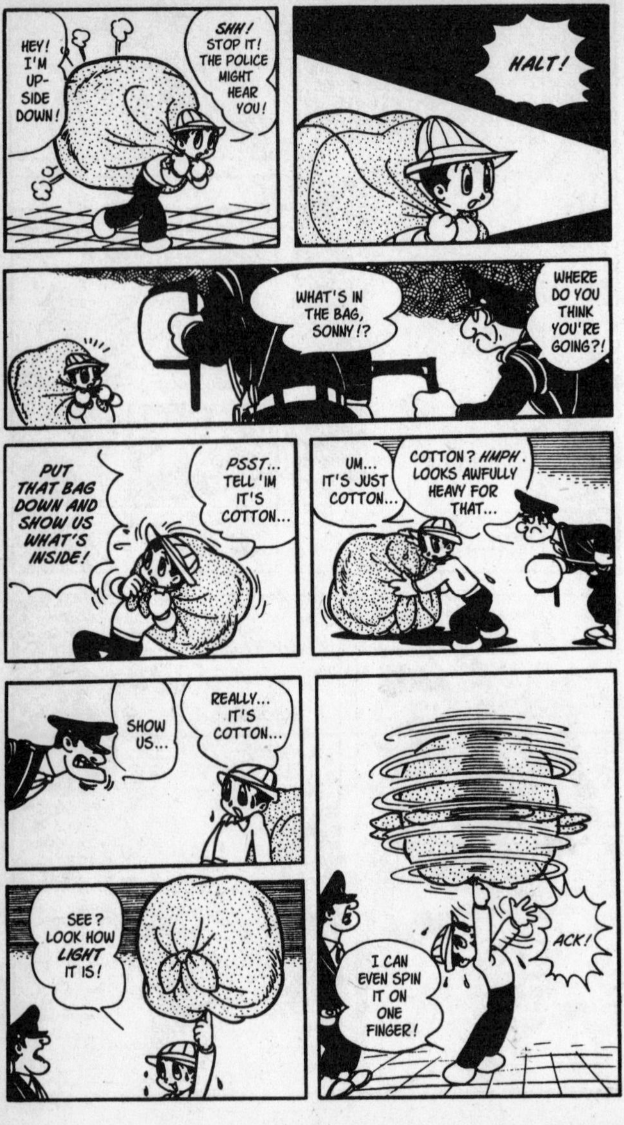
HEY! I'M UP-SIDE DOWN!
SHH! STOP IT! THE POLICE MIGHT HEAR YOU!
HALT!
WHAT'S IN THE BAG, SONNY!?
WHERE DO YOU THINK YOU'RE GOING?!
PUT THAT BAG DOWN AND SHOW US WHAT'S INSIDE!
PSST... TELL 'IM IT'S COTTON...
UM... IT'S JUST COTTON...
COTTON? HMPH. LOOKS AWFULLY HEAVY FOR THAT...
SHOW US...
REALLY... IT'S COTTON...
SEE? LOOK HOW LIGHT IT IS!
I CAN EVEN SPIN IT ON ONE FINGER!
ACK!

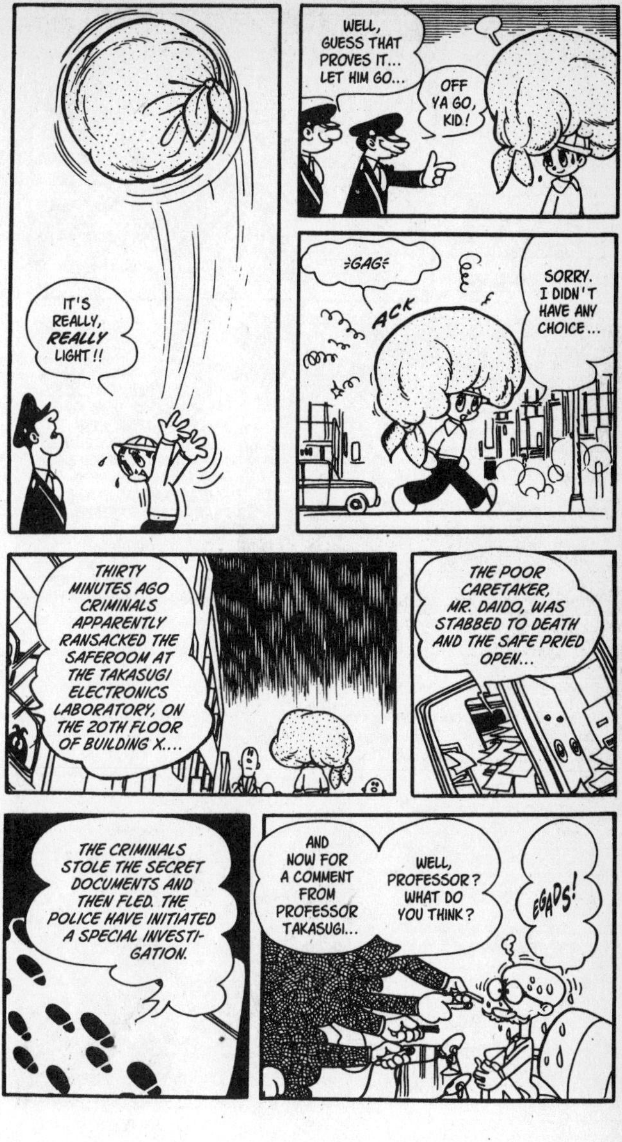
IT'S REALLY, **REALLY** LIGHT!!
WELL, GUESS THAT PROVES IT... LET HIM GO...
OFF YA GO, KID!
⚟GAG⚞
ACK
SORRY. I DIDN'T HAVE ANY CHOICE...
THIRTY MINUTES AGO CRIMINALS APPARENTLY RANSACKED THE SAFEROOM AT THE TAKASUGI ELECTRONICS LABORATORY, ON THE 20TH FLOOR OF BUILDING X....
THE POOR CARETAKER, MR. DAIDO, WAS STABBED TO DEATH AND THE SAFE PRIED OPEN...
THE CRIMINALS STOLE THE SECRET DOCUMENTS AND THEN FLED. THE POLICE HAVE INITIATED A SPECIAL INVESTI-GATION.
AND NOW FOR A COMMENT FROM PROFESSOR TAKASUGI...
WELL, PROFESSOR? WHAT DO YOU THINK?
EGADS!

THE CRUSH OF REPORTERS BEGAN QUESTIONING THE POOR SCIENTIST.

"AND WHAT WERE THE SECRET DOCUMENTS, PROFESSOR?"

"*UM, ER,* THEY WERE PLANS FOR A SPECIAL ENERGY TUBE THAT WE DEVELOPED..."

"AN ENERGY TUBE?"

"WELL, SIMPLY PUT, IT'S, *EM,* A DEVICE USED TO INJECT ENERGY INTO ATOMIC POWERED ENGINES. IF ATOMIC POWERED CARS ARE EVER DEVELOPED, FOR EXAMPLE, IT'D BE AN IDEAL WAY TO REFUEL THEM."

"SO IT COULD ALSO BE USED FOR ATOMIC SUBMARINES AND MILITARY WEAPONS, RIGHT?"

"IT CERTAINLY COULD, WHICH IS WHY WE WANTED TO KEEP IT SECRET UNTIL THE TIME CAME WHEN IT COULD ONLY BE USED FOR PEACEFUL PURPOSES. NOW THAT IT'S BEEN STOLEN, THERE IS A REAL DANGER THAT IT MIGHT BE USED FOR MILITARY PURPOSES..."

MEANWHILE, IN A RUN-DOWN BUILDING BY THE HARBOR, IN THE SHINAGAWA AREA OF TOKYO...

"WHERE ARE YOU JOE? I'VE BEEN WAITING FOR YOUR CONTACT! WE WERE AFRAID YOU'D BEEN CAUGHT!!"

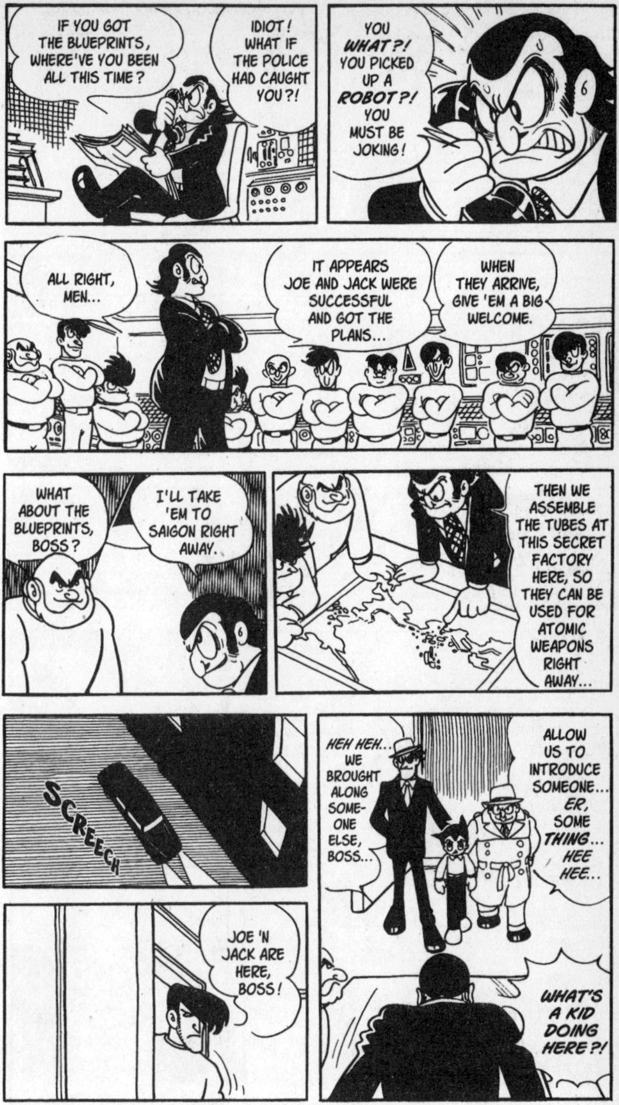
IF YOU GOT THE BLUEPRINTS, WHERE'VE YOU BEEN ALL THIS TIME?
IDIOT! WHAT IF THE POLICE HAD CAUGHT YOU?!
YOU WHAT?! YOU PICKED UP A ROBOT?! YOU MUST BE JOKING!
ALL RIGHT, MEN...
IT APPEARS JOE AND JACK WERE SUCCESSFUL AND GOT THE PLANS...
WHEN THEY ARRIVE, GIVE 'EM A BIG WELCOME.
WHAT ABOUT THE BLUEPRINTS, BOSS?
I'LL TAKE 'EM TO SAIGON RIGHT AWAY.
THEN WE ASSEMBLE THE TUBES AT THIS SECRET FACTORY HERE, SO THEY CAN BE USED FOR ATOMIC WEAPONS RIGHT AWAY...
SCREEECH
JOE 'N JACK ARE HERE, BOSS!
HEH HEH... WE BROUGHT ALONG SOME-ONE ELSE, BOSS...
ALLOW US TO INTRODUCE SOMEONE... ER, SOME THING... HEE HEE...
WHAT'S A KID DOING HERE?!

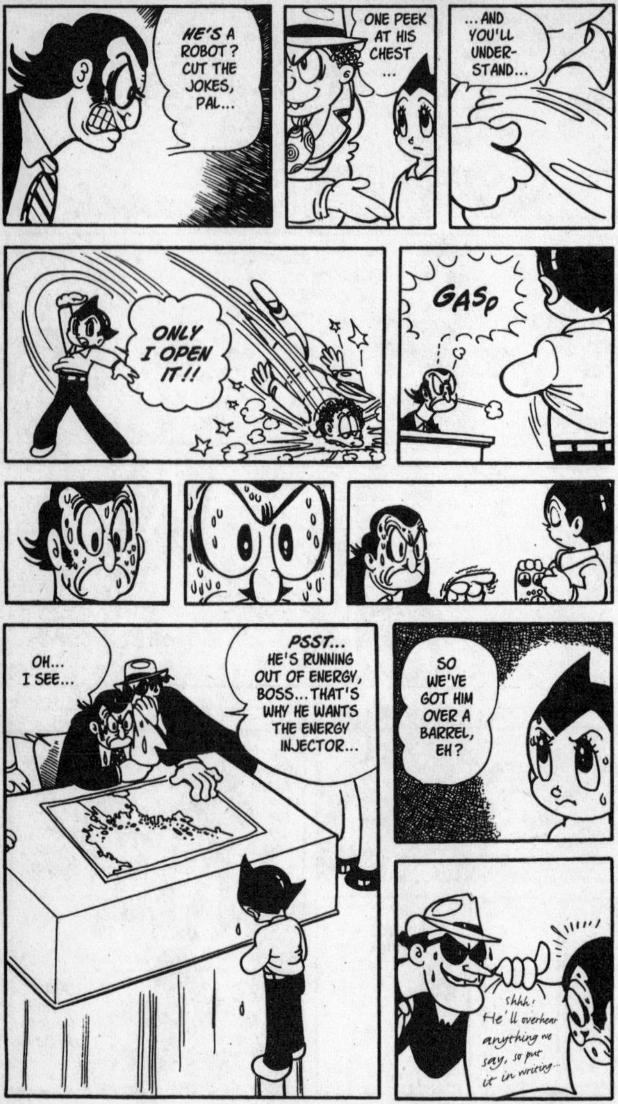
HE'S A ROBOT? CUT THE JOKES, PAL...
ONE PEEK AT HIS CHEST ...
...AND YOU'LL UNDER-STAND...
ONLY I OPEN IT!!
GASP
OH... I SEE...
PSST... HE'S RUNNING OUT OF ENERGY, BOSS... THAT'S WHY HE WANTS THE ENERGY INJECTOR...
SO WE'VE GOT HIM OVER A BARREL, EH?
Shhh! He'll overhear anything we say, so put it in writing...

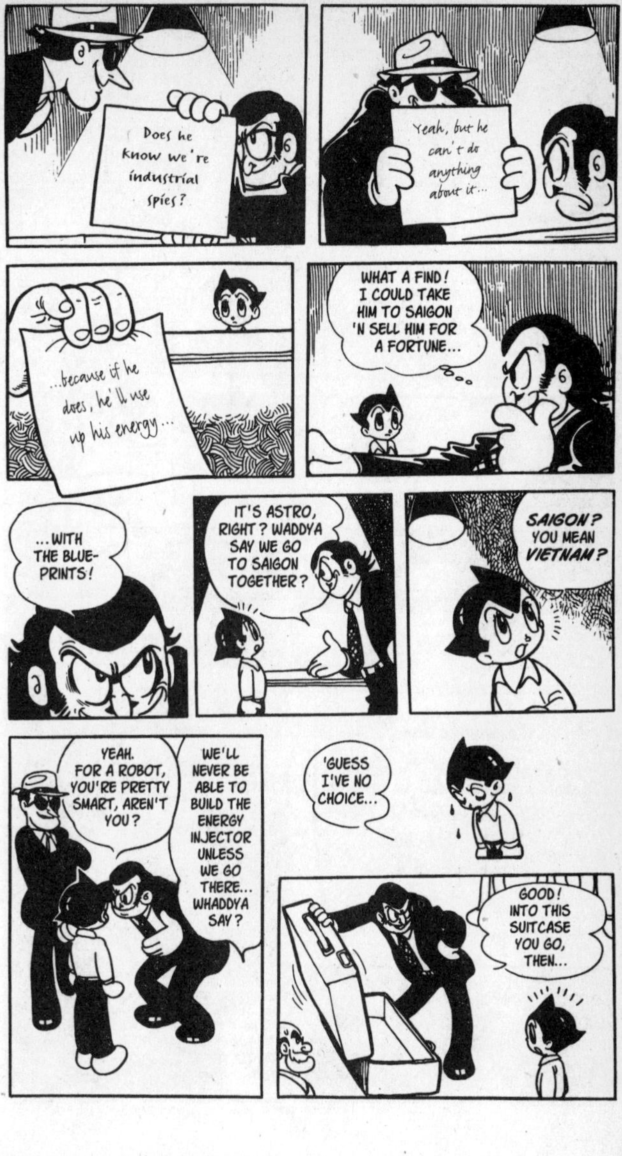
Does he know we're industrial spies?
Yeah, but he can't do anything about it...
...because if he does, he'll use up his energy...
WHAT A FIND! I COULD TAKE HIM TO SAIGON 'N SELL HIM FOR A FORTUNE...
...WITH THE BLUE-PRINTS!
IT'S ASTRO, RIGHT? WADDYA SAY WE GO TO SAIGON TOGETHER?
SAIGON? YOU MEAN VIETNAM?
YEAH. FOR A ROBOT, YOU'RE PRETTY SMART, AREN'T YOU?
WE'LL NEVER BE ABLE TO BUILD THE ENERGY INJECTOR UNLESS WE GO THERE... WHADDYA SAY?
'GUESS I'VE NO CHOICE...
GOOD! INTO THIS SUITCASE YOU GO, THEN...

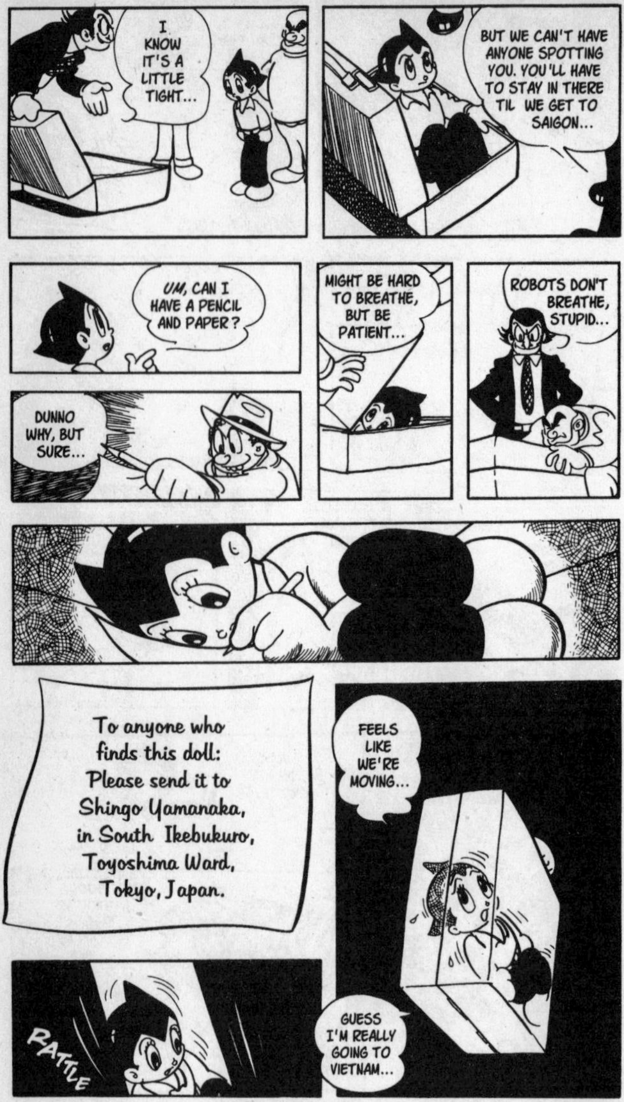
I KNOW IT'S A LITTLE TIGHT...
BUT WE CAN'T HAVE ANYONE SPOTTING YOU. YOU'LL HAVE TO STAY IN THERE TIL WE GET TO SAIGON...
UM, CAN I HAVE A PENCIL AND PAPER?
DUNNO WHY, BUT SURE...
MIGHT BE HARD TO BREATHE, BUT BE PATIENT...
ROBOTS DON'T BREATHE, STUPID...
To anyone who finds this doll: Please send it to Shingo Yamanaka, in South Ikebukuro, Toyoshima Ward, Tokyo, Japan.
FEELS LIKE WE'RE MOVING...
RATTLE
GUESS I'M REALLY GOING TO VIETNAM...

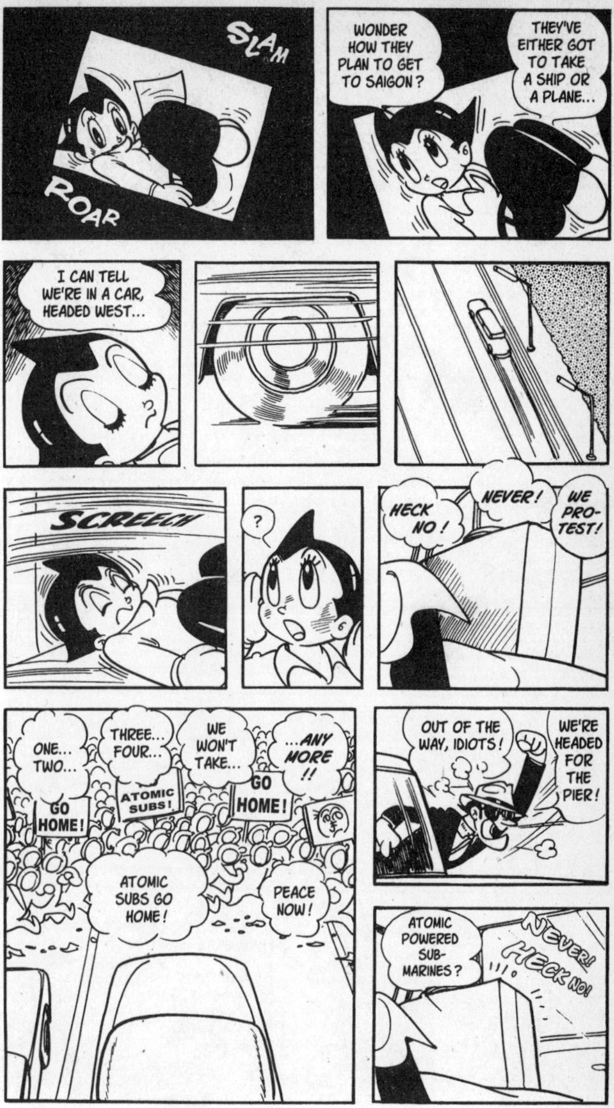
SLAM
ROAR
WONDER HOW THEY PLAN TO GET TO SAIGON?
THEY'VE EITHER GOT TO TAKE A SHIP OR A PLANE...
I CAN TELL WE'RE IN A CAR, HEADED WEST...
SCREECH
?
HECK NO!
NEVER!
WE PRO-TEST!
ONE... TWO...
THREE... FOUR...
WE WON'T TAKE...
...ANY MORE !!
GO HOME!
ATOMIC SUBS!
GO HOME!
ATOMIC SUBS GO HOME!
PEACE NOW!
OUT OF THE WAY, IDIOTS!
WE'RE HEADED FOR THE PIER!
ATOMIC POWERED SUB-MARINES?
NEVER!
HECK NO!

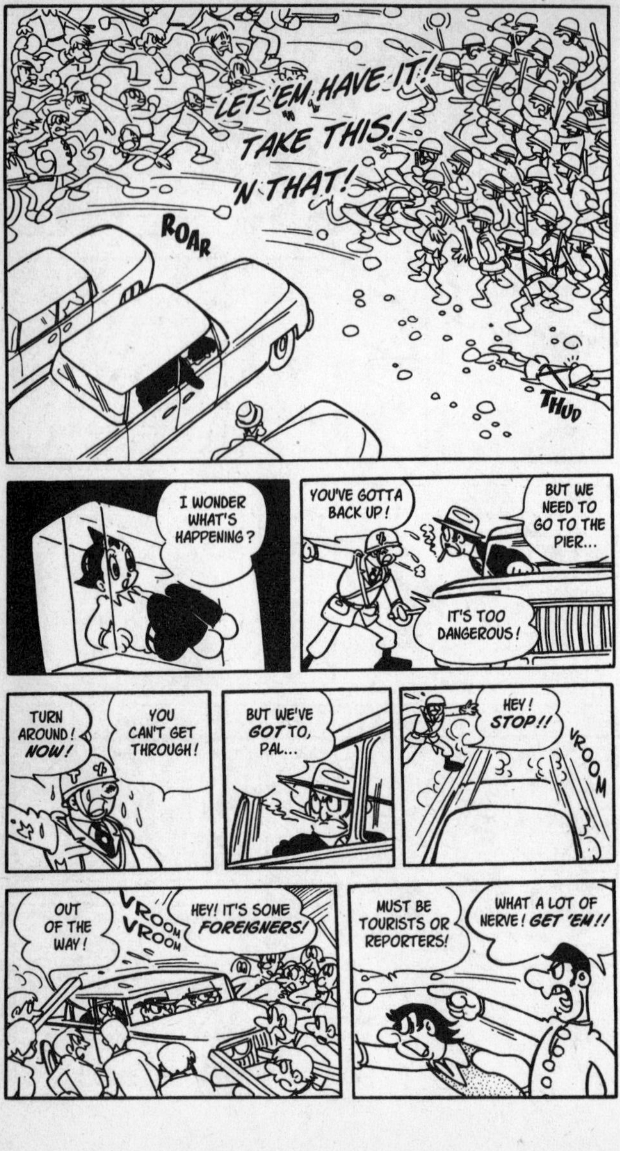
LET 'EM HAVE IT!
TAKE THIS!
'N THAT!
ROAR
THUD
I WONDER WHAT'S HAPPENING?
YOU'VE GOTTA BACK UP!
BUT WE NEED TO GO TO THE PIER...
IT'S TOO DANGEROUS!
TURN AROUND! NOW!
YOU CAN'T GET THROUGH!
BUT WE'VE GOT TO, PAL...
HEY! STOP!!
VROOOM
OUT OF THE WAY!
VROOM VROOM
HEY! IT'S SOME FOREIGNERS!
MUST BE TOURISTS OR REPORTERS!
WHAT A LOT OF NERVE! GET 'EM!!

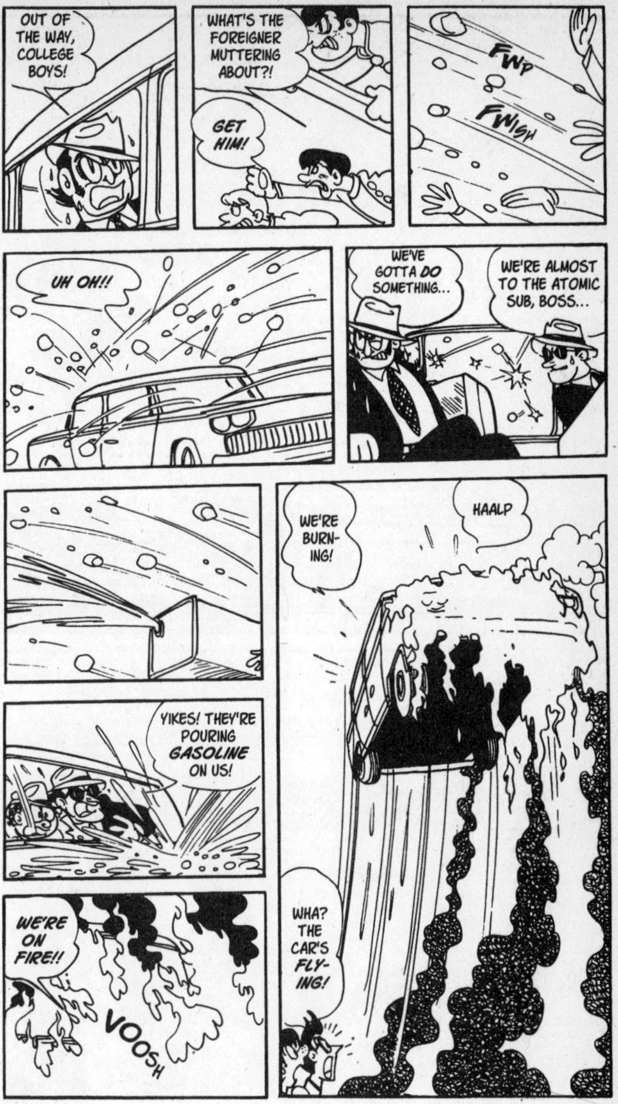
OUT OF THE WAY, COLLEGE BOYS!
WHAT'S THE FOREIGNER MUTTERING ABOUT?!
GET HIM!
FWP
FWISH
UH OH!!
WE'VE GOTTA DO SOMETHING...
WE'RE ALMOST TO THE ATOMIC SUB, BOSS...
WE'RE BURNING!
HAALP
YIKES! THEY'RE POURING GASOLINE ON US!
WE'RE ON FIRE!!
VOOSH
WHA? THE CAR'S FLYING!

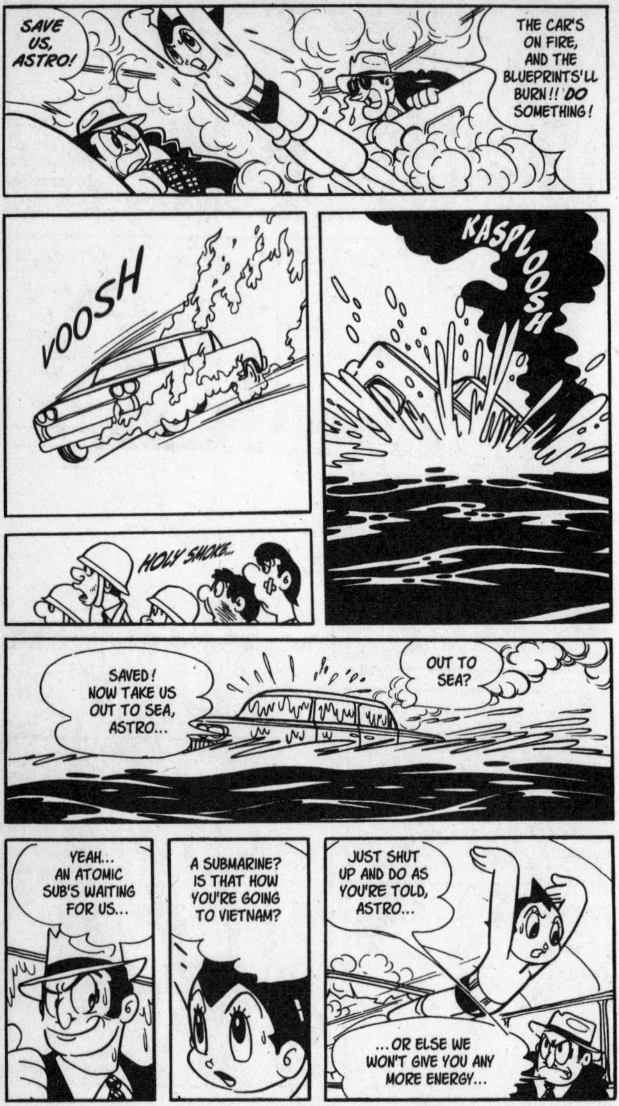
SAVE US, ASTRO!
THE CAR'S ON FIRE, AND THE BLUEPRINTS'LL BURN!! DO SOMETHING!
VOOSH
KASPLOOSH
HOLY SMOKE...
SAVED! NOW TAKE US OUT TO SEA, ASTRO...
OUT TO SEA?
YEAH... AN ATOMIC SUB'S WAITING FOR US...
A SUBMARINE? IS THAT HOW YOU'RE GOING TO VIETNAM?
JUST SHUT UP AND DO AS YOU'RE TOLD, ASTRO...
...OR ELSE WE WON'T GIVE YOU ANY MORE ENERGY...

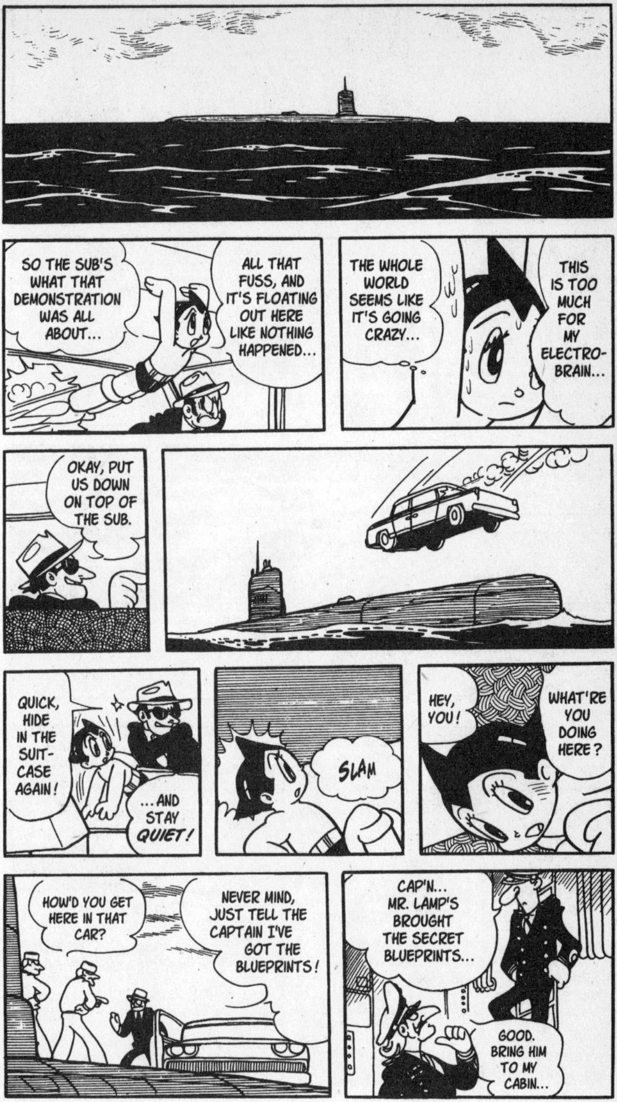
SO THE SUB'S WHAT THAT DEMONSTRATION WAS ALL ABOUT...
ALL THAT FUSS, AND IT'S FLOATING OUT HERE LIKE NOTHING HAPPENED...
THE WHOLE WORLD SEEMS LIKE IT'S GOING CRAZY...
THIS IS TOO MUCH FOR MY ELECTRO-BRAIN...
OKAY, PUT US DOWN ON TOP OF THE SUB.
QUICK, HIDE IN THE SUIT-CASE AGAIN!
...AND STAY QUIET!
SLAM
HEY, YOU!
WHAT'RE YOU DOING HERE?
HOW'D YOU GET HERE IN THAT CAR?
NEVER MIND, JUST TELL THE CAPTAIN I'VE GOT THE BLUEPRINTS!
CAP'N... MR. LAMP'S BROUGHT THE SECRET BLUEPRINTS...
GOOD. BRING HIM TO MY CABIN...

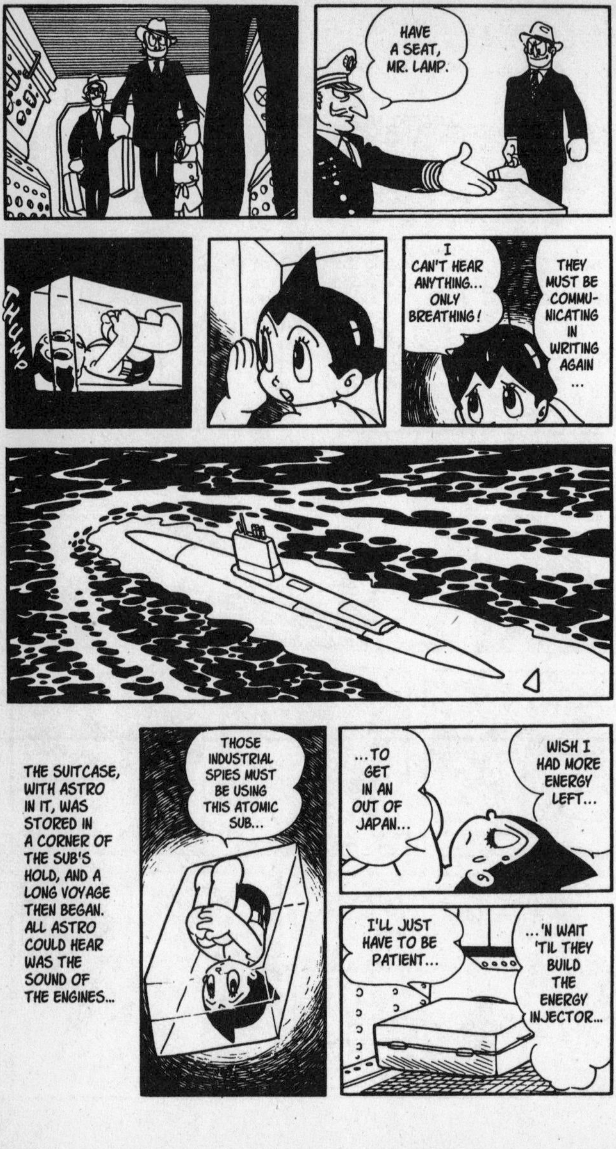
HAVE A SEAT, MR. LAMP.
THUMP
I CAN'T HEAR ANYTHING... ONLY BREATHING!
THEY MUST BE COMMUNICATING IN WRITING AGAIN ...
THE SUITCASE, WITH ASTRO IN IT, WAS STORED IN A CORNER OF THE SUB'S HOLD, AND A LONG VOYAGE THEN BEGAN. ALL ASTRO COULD HEAR WAS THE SOUND OF THE ENGINES...
THOSE INDUSTRIAL SPIES MUST BE USING THIS ATOMIC SUB...
...TO GET IN AN OUT OF JAPAN...
WISH I HAD MORE ENERGY LEFT...
I'LL JUST HAVE TO BE PATIENT...
...'N WAIT 'TIL THEY BUILD THE ENERGY INJECTOR...

THE ANGEL OF VIETNAM

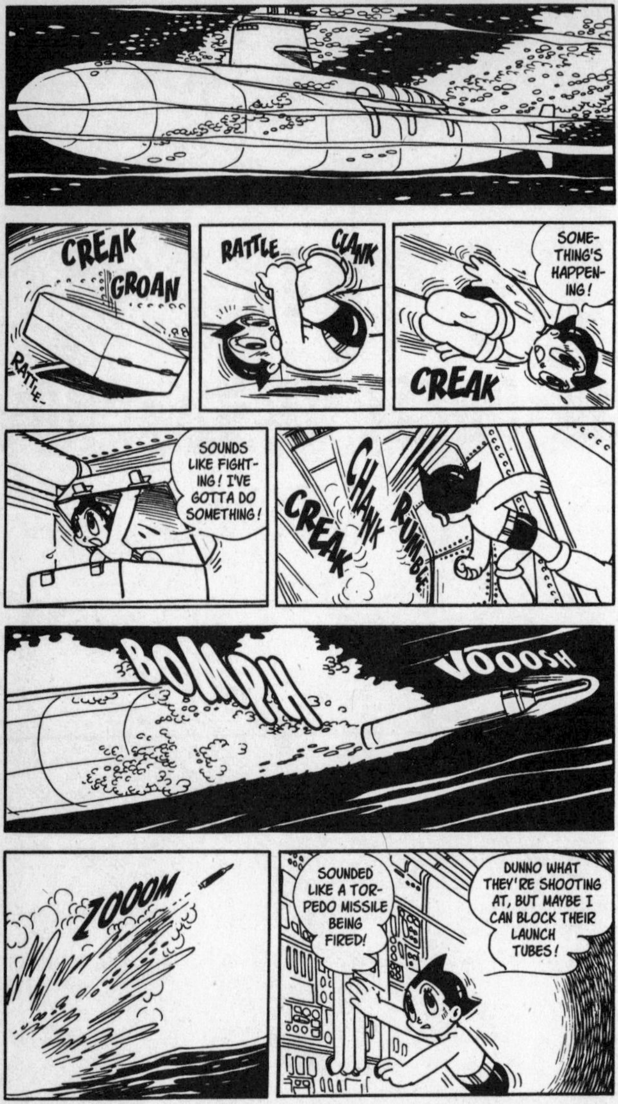

CREAK
GROAN
RATTLE-
RATTLE
CLANK
SOME-THING'S HAPPEN-ING!
CREAK
SOUNDS LIKE FIGHT-ING! I'VE GOTTA DO SOMETHING!
CREAK
CHANK
RUMBLE
BOMPH
VOOOSH
ZOOOM
SOUNDED LIKE A TOR-PEDO MISSILE BEING FIRED!
DUNNO WHAT THEY'RE SHOOTING AT, BUT MAYBE I CAN BLOCK THEIR LAUNCH TUBES!

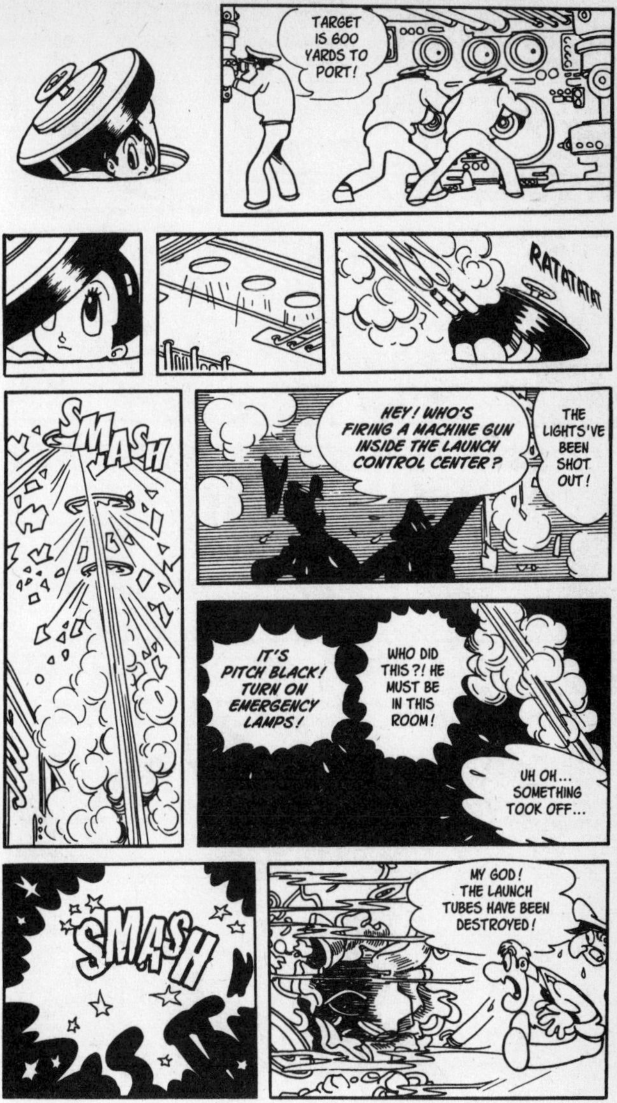
TARGET IS 600 YARDS TO PORT!
RATATATAT
SMASH
HEY! WHO'S FIRING A MACHINE GUN INSIDE THE LAUNCH CONTROL CENTER?
THE LIGHTS'VE BEEN SHOT OUT!
IT'S PITCH BLACK! TURN ON EMERGENCY LAMPS!
WHO DID THIS?! HE MUST BE IN THIS ROOM!
UH OH... SOMETHING TOOK OFF...
SMASH
MY GOD! THE LAUNCH TUBES HAVE BEEN DESTROYED!

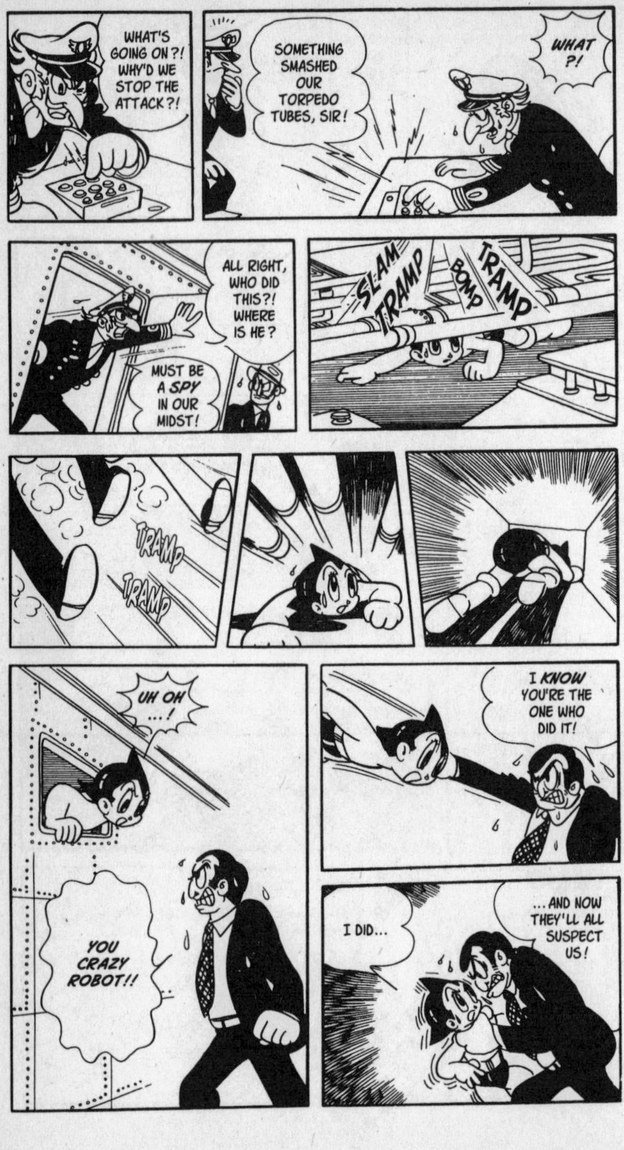
WHAT'S GOING ON?! WHY'D WE STOP THE ATTACK?!
SOMETHING SMASHED OUR TORPEDO TUBES, SIR!
WHAT ?!
ALL RIGHT, WHO DID THIS?! WHERE IS HE?
MUST BE A SPY IN OUR MIDST!
SLAM
TRAMP
BOMP
TRAMP
TRAMP
TRAMP
UH OH ...!
YOU CRAZY ROBOT!!
I KNOW YOU'RE THE ONE WHO DID IT!
I DID...
...AND NOW THEY'LL ALL SUSPECT US!

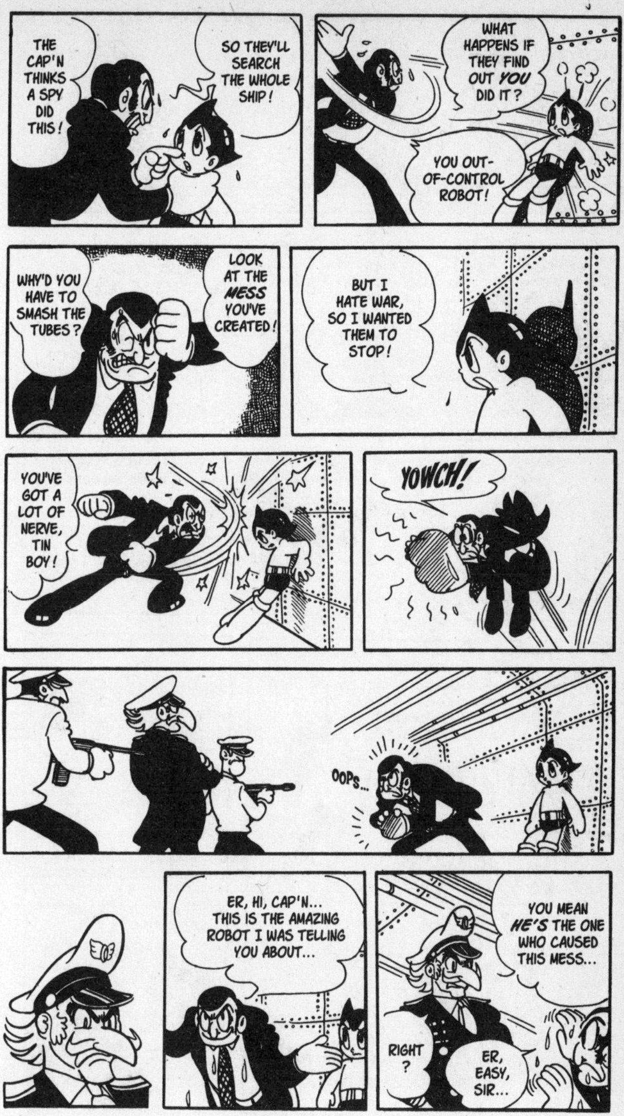
THE CAP'N THINKS A SPY DID THIS!
SO THEY'LL SEARCH THE WHOLE SHIP!
WHAT HAPPENS IF THEY FIND OUT *YOU* DID IT?
YOU OUT-OF-CONTROL ROBOT!
WHY'D YOU HAVE TO SMASH THE TUBES?
LOOK AT THE *MESS* YOU'VE CREATED!
BUT I HATE WAR, SO I WANTED THEM TO STOP!
YOU'VE GOT A LOT OF NERVE, TIN BOY!
YOWCH!
OOPS...
ER, HI, CAP'N... THIS IS THE AMAZING ROBOT I WAS TELLING YOU ABOUT...
YOU MEAN *HE'S* THE ONE WHO CAUSED THIS MESS...
RIGHT?
ER, EASY, SIR...

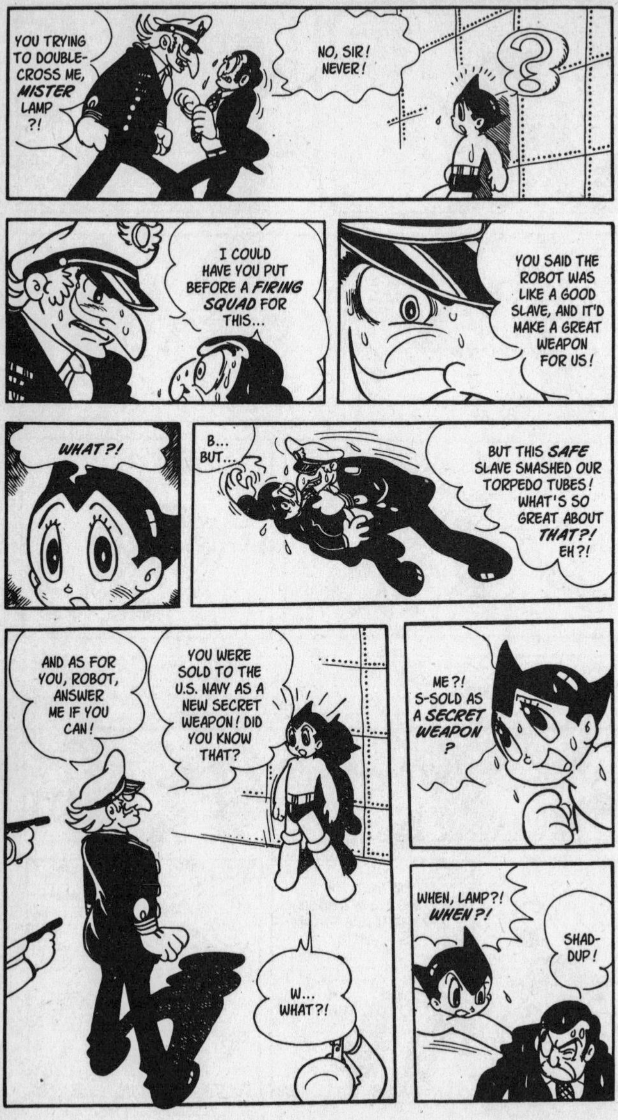
YOU TRYING TO DOUBLE-CROSS ME, MISTER LAMP ?!
NO, SIR! NEVER!
?
I COULD HAVE YOU PUT BEFORE A FIRING SQUAD FOR THIS...
YOU SAID THE ROBOT WAS LIKE A GOOD SLAVE, AND IT'D MAKE A GREAT WEAPON FOR US!
WHAT?!
B... BUT...
BUT THIS SAFE SLAVE SMASHED OUR TORPEDO TUBES! WHAT'S SO GREAT ABOUT THAT?! EH?!
AND AS FOR YOU, ROBOT, ANSWER ME IF YOU CAN!
YOU WERE SOLD TO THE U.S. NAVY AS A NEW SECRET WEAPON! DID YOU KNOW THAT?
W... WHAT?!
ME?! S-SOLD AS A SECRET WEAPON ?
WHEN, LAMP?! WHEN?!
SHAD-DUP!

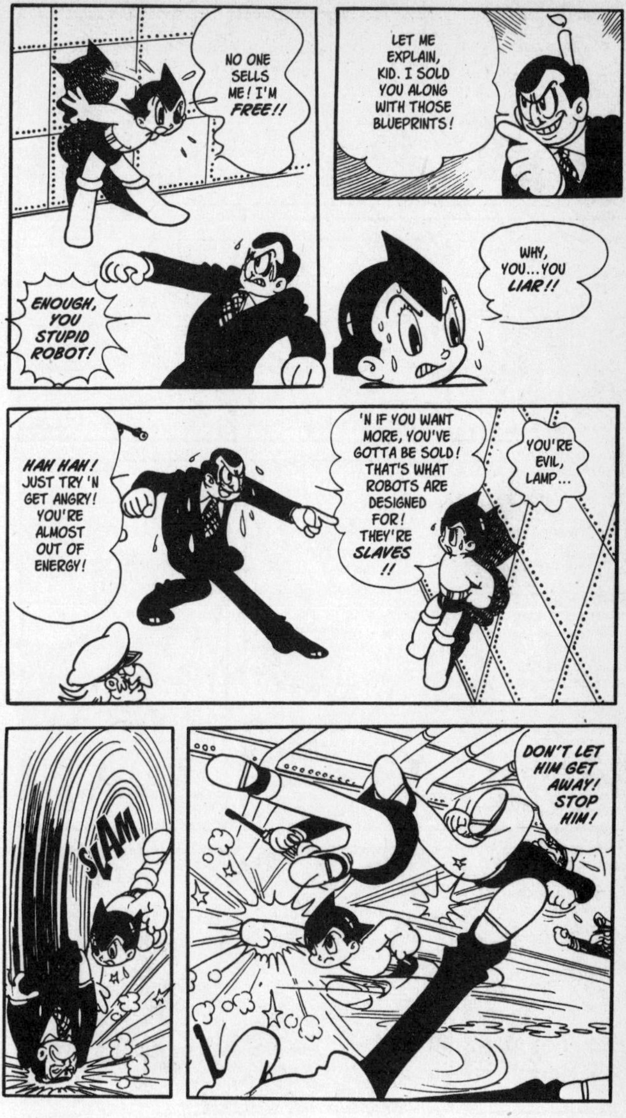
NO ONE SELLS ME! I'M FREE!!
LET ME EXPLAIN, KID. I SOLD YOU ALONG WITH THOSE BLUEPRINTS!
ENOUGH, YOU STUPID ROBOT!
WHY, YOU...YOU LIAR!!
HAH HAH! JUST TRY 'N GET ANGRY! YOU'RE ALMOST OUT OF ENERGY!
'N IF YOU WANT MORE, YOU'VE GOTTA BE SOLD! THAT'S WHAT ROBOTS ARE DESIGNED FOR! THEY'RE SLAVES!!
YOU'RE EVIL, LAMP...
SLAM
DON'T LET HIM GET AWAY! STOP HIM!

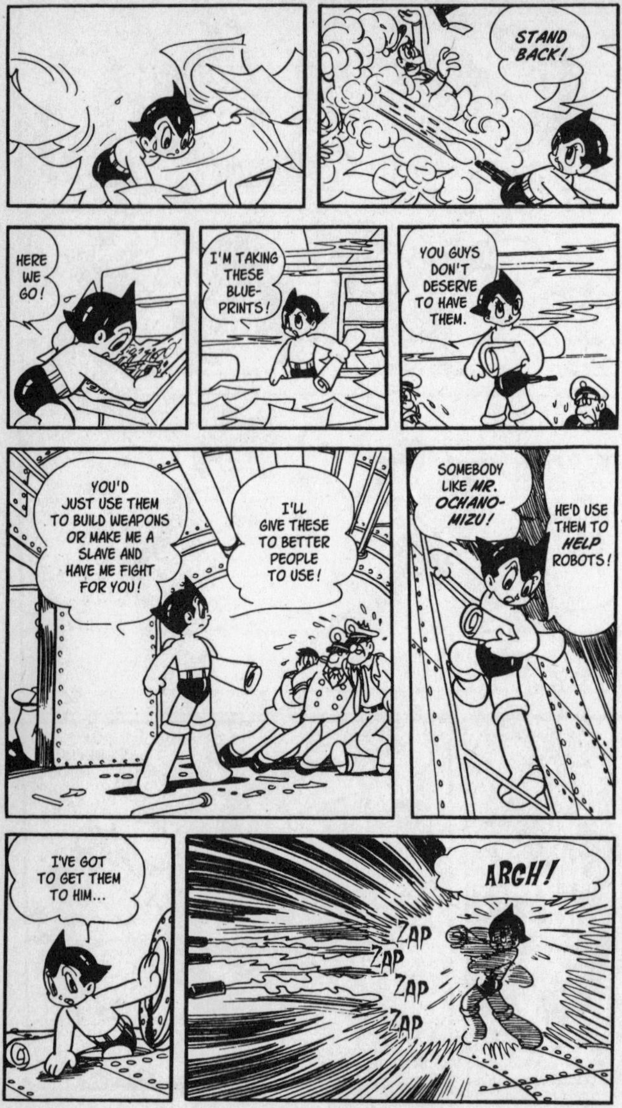
STAND BACK!
HERE WE GO!
I'M TAKING THESE BLUE-PRINTS!
YOU GUYS DON'T DESERVE TO HAVE THEM.
YOU'D JUST USE THEM TO BUILD WEAPONS OR MAKE ME A SLAVE AND HAVE ME FIGHT FOR YOU!
I'LL GIVE THESE TO BETTER PEOPLE TO USE!
SOMEBODY LIKE MR. OCHANO-MIZU!
HE'D USE THEM TO HELP ROBOTS!
I'VE GOT TO GET THEM TO HIM...
ARGH!
ZAP
ZAP
ZAP
ZAP

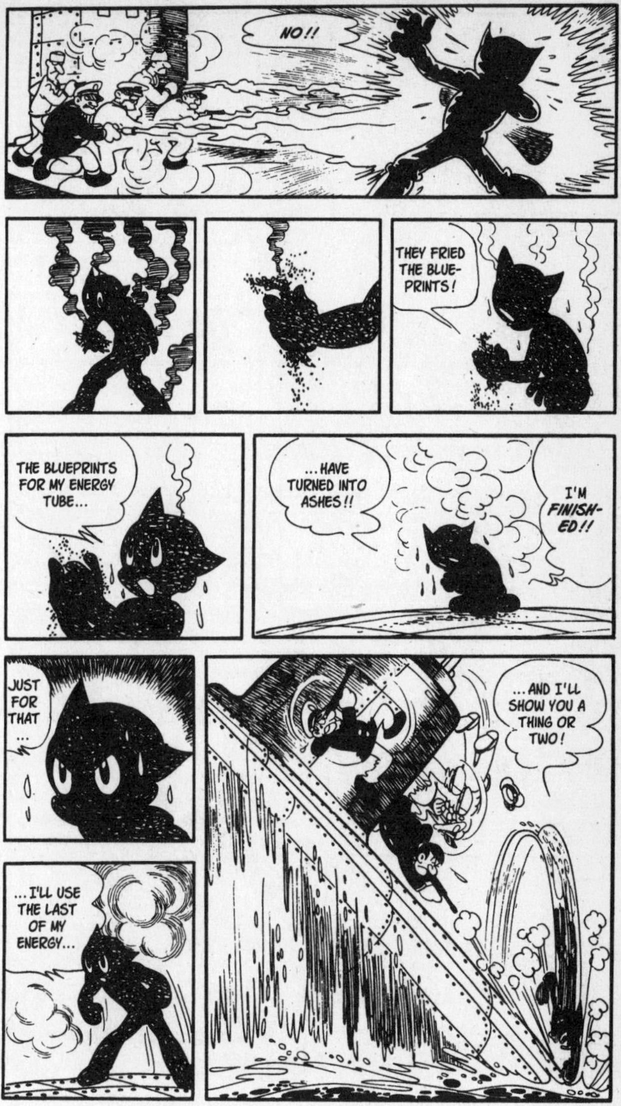
NO!!
THEY FRIED THE BLUE-PRINTS!
THE BLUEPRINTS FOR MY ENERGY TUBE...
...HAVE TURNED INTO ASHES!!
I'M FINISH-ED!!
JUST FOR THAT ...
...I'LL USE THE LAST OF MY ENERGY...
...AND I'LL SHOW YOU A THING OR TWO!

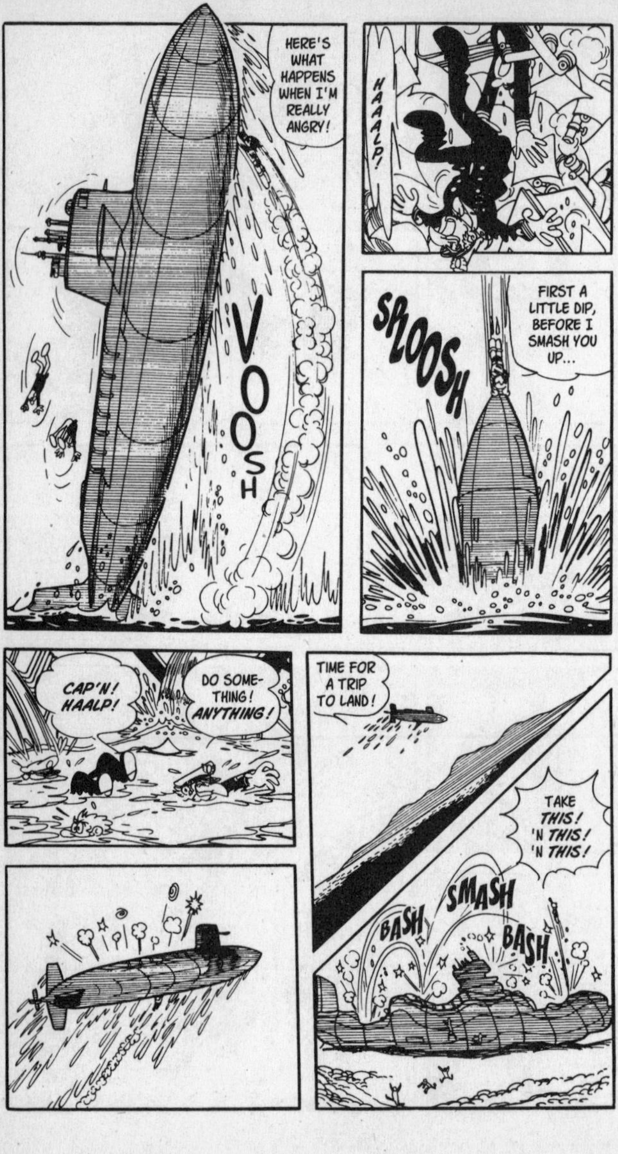
HERE'S WHAT HAPPENS WHEN I'M REALLY ANGRY!
VOOOSH
HAAAALP!
SPLOOSH
FIRST A LITTLE DIP, BEFORE I SMASH YOU UP...
CAP'N! HAALP!
DO SOME-THING! ANYTHING!
TIME FOR A TRIP TO LAND!
TAKE THIS! 'N THIS! 'N THIS!
BASH
SMASH
BASH

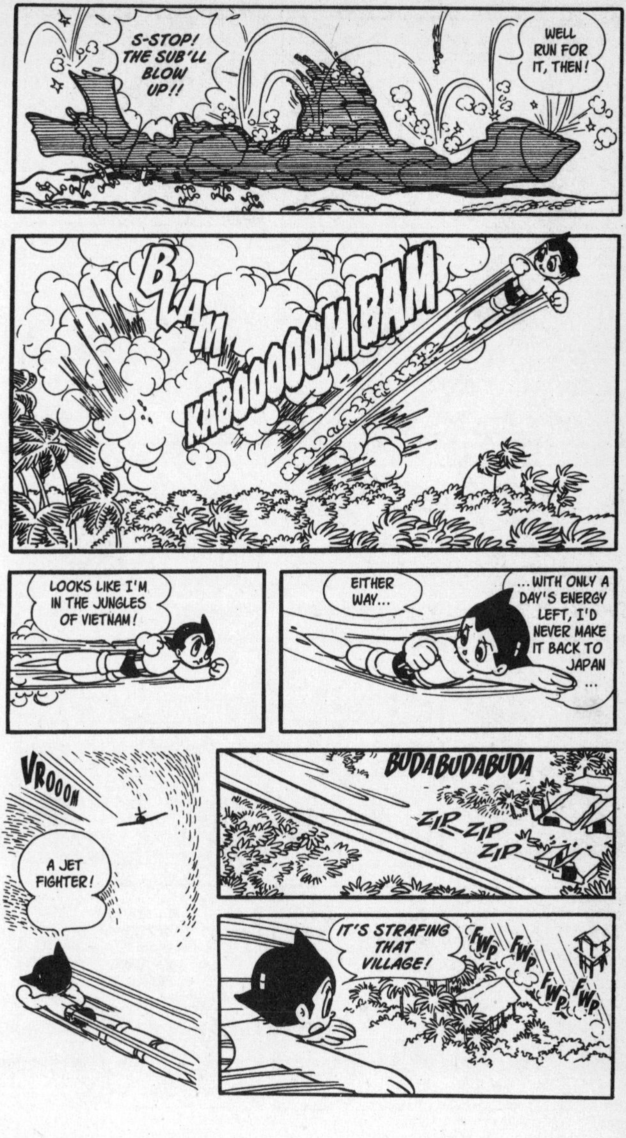
S-STOP! THE SUB'LL BLOW UP!!
WELL RUN FOR IT, THEN!
BLAM
KABOOOOOM BAM
LOOKS LIKE I'M IN THE JUNGLES OF VIETNAM!
EITHER WAY...
...WITH ONLY A DAY'S ENERGY LEFT, I'D NEVER MAKE IT BACK TO JAPAN ...
VROOOM
A JET FIGHTER!
BUDABUDABUDA
ZIP ZIP ZIP
IT'S STRAFING THAT VILLAGE!
FWP FWP FWP FWP

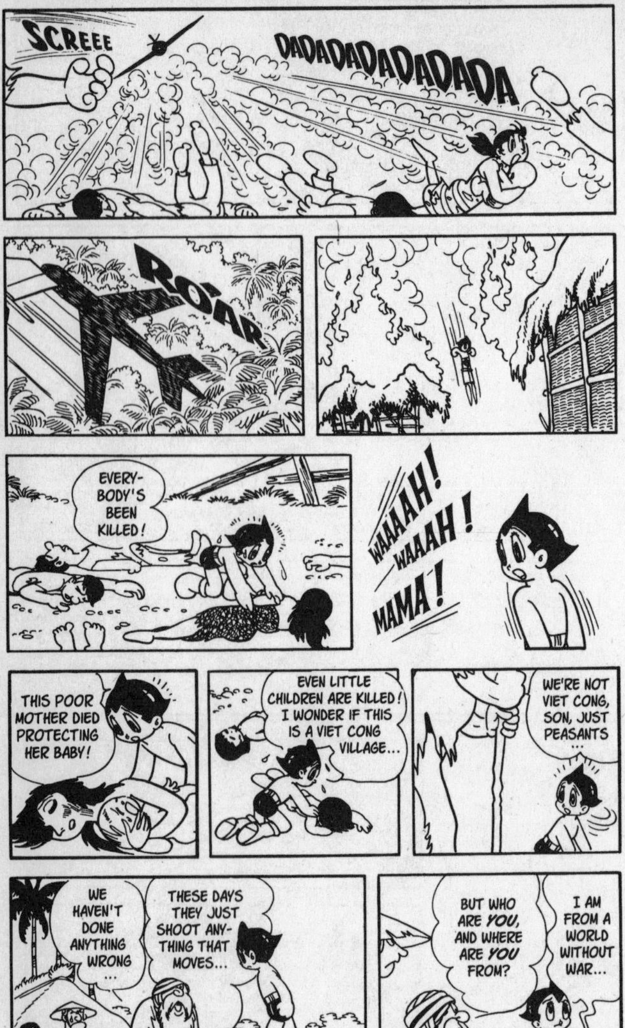

SCREEE
DADADADADADADA
ROAR
EVERY-BODY'S BEEN KILLED!
WAAAAH! WAAAH! MAMA!
THIS POOR MOTHER DIED PROTECTING HER BABY!
EVEN LITTLE CHILDREN ARE KILLED! I WONDER IF THIS IS A VIET CONG VILLAGE...
WE'RE NOT VIET CONG, SON, JUST PEASANTS ...
WE HAVEN'T DONE ANYTHING WRONG ...
THESE DAYS THEY JUST SHOOT ANY-THING THAT MOVES...
BUT WHO ARE *YOU*, AND WHERE ARE *YOU* FROM?
I AM FROM A WORLD WITHOUT WAR...

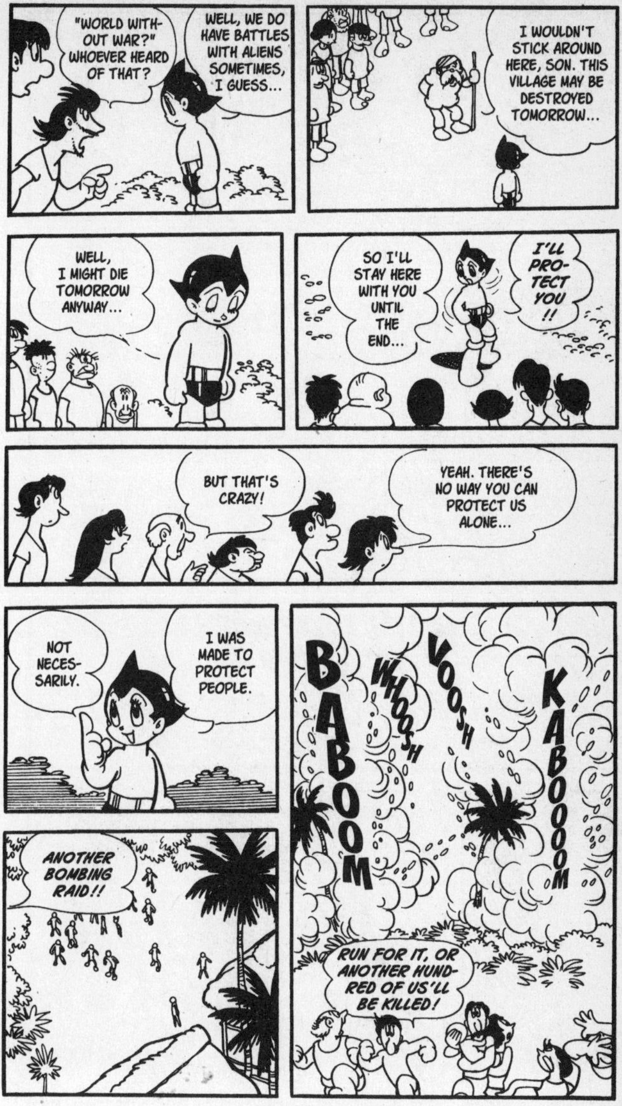
"WORLD WITH-OUT WAR?" WHOEVER HEARD OF THAT?
WELL, WE DO HAVE BATTLES WITH ALIENS SOMETIMES, I GUESS...
I WOULDN'T STICK AROUND HERE, SON. THIS VILLAGE MAY BE DESTROYED TOMORROW...
WELL, I MIGHT DIE TOMORROW ANYWAY...
SO I'LL STAY HERE WITH YOU UNTIL THE END...
I'LL PRO-TECT YOU !!
BUT THAT'S CRAZY!
YEAH. THERE'S NO WAY YOU CAN PROTECT US ALONE...
NOT NECES-SARILY.
I WAS MADE TO PROTECT PEOPLE.
ANOTHER BOMBING RAID!!
BABOOM
WHOOSH
VOOSH
KABOOOOOM
RUN FOR IT, OR ANOTHER HUND-RED OF US'LL BE KILLED!

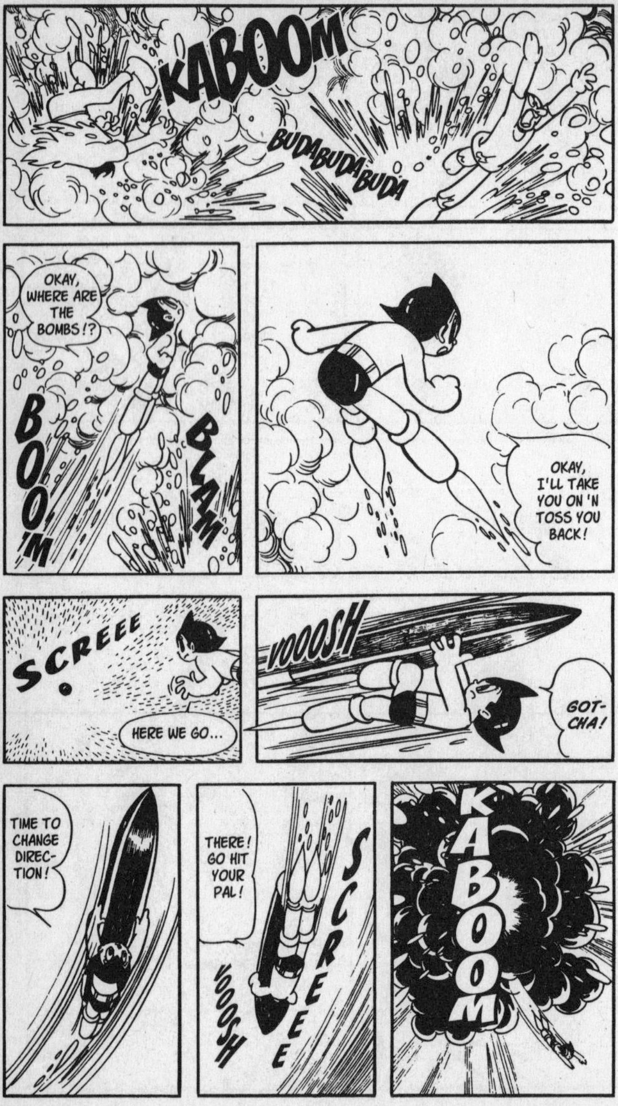
KABOOM
BUDABUDABUDA
OKAY, WHERE ARE THE BOMBS!?
BOOOOM
BLAM
OKAY, I'LL TAKE YOU ON 'N TOSS YOU BACK!
SCREEE
HERE WE GO...
VOOOSH
GOT-CHA!
TIME TO CHANGE DIREC-TION!
THERE! GO HIT YOUR PAL!
SCREEEEE
VOOOSH
KABOOM

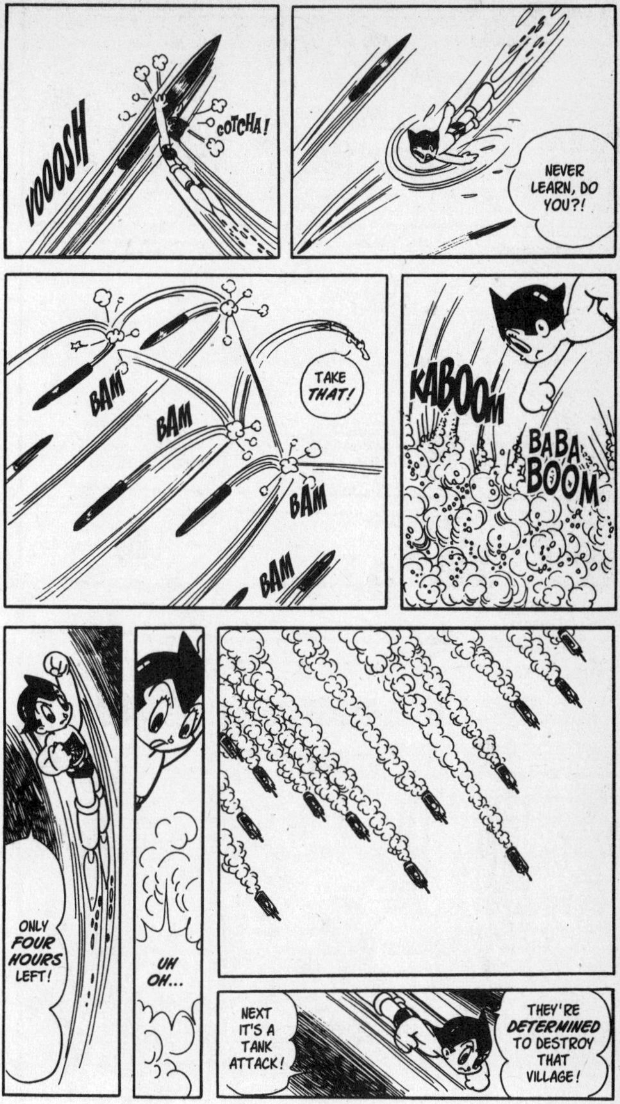
VOOOSH
COTCHA!
NEVER LEARN, DO YOU?!
BAM
BAM
TAKE THAT!
BAM
BAM
KABOOM
BABA BOOM
ONLY FOUR HOURS LEFT!
UH OH...
NEXT IT'S A TANK ATTACK!
THEY'RE DETERMINED TO DESTROY THAT VILLAGE!

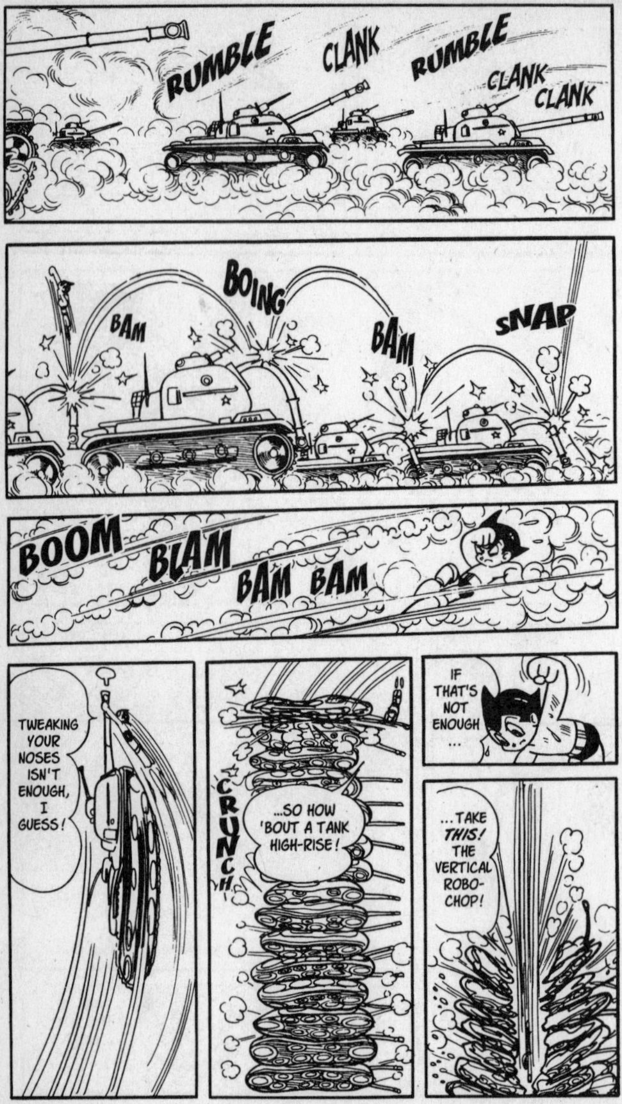
RUMBLE
CLANK
RUMBLE
CLANK
CLANK
BAM
BOING
BAM
SNAP
BOOM
BLAM
BAM BAM
TWEAKING YOUR NOSES ISN'T ENOUGH, I GUESS!
CRUNCH
...SO HOW 'BOUT A TANK HIGH-RISE!
IF THAT'S NOT ENOUGH ...
...TAKE THIS! THE VERTICAL ROBO-CHOP!

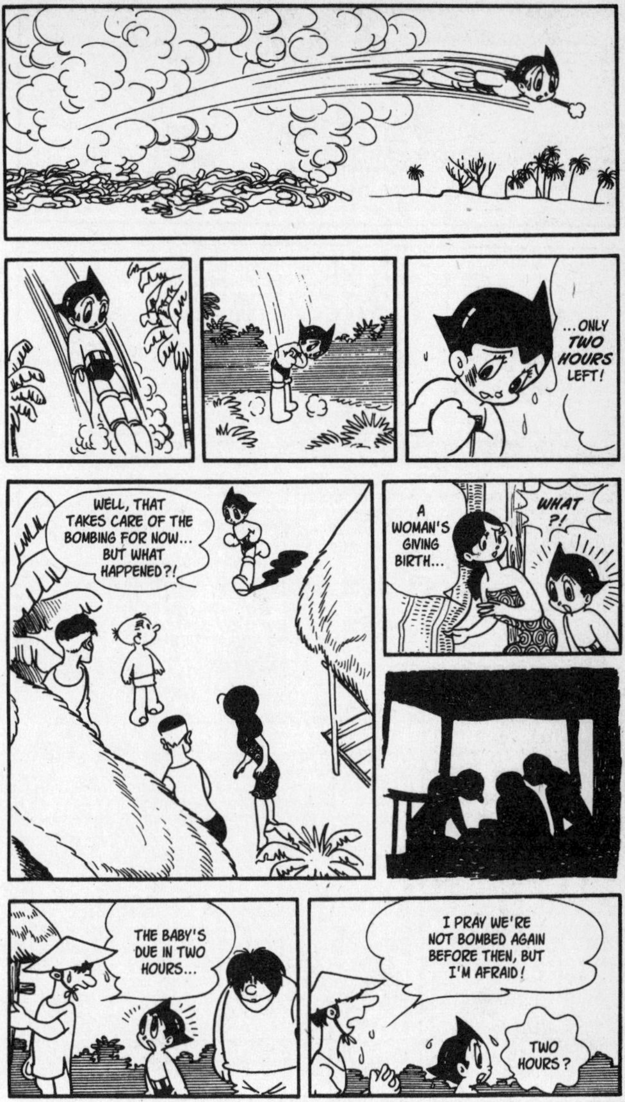
...ONLY TWO HOURS LEFT!
WELL, THAT TAKES CARE OF THE BOMBING FOR NOW... BUT WHAT HAPPENED?!
A WOMAN'S GIVING BIRTH...
WHAT ?!
THE BABY'S DUE IN TWO HOURS...
I PRAY WE'RE NOT BOMBED AGAIN BEFORE THEN, BUT I'M AFRAID!
TWO HOURS?

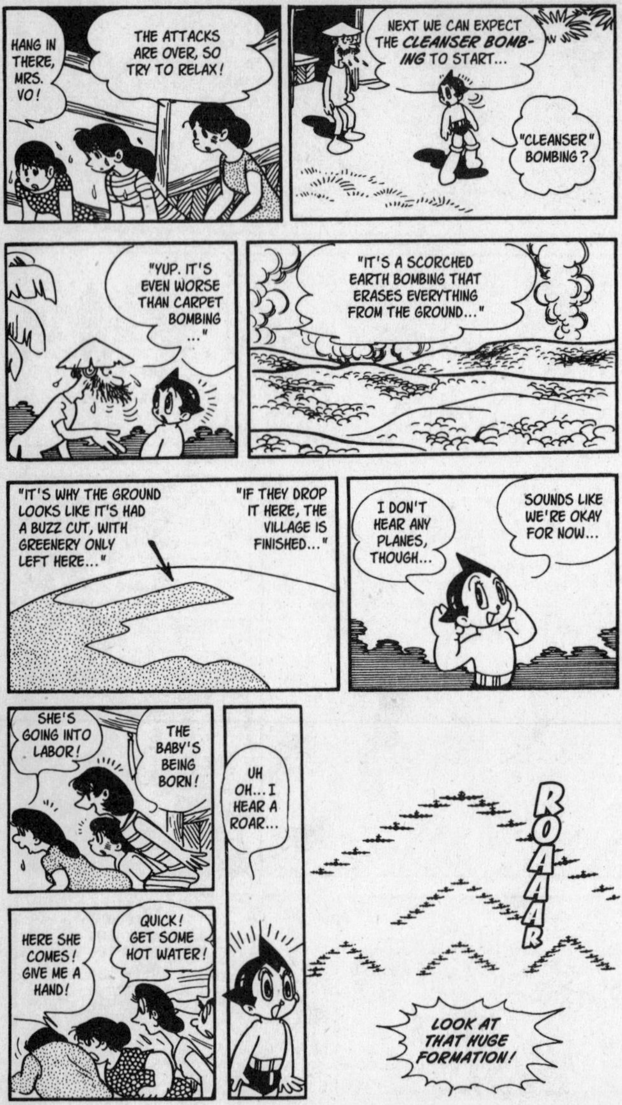
HANG IN THERE, MRS. VO!
THE ATTACKS ARE OVER, SO TRY TO RELAX!
NEXT WE CAN EXPECT THE *CLEANSER BOMBING* TO START...
"CLEANSER" BOMBING?
"YUP. IT'S EVEN WORSE THAN CARPET BOMBING ..."
"IT'S A SCORCHED EARTH BOMBING THAT ERASES EVERYTHING FROM THE GROUND..."
"IT'S WHY THE GROUND LOOKS LIKE IT'S HAD A BUZZ CUT, WITH GREENERY ONLY LEFT HERE..."
"IF THEY DROP IT HERE, THE VILLAGE IS FINISHED..."
I DON'T HEAR ANY PLANES, THOUGH...
SOUNDS LIKE WE'RE OKAY FOR NOW...
SHE'S GOING INTO LABOR!
THE BABY'S BEING BORN!
HERE SHE COMES! GIVE ME A HAND!
QUICK! GET SOME HOT WATER!
UH OH... I HEAR A ROAR...
ROAAAAR
LOOK AT THAT HUGE FORMATION!

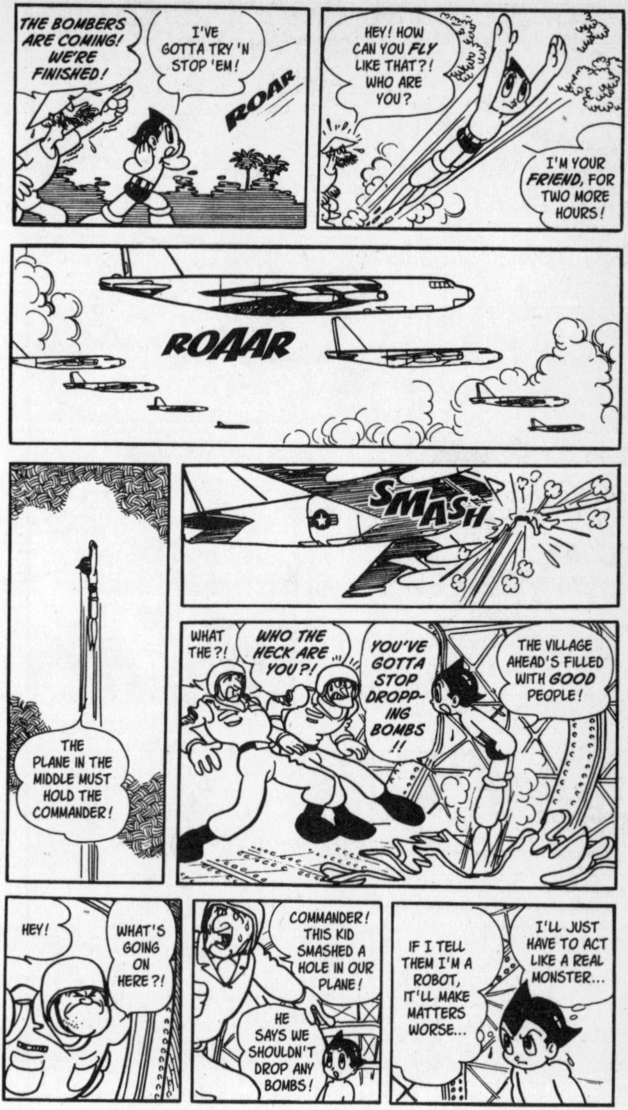
THE BOMBERS ARE COMING! WE'RE FINISHED!
I'VE GOTTA TRY 'N STOP 'EM!
ROAR
HEY! HOW CAN YOU FLY LIKE THAT?! WHO ARE YOU?
I'M YOUR FRIEND, FOR TWO MORE HOURS!
ROAAR
THE PLANE IN THE MIDDLE MUST HOLD THE COMMANDER!
SMASH
WHAT THE?!
WHO THE HECK ARE YOU?!
YOU'VE GOTTA STOP DROPP-ING BOMBS!!
THE VILLAGE AHEAD'S FILLED WITH GOOD PEOPLE!
HEY!
WHAT'S GOING ON HERE?!
COMMANDER! THIS KID SMASHED A HOLE IN OUR PLANE!
HE SAYS WE SHOULDN'T DROP ANY BOMBS!
IF I TELL THEM I'M A ROBOT, IT'LL MAKE MATTERS WORSE...
I'LL JUST HAVE TO ACT LIKE A REAL MONSTER...

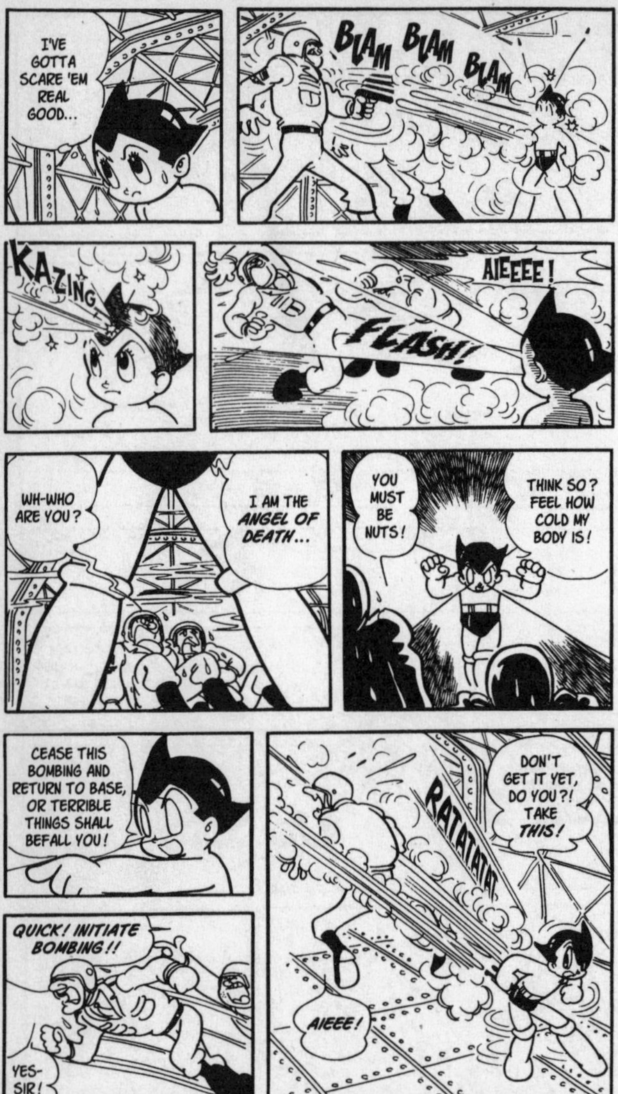
I'VE GOTTA SCARE 'EM REAL GOOD...
BLAM BLAM BLAM
KAZING
AIEEEE!
FLASH!
WH-WHO ARE YOU?
I AM THE *ANGEL OF DEATH...*
YOU MUST BE NUTS!
THINK SO? FEEL HOW COLD MY BODY IS!
CEASE THIS BOMBING AND RETURN TO BASE, OR TERRIBLE THINGS SHALL BEFALL YOU!
QUICK! INITIATE BOMBING!!
YES-SIR!
DON'T GET IT YET, DO YOU?! TAKE *THIS!*
RATATATAT
AIEEE!

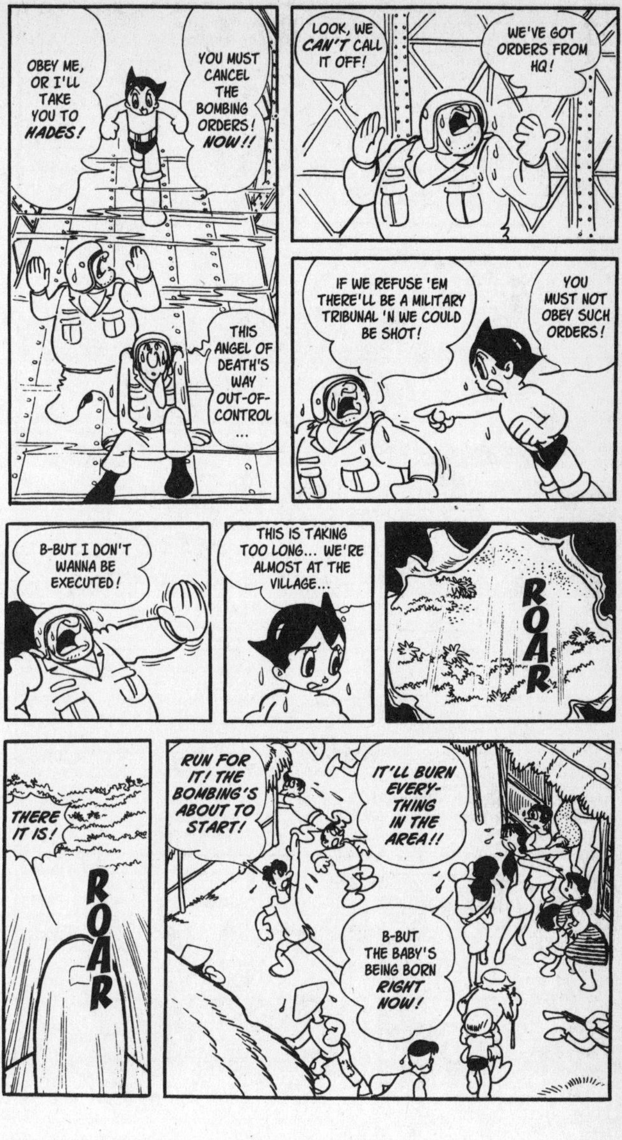
OBEY ME, OR I'LL TAKE YOU TO HADES!
YOU MUST CANCEL THE BOMBING ORDERS! NOW!!
THIS ANGEL OF DEATH'S WAY OUT-OF-CONTROL ...
LOOK, WE CAN'T CALL IT OFF!
WE'VE GOT ORDERS FROM HQ!
IF WE REFUSE 'EM THERE'LL BE A MILITARY TRIBUNAL 'N WE COULD BE SHOT!
YOU MUST NOT OBEY SUCH ORDERS!
B-BUT I DON'T WANNA BE EXECUTED!
THIS IS TAKING TOO LONG... WE'RE ALMOST AT THE VILLAGE...
ROAR
THERE IT IS!
ROAR
RUN FOR IT! THE BOMBING'S ABOUT TO START!
IT'LL BURN EVERY-THING IN THE AREA!!
B-BUT THE BABY'S BEING BORN RIGHT NOW!

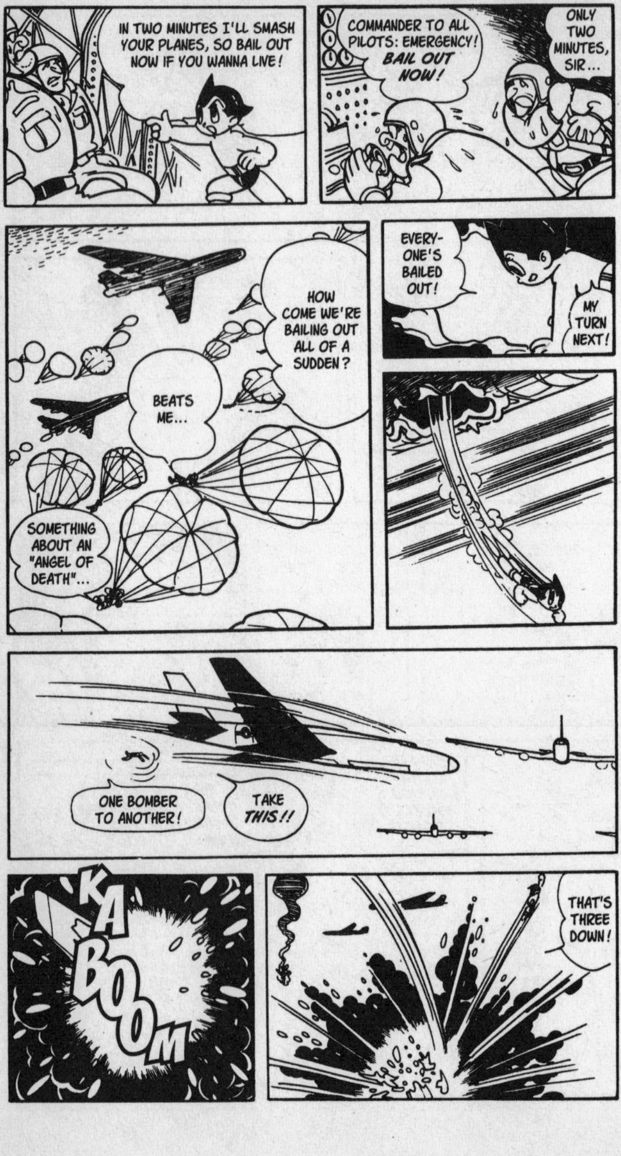
IN TWO MINUTES I'LL SMASH YOUR PLANES, SO BAIL OUT NOW IF YOU WANNA LIVE!
COMMANDER TO ALL PILOTS: EMERGENCY! BAIL OUT NOW!
ONLY TWO MINUTES, SIR...
HOW COME WE'RE BAILING OUT ALL OF A SUDDEN?
BEATS ME...
SOMETHING ABOUT AN "ANGEL OF DEATH"...
EVERY-ONE'S BAILED OUT!
MY TURN NEXT!
ONE BOMBER TO ANOTHER!
TAKE THIS!!
KA BOOM
THAT'S THREE DOWN!

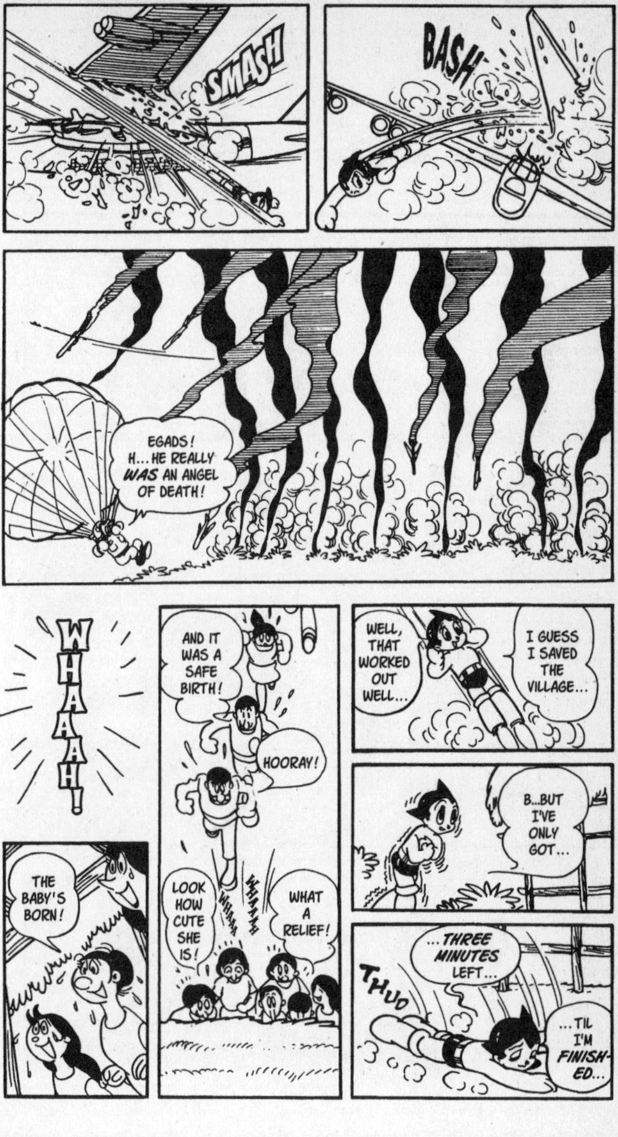
SMASH
BASH
EGADS! H... HE REALLY *WAS* AN ANGEL OF DEATH!
WHAAAAH!
AND IT WAS A SAFE BIRTH!
HOORAY!
WELL, THAT WORKED OUT WELL...
I GUESS I SAVED THE VILLAGE...
B...BUT I'VE ONLY GOT...
THE BABY'S BORN!
LOOK HOW CUTE SHE IS!
WHAAA
WHAAAA
WHAT A RELIEF!
...*THREE MINUTES* LEFT...
THUD
...TIL I'M *FINISHED*...

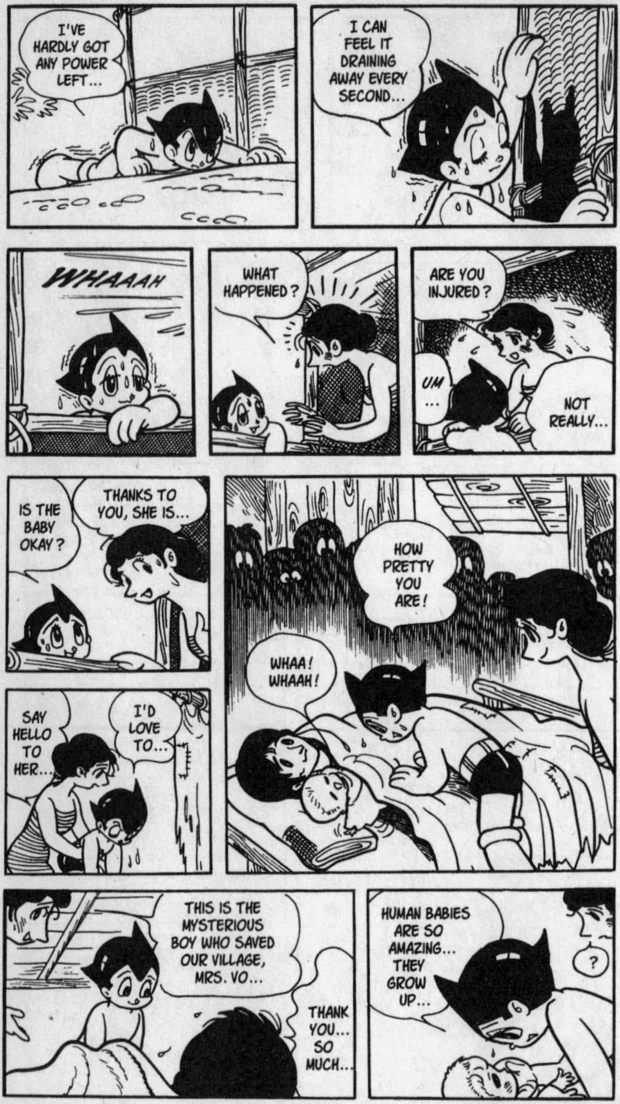
I'VE HARDLY GOT ANY POWER LEFT...
I CAN FEEL IT DRAINING AWAY EVERY SECOND...
WHAAAAH
WHAT HAPPENED?
ARE YOU INJURED?
UM ...
NOT REALLY...
IS THE BABY OKAY?
THANKS TO YOU, SHE IS...
SAY HELLO TO HER...
I'D LOVE TO...
HOW PRETTY YOU ARE!
WHAA! WHAAH!
THIS IS THE MYSTERIOUS BOY WHO SAVED OUR VILLAGE, MRS. VO...
THANK YOU... SO MUCH...
HUMAN BABIES ARE SO AMAZING... THEY GROW UP...
?

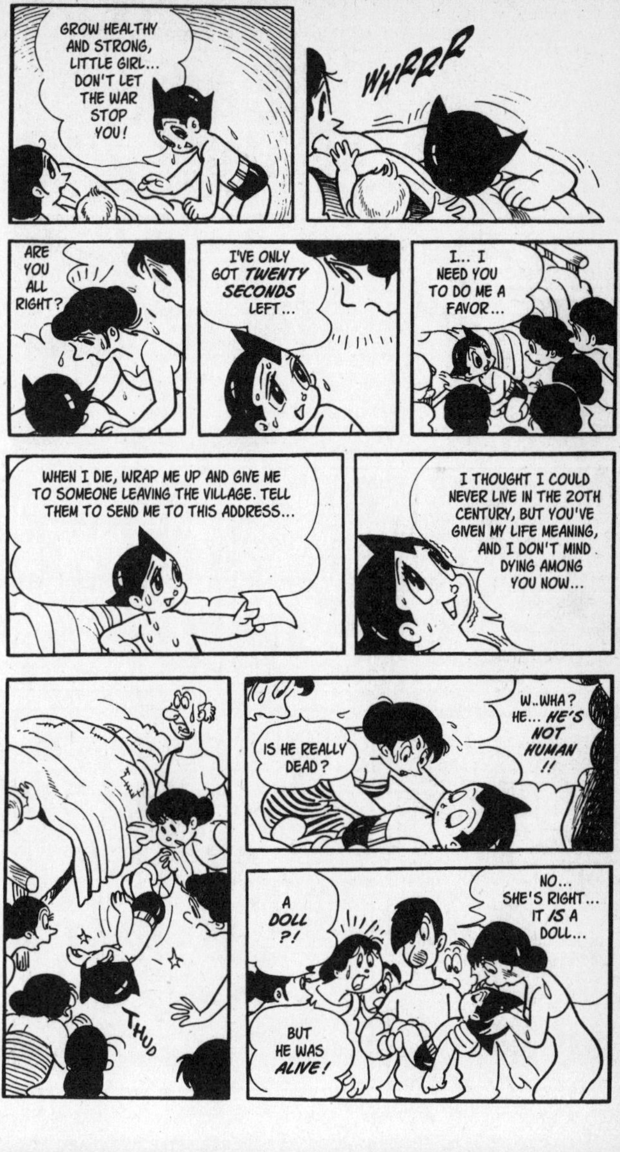
GROW HEALTHY AND STRONG, LITTLE GIRL... DON'T LET THE WAR STOP YOU!
WHRRR
ARE YOU ALL RIGHT?
I'VE ONLY GOT TWENTY SECONDS LEFT...
I... I NEED YOU TO DO ME A FAVOR...
WHEN I DIE, WRAP ME UP AND GIVE ME TO SOMEONE LEAVING THE VILLAGE. TELL THEM TO SEND ME TO THIS ADDRESS...
I THOUGHT I COULD NEVER LIVE IN THE 20TH CENTURY, BUT YOU'VE GIVEN MY LIFE MEANING, AND I DON'T MIND DYING AMONG YOU NOW...
THUD
IS HE REALLY DEAD?
W..WHA? HE... HE'S NOT HUMAN!!
A DOLL?!
NO... SHE'S RIGHT... IT IS A DOLL...
BUT HE WAS ALIVE!

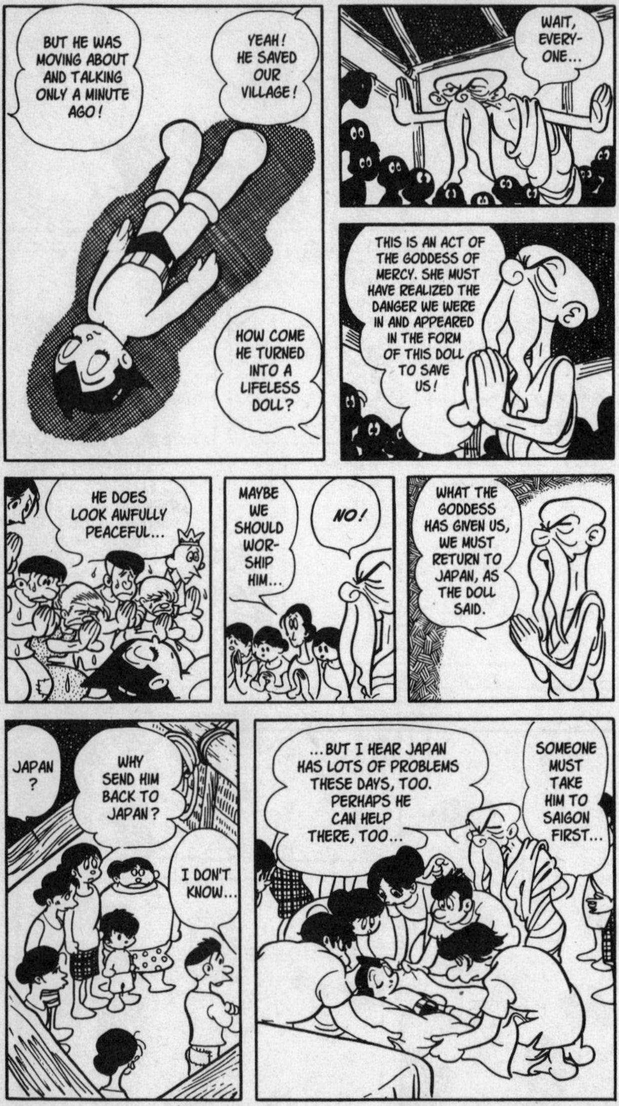
BUT HE WAS MOVING ABOUT AND TALKING ONLY A MINUTE AGO!
YEAH! HE SAVED OUR VILLAGE!
HOW COME HE TURNED INTO A LIFELESS DOLL?
WAIT, EVERY-ONE...
THIS IS AN ACT OF THE GODDESS OF MERCY. SHE MUST HAVE REALIZED THE DANGER WE WERE IN AND APPEARED IN THE FORM OF THIS DOLL TO SAVE US!
HE DOES LOOK AWFULLY PEACEFUL...
MAYBE WE SHOULD WOR-SHIP HIM...
NO!
WHAT THE GODDESS HAS GIVEN US, WE MUST RETURN TO JAPAN, AS THE DOLL SAID.
JAPAN?
WHY SEND HIM BACK TO JAPAN?
I DON'T KNOW...
...BUT I HEAR JAPAN HAS LOTS OF PROBLEMS THESE DAYS, TOO. PERHAPS HE CAN HELP THERE, TOO...
SOMEONE MUST TAKE HIM TO SAIGON FIRST...

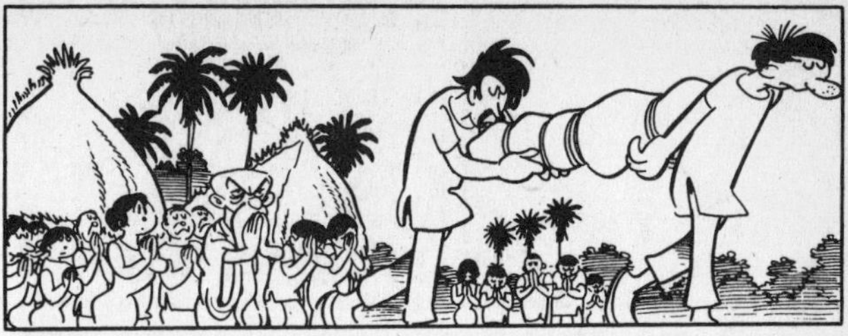

ASTRO WAS THEREUPON WRAPPED TIGHTLY IN WHITE FUNERAL CLOTH. TWO VILLAGERS WERE ELECTED TO PLACE HIS BODY ONTO A CART AND CARRY HIM TO SAIGON. THE WHOLE VILLAGE TURNED OUT TO SAY FAREWELL, THEIR HANDS CLASPED IN RESPECTFUL PRAYER. IT WAS A SOLEMN, ALMOST RELIGIOUS SIGHT, LIKE WITNESSING THE FUNERAL OF A HERO OR GREETING A TRUE SAINT.

THE MOTHER OF THE NEW BABY BID ASTRO FAREWELL FROM HER BED AND WATCHED AS HE SLOWLY DISAPPEARED FROM VIEW. "I SHALL NEVER FORGET WHAT YOU SAID," SHE WHISPERED, "AND I SHALL RAISE A HEALTHY AND STRONG CHILD, DESPITE THE WAR..."

WITH ASTRO ON IT, THE CREAKING AND RATTLING CART THEN FADED FROM SIGHT AMONG THE PALM TREES.

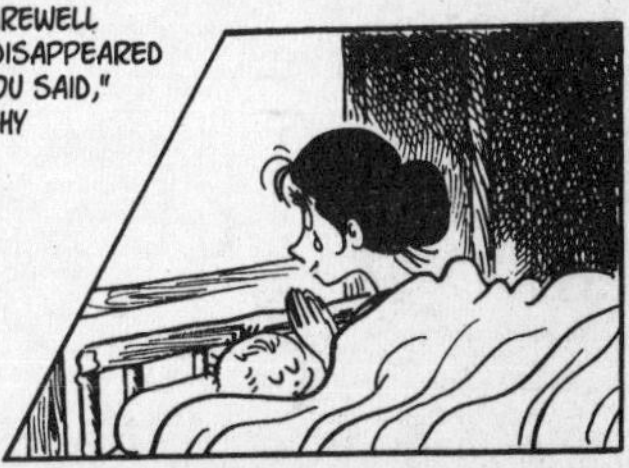

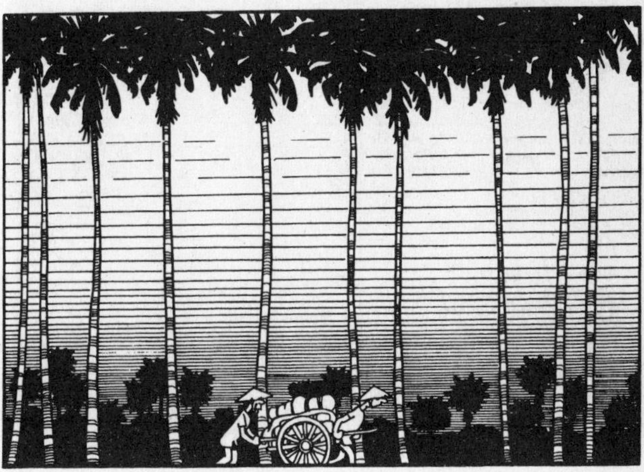

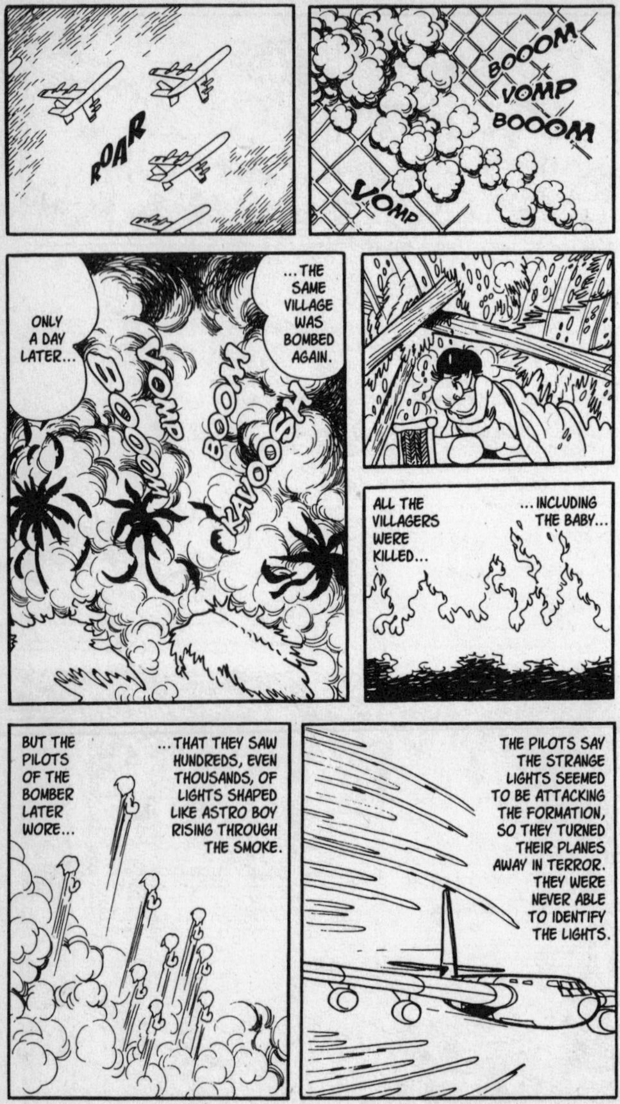

ROAR
BOOOM
VOMP
BOOOM
VOMP
ONLY A DAY LATER...
...THE SAME VILLAGE WAS BOMBED AGAIN.
VOMP
BOOOOM
BOOM
KAVOOOSH
ALL THE VILLAGERS WERE KILLED...
...INCLUDING THE BABY...
BUT THE PILOTS OF THE BOMBER LATER WORE...
...THAT THEY SAW HUNDREDS, EVEN THOUSANDS, OF LIGHTS SHAPED LIKE ASTRO BOY RISING THROUGH THE SMOKE.
THE PILOTS SAY THE STRANGE LIGHTS SEEMED TO BE ATTACKING THE FORMATION, SO THEY TURNED THEIR PLANES AWAY IN TERROR. THEY WERE NEVER ABLE TO IDENTIFY THE LIGHTS.

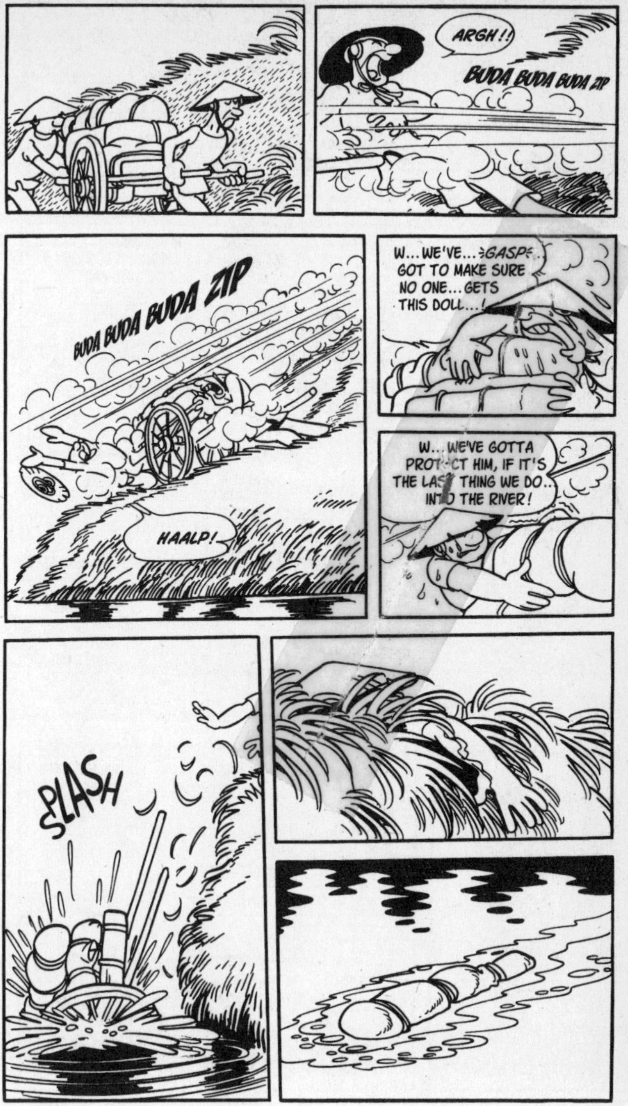
ARGH!!
BUDA BUDA BUDA ZIP
BUDA BUDA BUDA ZIP
HAALP!
W... WE'VE... ⋛GASP⋚... GOT TO MAKE SURE NO ONE... GETS THIS DOLL...!
W... WE'VE GOTTA PROTECT HIM, IF IT'S THE LAST THING WE DO... INTO THE RIVER!
SPLASH

ASTRO SLOWLY FLOATED DOWN THE MEKONG RIVER...

...ALONG WITH THE VICTIMS OF WAR.

BUTTERFLIES PLAYFULLY LANDED ON TOP OF HIM...

AND HE SAILED THROUGH BURNING OIL...

FOR A LONG, LONG TIME...

...ASTRO WAS UNCONSCIOUS, AWARE OF NOTHING, NOT EVEN DREAMING...

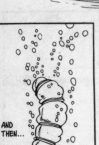

AND THEN...

...FINALLY...

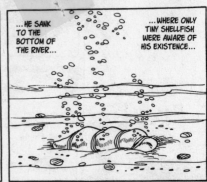

...HE SANK TO THE BOTTOM OF THE RIVER...

...WHERE ONLY TINY SHELLFISH WERE AWARE OF HIS EXISTENCE...

TO BE CONTINUED...

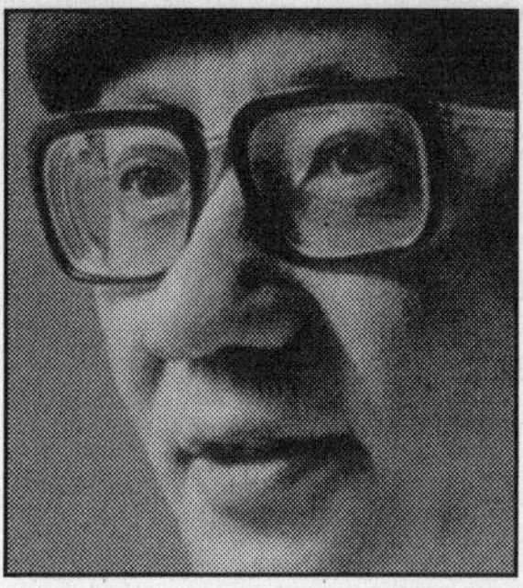

Osamu Tezuka was born in the city of Toyonaka, in Osaka, Japan, on November 3, 1928, and raised in Takarazuka, in Hyogo prefecture. He graduated from the Medical Department of Osaka University and was later awarded a Doctorate of Medicine.

In 1946 Tezuka made his debut as a manga artist with the work *Amachan's Diary*, and in 1947 he had his first big hit with *New Treasure Island*. Over his forty-year career as a cartoonist, Tezuka produced in excess of an astounding 150,000 pages of manga, including the creation of *Metropolis*, *Mighty Atom* (a.k.a. *Astro Boy*), *Jungle Emperor* (a.k.a. *Kimba the White Lion*), *Black Jack*, *Phoenix*, *Buddha*, and many more.

Tezuka's fascination with Disney cartoons led him to begin his own animation studio, creating the first serialized Japanese cartoon series, which was later exported to America as *Astro Boy* in 1963. Tezuka Productions went on to create animated versions of *Kimba the White Lion* (*Jungle Emperor*) and *Phoenix*, among others.

He received numerous awards during his life, including the Bungei Shunju Manga Award, the Kodansha Manga Award, the Shogakukan Manga Award, and the Japan Cartoonists' Association Special Award for Excellence. He also served a variety of organizations. He was a director of the Japan Cartoonists' Association, the chairman of the Japan Animation Association, and a member of the Manga Group, Japan Pen Club, and the Japan SF Authors' Club, among others. Tezuka became Japan's "comics ambassador," taking Japan's comics culture to the world. In 1980, he toured and lectured in America, including a speech at the United Nations.

Regarded as a national treasure, Osamu Tezuka died on February 2, 1989 at the age of 60. In 1994, the Osamu Tezuka Manga Museum opened in the city of Takarazuka, where he was raised. His creations remains hugely popular in Japan and are printed in many languages throughout the world, where he is acclaimed as one of the true giants of comics and animation, his work as vital and influential today as it was half a century ago.

"Comics are an international language," Tezuka said. "They can cross boundaries and generations. Comics are a bridge between all cultures."

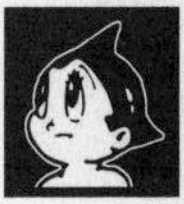

OSAMU TEZUKA'S ORIGINAL

ASTRO BOY®

JET-POWERED!
SUPER-STRONG!
EVIL-ROBOT-BASHING!
ALIEN-INVASION-SMASHING!

Each volume retails for $9.95!
New volumes available every month!

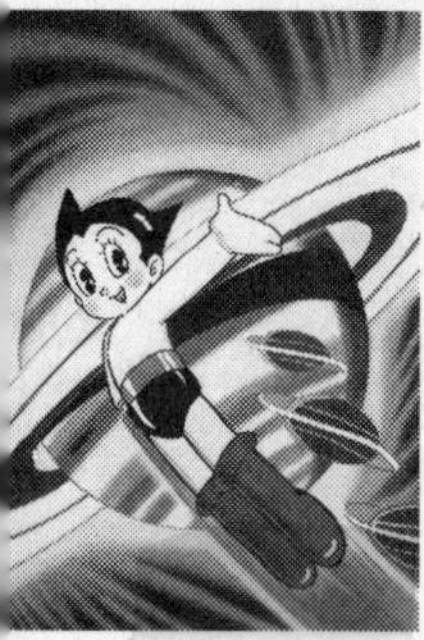

Volume 1
1-56971-676-5

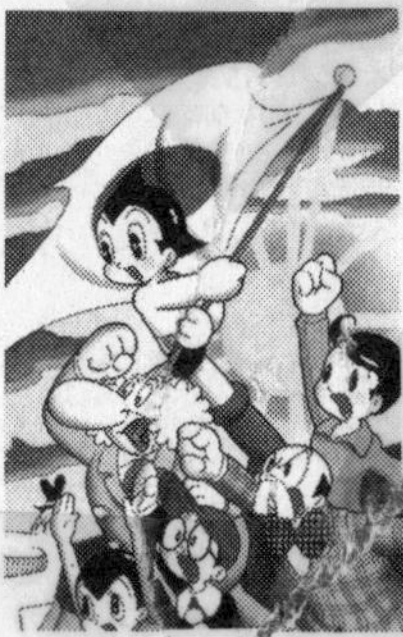

Volume 2
1-56971-677-3

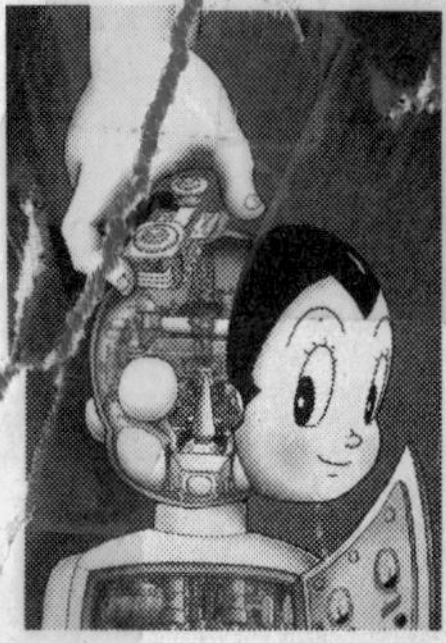

Volume 3
1-56971-678-1

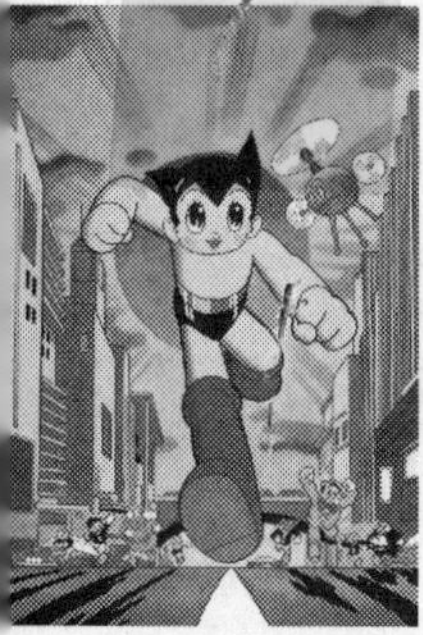

Volume 4
1-56971-679-X

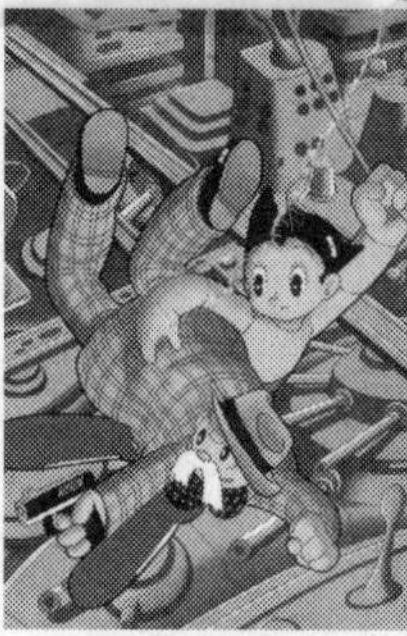

Volume 5
1-56971-680-3

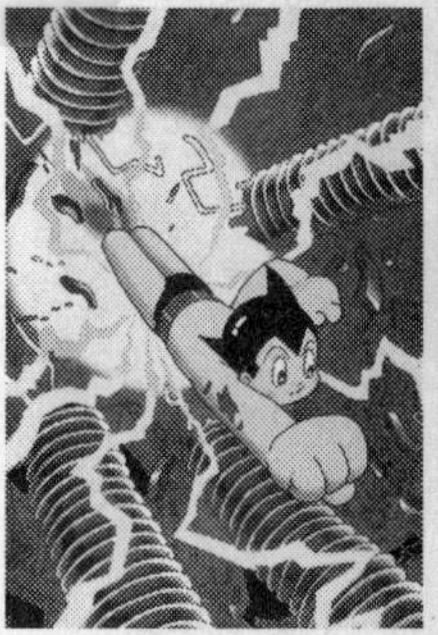

Volume 6
1-56971-681-1

AVAILABLE AT YOUR LOCAL COMICS SHOP OR BOOKSTORE
To find a comics shop in your area, call 1-888-266-4226

For more information or to order direct:
- On the web: www.darkhorse.com
- E-mail: mailorder@darkhorse.com
- Phone: 1-800-862-0052 or (503) 652-9701 Mon.-Sat. 9 A.M. to 5 P.M. Pacific Time

DARK HORSE COMICS®

MANGA! MANGA! MANGA! DARK HORSE HAS THE BEST IN MANGA COLLECTIONS!

AKIRA
Katsuhiro Otomo
BOOK 1
ISBN: 1-56971-498-3 $24.95
BOOK 2
ISBN: 1-56971-499-1 $24.95
BOOK 3
ISBN: 1-56971-525-4 $24.95
BOOK 4
ISBN: 1-56971-526-2 $27.95

APPLESEED
Masamune Shirow
BOOK ONE
ISBN: 1-56971-070-8 $16.95
BOOK TWO
ISBN: 1-56971-071-6 $16.95
BOOK THREE
ISBN: 1-56971-072-4 $17.95
BOOK FOUR
ISBN: 1-56971-074-0 $17.95

BLADE OF THE IMMORTAL
Hiroaki Samura
BLOOD OF A THOUSAND
ISBN: 1-56971-239-5 $14.95
CRY OF THE WORM
ISBN: 1-56971-300-6 $14.95
DREAMSONG
ISBN: 1-56971-357-X $14.95
ON SILENT WINGS
ISBN: 1-56971-412-6 $14.95
ON SILENT WINGS II
ISBN: 1-56971-444-4 $14.95
DARK SHADOWS
ISBN: 1-56971-469-X $14.95
HEART OF DARKNESS
ISBN: 1-56971-531-9 $16.95
THE GATHERING
ISBN: 1-56971-546-7 $15.95
THE GATHERING II
ISBN: 1-56971-560-2 $15.95

THE DIRTY PAIR
Adam Warren • Toren Smith
BIOHAZARDS
ISBN: 1-56971-339-1 $12.95
DANGEROUS ACQUAINTANCES
ISBN: 1-56971-227-1 $12.95
A PLAGUE OF ANGELS
ISBN: 1-56971-029-5 $12.95
SIM HELL
ISBN: 1-56971-159-3 $13.95
FATAL BUT NOT SERIOUS
ISBN: 1-56971-172-0 $14.95

DOMINION
Masamune Shirow
DOMINION
ISBN: 1-56971-488-6 $16.95

DOMU: A CHILD'S DREAM
Katsuhiro Otomo
ISBN: 1-56971-611-0 $17.95

GHOST IN THE SHELL
Masamune Shirow
ISBN: 1-56971-081-3 $24.95

GUNSMITH CATS
Kenichi Sonoda
BONNIE AND CLYDE
ISBN: 1-56971-215-8 $13.95
MISFIRE
ISBN: 1-56971-253-0 $14.95
THE RETURN OF GRAY
ISBN: 1-56971-299-9 $17.95
GOLDIE VS. MISTY
ISBN: 1-56971-371-5 $15.95
BAD TRIP
ISBN: 1-56971-442-8 $13.95
BEAN BANDIT
ISBN: 1-56971-453-3 $16.95
MISTER V
ISBN: 1-56971-550-5 $18.95

INTRON DEPOT
Masamune Shirow
INTRON DEPOT 1
ISBN: 1-56971-085-6 $39.95
INTRON DEPOT 2: BLADES
ISBN: 1-56971-382-0 $39.95

LONE WOLF AND CUB
Kazuo Koike and Goseki Kojima
New volumes released monthly!
Collect the complete 28-volume series!
VOLUME 1: THE ASSASSIN'S ROAD
ISBN: 1-56971-502-5 $9.95
VOLUME 2: THE GATELESS BARRIER
ISBN: 1-56971-503-3 $9.95
VOLUME 3: THE FLUTE OF THE FALLEN TIGER
ISBN: 1-56971-504-1 $9.95
VOLUME 4: THE BELL WARDEN
ISBN: 1-56971-505-X $9.95
VOLUME 5: BLACK WIND
ISBN: 1-5671-506-8 $9.95
VOLUME 6: LANTERNS FOR THE DEAD
ISBN: 1-56971-507-6 $9.95
VOLUME 7: CLOUD DRAGON, WIND TIGER
ISBN: 1-56971-508-4 $9.95
VOLUME 8: CHAINS OF DEATH
ISBN: 1-56971-509-2 $9.95
VOLUME 9: ECHO OF THE ASSASSIN
ISBN: 1-56971-510-6 $9.95
VOLUME 10: HOSTAGE CHILD
ISBN: 1-56971-511-4 $9.95
VOLUME 11: TALISMAN OF HADES
ISBN: 1-56971-512-2 $9.95
VOLUME 12: SHATTERED STONES
ISBN: 1-56971-513-0 $9.95
VOLUME 13: THE MOON IN THE EAST, THE SUN IN THE WEST
1-56971-585-8 $9.95
VOLUME 14: DAY OF THE DEMONS
1-56971-586-6 $9.95
VOLUME 15: BROTHERS OF THE GRASS
1-56971-587-4 $9.95

OH MY GODDESS!
Kosuke Fujishima
1-555-GODDESS
ISBN: 1-56971-207-7 $14.95
LOVE POTION NO. 9
ISBN: 1-56971-252-2 $14.95
SYMPATHY FOR THE DEVIL
ISBN: 1-56971-329-4 $13.95
TERRIBLE MASTER URD
ISBN: 1-56971-369-3 $14.95
THE QUEEN OF VENGEANCE
ISBN: 1-56971-431-2 $13.95
MARA STRIKES BACK!
ISBN: 1-56971-449-5 $14.95
MISS KEIICHI
ISBN: 1-56971-522-X $16.95
ADVENTURES OF THE MINI-GODDESSES
ISBN: 1-56971-421-5 $9.95
THE DEVIL IN MISS URD
ISBN: 1-56971-540-8 $14.95
THE FOURTH GODDESS
ISBN: 1-56971-551-3 $18.95

3x3 EYES
Yuzo Takada
HOUSE OF DEMONS
ISBN: 1-56971-059-7 $12.95
CURSE OF THE GESU
ISBN: 1-56971-175-5 $12.95

WHAT'S MICHAEL?
Makoto Kobayashi
OFF THE DEEP END
ISBN: 1-56971-249-2 $5.95
MICHAEL'S MAMBO
ISBN: 1-56971-250-6 $5.95

Available from your local comics shop or bookstore!

To find a comics shop in your area, call 1-888-266-4226 • For more information or to order direct:
•On the web: www.darkhorse.com •E-mail: mailorder@darkhorse.com
•Phone: 1-800-862-0052 or (503) 652-9701 Mon.-Sat. 9 A.M. to 5 P.M. Pacific Time
*Prices and availability subject to change without notice